$2.2

Florestan: The Life and Work of
ROBERT SCHUMANN

By Robert Haven Schauffler

Dover books on music

(continued on back flap)

Robert Schumann
Lithograph by Kaiser

FLORESTAN

THE LIFE AND WORK OF

ROBERT SCHUMANN

1344

BY ROBERT HAVEN SCHAUFFLER

DOVER PUBLICATIONS, INC.
NEW YORK   NEW YORK

Library of Congress Catalog Card Number: 63-17930

Manufactured in the United States of America

Dover Publications, Inc.
180 Varick Street
New York 14, N. Y.

To

CONSTANCE LILY MORRIS

*who first suggested this book,
and helped me to begin it.*

CONTENTS

PART II
THE MUSIC

ILLUSTRATIONS

OVERTURE

AS yet no biographer has painted the character of Robert Schumann without dipping his brush in either whitewash or tar. But the character of Clara has been worse falsified. The sympathetic consideration due to such a great keeper of the flame—a beautiful, talented, and heroic woman who suffered a tragic loss—has gone too far and obscured her real personality under gross layers of whitewash.

No other famous character in the history of music has been more consistently prettified than Clara. With one consent, the Schumann biographers have ignored the unfortunate traits which she inherited from that old scoundrel, her father, and have idealized her into a sort of secular Madonna of Music.

It is true that the scribes have also been blind to certain blemishes in the more admirable character of Robert. They have, for instance, not noticed his caddishness in dedicating to the girl whom he had cruelly jilted, songs with insulting words. They have overlooked his thoughtlessness in depriving Franz Schubert's poverty-stricken brother, for selfish reasons, of an adequate recompense for the publication rights of Franz's great C Major Symphony. But the biographers have handled his defects with more truth than those of Clara.

The world has about as accurate a notion of what this great woman was really like as one can get of the personal appearance of the masters of music from the little white plaster busts of them which are hawked about the streets by Italian peddlers. After many years of study, I have tried both to do the virtues of the Schumanns full justice, without idealization or unfair detraction, and to depict them as Cromwell wished to be painted, "warts and all."

The picture of Clara here offered may shock and offend a great many people who will declare that it does her wrong. They will be certain of this because their ideas have been formed by the very writers whose false accounts of Clara as the Madonna of Music this book endeavors to correct. If they will study without bias such original sources as the letters and diaries, they will find that the biographers have misled them.

One reason why Schumann's music is not so widely appreciated as it deserves to be is that it has never yet been adequately treated by the musical scribes; while those slaves of fashion, the pharisees, think it *comme il faut* to turn up superior noses. Another reason is that such a composer can never be fully appreciated in a barren time of brutal authoritarianism like the present, nor in a time of individualism gone rampant such as preceded the First World War and precipitated the Second. We are now, in the summer of 1945, approaching a period when unbridled authority will decline, as it is bound to do at this phase of the eternal historic cycle, to a point where authority and individualism will balance one another in some sort of equipoise. In that millennial day Schumann's music—where that very thing happens—will come into its own.

For brevity the title of this biography uses only one of Robert's self-imposed nicknames. "Florestan" has been preferred because he used it more often than "Eusebius." All foreign letters and documents quoted here have been freshly translated.

During four long summers I scribbled a good deal of this book on the Maine coast, clad in bathing trunks and with my back against a log of driftwood. Now, to write anything on a windy beach that involves so many musical and wordy documents demands the technic of the traditional one-armed paperhanger. But the business should enjoy compensating advantages. The salt wind should blow the dust from the documents; and a bit of the music of tern and wave and some of the bright spaciousness of ocean and sky should steal into the manuscript.

Acknowledgments of indebtedness will be found at the close of the volume.

R. H. S.

Ogunquit, Maine
June 1, 1945

PART I

THE MAN

*I do not care for the man whose life
is not in harmony with his work.*

ROBERT SCHUMANN:
Gesammelte Schriften, II, 262.

CHAPTER 1

SMALL-TOWN WONDER-CHILD

JUNE eighth, 1810, at Zwickau in Saxony. If ever a time and a place were calculated to fire the imagination of a genius, here they were.

In the months before Robert Schumann's birth, King Jerome Bonaparte, with sixteen thousand soldiers, was quartered in Zwickau. At that moment, his brother Napoleon was balancing upon the dizziest pinnacle of his career. He had smashed the little German states to their knees, lending them, through the misery which loves company, an incentive to work towards a united Germany. Four years before, at Jena, only forty miles northwest of Zwickau, the tiny Corporal had drubbed the Prussians. When Robert was two, he saw a hundred and fifty thousand French soldiers parading exuberantly through the streets on their confident way to conquer Russia; and it may have been this hearing of martial music in 4/4 time, when he was hardly more than a baby, which implanted his love of marches. As the climax of the show came the Emperor himself, with his Empress and a brilliant retinue. The world had become a dazzling contemporary legend of the infallible one's prowess.

Then suddenly—as in those later days of 1943—the legend collapsed, like a palace gnawed too long by termites. Tattered, starved, and frost-bitten fragments of the Grand Army began to struggle westward across central Europe, and presently through Zwickau, requisitioning most of the town's food and leaving pestilence in exchange. A few months later, for three whole days, Robert heard the dull booming of big guns fifty miles to the north. Napoleon was being crushed—though still not finally—in

3

the battle of Leipzig. (Let us hope that the child was spared the sight of the heaps of severed arms and legs in the streets outside the Zwickau hospitals!) Two years later, at Waterloo, the one-time conqueror of Europe was finished off.

Robert's father, August Schumann, felt a devoted—if short-lived—admiration for Napoleon, and the small boy, while in the nursery, must have heard from his father's lips the current Napoleonic legends, and been fascinated by them; and then, childlike, must have been thrilled by their disintegration into tales of defeat and disaster.[1]

This period, when the first decade of the nineteenth century was moving into the second, was one that tended to nourish sensitive imagination. It has been noted as a curious coincidence that so many great men were born during these stimulating years. Look at a few of them:

> 1809—Lincoln, Darwin, Gladstone, Gogol, Poe, Tenny-
> son, O. W. Holmes, Mendelssohn
> 1810—Cavour, Musset, Chopin, Schumann
> 1811—Thackeray, Gautier, Liszt, Greeley
> 1812—Dickens, Browning
> 1813—Livingstone, Verdi, Wagner

In esthetic development it was a crucial moment. Inspired by political upheavals, the world of the arts was turning away from austere, form-loving Classicism to the individualistic freedom of the Romantic period. German literature had already shown the way with Novalis, Tieck, Schlegel, the luxuriant fantasies of Jean Paul Richter, and the fevered fictions of E. T. A. Hoffmann. In music, young Franz Schubert and Carl Maria von Weber were beginning to follow suit, seeking escape from the miseries of the present indicative in the enchanted forests and Cloud-Cuckoo lands of fancy, peopled by elves, pixies, good fairies, wise swans, winged steeds, magic casements, and all the other apparatus of folklore.

The place of Robert's birth bore a name befitting the home

[1] No one has more poignantly expressed the loyalty and the grief of the Old Guard than did Robert long afterwards in the music to *The Two Grenadiers*.

of a Romantic poet and musician. Zwickau was fancifully derived from the Latin word *cycnea;* for tradition said that its site had once held a "swan lake," which restored the youth of those who bathed in it. How suitable that its most eminent son should have written music distinguished for eternal youth!

Schumann, however, was not the only local celebrity. In 1525, under the inspiration of the "Zwickau prophets," the town had given birth to the Anabaptist movement in opposition to Martin Luther.

The year 1810 saw the place a small provincial town of four thousand souls, at the junction of two important post roads. Two centuries before, it had boasted ten thousand inhabitants. But so severely had it been mauled by wars—the Thirty Years', the Seven Years', and the Napoleonic—that there had lately been no hope of progress until, when Robert was thirteen, the adjacent coal mines began active operations. Zwickau boasted a picturesque Cloth Hall (or Gewandhaus), two Gothic churches, paintings by Wohlgemuth and Cranach the Elder, and a remarkable wooden Pietà by Veit Stoss. From that day to this, the population has increased more than tenfold. A pharmaceutical industry was soon added. Brewers came, then tanners, nailsmiths, and an organ builder. The arrival of August Schumann's publishing house had been a noteworthy event in the local annals.

It was a dull, conservative, sleepy, countrified little provincial nest; but there was one emphatic thing to be said for it: the immediate environs were charming. The River Mulde flowed through agreeable gardens and meadows. The nearby Bridge Mount offered wide and engaging views. This hill, and the higher, well-wooded Windberg were two of Robert's favorite resorts, and doubtless inspired many a page of his music.

Robert's parents hailed from Thuringia. This accounts for much in his character, even though he happened to be born just over the line, in Saxony, to which the family had moved two years before. The Thuringians are the kindest, most charming, cultivated, fine-feeling, and generally attractive of all the Teutonic strains. They combine the choicest qualities of north and south Germany, and miss most of the defects. That they have music in their veins is shown by the fact that the region in and near Thuringia produced Schütz, Handel, J. S. Bach, with most of his tribe, and Wagner.

Robert's father, Friedrich August Gottlob Schumann, was a remarkable person. He was born into that domestic environment which has often produced such a disproportionate amount of ability, a poor pastor's large family. By clerking and by writing books, he forced his way up and, for a few months, managed to attend Leipzig University. While assistant in a bookstore at Zeitz, he fell in love with Johanna Christiane Schnabel. Her father was callous enough to insist that, if the young fellow wanted the girl, he must—of all things on earth—start a grocery store!

So August went home—and proceeded to write his head off. In the next year and a half he performed the miracle of finishing seven novels. Still more surprising, these brought him a thousand thalers—in that age, a phenomenal sum for an unknown author. Incidentally, this spurt of creativeness ruined his health.

Then, in 1795, he went to Ronneburg, set up the hated grocery, and married Johanna. However, the itch for literature persisted. With his own private collection of 4000 volumes as a nucleus, he installed a lending library in the store, to make it less obnoxious. Thereupon he retired to literary work in the back room, leaving Johanna to measure flour, weigh cabbages, and give out books.

This lasted four years. Then, despite the angry expostulations of old Schnabel, and with a tremendous sigh of relief, August kicked the grocery business out of doors. In its place appeared a publishing house which, in 1808, he transferred to Zwickau.

Though handicapped by impaired health, and in spite of his temperament, he made a success of the new venture. Indeed, he was an industrious and excellent man of business. His chronicle reads like a Horatio Alger story. He devised and brought out the first German pocket edition of world classics. He edited and published provincial papers as well as important works of reference. In view of Robert's later preoccupation with Byron,

Portraits of Robert Schumann's Parents
Painted by Glaeser

it is worth noting that August's last literary work was a translation of *Beppo* and of three cantos of *Childe Harold*.

Quiet and somewhat reserved, just as Robert was to be,
August was a man of immense ambition and drive. Although
he was a nervous invalid when Glaeser painted him and Johanna,
in the year of Robert's birth, we can see his energy, charm,
humor, and enthusiasm leaping out of the portrait. And in ·his
wife, too, what appears in the canvas is confirmed by the reports of contemporaries.

Johanna looks like a woman of excellent natural understanding, typically small-town in mind, manners, and culture, but
dependable, kind, full of sense and strength. All of these are
qualities desirable in the wife of an imaginative dreamer like
August, and the mother of a genius. Her somewhat stolid practicality offset her husband's daring initiative, checked him when
he would fly off on audacious adventures. There she stood, ready
to curb August's transports and inject the cool sedative of common sense into his high-flown plans. She was—as one would
expect her to be—an excellent housekeeper.

The two met on the congenial common ground of taste and
refinement. And they were both good-looking. One can see
Robert in his mother. And August's striking pulchritude cannot
be marred even by the fantastic coiffure of thick locks that
tumble every which way over his brows. Robert inherited from
him the strong nose and jaw and the agreeable harmony of
feature,[2] as well as his ambition, pertinacity, business sense, and
industry, his patience, his instinct as a pioneer of culture, and a
magnanimous freedom from envy and jealousy almost unheard-
of in a musician.

Even the literary styles of the two men were similar in facility,
compression, and variety, and in their way of passing from the
descriptive to the dramatic. Some of the mordant satire and just
criticism in the father's novel, *Junker Kurl von Kotenstein's
Verliebte Heldenfahrt*, might almost have been written by his
son.

When Robert grew up, his choice of a wife was destined to
parallel, and improve upon, this marital combination. Perhaps

[2] Compare Robert's portrait following p. 48 with those of his parents.

because Johanna spoiled him, the youngster developed such a fixation upon her that he later anticipated that modern Freudian song:

> I want a girl
> Just like the girl
> That married dear old Dad!

Robert was the youngest of five children. Now, a youngest child is apt to be spoiled. He may be given an inferiority complex by the older brothers and sisters, who build their own personalities up at Junior's expense by ridiculing him and painting blood-curdling pictures of the difficulties lurking ahead. Or else he may be spoiled by all hands' yielding to his every whim and making him believe that his word is law.

The latter is what happened to Robert. Father was too absorbed in business and writing to give the boy regular attention; though he was deeply interested in this one child whom he had destined for an artistic career. He helped Robert to collect coins, urged him to learn modern languages, often chatted about literature, and later, when the boy was fourteen, allowed him to become a fellow-contributor to an ambitious work which the firm was getting up: *Portraits of the Most Celebrated Men and Peoples of All Times,*—an early forerunner of such books as *Van Loon's Lives.*

However, the child was brought up largely by three women: his mother, his sister, and the wife of Burgomaster Ruppius, who took a fancy to him as a baby, and often had him at her house for whole days and nights. They spoiled him all the more because he was handsome and amusing, and he soon learned to turn on his charm to get whatever he wanted. Two bad results of this treatment were that, until nearly the end of his life, he never learned to brook contradiction or any sort of opposition, and that, until maturity, he had no sense of the value of money.

In the matter of health, Robert's inheritance was not fortunate. Toward the end of their lives, both parents were subject to morbid attacks of melancholy. August, indeed, had never been the same again after his eighteen months' orgy of fiction writing. By his own admission, Edward Young's works excited him to such a pitch that they sometimes drove him "to the verge of madness." Now, any man who can be thus affected by the milk-and-water sentiments of *Night Thoughts* must indeed have a shaky nervous organization to hand on to his progeny.

In her last years, Johanna was attacked by moods of deep depression, alternating with states of sentimental enthusiasm. And these often foamed over into crises of violent anger.

The harmony between these emotionally unstable parents seems to have been somewhat dissonant. In a town where the social distinctions of petty officialdom were absurdly exaggerated, Johanna took it hard that she, the daughter of the Municipal Surgeon, should have been made to keep a grocery. But, when the grocery was metamorphosed into a publishing house—surely a step up in society—she inconsistently regretted having given up the fancied greater security of the carrots, onions, and coffee. Perhaps it was this regret that turned her against the arts, especially August's ambition, a musical career for Robert. In fact, she grew to be a rather difficult person.

No matter how queer and difficult Johanna Schumann might have appeared to her husband and her contemporaries, her youngest son considered her an almost perfect being who needed encouragement. His letters home from Leipzig and Heidelberg were always trying to cheer her up. And he complained that her melancholy left "a terrible discord behind" in his soul. In 1829, three years after she had lost her husband and her only daughter, he wrote her these lines:

Oh, Mother, you have been sitting [in the grandfather chair] for two mortal hours, saying not a word, singing a dead old song, stroking the window up and down with your hand.

Robert's concern was justified. The shock had been too much. After that double blow the poor soul never won back to normal. But from first to last she always referred to Robert, in her somewhat euphuistic style, as "my high-light."

Johanna and August left their five children a dubious physical heritage. All of them were to be short-lived.

Eduard, Carl, and Robert died in their forties; Julius, a lad with a delicate constitution, at 28; and beautiful, bright, and vivacious Emilie, at 19. The girl had developed a mysterious and terrible skin disease. Melancholia set in, and, during an attack of typhus, she drowned herself. A blood relation, Dr. Georg Ferdinand Schumann, also committed suicide.

Few great composers have, like Schumann, begun to love and write poetry before they began to love and write music. This circumstance added to the originality of his equipment, and to the contrast between him and earlier artists. Bach, Mozart, and Beethoven were not his first loves, nor even Goethe and Shakespeare; but minor poets like Uz and Gleim; though he merely used these gentry as a springboard to the immortals of both arts. While his verse never attained any considerable heights, the poet in him was always prompting and inspiring those other selves, the critic and the composer.

He began his education under a pupil of the local High School, who boarded with the Schumanns and taught the boy some of the rudiments of music. At six he was sent to a private school, where for four years he was to distinguish himself in only one way. The habit of being the most important person at home combined, with his charm, ability, and ambition, to make him the leader of the boys of his own age, and foreshadowed the time to come when he was to lead the musical revolution.

But he early began to have a vivid interior life of his own. Once, as a fairly young lad, he woke up in the small hours, crept downstairs to the piano, and was found playing a series of chords and weeping heartily. The family began to realize that little Robert had a distinct leaning towards the keyboard.

At seven he was sent for music lessons to a schoolmaster and organist named Kuntsch, a humble performer and a stranger to the sciences of harmony and counterpoint, who soon taught him all he knew. Realizing Kuntsch's limitations, the ambitious and indulgent father corresponded with Carl Maria von Weber. That famous composer agreed to teach the lad; but in the end the plan fell through, and Kuntsch still reigned supreme over an urchin who played the piano better than he himself could. Such superiority, though, did not save Robert from an occasional box on the ears. And once his faulty rhythm acquainted him with Kuntsch's blackthorn cudgel.

This painful episode, however, must have been kept from the ears of Father. August Schumann had no great liking for music; but he would do anything for his son. At nine he took Robert in the post-chaise all the forty miles to Karlsbad in Bohemia to hear a real virtuoso—Ignaz Moscheles, the friend and protégé of Beethoven. This was an epoch-making experience for a lad who had never dreamed that so much beauty, excitement and wonder could be got out of a box of wires. He returned treasuring the concert program as a sacred memento, and, of course, fully determined to become a virtuoso himself. Thirty years later, in thanking Moscheles for the dedication of his E Major 'Cello Sonata, Schumann recalled the event: "At that time I never dreamed that I should ever be thus honored by so famous a master."

Before long Robert was taking deep headers into the classics. He played Haydn, Mozart, Beethoven, Weber, Hummel, and Czerny. And with another boy named Piltzing, he reveled in symphonies and overtures for four hands.

His doting father bought him all the music he wanted to own. And he was privileged to borrow what he wished from the library of a local church.

When Kuntsch got up a performance of Schneider's *Last Judgment*, the eleven-year-old Robert was allowed to stand at the piano and play the accompaniment. He stood so that his foot might reach the pedal.

In his father's shop, one day, he made an exciting discovery: the complete printed orchestral parts of the overture to Righini's *Tigranes*, which had probably been sent there by mistake. With shouts of glee the boy pounced upon them. Now, nothing would do but to get together an amateur orchestra and have a go at the treasure.

After the manner of amateur orchestras, the body of instrumentalists turned out to be somewhat on the shrill side. There were two flutes, two fiddles, two horns (for a wonder!), and a clarinet. Robert was kapellmeister *ex officio*. With his whole heart and soul he conducted his cohort. On the keyboard his free hand filled in the bass and the other missing parts.

For the occasion the good August had bought music stands

and a new Streicher piano. He was the only listener present. Johanna, even less musical than her husband, would lend no countenance to such goings-on. All through Robert's youth she never lost a chance to scoff at what she called "the breadless art" and to paint lurid pictures of the poverty of great musicians.

When the store of orchestral music gave out, Robert undertook to furnish what was needed. From the time when he was seven or eight, he had composed little piano pieces; but now he embarked on something more ambitious, a setting of the *150th Psalm* for voices and orchestra. We can imagine a haphazard double-quartet of neighbors packed into the Schumanns' front room behind the shrill orchestra, the flushed cheeks and brilliant eyes of the little maestro, and the group of Zwickauers standing down there in the market-place, looking up and wondering what all the unholy row was about.

Robert was nobody's fool. Once, when he was ten or eleven, he promised to appear in a public concert. Then it developed that the piano was impossible. Having heard that the best instrument in those parts was owned by a certain Herr Schiffner, he boldly called and asked the loan of it for the occasion.

Schiffner was shocked. He loved his treasure, and was not prepared to lend it to every urchin who turned up. So he set a trap for this one.

"Would you play on it yourself?"

Robert nodded.

"Well, let's hear what you can do."

He set upon the rack a very difficult sonata movement which contained a typographical error.

"Can you read that at sight?"

"Certainly!"

Robert clambered upon the stool and read the movement perfectly, without letting the printer's mistake be heard.

"How's this?" cried Schiffner, stabbing the spot with an accusing finger. "You didn't play that as it's written!"

"Oh," said the lad scornfully, "*that's* nothing but a typographical error. A *musician* couldn't play a thing like that!"

P.S. He got the piano.

CHAPTER 2

ROBINSON CRUSOE

VERY early Robert won considerable prestige among even the less musical school-fellows by his knack at humorous improvisation. An anonymous essay published in 1850 by Breitkopf and Härtel says that

even as a boy, Schumann had a special inclination and gift for painting feelings and characteristics in tones; indeed, it is said that he was able by certain figures and passages to depict on the piano so exactly and comically the various personalities of the comrades there beside him, that they doubled up with howls of laughter on recognizing the resemblance of the portraits.

Fortunately this rare gift ripened as he grew up. It was to stand him in good stead in many of his piano pieces, such as those for and about children, and in the *Chopin* and *Paganini* movements of *Carnaval*. And one of his most popular "stunts" was to perform in the manner of famous keyboard athletes like Döhler and Thalberg.[1] Despite the fact that he was allergic to opposition of all kinds, this talent joined with his other gifts to make Robert one of the most popular boys in the school. Naturally, he would not have been a success as a subordinate. There was room for a nature like his in only one place—at the top. But there his contemporaries were delighted to install him. When they played soldiers, he was Napoleon Bonaparte. When they sailed their toy boats on the Mulde, his was the admiral's flagship.

Like most boys, they had a pirates' and smugglers' den. It

---

[1] This is the sort of thing that Hans Kindler and Erich Simon do so consummately today in their imitations of eminent conductors.

was a cave on the outskirts of town, and was called *Sansouci*. There the gang roasted potatoes in the hot ashes of their fire, and carried out what they called "Robinsonades." These were inspired by a beloved volume, the title of which they pronounced "Roh'been-sohn Crew-so-ā'." Robert was always Robinson, while the rest of the gang constituted his Man Friday. The marked plurality of this singular Friday did not disturb them, for they were far above paltry and cheese-paring literalness.

The earliest bit of Schumann's handwriting known to exist is a page of his friend Herzog's autograph album. It begins with a quotation, in the original Latin, from Cicero's essay on friendship. Then it continues:

Zwickau
on the 20th of January
1823

Sansouci vivat!

When you read these few lines,
think of your faithful friend and fellow-student
Rob. Alex. Schumann
Pupil of the third class of the Zwickau Lyceum.

There is a crude drawing of a pair of scales, which may symbolize the even-handed justice that Robinson was supposed to mete out to all offenders against his rule.

At fifteen, Robert organized a German Literary Society among the Lyceum students, and became its life and soul. The statutes which he drew up declared that "it is the duty of every cultured man to know the literature of his country." The boys would read a portion of some masterpiece in prose or verse, then a brief biography of a famous author. After discussing these items, the members would offer original poems for criticism. In running this club for more than two years, Robert already showed his inherited talent for businesslike organization, management, and clear, concise expression. It is probable that he led his merry men a good deal better then than he would have later in life, when he became a dreamy, absent-minded, and inarticulate conductor of symphony orchestras.

The piano lessons with Kuntsch came abruptly to an end when the pedagogue declared that Robert, with his chamber-music and orchestral side-activities, his public appearances, and his eternal composing, was too independent by half. That, very probably, was only a pretext. In musical knowledge and prowess, the lad had already outdistanced the teacher. And the leading professional of Zwickau, whose very livelihood depended on his reputation and authority, shrank from being shown up by a mere youthful amateur.[2] However, in 1832, the large-hearted Schumann sent Kuntsch the following pleasant tribute:

You will scarcely believe, my most honored teacher and friend, how frequently and gladly I think of you. You were the only one who recognized the predominant musical talent in me and showed me in time the path along which, sooner or later, my good genius was to guide me.

And much later he inscribed to Kuntsch a work by which he set great store, the *Studies for Pedal-piano,* Op. 56.

In the Lyceum Robert developed a taste for such authors as Horace, Tacitus, and Sallust. Plato left him cold—and no wonder, at his age! Cicero he put down as a "pettifogger, charlatan, and windbag." Sophocles was "the glowing South Pole" of his life and endeavor, in contrast to geometry which was "the icy North Pole." In those days, the notion was not uncommon that the farther south you go, the hotter it gets.

In 1826, when Robert was sixteen, his sister Emilie killed herself. Not long after that, his beloved father died. At the time, Mother Johanna was away from home and the boy's encounter with the stark realities of the situation gave him a shock which ever afterwards made him incapable of facing deaths and funerals.

His bereavement was all the more bitter because August Schumann had intended Robert for a musician's career. But now the choice of his life-work lay with a hard-headed man of affairs named Rudel who had been appointed Robert's guardian, and with Johanna, who feared what she still persisted in calling "the

[2] Later on in Leipzig, Master Dorn was to stop the theory lessons he was giving Robert, on account of this same Schumannian independence.

breadless art," for her boy. Despite the fact that the prosperous August had left enough of a fortune to buy Robert and the rest of the family not only bread, but even cake, Johanna and Rudel determined that the lad should become a lawyer.

Karl Carus's was one house in Zwickau where Robert loved to go. Carus was a leading man of business and an ardent amateur fiddler with a passion for string quartets. There the boy first enjoyed such works of Haydn, Mozart, and Beethoven as were —and are—seldom heard in small towns; and from time to time was allowed to play along with the strings.

Robert, however, was still unsatisfied. He longed to find a musical kindred spirit. And presently something happened that left an indelible mark on his creative life. Carus had a nephew, Dr. Ernst Carus, who practiced medicine in nearby Colditz. His young wife, a singer, was also a real musician. And when she came to visit her husband's Zwickau relatives, and Robert heard from her lips his first Schubert song, he found his dream coming true.

Naturally, he fell in love with the lady; and his struggles to hide it gave his elders secret amusement. The two had glorious hours together, playing four-hands and doing Schubert. Later he spent many a vacation in Colditz with the Carus family.

This puppy-love was sexually awakening. Robert fell further in love with two Zwickau maidens, Nanni Patsch and Liddy Hemper—and at the same time. (Otherwise he was never a lad to do things by halves.) The crudity of his epistolary confidences, with their silly assumption of superiority and world-weary maturity, are delicious specimens of the effusions of a provincial lad of seventeen, and of the tastelessness one would expect in a sentimental epoch.

With Liddy he climbed a mountain at sunset. Pointing to the wild western clouds, he was about to make the profound observation: "That is our life!"—when she suddenly began derogatory remarks about Robert's wild new literary enthusiasm, Jean Paul Richter, a writer whom he idealized even above Goethe.

And now [he wrote Flechsig] the exalted picture of the ideal has vanished *whenever I think of the way she talked about Jean Paul.* Leave the dead to rest in peace!

As for the other flame, he wrote in 1827:

Nanni was my guardian angel. The dirt of vulgarity had already gathered thick about my youthful soul. This good girl appears before me as if adorned with a halo. I should like to sink at her feet and worship her like a Madonna.

Note the last sentence well. It is the first hint of a fixation that was to have a profound effect upon his whole life.

Boylike, however, he very soon forgot both girls. For he discovered that feminine beauty could be only face-deep.

Still seventeen, he wrote Flechsig as if he were at least seventy:

Passions even yet boil up too mightily in me. I have hard fights with myself. . . . Passions are almost always poetic licenses that moral freedom takes.

Now a new taste developed, which he was never to lose:

I should like to drink champagne every day as a stimulus. . . . To ascend the many-fountained regions of sunny Pindus, one must have a friend, a lady-love, and a glass of champagne.

Robert also accused himself of another weakness which he never had, a want of "*Sitzfleisch*," or "sitting-flesh." Which recalls Mary Heaton Vorse's remark that genius is nine-tenths "the art of applying the seat of the pants to the seat of the chair." But Robert was unjust to himself. Many and grievous though his faults were, he was always a model of industry.

The teacher who had the most influence over him was Master Karl Ernest Richter, the Vice Principal. (Perhaps his ascendancy was partly due to his having the same surname as the boy's literary idol, Jean Paul Richter.) He wrote a biography of August Schumann, and continued that writer's *Leaves of Memory for Cultivated Readers,* in the form of a weekly magazine called *The Bee.* At twenty-three, Robert made a thumbnail sketch of his old master:

Richter, commonly called Bee-Richter. Not without influence upon my earlier education. Betimes recognized the musician in me. Moved among us like a regular Talleyrand. In his presence I always felt like a pupil. A man who succeeded wonderfully in everything. Draftsman, musician, merchant, preacher, philologist, politician, bookseller, solicitor. Poetic genius.

The boy was indeed lucky to be taught by such a myriad-minded man.

When he graduated from this school at seventeen, he had for years been writing poems. Now he attempted to deliver one of them, *The Death of Tasso*, in public, and unfortunately from memory. Part way through, to his painful embarrassment—he stuck. Articulateness was never his strong point, anyway. And in this incident we may perhaps find the first symptom of the inhibition that was destined to make him such a preternaturally silent person.

For all his precocious talents, he could amuse himself like an ordinary boy. In December 1827 Robert and his two friends, Walther and Rascher, floundered through two feet of snow on an excursion to the neighboring village of Haslau. Once there, they order roast pork and pickles, and have just money enough left for a long glass of grog apiece. They burst into student songs.

The inn is full of peasants. A fat one approaches and politely begs them to declaim poetry, which the two other boys do with loud applause. Robert improvises at the piano instead; and the peasants prop their mouths wide open as he tornadoes "so drunkenly over the keys." A dance is organized. While the audience shout in jubilation, the young gentlemen swing the peasant maidens with might and main; and, as a final cadence, bestow a loud smack upon the lips of each. "At midnight we reached Zwickau, still very swervy and wobbly. That was indeed a highly genial evening, one worthy of a Van Dyke!!"

After graduation he wrote to his young friend Flechsig on March 18th, 1828:

School is now behind my back and the world lies ahead. As I went out of school for the last time, I could scarcely suppress my tears; but the joy was still greater than the pain. Now the true inner man must come forward and show who he is.

Compare this resolution with one which young Beethoven scribbled on the margin of a sketch-book:

Courage! Despite all the weaknesses of the body, my spirit shall rule! Here I am, twenty-five years old. This year must bring out the complete man.—Nothing must remain over.

During such an era of sentimental gush, it is amusing to find Robert, in this same letter, accusing his fellow-creatures of inability to express their feelings:

Ah, friend, on this earth love and friendship go among men with veiled head and silent mouth, and nobody is able to *tell* another *how* he loves him; but he *feels that* he loves him: for the inner man has no tongue and cannot speak.

The above is clear evidence that Robert has fallen mightily under the influence of Jean Paul Richter, the much-adored Romantic story writer who was, in his day, even more widely read than Goethe, but whose emotional tone, like that of many other European scribes, had been taken from that poet's *Werther*. He was an artist of superb imaginative quality, with a leaning toward the sentimental which appealed to his own age but which annoys ours. Robert, however, fortunately shows no tendency to imitate one of his hero's worst faults, the centrifugal impulse which cannot keep to one subject for five minutes on end. But, in closing this epistle, the boy almost goes Jean Paul one better in the matter of sentimentality:

Pray to the guardian geniuses of friendship not to part us for ever and to let no discord grieve our souls, and to let each fit of weeping that life brings us be short, and be dried on the friend's breast.

Years later he was still getting off good Jean Paul when he called the nightingale "an artist's soul."

On June 5th he wrote from Leipzig to a comrade in Heidelberg:

Perhaps you are now sitting on the ruins of the old mountain castle and, pleased and gay, are smiling at the blossoms of June; while I stand weeping on the collapsed ruins of my air-castles and my dreams, and gaze through tears into the gloomy heavens of the present and the future.

Outpourings like the following are laughable—when they are not downright irritating:

Ah, friend! were I a Smile I would flutter around her eyes; were I Joy I would skip softly through her pulses; were I a Tear, with her would I weep; and if she then smiled again, I would gladly die on her eyelash, and gladly—yes, gladly—be no more.

During this lachrymose period, the quantity of tears shed annually in Central Europe would have floated a navy.

Here is a lush letter which Robert wrote his mother on August 3rd, 1828:

Nature is the great handkerchief of God, spread forth and embroidered with His eternal name, on which man can dry all his tears of anguish; but also of joy; and where every tear drops away into a weeping rapture, and the heart is attuned silently and gently, but piously, to devotion.

However, it would be unfair to be harsh with Jean Paul Richter as young Schumann's literary bad example. After all, the man was a rare soul, capable of writing lines which must have brought Robert genuine and valuable inspiration: "Music is a holy thing that shows mortals a past and a future which they never experience."

And let us not forget that the cult of this poet was actually good for Schumann the composer. While still a young man, he confessed about Jean Paul:

He often brought me near to madness; but the rainbow of peace . . . always floats softly above all tears, and the heart is wonderfully lifted and mildly transfigured.

One ought to forgive Jean Paul his sentimentality, and be grateful to the man. For, under the influence of his dithyrambics, his chief disciple was to compose some of the greatest piano music ever written.

Robert's first brief visit to Leipzig took place just before graduation from the Lyceum. He went to make arrangements for entering the law school of the University. Having agreed to room with Emil Flechsig, a student of theology, he visited his old friends, the Carus family. The doctor from Colditz and the lady with the lovely voice had now moved to Leipzig. And "Fridolin," as they had nicknamed Robert after a character in a ballad of Schiller's, was given a heart-warming welcome.

Frau Agnes was not a little proud of the talent she had discovered in such an unlikely part of the provinces as Zwickau. She thought, too, that he looked extremely presentable in his blue coat, well fitted around the waist, the lapels very broad, a black velvet collar and black satin stock—to say nothing of the dreamy blue eyes, the becoming dimple in his chin, and the satiny lights in his wavy hair.

As for Robert, he had not yet entirely outgrown his calf-love for Agnes, and had little attention to spare for an eight-year-old girl named Clara Wieck. This creature's eyes were much too large for her face, and her nose much too long. But she played the piano part of a Hummel trio amazingly well for her years.

Robert found her father and teacher, the hard-faced Friedrich Wieck, more interesting. Perhaps scenting a pupil, Wieck drew the young fellow out. Gradually the truculence and suspicious defiance of the man's manner moderated. Gleams of humor crept in. In the end, when each acknowledged the same ardent love of Schubert, they found each other congenial. The boy was glad when the man invited him around to the Salzgässchen on his return to Leipzig.

All this, however, was temporarily driven from Robert's mind by a sudden, whirlwind friendship with a fascinating boy named Gisbert Rosen. This fellow law-student was congenially crazy about Jean Paul. He presently visited Robert in Zwickau, broke the news that he was leaving Leipzig for Heidelberg University, and made his friend long to follow him there.

Having been graduted *"eximie dignus,"* Robert sentimentally meditated on paper. Facing the struggle for existence, he might well have echoed the Gascon who was about to charge the enemy: "I tremble at the perils to which my courage is about to expose me!"

Thrown out into existence, flung into the night of the world, without guide, teacher and father, here I stand. And yet the whole world never appeared to me in a lovelier light than now as I face it and, rejoicing and free, smile at its storms.

"Rejoicing and free." By a curious coincidence, this almost exactly anticipates the device which Schumann's successor, young Brahms, was to adopt as his motto, soon after meeting him: *"Frei aber froh"*—"Free but rejoicing."

CHAPTER 3

THE SPENDTHRIFT

I T was the March of 1828. August Schumann had been dead
a year and a half. And now young Robert set out into the
world without the guidance of a father, a spoiled mamma's
darling, ready to use his undeniable charm deliberately to gain
his own self-indulgent ends. For an ordinary youth in these circumstances, there would have been slight hope. But Robert had
inherited three things that were to save him: latent nobility of
character, industry, and genius.

Rejoining Gisbert Rosen, he found it impossible to tear himself away after only a brief visit with that engaging youth, and
arranged to bear him company part of the way to Heidelberg.
The boys chalked out an itinerary that made the trip almost
twice as long as it need have been.

First they stopped at a town which, half a century later, was
to be celebrated as the headquarters of a far greater man than
Jean Paul Richter. At that time, however, the friends had never
heard of Richard Wagner, who was a fourteen-year-old schoolboy. To them Bayreuth meant their little god, Jean Paul, who
had spent there his last twenty-one years.

At his grave they worshiped for an hour, making vows to
remain true to his spirit. Then they called on Frau Rollwenzel,
who had kept the tavern where Jean Paul had done a great deal
of his writing. For two hours the youngsters eagerly questioned
her. Finally, from Richter's widow, their youthful fervor ex-
tracted a portrait of their hero.

In Augsburg the susceptible Robert promptly fell in love with
Clara, the daughter of his father's old friend, Dr. Kurner. But

she turned out to be engaged. The lucky rival, however, was a good sportsman. He sent the boys to Munich with a letter to Heinrich Heine, already famous for his *Buch der Lieder*. The poet showed them more hospitality than, in the circumstances, they had any right to count on; but both sides parted without too much regret. How could Heine have foreseen that his poems were destined for even greater fame at Robert's hands than they would otherwise have achieved? As for Robert, his head was still too full of Jean Paul, and his heart of Clara Kurner, even to guess at the importance of the poet he had just met.

At this point the friends separated with sorrow and vows to reunite soon in Heidelberg. On the way home, Robert had "visions of the lovely Clara" before his eyes, "waking and sleeping." This love-disappointment may have made him a bit cross-grained when he reached Zwickau. For, despite the entreaties of Mamma and the rest of the family who wanted to hear about the trip, he hastily repacked, and in three hours was on his way to Leipzig, and the law studies to which he looked forward with such hearty distaste. We can visualize him in the post-chaise as [1]

a strongly built but slender young man with a blooming complexion, not exactly red-cheeked, but colorful. This was well matched by dark hair worn rather long, that curled on the side from ear to temple. His dark eyes lay deep and sparkled with enthusiastic fire. His whole appearance was noble throughout. He carried himself elegantly; and at the same time the entire man expressed such goodness of heart that one was unconsciously prepossessed in his favor.

Schumann an embryo lawyer! He was as far out of his element as a hundred-per-cent football player in a required course in esthetics. For an equally absurd misfit we would have to visit the eighteenth century and discover, on the hard benches of law schools, two lads named George Frederick Handel and François Arouet (better known as Voltaire); then sail across the Channel to nineteenth-century Scotland, and find in that same uncongenial air a Robert who had for the rest of his name Louis Stevenson. In her determination to force her son into the legal profession, Frau Schumann was like the A.E.F. in the First

[1] According to Täglischbeck's word-portrait of him at this time.

World War, which made scientists into muleteers, and philosophers into cooks, and knew but one destination for a square
peg—a round hole.

It is likely that Robert himself saw the absurdity of the situation, and went to Leipzig with his tongue in his cheek, waiting
only for a favorable opportunity to turn musician. Indeed, what
could be more absurd than to take a wild, airy, undisciplined
imagination, a sparkling wit, a well-winged fancy and high
musical originality, and make an ass of the combination by
tying upon it a nosebag composed of the Pandects of Justinian?

Fresh from the country, Robert was overwhelmed by Leipzig.
Though a small city of only forty thousand, to the very-small-
town lad it seemed a huge metropolis. In a letter to Rosen we
have already seen him compare the city to ruins. "Nature," he
complains in the first letter to Mother,

> Nature, where shall I find it here? All hidden by the flourishes and
> curlicues of art. No valley, no mountain, no forest where I can give
> free rein to my thoughts. No place where I can be alone but in
> my locked room. And even there I'm just above an eternal noise and
> fuss.

Poor young bumpkin! It is true that the country about Leipzig was more prosaic than that about almost any other city in
central Europe, and that the Pleisse could not compare in charm
with the Mulde outside Zwickau, flowing by tranquil meadows.
But this letter makes one wonder what he expected a city to be
like. However, Leipzig was at first harder for him to put up with
than it need have been. For Flechsig, the theology student, had
foolishly taken rooms for them in the Ghetto, and ground-floor
rooms at that. There, just beneath the windows, men hawked
goods in strident, passionate tones, and wrangled all day over
coppers.

To deepen the misery, there was always the hated law! In the
same letter he went on:

> This cold jurisprudence, which at the very start hurls one to earth
> with its icy definitions, cannot please me. I don't want medicine,
> and can't study theology. Here am I, in the midst of an eternal inner
> conflict, vainly seeking a guide who could tell me what I should do.

His loathing of Leipzig and law also embraced the student clubs, the *Burschenschaften,* with their rough crudity and boorishness. A *Bursch* might have intellectual interests of some kind, and if he successfully camouflaged them, while throwing himself heartily into drinking, fencing, and the pursuit of women, they were not held against him. But woe to the poor fellow if they were discovered!

Public opinion compelled Robert to join a fencing society. But he found he was not built on swashbuckling lines, and soon withdrew. In a letter to Rosen he cried:

I hate it here; and student life seems to me too base to tempt me to plunge in.

So he avoided most of his fellow-students. "I go out very little, and sometimes feel quite crushed by the pettinesses and miseries of this egotistical world." He conceived himself a better man than the other students—and he was right.

But nobody is quicker to spot such assumptions of superiority than a student, especially if their owner is a *Fuchs,* or Freshman. Probably it did not take Robert long to "queer" himself pretty thoroughly with the regular gang; which made him all the more eager to run away and join Rosen in Heidelberg.

The process of "queering" was aggravated by the patent fact that he was a spoiled lad who had been brought up by doting women. (If Robert had only given the fellows a chance, they might have counteracted some of the spoiling.)

On August 22, 1828, a piteous wail went to Mamma:

If only I had somebody here who rightly and wholly understood me, and did everything for my sake out of love for me! With Flechsig I get on well; but he never cheers me up. If sometimes I am melancholy, he ought not to be melancholy also, but should have humanity enough to stir me up. Often I am conscious that I need cheering up.

How much further could the expression of mawkish and egotistical self-pity go?

Another aspect of Robert's spoiling was financial. He was a sad spendthrift. In fact, he had no idea of the value of money. This led him on to become a champion hornswoggler and virtuoso in the composition of begging letters. How deftly he could turn on the spigot of charm and extract gold from his family, from his friends, and even from his hard-boiled guardian, Herr Rudel! Robert assuredly shared the sentiments of that young rascal, Peter Simple, in Captain Marryat's novel, who exclaims: "What a pleasure to receive a letter from one's friends when far away, especially when there's some money in it!"

One of Robert's cleverest appeals to Rudel is the careless mention, and veiled threat, of credit:

March 26, 1830

What an obligation you would place me under, most honored Herr Rudel, if you would send me as quickly as possible as much as possible! Please believe me when I tell you that a student never spends more than when he hasn't a *Kreuzer* in his pocket, especially in the small university towns, where he gets as much credit as he likes. During the last seven weeks there were two when I didn't possess a copper; and I can honorably admit that I've never spent as must as in these seven weeks. The inn-keepers write your debt with double chalk, and one has to pay with double crown-dollars.[2]

One can see Rudel cursing and bounding in his chair—and paying.

Another effective dodge of Robert's was frankly to admit his own shortcomings. He wrote Mamma:

This contempt for money and this squandering of it is pitiful in me. You would scarcely believe how frivolous I am and how often I just throw money out of the window. I always curse myself and make the finest of resolutions; but the next minute I have forgotten them and again give an eight-groschen tip. . . . I fear I am incorrigible.

In another letter to her:

I am not a practical person. . . . Really it is nobody's fault but heaven's itself.

And to the wife of his brother Eduard he mails this gem:

I shall even have to sell or pawn my watch. If God would only let it rain ducats! Then there would be no more tears and letters to guardians and brothers.

[2] A Kronenthaler then represented about a dollar in our money.

However, to labor this point can give no pleasure to anybody who loves Schumann's music. In the matter of his youthful foibles there is no reason to be as grim as one disapproving biographer, Herbert Bedford,[3] who calls him, in the words of Sir Toby, "a very dishonest paltry boy." Happily the German proverb, "End good, all good," applied here. In the end, Robert's economic life was saved by a prudent mate, plus his own innate integrity.

As a matter of fact, Schumann came to maturity with as few faults and as many admirable qualities as any other of the great composers. Think of the overbearing bad temper of Bach, Brahms, and Beethoven, and the downright dishonesty of the last-named, as when he represented himself a pauper on his death-bed. Think of Wagner's despicable personal character. Schumann turned out to be a person of a quite different moral stamp.

Fundamentally honest though he was to prove himself to be, Robert was not above another sort of misrepresentation at this period in his life. Frequently he wrote home professing that he was pursuing jurisprudence industriously, and attending classes as regularly as clockwork. As a matter of fact, he was doing nothing of the sort. His days were spent in practicing, reading, and walking in the country. With a couple of fiddlers, he became enthusiastic about Schubert's E Flat Trio, the one with the exciting funeral march. So he gave an evening party for it. Wieck was invited as guest of honor. Champagne flowed as from a tap. And everyone got drunk except the host and the theological student.

When the largely self-taught Robert first went to Wieck for piano lessons, he was in dire need of precisely such a half-pedantic pedagogue. His ardent temperament and natural talent might serve to screen his lack of clarity, accuracy, and thoroughness; but the just judge, and even his own better self, could not be fooled. Later, in writing of this period, he confessed: "I could play all concertos at sight [did he really believe that one?], but had to get down to bedrock and start with the C major scale."

[3] *Schumann*, Harper, 1925.

At last the boy was getting a little sorely needed discipline. And how hard it came!

My most fatal crisis [he wrote] was this business of standing in the middle between art and nature. I was always a fiery performer; but my technic was full of holes. So I had to take everything slowly and clearly. The consequence was a hesitation that made me doubt my own talent.

Perhaps as a result of this grilling, he felt that he was faring badly in Leipzig and becoming "quite soured." At the end of August he wrote Mamma: "I am too soft. I realize it clearly." One common trait, however, subconsciously worked for congeniality between pupil and master. Robert was a notable innovator. And, in his lesser way, Wieck was another.

The boy found it difficult enough to swallow Wieck's technical regimentation, and he was still too soft to acknowledge the need for studying harmony, counterpoint, and form. That would come later, and would go much against the grain.

Meanwhile he had become enamored of some compositions by a then famous, now forgotten, composer. Wiedebein was director of the orchestra at Brunswick, and an acquaintance of Beethoven's. Robert sent him some songs for criticism, and received one of the wisest and most charming letters ever written by a mature composer to a young one. Here are a few lines of it:

                                                                August 1, 1828.

In moments of divine consecration, we should give ourselves completely up to beautiful enthusiasm. But afterwards calmly-weighing reason must come into its own and, with its bear's paw, mercilessly scratch out any imperfections that have smuggled themselves in. . . .

Above all, lay stress on truth: truth of melody, of harmony, and of expression—in a word, poetic truth. Whenever you do not find this, whenever you find it even threatened, tear it out, even though it should be your dearest. . . .

From nature you have received much, very much. Make use of it, and the world's respect will not pass you by.

Even at eighteen, Robert was scarcely what could be called a mixer or a royal good fellow. Already he had developed a remarkably sensitive technic in avoiding whatever threatened to upset his inner equilibrium. He early acquired a habit of silence which grew on him progressively. Perhaps he felt that the more you have to say with your lips, the less you have to say with your pen. Often he would sit through a supper party without making more than two or three remarks.

Henriette Voigt, a young matron with whom he had a romantic friendship of an odd sort, testified:

One summer evening we made music together, then took a boat ride on the river. During an hour, Robert kept complete silence. Then he pressed my hand tenderly with the words, "And now we perfectly understand one another."

During the first months when Robert was still an outsider in Leipzig, he must have led a rather poverty-stricken musical life. His letters mention only the concerts of the Gewandhaus, the time-honored symphony orchestra established in 1781. Not a word about the opera, nor the weekly motet at St. Thomas's where Johann Sebastian Bach had been cantor, nor about the "academies," as the concerts of the Matthäi Quartet were still called.

His homesickness lasted long, as was natural for a boy with a mother-fixation. On October 24th he wrote Mamma:

Oh, I have enjoyed *hours* in Zwickau that tip the balance against *days* in Leipzig. I mean those quiet autumn evenings at home which are at the same time rapturous evenings of the heart, those gilded heights and the valleys in full bloom. Oh, Leipzig, with all its concerts, theater, and so on, cannot compensate me for that whole still-life of nature and friendly humanity.

Tenderness for his birthplace and his mother also breathes through the next letter, written a month later:

This, my dear Mother, is the first of your birthdays when I have not been able to press your hand. And yet I celebrate it as sacredly as in my childhood days, when I brought you a bouquet of flowers and shyly stammered my childish good wishes.

During those years Robert's impressionable heart was still in a highly volatile state. By April 1829, having already forgotten

Clara of Augsburg, he wrote to Gisbert before joining him in Heidelberg:

In the last while, it seemed terribly hard to think of leaving Leipzig. Recently . . . a feminine soul, beautiful, gay and devout, enchained my own. It cost me a fight; but now it's all over. I stand here strong, with unshed tears in my eyes, and look with hope toward my Heidelberg blossoms and mayflowers. The first thing that I shall seek in Heidelberg is—a sweetheart.

Who was the Leipzig lady? It could scarcely have been Agnes Carus, for she had enchained his heart back in Zwickau. Was it Henriette, to whom, on the water, he had sung silent songs without words?

Of this we may be certain: the young law student had one mistress to whom he was more devotedly attached than to any of flesh and blood. Whenever, in his letters, the subject of music comes up, we feel his spirit flaming. And the sparks form a momentary halo about the passionate young face.

CHAPTER 4

LAWYER INTO MUSICIAN

THE law school at Leipzig shut up shop for vacation. Now on to Heidelberg! But first a few days of joy at home.

In Zwickau, however, disaster threatened the student. Brother Julius fell seriously ill. In case of his death, Johanna declared, Robert would have to stay at home with her. The two-way fixation of mother on son and son on mother was now threatening the youth's career as dangerously as was her distrust of "the breadless art." But the patient recovered, and high old times began.

I can't get away at all at all from the joy and delight of celebrations [he wrote Gisbert]. Day before yesterday there was a most brilliant concert in Zwickau, where 800 to 1000 people got together. Naturally I let my own fingers also be heard.

The middle of May he started south. The coachman of the diligence was charmed into giving him the reins. He made friends with a best-selling novelist whose pen name was Willibald Alexis, and whose real name was Georg Wilhelm Häring. This gay and charming gentleman had won fame and fortune by imitating the then booming *Waverley* novels of Sir Walter Scott. It was a new idea to Robert that one could be a celebrated literary person and yet not stalk through life wrapped in the melodramatic gloom which the late Lord Byron had made fashionable.

Häring took a fancy to Robert. In Frankfort he introduced him to Ferdinand Ries, the pupil of Beethoven. The musician's English wife had features so lovely that they made the lad's

31

head spin, and his susceptible heart pump *accelerando*. "When she spoke English," he confessed, "it fell on my ears like the lisping of an angel."

The novelist also showed him the gentle art of wandering planless through the picturesque courtyards and hidey-holes of ancient cities. In the spirit of the future Vagabondia school of poetry, he urged that they should

> loose reins upon the neck of fate, and forth

to new adventures around the next corner. Frankfort was not a bad practice-ground for that sort of errantry. Goethe's birthplace and the Städelsche Museum were milestones on the way.

Häring taught the lad "the possibility of enjoying beauty without tears"; and from then on our hero grew less lachrymose at a gratifying rate. Under this bracing influence he laid aside his morbid posing and became a natural, healthy young fellow, enjoying himself to the utmost, and cavorting triumphantly on top of the world.

He compared the journey to "a flight through hundreds of Spring skies." But, with a sudden premonitory catch at the heart, we read these light words from Frankfort:

> In passing let it be remarked that my lodging has an insane asylum on the right and a Catholic church on the left; so that I'm really in doubt whether I ought to go mad or Catholic.

There he suddenly felt an imperious desire to get his hands upon a piano. So he dropped in at a dealer's and claimed to be the master of ceremonies of an English lord who wanted to buy a grand. For three hours he performed with great applause, and said he would let them know the lord's decision in two days. "By then I was already long in Rüdesheim, drinking Rüdesheimer."

Then he met the river that was always to be linked in intimate association with his art and his fate.

> I closed my eyes in order to enjoy the first view of the majestic old father Rhine with the whole of my fasting soul.—And when I opened them, it lay before me, quiet, still, earnest and proud like an old German god.

Finding that Häring was Paris-bound, Robert turned his back on Heidelberg to accompany him as far as Coblenz. Not until he arrived there did he count his money to see whether he could afford the trip—and found that he could not. But he did not let this fact spoil the sport.

He mailed his mother zestful thumbnail vignettes of miscellaneous fellow travelers. They show a pretty gift for the observation of human types. For such an introvert, Robert now brought to light an extraordinarily extroverted interest in all kinds of folk, from a drunken dancing master, and old soldiers who told him how it went at Waterloo, to a kindly fat man encountered at sunrise on the ruins of Stolzenfels. It afterwards developed that this person was Frederick, Crown Prince of Holland. And Robert learned about people from everybody. As this is, in all his correspondence, the one instance of such a broad and eager interest in the human kaleidoscope, it brings up the question whether Robert may not have caught it, like a swiftly passing contagion, from his novelist traveling companion.

Though so poor that he had to trudge the last dozen miles, he reached Heidelberg in exuberant spirits. Here in this lovely town, between the mountain and the River Neckar, as a student in the oldest of German universities, Robert was to be happy, and to make the most momentous decision of his career.

He was received with open arms and purses by Gisbert Rosen and a new friend named Semmel. Presently he wrote:

Rosen stands as a fine, upright conciliator of my world of feeling with Semmel's world of reason. And together we make a right harmonious clover-leaf.

The clover-leaf devoted itself with energy and success to having a good time. Though Robert wrote home that the law tasted excellent, and that he felt "the true worth of jurisprudence and how it furthers all the holy interests of humanity," his tongue was doubtless in his cheek.

In the summer vacation he yearned to see the Alps and northern Italy. Mother and guardian balked and refused to put up the money for the trip. He won by threatening to borrow at a ruinous rate of interest.

In Switzerland, where he caught "beautiful glances from a beautiful English girl," this was his reaction to the mountains: "Man is not so unhappy as he thinks he is. He has his heart, which finds its loveliest echo in nature." Conscious of his subjective advantages over other wanderers, he exulted: "The poet's eye is the richest and most beautiful."

In Italy he was fleeced by fellow-travelers and shopkeepers. Then he corrected the equilibrium by the schoolboy trick of giving himself out as a Prussian, because there the Prussian was more highly considered than the Saxon. He borrowed sixteen gold napoleons from a sympathetic merchant in Milan, and raised further loans from family and friends.

Yes, at this time he was the perfect hornswoggler. However, instead of worrying about lads like him, the moralist ought rather to worry about the young fellow who is so good that he worries nobody. There is something in Robert's later aphorism:

> One forgives the diamond its sharp points. It is very costly to round them off.

Later on, a brilliant girl called Clara was to round off some of Robert's, and make the art of music the sufferer. Fortunately she did not, into the bargain, round off his susceptibility to impressions, the vividness of his "Florestan" and "Eusebius" moods, his generous impetuosity, his mysticism, humor, nobility, and his utter devotion to beauty.

Robert praised the fire of the Italian orchestras, but deplored their slovenliness. In La Scala everything must have been set fair to give him a single memorable experience. He wrote Wieck:

> There has been only one evening in my life when it was as if God stood before me and let me . . . look for a few moments into his face—and that was in Milan when I heard Pasta—and Rossini.

It speaks for the strength of Robert's personality that, after such an exaggerated outburst, one searches his music almost in vain for any trace of Italian influence.[1]

---

[1] Later on in Leipzig, after he had heard Francilla Pixis sing an aria by Donizetti, "something very wet" was noticed on his cheeks, which he

But Italy itself, like all his experiences, turned to melody and harmony within him. He called the Italian language "an eternal music," and agreed with an acquaintance that it was "a long-drawn-out A minor chord."

After visiting Vicenza, Verona, Padua, and Venice (where he was ill for a few days), he returned to Heidelberg on October 20th, 1829. In seven weeks he had developed a love of Italy which was never to leave him. Perhaps this love was part of the inheritance which he would pass on to a boy named Johannes Brahms, who was to enter the world four years later.

One of the Heidelberg professors, an enthusiastic musical amateur named Thibaut, made a deep impression on Robert. And the boy wrote his mother:

> Thibaut is a splendid, godlike man at whose house I enjoy my most delightful hours. When he gives one of Händel's oratorios (every Thursday more than seventy singers gather there), and accompanies so enthusiastically at the piano, finally two great tears roll out of his lovely large eyes beneath the beautiful silvery white hair, and then he comes to me so delighted and gay and presses my hand and is silent because there's too much emotion in that big heart. And often I am at a loss to know how a beggar like me has the honor to be let in to listen in such a holy house. You can scarcely imagine his wit, acuteness of perception, depth of feeling, pure artistic sense, kindness, tremendous eloquence, and breadth of outlook.

Later on, however, when satiated with a little too much Händel, Robert nimbly modified these early transports, and bore hard on the professor's painful one-sidedness and limited, pedantic outlook upon music: "Under the table with Thibaut and his Händelian operatic tunes!"

After performing once in public, Robert received so many invitations to play that he had to decline them all. By his own admission, he was the favorite of the Heidelberg public. Life became a round of parties and balls; but he informed Mamma

explained away as "drops of perspiration." He rushed to his room, turned the key in the lock, and was then heard to rage furiously against his own weakness; after which he stormed to the piano, improvised a consummate parody of Donizetti, and assured himself in a passionate voice that it was nothing but the singer's quality of tone that had so moved him.

that he got to work every morning at four. If this was true, lack of sleep may later have been one important cause of his recurrent nervous troubles.

At Easter 1830, an overwhelming impression was made on him by the sensational violin virtuoso Paganini. Here are a few extracts from his telegraphically brief account of the pilgrimage to Frankfort:

Mountain-road unexpectedly vile—the little waitress—Malaga—drinks—caroms in the vestibule, etc.—*Easter Sunday*—Töpken's curses —April weather, blue and black—the watch-tower outside Frankfort—arrival at The Swan—in the evening Paganini—far music and blessedness in bed—*Easter Monday*—the beautiful girl in Weidenbusch—evening "*Tell* by Rossini"—hustling to Weidenbusch—the beautiful girl—lorgnette-bombardment—champagne—*Easter Tuesday*—departure from Frankfort, perhaps forever—my artistic evasion in the Frankfort tenderloin—Darmstadt—exquisite state after a bumper of wine———wine in belly—getting the reins crossed—at last arrival in Auerbach—little Lottie————*Easter Wednesday*—bad weather—lovely blossoms on the mountain road—the profligate Prussian freshman in Handschuchsheim—arrival in Heidelberg—End—.

The experience of hearing Paganini was decisive. It broke down the last hesitation about his career. He sent Mamma an eloquent letter, at last coming squarely out into the open and playing on her heart-strings with virtuosity. Indeed, so skillfully did he marshal his arguments, and so convincingly set them forth, that one wonders whether, after all, he did not have in him the makings of a brilliant criminal lawyer.

He reminded Mother how Father had destined him for an artistic career, but how she had always stood firmly in the way. He declared that in six years he could be as good a piano virtuoso as there was in the world, bar none. It touches us to find him continuing: "Here and there I also show imagination and perhaps a disposition for creative work of my own."

He drew a vivid contrast between the hated treadmill of law and the Elysium of art; and begged her to leave the decision to Wieck. She consented to this; and the pedagogue's verdict was, of course, favorable.

Considering your son Robert's talent and fantasy, within three years I guarantee to make of him one of the greatest living pianists, who will play with more imagination and warmth than Moscheles, and more splendidly than Hummel.

The only doubts which Wieck permitted himself to express were not about Robert's artistic promise, but about his moral qualifications.

And so Robert crossed the Rubicon. By coincidence, he won his musical independence just when Chopin was settling down to an artistic career in France, and when Berlioz was struggling free of the hated Conservatoire.

As he shook from his feet the very moderate amount of legal dust that may have collected there, he gratefully and jubilantly wrote Wieck:

I trust you wholly and give myself entirely into your hands. Take me as I am. In everything have patience with your pupil. No censure will discourage me, and no praise will make me relax. I wish you could look inside me. It is quiet there, and over my whole world lies the gentle, bright perfume of morning. So, trust me. I will earn the honor of being your pupil.

And to his family: "Surely you would all rather see me poor and happy in art than poor and unhappy in the law."

Thus Robert joined the illustrious company of the ardent souls who have burst from the cell of the law. As he wrote Lemke, the parting from Heidelberg hung in his mind "like the rain-clouds, out of which, from time to time, the lovely Philippine protruded her little angel's head." Who Philippine was we do not know.

On the way to Leipzig, with characteristic indirection, and as usual regardless of expense, he made the long trip down his favorite Rhine. And on September 27th, 1830, from Wesel near the Dutch border—already inconstant to Philippine—he wrote Mamma of all the English people he had met on the boat. Memories of Frau Ries may have supervened, for he exclaimed: "If ever I marry, it will be an English girl!"

CHAPTER 5

THE CRIPPLED HAND

FINANCIAL worries accompanied Robert from Heidelberg to Leipzig. His brothers grimly disapproved of his change of profession. His habit of begging them to send him money and keep the transaction dark from Mother did nothing to sweeten their tempers—especially as he would promptly try the identical game with Mother. This led to bold dissonances, so that he wrote her: "A long-suppressed discord between two human hearts is far more wounding and dangerous than an open, direct reproach."

Robert recognized, moreover, that his deplorable prodigality extended beyond financial to spiritual concerns. "If my talent for poetry and music were only focused upon one point, the light would not be so much broken up."

He was always a creature of kaleidoscopically shifting moods; but at this time they seemed to change with more than customary agility. One moment he deplored the poverty which kept him from buying a pistol to shoot himself. The next, he exulted:

I am so fresh in soul and spirit that life gushes and bubbles around me in a thousand springs. This is the work of divine fantasy and her magic wand.

One day, hypochondria made him fear blindness. The next, he was "uncommonly free in a light and divine mood." Then panic pounced. He dreaded cholera, and planned to flee as far as Naples or Sicily, first making his will, and leaving his most important papers in his mother's hands. But, presto change, he felt "healthy as a fish," and abandoned all thoughts of flight.

Such a volatile nature is peculiarly open to the temptations of alcohol; and, during these critical days of 1831, Robert was in danger of forming an unbreakable habit. His theory teacher, Dorn, told about their combining counterpoint and champagne. And a few months later, with admirable candor, Robert wrote his mother:

You yourself have asked Rascher if I really drink so much. I believe he defended me. I myself would not have done so; for there is something in it. However, as Bavarian beer is more a prosaic habit than a poetic passion, swearing off was not easy. For a passion is no end easier to get rid of than an old habit. But if you ask whether I've gotten rid of it, I say in a firm voice: Yes.

Perhaps all that saved him from becoming a dipsomaniac was his creative gift. Instinctively he felt that for its sake he must take care of himself.

One of Robert's most attractive traits was his love and understanding of children. At the Wiecks', where he lodged for the first year after his return from Heidelberg, he was a prime favorite with the youngsters. He turned the boys into amateur magicians and made them perform tricks for coppers. He was a champion concocter of riddles and organizer of charades. And his humor kept the air full of shrill, delighted laughter.

He had no awe whatever for little Clara, the wonder-child whom Goethe complimented, and who could make strong musicians tremble. Why, the year before, even the famous Reissiger, who had stepped into Carl Maria von Weber's shoes as conductor of the Dresden Opera, had declared that it made him dreadfully nervous to play before her! Once when she was away on a concert-tour, Robert wrote her such a letter as a child would dote on:

During your absence I paid a visit to Arabia to gather all sorts of stories that would please you—six new doubleganger [1] tales, one hundred and one charades, eight amusing riddles, and then the frightfully lovely robber stories, and those about the white ghost—guroo-oo, how I shudder! . . .

[1] This word, which is good English, refers to the weird stories of the wraiths of the living which Robert used to concoct for the Wieck children.

Like his successor, Brahms, Schumann was especially charming to poor children. One afternoon, in his favorite café, The Coffee Tree, he noticed a hungry-looking urchin of ten, hawking hard-boiled eggs. He called the lad to his table:

"Wouldn't you like to eat a couple yourself?"

"Yes, indeed, but I'm not allowed."

"Well, how many could you get outside of? I'll pay for them."

In embarrassment the boy dug a grubby fist into his eye. "Dunno, *mein Herr.*"

Robert clapped the little fellow on the shoulder. "All right; start in!"

The first three eggs vanished in a trice. With the fourth there came a *rallentando.*

"That's too dry for him; he must have butter. Waiter, some butter!"

This improved the rate of consumption; but six were enough. "Now he must drink. Waiter, bring the lad a glass of beer!"

And the gamin's pleasure was exceeded only by that of his new idol, Robert Schumann.

Here in the world of those little folks who invariably became his idolaters, the young musician discovered an unsuspected mine of gold and jewels. "In every child," he said, "there lie wonderful depths." As we shall see, he was the first composer ever to explore those depths, and to write music with, and about, children that was worthy of its subject.

It is not known when Robert resumed his lessons with Wieck, or for how long, or just when further lessons were put out of the question by that most terrifying of all catastrophes for a pianist, the injury to his hand which will presently be described. What is sure is that, before the accident, he was not fully satisfied with his master. Clara's father often took her away on tour, and Robert undoubtedly felt that his progress was too slow. He had solemnly bound himself to work under Wieck for three years. But one day he casually informed the pedagogue of a plan he had for studying with Hummel in Weimar. The egotistic and tempestuous music-master burst into a paroxysm of rage, and offered Robert a foretaste of those tongue-lashings to which, in the future, Clara's father was to treat him. Robert sought to appease the fury by explaining that he had thought of the plan merely on account of Hummel's exalted name. But this tactless remark only made matters much worse.

"Name?" shrieked the other. "And what of *mine?* Haven't I the name of being the greatest piano teacher in the world?"

Robert wrote Mamma:

I was visibly terrified at his premature anger; but now we are on friendly terms again, and he treats me affectionately like his own child.[2] You can have scarcely an idea of his judgment and his grasp of art; but if he talks in his own interest or Clara's, he gets wild as a peasant.

And this lad of twenty showed how young he really was by ending with a request for specific Christmas presents: a fur rug, cigars, boots, and a pair of artist's cuffs.

On January 11th, 1831, we find the first mention in his correspondence of a published composition. It is the postscript of a letter to his friend Lemke in Heidelberg: "The *Abegg Variations* will very soon be printed. Are you scared? The whole of Heidelberg will get free copies."

This work, Robert's Opus 1, was fancifully dedicated "to Mademoiselle Pauline Countess Abegg." In reality there was no Pauline and no countess, and Abegg was the surname of Meta, who lived in Mannheim. She was a girl admired by one of his friends. Here is the first instance of his pet habit of making words out of notes which correspond to letters of the alphabet. As B flat is called B in German, the name-theme runs—

We shall see more of this musico-alphabetical habit.

Among all delights there are few to compare with the rapture felt by a budding author or composer on the publication of his

[2] We shall presently see how affectionately Wieck was to treat his own child.

first book or piece. Before the appearance of Opus 1, Robert wrote his mother:

> You can scarcely believe what a feeling it is when a young composer can say to himself: "This work is all yours; nobody will take this possession away from you, nor can take it, for it is wholly your own." Oh, if you could feel this "wholly"!

And, after publication, he exulted:

> I doubt if being a bridegroom will be in the same class with these first joys of being a composer. The entire heavens of my heart are hung full of hopes and presentiments. As proudly as the doge of Venice once married the sea, I now, for the first time, marry the wide world.

During the last two years before his publishing debut, Robert had been composing with enthusiasm: various starts for a symphony, small piano pieces which were to become numbers 1, 3, 4, 6, and 8 of the *Papillons,* Op. 2, the beginning of a piano concerto in F, and the earliest form of the much-to-be-revised *Toccata,* Op. 7.

In 1831, having made his bow as a composer, he proceeded to make an even more brilliant bow as a critic, by publishing in the *Allgemeine Musikalische Zeitung* a review of the Opus 2 of a youth as unknown as himself, born in the same year, and named Frédéric Chopin. "Gentlemen," cried Robert, "hats off! a genius!"

The large-heartedness of this gesture, its entire lack of the professional jealousy only too common among creative artists, showed that, in this respect at least, the generous Schumann's life was, to use the words of his own epigram, "in harmony with his work." The same review also provided a debut for two imaginary personages, Florestan and Eusebius, who, in his writings, were to represent respectively the dashingly active and the dreamily reflective—the manic and the depressive—sides of Robert's dual nature. Whatever the source of this personative device was in Schumann's case, it had already been used by his idol, Jean Paul. It gives a foretaste of that fantastic society, soon to be born of the composer's imagination, the Davidsbündler.

Robert wrote Mother that here and there people were beginning to recognize his talent and count on a future for him. He cannot, however, have had a very stimulating reaction from one Leipzig boy, three years his junior, to whom he played the *"Abegg" Variations.* "They were very much figurated," this lad afterwards observed. "I hated them!" His name was Richard Wagner; and he was never to find Robert or his music congenial. Nor was Robert to feel much fervid enthusiasm for Richard the Great. They were of mutually antagonistic breeds.

In Heidelberg he had begun a series of little dances inspired by the dance of the larvae at the close of Jean Paul's *Flegeljahre.* Now he completed and published them as *Papillons,* Op. 2, and wrote his mother, May 3, 1832:

In many a sleepless night I behold a far-away picture, like a goal.— While writing down the *Papillons* I truly feel a certain independence trying to develop itself. This is, however, the sort of thing that the critics usually reject.—Now the *Papillons* flutter in the wide, glorious world of Spring. Spring itself stands outside the door and gazes at me—a child with heavenly blue eyes.—And now I begin to comprehend my own existence.

At last Robert now had a home of his own where he could entertain. He had moved from the Wiecks' to two pleasant rooms with a view of foliage and water. Since the appearance of the *"Abegg" Variations,* people had begun to flock around him; so that almost the whole morning his place was full of singers, dilettantes, and all sorts of artists. But he was growing eclectic in his human contacts. He told Wieck: "I depend on being given a lift by certain people. With my equals, or with those whom I cannot permit to pass judgment on me, I am apt to grow proud and ironic."

On June 14th, 1831, we have the first word of that accident to his right hand which was, at the time, regarded as a calamity, but which proved to be a blessing in disguise. In a letter to his mother he refers to "the strange misfortune that has come upon me." Driven by impatient ambition, and perhaps stung by little Clara's easy technical superiority, he had invented a too ingenious apparatus for acquiring technic in a hurry. In order to make the fingers independent, he would hitch one of them up in a sling, while practicing. This resulted in laming for life the right ring finger, thereby shattering all his shining hopes of a virtuoso's career.[3]

On August 9th he wrote Mamma that his home was a chemist's shop, that Professor Kühl said he would be well in six months, and that he must keep applying raw meat, brandy, and herbs.

The cure is not the most charming procedure in the world, and I fear lest something of the nature of the cattle may pass into my own nature; but it is very strengthening, and my whole body is so strong and fit that I feel greatly disposed—to give somebody a sound thrashing.

How this last abrupt turn of thought resembles some surprising and capricious modulation in his own music! Three months later he sings her a different tune:

The doctor keeps on reassuring me about my hand. *As for me, I am completely resigned,* and regard it as unhealable. In Zwickau I will again take up the violincello (for which only the left hand is needed), which besides, will come in very usefully in writing symphonies.

It is probable that nothing came of this resolve; for no great composer has ever written more unidiomatically for the 'cello than Schumann. When he declared that that instrument needed only one hand, he meant, of course, one perfect hand.[4]

The courageous way in which Robert took this blow arouses surprise at such an admirable spirit of sportsmanship in a spoiled lad. In April 1833, he wrote Töpken that the injury was hopeless, but that it seemed "almost providential now," and that his present prospects looked "very rosy." To his mother he gaily referred to himself as "nine-fingered me." Later he enjoined her

[3] The venerable Dr. Alfred Meyer of New York tells me that in 1878, while a post-graduate student of medicine in Leipzig University, he was told by a German doctor that Schumann had cut the tissue between his fingers with the object of increasing his span.

[4] Note how he fell into the common error of misspelling "violoncello." By substituting i for the second o, he made the word mean "little violin," instead of what it really is: "little double-bass."

not to be uneasy about his finger. He could compose without it; nor did it handicap him in improvising. And he would not have been happier as a traveling virtuoso on account of having been spoiled as a child.

He must have felt his creativeness boiling up, and have had a presentiment of a greatness as a composer that would far out-shine the fame of any virtuoso. He wrote De Sire that, in compensation for the injury, "Heaven gives me now and then a strong thought, and so I have put the matter out of my mind."

It was fortunate that he traveled as far as he did on the road to virtuosity; for that gave him a grasp of the mechanics of piano-playing which proved of the utmost value in composition.

On the eighteenth of November he had the sort of experience that every young composer finds world-shattering. Parts of his first symphony, a composition destined never to see printer's ink, were performed, through the kindness of Wieck, in a Gewand-haus concert given by the thirteen-year-old Clara. Alas! it was only the Zwickau Gewandhaus. And doubly alas, from Robert's standpoint, the work found no favor. But from our standpoint, this may have been fortunate; for a success might have further encouraged the ignorant lad's coolness toward the study of musi-cal theory.

A few months later parts of the same work were performed in Leipzig; and of course Robert was in a daze of excitement. He wrote Mother: "When I introduced myself to Matthäi, the con-certmaster, something ridiculous happened. Absentmindedly I told him: 'My name is Matthäi.' Isn't that just like me?"

On his return from Heidelberg, Robert had met Dorn, the musical director of Leipzig's municipal theater. It was probably after the accident to his hand that everyone urged him to study theory with this authority. So at last, very much against the grain, sadly, and with violent mental reservations, he had given in. With Dorn he worked hard but uncongenially, struggling not to let the formalism of gray theory kill the freshness of his fancy. After a first dose of Dorn, his youthful cockiness noted: "I scarcely wish to know more than I know now. The poetry of imagination lies in the quality of mystery or unconsciousness."

One or two years later a wiser "Eusebius" wrote: "The silver thread of imagination must wind itself around the chains of the rules."

On January 11th, 1832, he sent this complaint to the absent Wieck:

> I shall never be able to get on with Dorn. He would have me believe that music is fugue—heavens! how different men are. All the same, I have the feeling that the study of theory has influenced me for good. Where everything used to be the inspiration of the moment, now I ponder more upon the play of my enthusiasm. Sometimes I pull up in the middle to take stock of where I am.

He went on to tell of sitting next to Dorn at a concert. During a fugue by Romberg (which must have been mortally dry!) he nudged his teacher and indicated the audience who were all chattering and coughing. This was as much as to say: "These people hardly share your convictions!" The lad did not see that it is no valid argument against the contrapuntal art to point to a desiccated fugue. It is good to know that, before too long, through an awakened passion for Bach and an intensive study of *The Well-tempered Clavichord,* Robert overcame his supercilious dislike of fugue.

Canon in double counterpoint had been reached when, for some unavowed reason, Dorn suddenly broke off the lessons, and did not reply to Robert's charming letter of modest entreaty to be taken on again. Despite the fact that his pupil always brought twice the assigned number of exercises, the dry but vain theoretician was too irritated by the enormous differences between himself and the freshly creative but undisciplined and ignorant pupil.

At any rate, Robert took this rebuff with good-humored sportsmanship. Two years later, he testified in print that Dorn had been the first to reach a helping hand to him as a young climber:

> and when I began to doubt my own ability, [he] drew me higher where I could see less of the common concerns of humdrum existence, and breathe more of the pure ether of art.

But Dorn never so imbued Robert with the sacrosanctity of the rules as to shake the boy's conviction that "whatever does not sound beautiful is false."

Once when his good mother counseled him to seek criticism from "some worthy man" and be guided by it, Robert replied that whenever he did this things went "crooked" and to the detriment of his self-reliance. "I follow my moral instinct, listen gladly and modestly to the judgment of experienced men, but do not trust it blindly."

It may even have been fortunate that Robert did not study more theory, and blindly follow criticism when very young. Who knows what a sterner, more ironclad regimentation might have done to the fresh, pioneering originality of his harmony and melody and form—even to those undeniable faults that were destined to yield such precious fruit? Surely he would not have been so incomparably the incarnation of what M. Hubert calls "the melancholy, agitated, dreamy, suffering, and extraordinarily sensitive soul of his century."

The year 1832 saw the completion of the *Intermezzi*, Op. 4. The third of these twice bears a motto from *Faust: "Meine Ruh' ist hin* (My peace is gone)." He had not yet encountered Ernestine; and Clara was still too young to sow unrest in his heart. Was it the mishap to his finger, his dread of cholera, or his calf-love for Agnes Carus that had destroyed his peace of mind?

Now Robert's barque was nearing the harbor's mouth, ready to sail out upon the seas of greatness. And all the alternations of light and dark which he had already experienced, his merry youth and the tragic death of his father, his love for Agnes Carus and the nightmare of law school, his triumph in winning the chance to be a piano virtuoso, the tragedy of the injured hand, the exultation of discovering that he could be something far greater than a mere virtuoso—all these experiences prepared him for the point counter point of a life of rapidly shifting chiaroscuro in which the gay sunlight of Florestan and the somber gloom of Eusebius were constantly to alternate.

CHAPTER 6

CLARA WIECK

U NLIKE so many of Robert's sudden attachments, the friendship between the elegant young music student and the little girl piano virtuoso developed with a gradualness that betokened depth and durability. It began with the tenderness and sympathy which this lover of children had for all youngsters, intensified in this case by the wistful admiration that he felt for her magical, twelve-year-old fingers. This was answered by a young girl's timorous respect for an impressive but entertaining grown-up gentleman who was always ready to lay himself out for the little Wiecks.

She felt a sort of proprietary interest and pride in her Herr Schumann, who had lived so long under the Wieck roof that he was almost a member of the family. She delighted in the "moonstruck concocter of charades," as he once called himself, and in the imagination that conjured up for her and the littler children those tales of wonder, fear, beauty, and laughter.

But what impressed and captivated her most was her gentleman's divine gift for pulling lovely melodies and harmonies right out of the sky, and setting them down on paper for her to play. When he did that, it was even more intimate and exciting than those country walks that they often took, hand in hand.

In the spring of 1832, Clara and her father were just back from a long concert tour which, for the first time, had included Paris. On the way they stopped at Weimar where, after many disheartening rebuffs, they finally won through Goethe's august gate. Wieck correctly gauged the great man's somewhat tawdry musical taste, and had Clara play him the *Bravoura Variations* by

48

Clara Wieck at Thirteen

Niccolò Paganini

Robert Schumann at Twenty and Twenty-nine

The Thomaskirche, Leipzig, in 1840

Herz. These tickled him so much that she was invited to repeat the visit. The aged poet was gracious. With his own hands he brought a cushion to raise her to the keyboard. He gave her a small bust of himself, and a written endorsement of her talent. "Why," he exclaimed, "the girl has more power than six boys put together!"

At Cassel the Wiecks broke the journey long enough to collect another testimonial from Spohr. These precious documents were a welcome addition to the tribute which, two years earlier, Paganini had written "to the singular merit of little Miss Wieck."

They went on, by way of Frankfort and Darmstadt, to storm the gates of Paris. But there, alas! the piano virtuosos were too numerous, the pianos too bad, the audiences too noisily rude. With characteristic humor, Wieck wrote home about his get-up. After having been strictly coached on what to wear, and how to comport himself in the musical soirees of Paris, he appeared

with yellow gloves and white neckcloth, my hat always in my hand, half German, half French, and half despairing. . . . You'd never recognize your Friedrich; for you've never seen a more interesting lackey.

To add to their difficulties, cholera was rampant. So that Clara's first attempt on the French capital had to be written down a dismal failure. She was relieved to turn her back upon the fatigue and annoyance and artificiality, the dressing-up and strain, the formality, jealous hostility, false glitter, and disappointments of such a tour.

May Day, 1832, her satisfaction on reaching home and slipping back into the old familiar life may be gathered from an entry in Wieck's diary: "Fifteen minutes after our arrival, Clara was back in the kitchen, cleaning the knives." The little Wieck boys, Gustav and Alwin, were dispatched on the run to fetch the indispensable Herr Schumann, who hastened around the corner from Neumarkt 641, to hear all about Paris, and to tell much of the *Papillons,* but little of the injured hand.

Two days later he confided to the diary which he called his *Leipzig Book of Life* how the girl had changed during these seven months: "Clara is bigger, better-looking, stronger and nimbler, and her German has taken on a French accent which Leipzig will cure in short order."

If he was right about this improvement in her looks, Clara must have been downright ugly the year before. For the Fechner portrait of her, dated 1832, shows her as still far from prepossessing, with eyes and nose several sizes too large for the insignificant rest of her face. In his charmingly written life of Clara,[1] Mr. John N. Burk says that Robert felt that she had now grown up to those eyes. But, if trustworthy, the evidence of the portrait is against this opinion.

Robert told his book that Clara played "like a hussar."[2] This may have been the result of long wrestling with the French pianos, whose action was so hard that Wieck cursed them as "tough bones."

Naturally no time was lost before setting Clara at the *Papillons*. And the diary noted with amusement that she preferred the third, which is the simplest and least interesting of the lot. "Her childish originality shows itself in everything."

After the long spell of work and absence, there came rest and country walks and picnics for all hands. Arm in arm, Robert and Clara took the boys to the menagerie. During an outdoor family supper in the Rosenthal, it was discovered, to everybody's delight, that Clara "did not know whether a duck was a goose or merely a duck." It is possible that her child's imagination conceived of a curious evolutionary process. She may have thought of maturity as bringing beauty, so that the ugly duckling becomes the lissome-necked goose, and the goose becomes the lovely swan. If so, it was a wish-thought, to be fulfilled by her own development from homely child to beautiful woman.

For that matter, Robert's own looks seem to have undergone a development somewhat similar to Clara's; although they were destined to turn downhill at a much earlier age than hers. When we compare his portraits at twenty and at twenty-nine, we are astounded to find in the former a somewhat poisonous-looking ruffian, with a double chin, a repulsive mouth, the arrogant ex-

[1] *Clara Schumann*, Random House, 1940.
[2] A peculiarity since perpetuated by nine pianists out of ten, for which the unfortunate construction of their instrument is partially responsible.

pression of a spoiled child, a dissipated look, and eyes almost
as much too large for the face as we found in the picture of
Clara at twelve. We marvel that anyone with features like that
could ever have had a beautiful thought.

Then we turn to the later portrait and—presto change—we
are attracted to it as strongly as we were repelled by the earlier.
Here is an ideally handsome and winning young fellow. He has
grown up to his eyes; his features now are almost flawless. And,
instead of the arrogance of a spoiled sprig, goodness, kindness,
sympathy, and lofty intelligence stream from the portrait. It is
to be hoped that the earlier picture is not a faithful likeness.

On May 9th Robert tells his *Book of Life* that Clara is "silly
and nervous"; on the 16th, that she plays the *Papillons* "unsurely
and without understanding." But it speaks for her gift of rapid
improvement that, ten days after, she comprehends those pieces
"rightly and with fire, and with few exceptions performs them
so." And the following day he notes: "I never heard Clara play
as she did today—everything masterly and beautiful. Also she
played the *Papillons* still better than yesterday."

The *Book of Life* would seem to suggest that Robert was not
yet in love with little Clara.

May 29. Gave a soft, lovely kiss to the Maid of Holland [his nickname for Agnes Carus], and when I got home I sat down at the piano
and felt as though flowers and gods were flowing out of my fingers,
so carried away was I by the stream of ideas.

He went on to say that this was when he first thought of the
theme in descending fifths (marked here by a bracket)

with which he preluded the *Impromptus on a Theme by Clara
Wieck,* Op. 5. He had unconsciously borrowed this from the
start of Haydn's *Quinten* Quartet, Op. 76, No. 2, and was to use
it so often that it became one of his chief idioms. Let us call it
the Haydn source-motive.[3] Though Agnes was the original in-

[3] Not wishing to resort to clumsy foreign expressions, the writer has,

spiration of this motive, the fact that Robert first used it in his
first variations on a theme by Clara probably led him later to
identify the Haydn source-motive with Clara instead of Agnes,
and to employ it throughout his music as a secret greeting to
the girl he loved best. One hopes that the jealous Clara never
learned the circumstances in which it had originally come into
his mind! Up to the time when Robert fell definitively in love
with her, his susceptible and capacious heart was easily thrilled
by more than one woman at a time.

Perhaps that "soft, lovely kiss" induced a detached mood
which made Robert unusually aware of the faults of the twelve-
year-old pianist; for he suddenly began to criticize Clara's character. Mr. Burk seems to be mistaken when he finds evidence
in the next entries that, at this time, Robert "hoped she would
shake off in some degree her subjection to her father," and that
he "was troubled by the submissiveness which the parent
exacted." On the contrary Robert actually appeared, for the
moment, to side with the parents against his little friend. On
June 1st he noted:

> Clara now shows great willfulness toward her stepmother, who is
> certainly a most estimable woman. The old man upbraided Clara.
> For all that, he'll soon knuckle under to a petticoat government.
> Already she issues commands like a Leonore. . . .[4]
>
> June 4. Clara was willful and teary. A rebuke delivered with proud
> superiority would have a good influence over her moods.

This phase of reaction against Clara, however, was as fleeting
as the kiss which may have caused it. While it lasted, it would
have been hard to say whether Robert cared more for the father
or the daughter. At any rate, he wrote Wieck: "Every day that
I can't talk with you or Clara makes a hole in my *Leipzig Book
of Life.*"

in earlier books, been driven to coining the terms source-motive and germ-
motive. The former is a musical phrase which recurs, more or less identically, in a number of distinct compositions, and produces in the group an
effect of thematic unity. A germ-motive is a germinal phrase, cyclically
used with more or less disguise, to interlock the parts of a sonata, symphony, etc., into a unified whole.

For the Haydn source-motive, see pp. 285, 344, 472, and 482.

[4] The strong-minded heroine of Beethoven's opera, *Fidelio.*

In July Clara gave two concerts in the Gewandhaus. They were so successful as to make her more Leonoresque than ever. Her introduction of the new French custom of playing without visible notes caused a profound sensation; though a few know-it-alls explained how much easier it was to do hard pieces if you could look all the time at the keys.

Her self-assurance, though, was taken down a peg on her thirteenth birthday, September 13th. During a musical guessing-game at a children's party, she stuck repeatedly while playing a small scherzo. But her defense was spirited. "No wonder! With nobody but a lot of little girls for an audience; and to have to play piano on my birthday!" She had already begun to realize that she was not a woman's woman.

The Zwickau concert on the eighteenth of November has already been mentioned. This was a memorable date in the annals of Clara and Robert. First, because she created such mad excitement with that old warhorse, the *Bravoura Variations* of Herz, that the enraptured hearers actually forgot themselves so far as to crowd between the orchestral stands and collide with the fiddle bows, in order to be nearer the little virtuoso. Secondly, because, for the first time, Robert's name appeared on a program with Clara's, when part of a never-to-be-published symphony of his was played; though, in the general frenzy over Clara—and Herz—it went unnoticed.

Thirdly, the wonder-child was introduced to Robert's family. And Frau Schumann had a flash of divination. Perhaps the good woman had some vague inkling that she had attached her youngest to herself with a too dangerous devotion. She must have had when he wrote her:

Like a good genius, you stand always before me in waking hours and in dreams, always tender, loving, and as if transfigured by youth. Believe me, I dream of you almost daily, and nearly always beautifully.

This woman knew that her son, with his erratic and sensitive nature, would after she was gone still need what she now gave him. And she recognized in this highly maternal type of girl the ideal substitute who could some day lavish on her Robert the love and sympathy and tender support which he must have.[5] As she and Clara stood at the window, Robert went by in the market-place below and waved to them. Frau Schumann drew the slender child to her and, yielding to a sudden, overmastering impulse, murmured: "One day you must marry my Robert."

Clara looked up in childish wonder. At the moment the words meant little to her; but she was never to forget them.

[5] Clara's maternal quality will be noticed in her young letters to Robert on pp. 55 and 64, and in the story of the stumbling blocks, p. 58.

Chapter 7

CLARA AND THE STUMBLING BLOCKS

U NTIL March of 1833, Robert stayed on in Zwickau and Schneeberg, working on his symphony. But he could never get the finale to suit him, and at last laid the whole thing upon the shelf.

A month after Clara's departure he received the first letter that she is known to have written him:

Dec. 17, 1832.

My dear Herr Schumann!

"Ha, ha!" I hear you say. "Now see what she's like! She, she is one who wastes no second, second thought upon her promises." Oh, but she still remembers them. Now just you read and hear why I haven't written before.

A few days after our return, the very day I was to have played in Molique's concert, I came down with scarlatina, and until a few days ago had to languish in my boresome bed. . . .

Listen here, Herr Wagner has gone you one better. A whole symphony of his was performed, that is said to resemble Beethoven's A Major to a hair. Father said that F. Schneider's symphony which was played at the Gewandhaus is like the heavy freight wagon that needs two days to reach Wurzen, and never leaves the ruts the whole way; and a boresome old teamster, wearing what looks like a great night-cap, keeps murmuring to the horses: "Ho, ho, ho, hotte, hotte." But Wagner [1] drives his one-hoss shay over stock and stone, spills over into the ditch every other minute, but somehow makes Wurzen in *one* day, although he looks black and blue.

In the same Euterpe concert, as well, the famous young Bahrdt played Herz's *Bravoura Variations* on a small piano in 5 *Adagios*

---

[1] Literally, wagoner.

fraught with disaster. . . . Father helped me with this part of my
letter. . . .

Well, you're a pretty person, to leave your linen behind in the
carriage! Have you got it back from the driver? . . .

Now greet everybody heartily from me, and write soon again; but
make it nice and legible.

In the hope of seeing you soon again at our house, I close my letter
and remain

Your friend

Clara Wieck.

Even without the honest Clara's confession, Robert would
have had no difficulty in recognizing the pun on Wagner's
name, and the bit about the variations as the Wieckian brand
of spiteful wit, reinforced by Clara's characteristic malice towards her rivals. The letter capitally hits off the light tone of
their personal relations. At the start, the child pertly imitates
the faults of Robert's slow, repetitive speech. And near the end
she gets in neat digs at his absence of mind, and his almost un-
decipherable handwriting. With womanly tenderness she tries
to console him for the failure of his symphony movement at
Zwickau by telling of young Richard Wagner's latest symphonic
venture, as tried out by the Euterpe Society of Leipzig. Robert
was delighted with her candor, and wrote his teacher:

The symphonic similes in Clara's letter raised much laughter in
Zwickau, especially the naïve aside, "Father helped me with this
part of my letter." It was just as if Clara had secretly whispered
something into my ear.

Although Clara here borrowed her out-and-out humorous
effects from her father, the whole touching and remarkable
letter has a crisp freshness that verges on laughter. As she grows
older, these qualities diminish. Clara steadily loses her ability
to originate or even appreciate humor until, in the end, her
family and friends, full of suppressed mirth, become as wary of
being funny in her presence as if they were the kind of corpora-
tion magnates who regard humor as so much T.N.T., because
they think it bad for business. So, as Robert's humor is a perpetually gushing fountain that may not be driven underground

and sealed up, this dissimilarity causes complications. A few years later, it becomes parlous for him to adopt the bantering tone which he can now with impunity use toward his thirteen-year-old friend.

In March 1833, Robert returned to Leipzig. After a long, despairing search, he finally found such a home as might make up to a provincial nature-lover for the barren, prosaic quality of urban existence. It was in Riedel's Garden: "a couple of charming, simple rooms, with all kinds of moon- and sunshine, giving upon green meadows and flowering gardens." The place was an ideal focus for his musical friends. Many of these were virtuosos; and their chief was Friedrich Kalkbrenner, whom he described as "the finest, most amiable, of Frenchmen (but vain.)" [2]

When Clara dedicated to Robert her *Theme with Variations*, Op. 3, he was gratified, but wrote her guardedly:

However, I can give you nothing but hearty thanks and, if you were here (even without your father's permission) I would press your hands. And I would express the hope that the union of our names on the title-page would mean that of our views and ideas in times to come. More than that, a poor devil like me cannot offer.

On recovering from a fever, Robert wrote her more in the old whimsical vein:

July 13, 1833.

The doctor, indeed, has forbidden me to yearn too hard, that is to say—for you; because it takes too much out of me. Today I ripped all the bandages from my wounds and laughed right in the doctor's face as he wanted to keep me from writing you. Indeed, I threatened to attack and infect him with my fever if he didn't leave me in peace to do what I wanted. So he did.

Then the young man went on to propose something in the spirit of the old ghost stories with which he had long delighted the Wieck children. It was an experiment in musical telepathy. Tomorrow at eleven sharp, he was to play the *Adagio* of the Chopin *Variations,* while thinking intently of Clara, and of none

[2] He was wrong. The famous pianist was a German.

but Clara. He begged her to do the like, so that in spirit they might see and meet one another. The point at which their second selves would encounter would probably be over the little portal of Bach's old church, St. Thomas's.

The same day she replied tenderly, but without answering humor:

> Surely you can imagine how I live. How can I live well if you do not visit us any more?! As for your request, I will grant it and be over the little portal of St. Thomas's tomorrow at eleven o'clock.
>
> [A postscript was significant:]
>
> If you should receive this letter without a seal, please write me so.

This probably means that Wieck was beginning a secret censorship of their correspondence. Until then the pedagogue had been blindly oblivious to what so often happens when a young, artistic, and temperamental man walks daily in the country hand in hand with a precocious adolescent girl of similar tastes and temperament, especially one whose imagination he captured when she was small.

A few days before this, Robert had written his mother a touching bit about Clara who, he said, was intimately attached to him:

> She is the old Clara—wild and enthusiastic—runs and jumps and plays like a child, and then will suddenly say the profoundest things. It gives one pleasure to see how her aptitudes of heart and head develop now, ever more rapidly, but, so to say, leaf by leaf. As we walked home from Connewitz the other day (we take two-to-three-hour hikes nearly every day), I heard her say to herself: "Oh, how happy I am! how happy!" Who wouldn't be glad to hear that?!— On this same walk some extremely useless stones lie in the middle of the foot-path. As it happens that, often in talking with others, I look up more than down, she always walks back of me and, at every stone, she gently tugs my coat, so that I may not fall. But sometimes she stumbles over these very stones herself.

Girl and woman, she was destined, as long as he lived, to go on making Robert's path safe and smooth for him, though at the expense of many a painful fall of her own. It may be that these stones on the way to Connewitz played an important role in starting the foundations of their love. Perhaps, as the Scriptures have it, the stone of stumbling was to become the cornerstone of the edifice.

For both Clara and Robert these were happy days, full of dim and wonderful presentiments. No word of love had yet passed between the brilliant girl just ripening to womanhood, and the brilliant youngster just ripening to genius. Upon both lives lay shimmering the poetry and promise of a Spring dawn. Both dreamily felt that some miracle was about to happen.

For the young composer this was a time of intense creative ardor. In 1833 he did the second book of Paganini transcriptions (published later as *Concert Etudes,* Op. 10), and the *Impromptus,* Op. 5, on the theme which Clara had recently varied and dedicated to him. He revised the *Toccata,* Op. 7, transposing it from D to C; and started the first two piano sonatas.

Without warning, tragedy descended upon him. It opened with that fever about which he had joked in his letter to Clara. He moved from Riedel's Garden to rooms four flights up, at Burgstrasse 21. But no sooner was he settled in them than he developed that dizzy fear of high places called hypsophobia, and had to take a friend, young Günther, to live with him.

News came of the death of Rosalie, the wife of his brother Carl. Robert was devoted to her; and the shock brought on an acute nervous breakdown, which was soon aggravated by the death of his brother Julius.

To his mother, who repeatedly urged him to come home during Julius's last illness, he complained of "fearful melancholy, violent rushes of blood, unutterable fear, lack of breath, brief lapses of consciousness." "I have not the courage to travel alone to Zwickau *for fear something might happen to me.*" "It might easily come about that I should have to go direct from the stagecoach to bed, perhaps never again to leave it."

When one is at a low nervous ebb, even his best friends and loved ones are a nuisance. What he wants is to be let alone. On November 27, 1833, after the funerals of Rosalie and Julius had taken place without him, he wrote his mother: "Of the past weeks, nothing. I was scarcely more than a statue, not cold, not warm; by dint of violent work, life gradually returned."

But it did not wholly return until well into the following year. On January 4, 1834, he wrote her:

As, just at present, the mere thought of the sorrows of others is so destructive to me that it robs me of all energy, please guard against letting me know anything that could in any way disturb me. *If not, I must deprive myself of your letters entirely.* . . .

I had never known pain. Now it has come; but I have not been able to crush it, and it has crushed me a thousand times over.

The Schumann family was short-lived and inclined to nervous diseases, insanity, and suicide. Walter Dahms [8] thinks that its strain of Wendish blood was an unhealthy factor. The Wends are the ancient Slavic people whom the incoming Germans found in what is now Saxony and Prussia, and conquered. By the time of this story, the stock had become somewhat degenerate and was beginning to die out.

Robert's mental abnormality was of a kind that often rhymes with the artistic temperament. He was of the manic-depressive type that Goethe so neatly characterized as

> *Himmelhoch jauchzend,*
> *Zum Tode betrübt.*

> (Thrilled to the sky,
> Ready to die.)

When thoughtfully read, Robert's whole correspondence graphically charts the ebb- and flood-tide rhythm of the spirit within him. The pattern of stimulation and depression is there, almost nakedly. Not that he himself was fully aware of this pattern; but it affected everything he did and felt until he could not help perceiving something of its effect upon his life. People of his type are apt to rationalize their sudden changes of mood as caused by something outside of themselves. And Robert once remarked how "the outer world, now beaming, now frowning, often lays violent hands upon the insides of the poet and musi-

[8] *Schumann,* Schuster und Loeffler, 1922.

cian." Litzmann [4] says of him in the summer of 1839 that gloomy moods almost always followed optimistic "moments of happy accomplishment."

But, when we plot the rhythmically alternating elations and depressions in Robert's correspondence, we find the cause of this seesaw within himself rather than without. Here is a sample.

He is at seventeen. Through the mawkish bravura of imitation Jean-Paulism, one feels the morbid contrast of manic and depressive phases:

July, 1827. My whole life blooms now in the mild rose-garden of memory, where I plucked many a lovely immortelle and, though they now are wilted, I press them forever upon my weeping bosom and kiss the faded buds of a happy life.

In 1828, after a page of high spirits, he suddenly begins a tirade against "the pettinesses and meannesses of this egotistic world," which he calls "a dreadful cemetery of sunken hopes."

On February 24, 1830, a threat of the depressive is instantly countered by an Irishism: "I could plunge into despair—if I were not already in it!"

November 16. "I am gay and well-disposed." Same letter: "Don't be angry at me if, in weak desperation, I up and run away to America."

December 15. Every word in your letters is full of bloom and vitality. . . . The great, great time in which we live and in which even old men are as glowing as youths. . . .

September 21, 1831. Without him [Lühe] perhaps I would long ago have been lost in melancholy or similar bilious fevers.

October 14. "How enchanting the world can sometimes be!"

November 27, 1833. You would surely forgive my not writing, if you had an idea of the profound slumber into which melancholy has plunged my soul.

Dateless, 1836. I have my glorious hours when . . . spiritual exaltation causes such high spirits that I fairly want to take the whole world by storm. Reaction promptly follows, and then, artificial means of bucking myself up. I know the right way of reconciling such dangerous extremes: a loving woman could do it.

[4] Berthold Litzmann: *Clara Schumann,* 3 vols. Breitkopf, 1906.

At the end of 1836, after the death of his mother, he turned for mothering to his sister-in-law Therese:

> Sometimes, when deadly terror of the heart attacks me, I have no one but you to take me, as it were, in your arms, and protect me.
>
> December 19. Often I am on the crest of the wave; but much oftener, so melancholy that I could shoot myself.

These extracts will suffice to indicate the perpetual trough-and-crest movement of his spirits.

Robert, as we have seen, was fond of representing the two opposing sides of his dual nature in the guise of two imaginary creatures. Florestan was the vigorous man of action, the up-and-comer. Eusebius was the dreamy, poetic man of reflection, somewhat addicted to sadness. This pair represented a charming wish-dream, a rationalization of what he wished his dimly realized manic-depressive make-up to be. More than once he struck nearer the actual truth when he likened himself to Janus, the two-faced Roman god.

In point of fact Eusebius was addicted not only to sadness but also to fear and terror. The fear and the terror were that the darkness would, as the pendulum swung into its half, destroy the light—that Eusebius would murder Florestan. And such a catastrophe is what always threatened Schumann at that point where the depression became itself manic in its power.

CHAPTER 8

ERNESTINE

O N April 21st my friend Ernestine von Fricken arrived to study with Father," wrote Clara in her diary for 1834. This entry showed no prophetic awareness on Clara's part of the drama that was to commence with Fräulein von Fricken's appearance in the Wieck home. Apparently she was happy about it, even to using the words "my friend," in the circumstances a generous phrase. The girls had first met only a few days before, at Clara's concert in Plauen.

Ernestine's ostensible father, the rich Baron von Fricken, was a passionate amateur of the flute, who lived just across the Bohemian frontier, at Asch. He had brought his seventeen-year-old girl to hear the fourteen-year-old wonder-child, and he had been so impressed by the efficacy of Wieck's methods that he had turned her over to the pedagogue as boarder and pupil.

Wieck soon saw that Ernestine and Robert were mutually attracted. He saw it with a good deal of pleasure and relief. For he had now at last begun to suspect the truth: that Clara was growing a little too fond of her Herr Schumann. So he bundled her off to Dresden to study theory with the mediocre tone-poet Reissiger (of all people!); but really to let Ernestine get in her full, deadly effect on the young man while he was undistracted by his little friend.

Four years later Clara wrote Robert how she had really felt about this episode. The letter throws a touching and admirable light upon her adolescence before jealousy had begun to rear its ugly triangular head.

I must let you know what a silly child I was in those days. When Ernestine came to live with us, I told her: "But just you wait till you come to know Schumann. I like him the best of all our friends."— However, she would not consider this; for she thought she knew a gentleman in Asch whom she liked much better. This embittered me awfully. But it was not long before she fell more and more in love with you; and pretty soon things got so far that I had to call her every time you came. This I was very glad to do; for I was only too happy that she loved you. That's what I wanted, and was satisfied. When she appeared, you talked to her alone, and me you merely entertained with all sorts of fun. [Could this have been one of the factors that gave Clara her lifelong distaste for humor?] Now, that hurt me not a little. But I comforted myself with the thought that this was only because you always had me. And besides, Ernestine was more grown up. The strangest feelings stirred my heart (young though it was, it already beat warmly) when we three went walking, and you talked to Ernestine and occasionally handed me some child-ish nonsense. On that account Father sent me to Dresden, where I recovered a bit of hope. Even as early as those days I already thought: "After all, it would be pretty nice if some day he were your husband."

From Dresden this child sent Robert a pert admonition that revealed an intimate knowledge of such peculiarities of his as contrariety, love of lifting his elbow, absent-minded bad man-ners, irregular hours, thoughtlessness in friendship, and blind handwriting. It was timed for his birthday—

the day when the dear God let fall from heaven such a musical spark. . . .

The first thing I write is to express my wishes, viz.: that you may not always do the contrary—drink less Bavarian beer—not keep on sitting when others take their leave—not turn day into night and vice versa—show your girl friends that you think of them—compose indus-triously—make the firm resolve to come to Dresden, etc.

Now, is that permitted, Herr Schumann, to show a girl friend so little attention that you do not write to her even once? . . .

Well, now I may beg for an original, but not originally written [i.e. illegible] little letter, mayn't I, Herr Schumann? This wise,

original, and witty letter recommends to your attention in all delib-
eration (as you don't like hurry)

Your friend

CLARA WIECK
CLARA WIECK
Doubleganger [1]

The epistle shows one of the last expiring sparks of Clara's
humor. The self-directed irony of its close looks as if the honest
girl were becoming conscious of her own deficiency in the field
of laughter, and even had the courage to poke fun at it. There
is in this effort something rather touching. It is evident that
Clara means to have Robert, plays her cards as best she knows
how, and tries to be ingratiating through flippancy. What probably appealed more, however, to the addressee was the strong
maternal feeling evident between the lines.

On the 25th of July, 1834, Clara came home for a brief fortnight to attend the christening of her half sister Cäcilie. She
found that the wily Wieck had arranged to have Robert and
Ernestine stand up side by side before the minister, as godfather
and godmother to the child. How powerfully suggestive the
effect of this was on their impressionable hearts may well be
imagined.

Robert's *Book of Life* is laconic about the ceremony and un-
sympathetic as regards his Doubleganger: "Christening at the
Wiecks'. Clara here from Dresden.—Returns sorrowful."

Once back there, she took a mild revenge by flirting with a
musician named Karl Banck, who made her stay "very agreeable." On September 4th, coming home for good, she found
Ernestine extremely close-mouthed (*kleinsilbig*, "little-syllabled,"
was her apt adjective) and suspicious, "for which, in my case,
she truly had no warrant."

As to that, time would soon show how much warrant Ernestine's feminine instinct had for being wary of little Clara. Robert,
moreover, was none too friendly with the child, who now heard,
and believed, that the two were secretly engaged. And she was
right.

[1] See p. 39, N.

Baron von Fricken's earlier anxieties about what was going on in Leipzig had been lulled by a letter from Wieck. It contained a fine testimonial to Robert, whom he called "a somewhat moody, headstrong, but noble, glorious, enthusiastic, highly gifted, deeply cultivated genius of a composer."

I will not say that Ernestine and Schumann are intimately—but they are without doubt strongly—attached to one another. . . . This inclination . . . , however, is of no unworthy kind. If I saw you, I could prove that no kiss, no caress has passed between them, but they are deeply interested in one another. . . . Now, my experienced friend, look at the restless Ernestine. How after ten or twenty minutes she springs up from the piano, goes to another one, chances to find herself by the window of the next room, wanders to her own chamber, looks at me with timid pleading and inquires if we are not taking our morning coffee in the Rosenthal tomorrow—and in her face one may read—Schumann. What does Ernestine do when not playing? Nothing wrong, ever! But often she hangs dreamily about, and has almost nothing to do with books, for she reads and studies Schumann's face too much for that; and what are lifeless letters to a living countenance?

Wieck was, however, somewhat less omniscient and omnipotent than he fondly imagined. As Anatole France's devil in disguise remarked to the holy and innocent St. Maël, a caress leaves as little trace as the passage of a fish through the sea. The pair were, in fact, meeting daily at the Voigts'; and there was no dearth of kisses. It may be that this entry in Robert's letter to Töpken on August 18th is about one of these meetings: "(Adieu—it is striking ten—I'm going now on a *beautiful walk*.) —[Later] I've got back from the beautiful walk—and it was good."

Buxom Ernestine's body, together with her vigorous emotional nature, had the charm of youth and of a fresh luxuriance that was lacking in her quite ordinary mind. But Robert, being in love and therefore not fully rational, failed to notice that she was not beautiful, and could not see that she was uninteresting. According to him, this "brilliant jewel" had "a Madonna head." Schumann reverted often, as here, to the mother image in his descriptions of women and their effect upon his heart and senses.

This time, his heart apparently went a bit further than usual in clouding one of his senses—that of hearing—for he even described Ernestine as "extraordinarily musical." That from the young man who had been for so long the friend of little Clara Wieck, was sheer besottedness. And he took his mother into his confidence about the girl: "just the one I might wish for a wife."

For all his infatuation with Ernestine, Robert continued impressionable. As has already been noted, his heart could sustain more than one tender passion. He had the talent, especially characteristic of his times, for sentimental relations with women on a multiple basis. And it still had some years to flourish. While under the spell of Ernestine, he was simultaneously inditing what look uncommonly like love letters to Frau Henriette Voigt. He called her "my A major soul," and drew a crescendo sign _____ in her autograph album, to indicate that their friendship was always growing. Here is one passage, written August 25th, 1834:

> When I had read your letter, I very softly shut it away and did not reread it, and have not to this moment, in order to carry along that first impression in all its purity, into the coming time. Ah! if a day should arrive that left me nothing but these lines, then I will seek them and bring them forth and press the shadow of this hand closely and fondly in mine.

Then, struck perhaps by misgivings about the propriety of such language in the circumstances, he added a postscript, as if trying to correct the impression his words may have made: "A girl must have written the foregoing lines—in another connection." Which suggests that he was conscious of the feminine streak that every creative man necessarily possesses.

In September, when Clara came home from Dresden, she found Baron von Fricken there. He had got wind of the true state of affairs and had hastened to investigate in person. From the tongue-tied Robert the Baron obtained little but an unusually intense silence. Ernestine denied everything, and was top-loftily difficult. So she was haled home to Asch; and we find Wieck making this relieved entry in Clara's diary:

We miss her not at all. In the last weeks she has become a stranger in this house. . . . She was like a young plant that has been scorched by the sun—that is—by Herr Schumann.

Just before a concert where Clara was to play his new *Toccata*, she was hurt by Robert's abrupt disappearance from Leipzig. He had learned that Von Fricken and Ernestine were to break their journey at Zwickau, and hastened there in order to have a final lovers' meeting and parting behind the Baron's back.

There was no formally announced engagement between Robert and Ernestine. But, since she left Zwickau with his ring, it is puzzling to find him writing so casually of the affair. In announcing his visit to Mamma, he mentioned "this summer romance" as 'perhaps the most remarkable of his life.'

Presently Ernestine wrote Robert blissfully that her parents would grant their consent. His waning ardor flickered up for the moment, as we see in a letter to his confidante Henriette:

Nov. 7, 1834.

My mental state gives me a shudder. I have a positive virtuosity in clinging to unhappy thoughts—it is the evil spirit which opposes and mocks at one's peace of mind. . . .

He [the Baron] gives her to me—Henriette, he gives her to me . . . do you feel what that means?—and nevertheless there is this torturing state of mind, as if I fear to accept this treasure because I know it to be in ill-starred hands. If you asked me to define my torture, I could not put a name to it. *I believe it is pain itself*—better than that I could not define it.

This reference to his bad mental state and to his "ill-starred hands" shows that he had not yet fully recovered from his breakdown of the year before, and was even then shuddering away from a vivid premonition of his own ultimate fate. Twice before Christmas he visited Asch, but without declaring himself or becoming formally engaged. There was a little girl pianist whom he could not get out of his mind.

Then he found that Ernestine had misled him. It came out that the poor girl was only an adopted daughter of the Baron's, was of illegitimate birth, and would inherit nothing. Here was a real facer for Robert!

In the meantime, Ernestine's letters had been getting in effective work. Their crude style and lapses in grammar and spelling, unneutralized by the glow of her living presence, were a torture to his sensitive soul; for he was the devoted son of a literary father and of a mother who had felt that it was an outrage to make a woman of her social standing keep a grocery store.

Realizing that this was not a girl with either the personality or the economic endowment to make him happy, Robert let the relationship die of its own inherent perishability. (In any case, it had never been viable.) And—triumph of tact—he did so without turning Ernestine against him. All he did, when the engagement was scrapped late in 1835, was to break her heart.

In 1838, in an intimately revealing confessional letter from Vienna, Robert was to tell Clara about these crucial months. In October 1833, he had been visited by "the most fearful thought with which heaven can punish a man"—the fear of losing his reason. In wild despair, he had rushed to a doctor and confessed that he was afraid he might commit suicide. The doctor was comforting, and said, with a smile: "Medicine is of no use here. Seek yourself out a woman. She will cure you at once."

This lifted a load from me. I thought, "That can be done." Just then you weren't bothering much about me. Besides, you were at the parting of the ways between childhood and girlhood.—Then came Ernestine—as good a girl as the world ever bore—"She is the one," thought I. "She will save you." I wanted to cling with all my strength to some feminine being. And this agreed with me.—I saw that she loved me—you know all about it. . . .

Now, when she had gone away, I began to wonder how this might end. When I learned of her poverty, and knew that I myself, with all my industry, earned but little, I began to feel as though fetters were pressing me. I saw no goal, no help. Then too, I heard about unhappy family complications in which Ernestine was enmeshed. And I must say that I took it ill of her to have kept them so long secret from me. Putting this all together—damn me—I must confess it—I cooled off. . . .

A few months later, again to Clara, he resumed the theme:

I feel it clearly, and cannot conceal it from myself that here a wrong has been committed. But the catastrophe would have been greater—it would have been *monstrous,* if it had once come to a union between her and me. Earlier or later, my old love and devotion for you would again have been awakened, and then what a calamity! The three of us would have been most horribly unhappy. So she is the victim of circumstances; and I in no way deny my own guilt in all this. But, Clara, let us do what we can to make this good. Ernestine . . . knows right well that in the first place she crowded you out of my heart, which loved you before ever I knew Ernestine. . . . She often wrote me: "I always believed you can love no one but Clara, and believe it even now."—Her vision was clearer than mine.

Perhaps the unfortunate young girl was somewhat to blame for not doing the almost impossible—for not having at once told her tragic secret to the man whom she adored. But to her credit we must place the fact that she always afterward remained on friendly terms with Robert and with her successful rival.

These extracts from Ernestine's letters to Clara will suggest a view of this affair somewhat different from that of Schumann's earlier biographers.

July 29, 1836.

[Schumann] has sunk deeply in my estimation. . . . o if only I had never come to know this Sch! [abbreviated] . . . I'll just tell you this much that I then loved Sch. unspeakably, I would have given my life for him, I could do nothing else but think of him, from each of his words his portrait looked out smiling so roguishly at me. Indeed, you know his smile, o it is enchanting!

Sept. 10 evening

. . . Life goes so against my grain, I wanted nothing but to be out of this world for in it one has nothing but anxieties, torments and cares. . . .

He wrote me I should save myself while there was still time, that is the whole of it, apart from this I know of no reason, for he did not write me any, and to begin by involving myself in long questions, no that I did not do, I set him *free at once, quite free*— . . .

Schumann is entirely to blame for my present misfortune, for I feel myself wholly abandoned and miserable. . . .

Sept. 11.

Also I never want to see him again, but with my whole heart I wish him everything good, and if I can do anything for him, it will be joyfully done.

Ernestine had real character, and the fact that her words were not simply idle words was made clear when Wieck sought her assistance in blackening Robert's name to prevent his marrying the girl for whom he had jilted Ernestine. Loyally she made good her promise and stood up on the side of Robert and Clara. With noble sportsmanship she wrote Wieck on October 3rd, 1838: "I was never engaged to Schumann," and went on to say that she had considered a permanent union with him as little as he had expected such a thing.

Four years after putting on Schumann's ring, she sought consolation on the rebound in marrying old Count von Zedwitz, who very soon left her a widow. And five years later, in 1844, she died of typhoid.

Ernestine was closely connected with four of Robert's compositions. Two of them constituted the first conclusive evidence of his real genius. *Carnaval,* Op. 9, was a suite of pieces most of which were variations on the letters ASCH.[2] By a neat coinci-

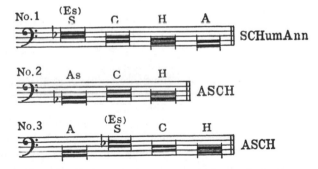

dence, these spelled out the name of Ernestine's home town, and at the same time were the only musical letters in the name **S C H** U M **A** N N—(here in bold type).

The other evidence of genius was the *Symphonic Etudes,* Op. 13. They were bold, sweeping, infectious variations on a theme which Ernestine's adoptive father had written for his own flute. But did Robert dedicate these to Ernestine? By no means.

[2] In German, S, or Es, is our E flat; As is our A flat; while H is our B natural.

Even musically he returned evil for good. Instead of inscribing her name on these masterpieces which were due to their love, he finally wrote it upon two others which were far from his best: the *Allegro*, Op. 8, for piano, a poor attempt with which he himself was dissatisfied, and the *Three Songs*, Op. 31, to words by Chamisso.

When Litzmann called this latter opus "a specially tender homage" and "a public token of lasting friendly feeling," he must have been indulging in the hazardous sport of writing about something with which he was not familiar. For he could not have read the words of these songs. Nor, apparently, has any other writer on Schumann appreciated their significance.

Opus 31 was, to say the least, a somewhat curious offering for the then lionized Schumann to lay at the feet of his poor, jilted love. The first song, a ballad called *The Lion's Bride*, tells of a maiden in bridal array coming to say farewell to her old friend the lion, who proceeds to slay her in the presence of the bridegroom.

In *The Fortune Teller*, the cards tell a maiden that she will be a rich widow. She will be one step from becoming a princess or a queen—when "a secret comes to light," and—"Farewell, ye splendors. Oh, that was a hard blow!"

In the last song, *Red Hannah*, a young and handsome suitor promises a maiden marriage, then jilts her, and, on the rebound, she marries a *Taugenichts*, a good-for-nothing.

Now, Schumann was a notoriously absent-minded, but also a highly generous, intelligent, sensitive, and fine-feeling man. In the circumstances, how could he have failed to perceive what a coarsely cruel, not to say caddish, thing he was doing in inscribing such all-too-appropriate songs to Ernestine? And how could Clara have permitted him to do it?

Chapter 9

THE DAVIDITES MARCH

Marche des "Davidsbündler" contre les Philistins

N EAR Leipzig stands an eminence which is known as
Barefoot Mountain, a wart of earth which would never
have achieved the dignity of mountainhood except
among flatlanders like the people of Leipzig. Not far from the
foot of this peak-by-default there was an inn known as The Sign
of the Coffee Tree. There, in the summer of 1833, a group of
musical enthusiasts used to gather for evenings of discussion and
good fellowship. Sooner rather than later, the talk would invariably veer around to the deplorable state of German musical
taste.[1]

It was a shame, they agreed one night, that so shortly after
the deaths of Beethoven and Schubert, the music which people
preferred was Rossini, the meaningless roulades of Herz and
Hünten, the Pleyel-Vanhal "nightcap-style"—and that all the
young girls were falling in love with Czerny. This deplorable

[1] "The beginning of the Nineteenth Century was an era of bad taste
that has never been equaled in history." HENDRIK WILLEM VAN LOON—
The Arts.

state of affairs was further vitiated by the base standards of
the musical journals. In the end, they grew so worked up that
Robert Schumann sprang excitedly to his feet. The usually
tongue-tied musician was so moved that he broke his customary
silence, and cried: [2]

"Gentlemen, we are always scolding about this state of affairs; but nobody *does* anything about it! Now I say—let's *do*
something to raise our country's musical standards. Let's organize
a movement against the silly finger-twiddling that generally
passes for music in Germany. Today the musical journals are all
run by amateurs. I say, let's found one edited and written by
professionals! Let's start something!"

Cheers. The proposal was adopted by acclamation, and
Robert's back resounded to the heroic slappings of his comrades. At once the Coffee Tree gang set about realizing their
dream.

On June 28th, 1833, Robert wrote his mother that his life of
late had been

not without charm and vivacity. A crowd of young, cultivated people,
mostly students of music, has formed a circle about me which I, in
turn, have formed about Wieck's house. We are chiefly possessed by
a plan for a great new journal of music, . . . prospectus and adver-
tisement of which will appear as soon as next month. Its tone and
color are to be fresher and better varied than the others. In particular we shall set up a dam against the even flow of the old, time-
honored routine; although I see little likelihood of ever bringing
Wieck (who, however, grows day by day more friendly) around to
my views on art. . . . The directors are . . . mostly executive musicians (nine-fingered me excepted) which at once gives the cause an
air. . . .

I may perhaps get something out of this enterprise for which my
real nature (which loathes everything disorderly) longs, like many
another artist: a more solid (bourgeois) background. This would serve
as a frame about the picture, or as a vessel containing the spreading
mass. To say nothing of the financial advantages— — —

So here was the dreamy, tongue-tied composer, functioning
as the real, though retiring, head of a doubtful literary enter-

[2] I give only the gist of his outburst.

prise. The prospects of success were indeed dubious. Robert needed editorial associates who knew how to edit, and write. But not one of them came up to these specifications.

Wieck, besides being a peripatetic concert manager, had very little time or inclination for that sort of thing. Julius Knorr, the nominal editor-in-chief during the first year, was a good piano teacher; but he liked skat and billiards better than music, or work of any kind. A talent wasted in dissipation. Ferdinand Stegmayer, conductor of theater orchestras, a notable ladies' man, refused to take the venture seriously, and amused himself on the side-lines. The same may be said of Ernst Ortlepp.

In December 1833 these collaborators were joined by a new-comer to Leipzig, a piano virtuoso and composer of talent named Ludwig Schunke. Between him and Robert it was a case of friendship at first sight. When he appeared at the comrades' table, with his "ardent eyes, aquiline nose, and finely ironic mouth," Schumann said to himself: "That's Thorwaldsen's Schiller to the life, only more so!" On March 19th, 1834, Robert wrote to his mother of the newcomer: "One patch of blue in the sky often gives more pleasure than a whole wide expanse of azure. I would give all my other friends for this one alone."

The two proved to be of the same age. They lodged in the same house, and were much together, walking and skating. Once Schunke, the frail little hothead, plunged into an argument with the composer Nicolai, and was kept from fighting a duel with him only by discovering that Robert was to be Nicolai's second.

Schunke threw himself ardently into the new project as direc-tor and contributor. But he was inexperienced in business, and so poor a stylist that Robert's copious revisions were the best part of the Schunke contributions.

He made up for this, however, by introducing his friend to the highly musical home of the Voigts, where such lions as Men-delssohn, Chopin, and Loewe were familiar figures. And, as we have seen, Henriette not only helped on Robert's courtship of Ernestine, but also, for good measure, got him more than half in love with herself.

When the eccentric, absent-minded young fellow became the

predominant figure in the new enterprise, the older men laughed, shook their heads, and wagered that *Die Neue Zeitschrift für Musik (The New Magazine for Music)* would not last more than half a dozen numbers. In fact, Wieck promised to be a director only on condition that Robert showed real industry. But he reckoned without the strong literary and publishing instinct which the boy had inherited from his remarkable father, together with other necessary qualities such as persistence and business acumen. What Robert needed was not threats but encouragement, strong support, and help in carrying the burden. Of these, however, his dear friends gave him all too little.

The youngsters were forging a new weapon to attack the old, wizened style of criticism, and the old indecisiveness that sought to conceal invertebracy behind the screen of impartiality. Down with the critics who dipped their pens, not in ink, but in honey! Down with everything morbid, inartistic, and ugly!

Robert boldly nailed his colors to the mast:

The age of mutual compliments is gradually sinking into its grave. Frankly, we are not minded to assist its resurrection. He who does not attack the bad, defends the good but halfway.—Our purpose . . . is to remind our readers emphatically of the distant past and its works. Then, to emphasize the fact that the contemporary artist can secure strength for the creation of new beauty only by drinking from such pure fountains. Then, to attack as inartistic the immediate past, which is concerned merely with encouraging superficial virtuosity. Lastly, to help prepare and hasten the coming of a new poetic era.

From amid the preparations for the venture, he jubilantly wrote his friend Töpken: "Just now we are living a romance such as has never perhaps been told in any book."

Schumann's own contributions to the periodical were extraordinarily important, and were destined to exert a very real influence upon his times. Music itself owes a large debt to his literary and critical gift. He sold his contemporaries the idea of really good music. This magazine venture became a truly creative thing, and produced results. His sympathetic treatment of contemporary composers also showed the generous, constructive streak in his nature.

Besides all this lofty idealism, more personal and practical interests entered into Robert's plan. In the prospectus he forecast a magazine in which the artist "can defend himself against one-sided or false criticism, in so far as this is compatible with justice and lack of bias." When he wrote "the artist," he of course included himself; and under "false criticism" he included that deadliest sort, complete silence and indifference. The publishers were turning such a hard-boiled eye upon his compositions that he had to bring out a number of them at his own expense. But if he were an editor, and could review their publications as he saw fit, he knew they would take him more seriously as a composer.

And so it came to pass. "If the publishers didn't fear me as an editor," he confided later to Dorn, "the world would never get to know anything about me." This, unfortunately, is the sort of thing that has always lain, a sinister shadow, over the world of the arts—a kind of genteel seventh cousin of blackmail.

But Robert resolutely refused to share the fate of Schubert, whom the *Allgemeine Musikalische Zeitung* under Fink mentioned only twice in the decade beginning 1830. The first time was in connection with a song; the second, with Schumann's discovery of the great C Major Symphony. Rellstab, who then dominated music criticism in Germany, had proclaimed himself "Schubert's most implacable foe," and detested Chopin. In such precarious conditions, Robert's instinct for survival prompted him to provide himself with a stout weapon of offense and defense.

After he had, by such means, secured his own position, his indignation at the rank injustice meted out to less doughty warriors made him sometimes over-appreciative in his editorial eagerness to do full justice to composers of promise who were defenseless.

For himself, he used his advantages with much delicacy and moderation. And his circle had nothing in common with the literary gangsters who organized soon after the First World War for mutual glorification, the browbeating of editors, and hostilities against all writers not in the gang. Such was Schumann's discretion that, during the decade when he was in charge of the magazine, he allowed but five of his forty-four then published compositions to be mentioned, and these in terms far from fulsome.

Three years before the birth of the *New Magazine*, Florestan and Eusebius had made their bow in the article heralding the advent of Chopin. These two imaginary personages, who often appeared in Schumann's earlier articles and piano pieces, formed the nucleus about which was built the bizarre association called the Davidsbündler, or Davidites. It began as a fanciful Jean-Paulian device for allegorizing Schumann's wishful idea of the contrasting aspects of his own dual nature.

This was indeed a strange, original business! Every man is made up of different personalities; but who had ever before made artistic capital of the fact, or even admitted it? [3] Schumann's dual personality played such a tremendous role in his own life, and his minting of it loomed so large in his music, that in any estimate of the man and his work it should be taken seriously into account.

At the start the Davidsbündler was a purely subjective association. The club premises were all contained within Robert's capacious skull. This is how he described the germinating idea:

> In order to express contrasting points of view about art, it seemed not unfitting to invent antithetical artistic characters, of which Florestan and Eusebius were the most important, with Master Raro as intermediary. This "Davidsbündler" idea runs like a red thread through the paper [the *N. Mag. for M.*], humorously combining *"Wahrheit"* and *"Dichtung."* [4]

The idea of such an association was not brand new; for, in the year of Robert's birth, Carl Maria von Weber had wished to start a "Harmonic Club" with similar ideals. But the elder composer's devotion to music was too single-minded for any

---

[3] Half a century was to pass before *The Strange Case of Dr. Jekyll and Mr. Hyde* created a sensation. And the coincidence is worth noting that this story was written by the same author whose *Child's Garden of Verses* formed the first literary parallel to Schumann's pioneer *Scenes from Childhood.*

[4] An allusion to Goethe's autobiography, *Truth and Poetry.*

such literary and organizing activities. So it was left for Robert to realize Weber's dream.

When the *New Magazine* project was inaugurated, its sponsors automatically became members of this fantastic organization, and a number of the contributing members were elected. The club's remarkable name *"Davidsbündler"* was one of Schumann's happiest inventions. For old King David, poet, composer, harp virtuoso, and inventor of the music cure for mental complaints, was not only the ablest and most serious musician of his country and time; but he also smote those barbarians, the Philistines, hip and thigh. Long afterwards, the name of David's foes came to be applied by German university students to the townsfolk, the "outsiders," who were the enemies of the chosen people. In Jena, towards the end of the seventeenth century there was a fight between "town and gown," in which a student was killed. Whereupon a sermon was preached in a local pulpit on the text "the Philistines be upon you, Samson." After that the cultured contemptuously called those people "Philistines" whose taste and intellect they held to be inferior to their own.

The Davidsbündler gang was a natural continuation of Sansouci, the pirates' cave-clan of Robert's youth; and its headquarters should by rights have been called the "Cave of Adullam." [5] Over the entrance should have been blazoned these words from I Samuel, 22:

David therefore departed thence, and escaped to the cave of Adullam. . . . And every one that was in distress . . . and every one that was discontented gathered themselves unto him; and he became a captain over them.

Schumann had a natural tendency to drape the commonplace of every day in the veils of poetic mystery. When he was young and strong, this tendency made him turn the editors and contributors of the *Magazine* into a fantastic club. At the time of his tragic break-up, this same impulse, exaggerated by illness, made him an enthusiast for table-tipping, and led him to at-

[5] As Mr. Norman Hoyte happily suggests to me. This was David's hideout when he "was sore afraid of Achish the king of Gath. And he . . . feigned himself mad . . . and scrabbled on the doors of the gate, and let his spittle fall down upon his beard."

tribute melodies of his own creation to the spirits of other composers.

He delighted in mystifying the reader, and felt that the reader liked it too. When subscribers wrote in to ask just what this strange association was, he inserted the following notice:

Various rumors are floating around in regard to the undersigned association. As we unfortunately must, for the time being, withhold our reasons for veiling this matter, we beg Herr Schumann (in case such a person is known to the honorable board of editors), if circumstances demand it, kindly to represent us with his name.

THE DAVIDSBÜNDLER.

I'll do it with pleasure. *R. Schumann.*

As a matter of fact, even today the Davidites retain some of the blurred outlines dear to Robert's heart. His various definitions give but a nebulous idea of the organization. From the vantage ground of 1854, he described it as "more than a secret one, for it existed only in the head of its founder." But in his young days, he called it a spiritually romantic club "of all those artists who approached art from higher viewpoints." . . . "Mozart was just as great a *Bündler* as Berlioz is now."

The men of today, however, can form a clearer picture of it than could the first subscribers to the *Magazine;* for the natures of Florestan and Eusebius are now understood. From the fact that the Davidite nickname of Robert's bosom friend Schunke was Jonathan, it may be gathered that Robert, secretly but appropriately, considered himself David.

Schumann's biographers have inherited from one another the theory that Meister Raro was the nickname of Clara's father. But, in view of Robert's despair, already mentioned, of ever bringing Wieck to see eye to eye with him on important musical questions; and considering the quarter-century difference in the ages of the two, which would account for this despair, the idea must be rejected that there is much of Wieck in Raro —except perhaps at second-hand, through his daughter. For Riemann has made the interesting discovery that when you join the two lovers' names, end to end,

claRARObert

Ludwig Schunke on His Deathbed

Clara Wieck at Sixteen

the four linking letters spell RARO. So perhaps this imaginary character meant to Robert the balanced wisdom of perfect sanity to which he wistfully aspired, enriched and corrected by the common sense of the girl he loved. Naturally, Raro became the conciliator and arbiter in the frequent clashes between Florestan and Eusebius.

Most of the Davidites had nicknames. "Fritz Friedrich" was Johann Peter Lyser, the dumb eccentric who wrote fiction about the great composers, but was best known for his striking imaginary pen caricatures of Beethoven. His affliction must have endeared him to the almost wordless Schumann.

Karl Banck, pupil of Goethe's friend Zelter, composer and rival for Clara's favor, whose devious, intriguing nature made trouble for Robert, was tellingly named "Serpentinus"; and one wonders why he stood for thus being called a snake in the grass. "Vult" and "Walt" were aspects of the idolized Jean Paul; and "Walt" was also occasionally applied to Rakemann, the pianist.

The humorous "Jeanquirit" was the piano virtuoso and composer Stephen Heller, then living in Paris, a friend of Chopin, Berlioz, and Liszt, and a favorite of Robert. "Knif," a name with which the editor-in-chief had great fun, was reversed writing for Fink, editor of Leipzig's other music magazine, who now ignored his competitor's existence. The latter wrote home:

Fink's in a bad way. He is already furious. . . . If it comes on to rain mental stones, five backs can always endure more, especially as there's youth among them, than a single old one that's already very much bowed.

This calculation, however, turned out to be rank optimism. For it was not long before Robert's back stood alone under the stony downpour. Somewhat abruptly disturbed in his mossy rut by the youngsters of the new day, music-pope Fink lost control of himself, and burst out with:

Bündler to right of us, *Bündler* to left of us, Figaro here, Figaro there [I suppose this reference to the libretto of Rossini's ubiquitous *Barber of Seville* is intended as a dig at Florestan's imaginatively humorous style]. . . . But to date we are still here at the old stand, eager to say a little word of our own, and that with a vengeance.

It seemed, though, that old Fink's little word could make but feeble headway against the charm, the talent, and the brilliant, amusing impetuosity of the Davidites.

Clara was known as "Chiara," "Chiarina," or "Zilia." Henriette Voigt was "Eleanore"; Mendelssohn, "Felix Meritis," and Leipzig became "Firlenz." "St. Diamond" was Zuccalmaglio, the poet and folklorist whose carelessly compiled anthologies were destined to mislead Brahms.

Ernst Ortlepp, of the original board of directors, soon stepped down from that eminence to become an occasional contributor. He was another Davidite who wrote fiction about the great composers. Later he took to drink, and was literally brought down to the gutter; for he was drowned in one. He was one of the very few Davidites without a nickname. This distinction he shared with Richard Wagner,[6] and with old Ignaz von Seyfried, pupil of Haydn, close friend of Mozart, and an acquaintance of Beethoven. He had lived in the same house with L. v. B. and dined with him almost daily.

There was Joseph Mainzer, successively priest, abbé, singing teacher, and revolutionist. Seven years after helping to start the *New Magazine,* he went to England and founded a magazine of his own, which was the genesis of the present *Musical Times.* The most picturesque figure of them all was the highly eccentric Johann Ludwig Böhner. He was no less a personage than the original of "Kapellmeister Kreisler," that favorite invention of E. T. A. Hoffmann, whose *Tales* were to inspire Offenbach to write his most popular opera. Böhner was a highly talented composer-errant, and the most peripatetic of artists. His love of roving enriched the *Magazine* with many a quaint report from out-of-the-way nooks and corners of the musical world. As in the cases of Knorr and Ortlepp, drink hastened his demise.

These, then, were the chief Davidites. Schumann was no milk-and-water editor. He held lofty ideals and could fight formidably for them. Wordy polemics, however, were not to his taste. He preferred to furnish example rather than precept:

[6] A contributor to the *Magazine,* but a lukewarm and temporary adherent.

I have long had it in mind [he wrote Hirschbach] to take the field against certain theories. . . . Like you, though, I would prefer to demonstrate my meaning at once, practically. That is to say, I write letters of the alphabet only under compulsion, and prefer the direct method of writing sonatas and symphonies.

He must have been that inspiring sort of person, met but once in a blue moon in editorial chairs, who brings out the best in his contributors. And he was far removed from the daily-tabloid-minded type of magazine editor, justly loathed by good writers, who is always eager to sacrifice quality and lasting value for a picayune timeliness. When Joseph Fischhof feared that his article would be out of date if he should stop to rewrite it, Schumann exclaimed: "The good is always timely!"

CHAPTER 10

DIAMOND FACETS

O N February 4th, 1836, Johanna Schumann died. To her youngest son this was a staggering blow. The mother upon whom Robert's affections had so long been fixed left him alone. Suddenly the fixation focus was removed and the young man's whole life was changed.

From this moment a particular aspect of his personality became more sharply defined. Robert's character was one of contrasts, but none more remarkable than the contrast between the prodigality of his youth and his increasingly sound, prompt, accurate, far-sighted, honest and thorough business relations with the *Magazine* and with music publishers. From the moment he became an editor, he wrote home for money less and less frequently. This can hardly be accounted for by the fact of his having come into possession of a modest fortune at the death of his mother, since at the time of her death he had for two years been a successful editor; and, at the rate he had squandered money in Heidelberg, he would have run through that inheritance in short order.

There may be another explanation for this stiffening of his backbone. When an event like a mother's death happens to a character like this there is usually a period of premature or superficial maturity which is due to an anxiety to prove oneself against the memory of the departed: "Mother loved me, so I must be a man now."

There is another striking contrast between the wildness and luxuriant delicacy of his Jean-Paulian dreaming, and the stern, almost incredibly industrious application with which he constantly dispatched whole mountain ranges of work, both journalistic and creative. Franz Brendel gave a striking instance of his conscientiousness in practical matters.

Schumann bound all incoming letters, and had these before him in a series of volumes. Why, at the close of every semester, he himself undertook the dismal task of indexing them; and later sometimes asked me, in fun, how this work tasted to me.

Any journalist knows that to edit a magazine year in, year out, and maintain a consistently high standard, would be impossible for any mere fit-and-start dreamer. With all his dreaminess, Schumann was far abler in practical matters than almost any other composer before or since. Taken alone, either the Florestan or the Eusebius in him would have made an outstanding person. But the fusion of the two with the portion of Raro at his disposal created an editorial combination unique in history. He was diplomatic and charming with contributors, publishers, and printers. He was conscientious in keeping promises and engagements. He was far-seeing about writing to distant places in plenty of time to make and carry out plans with no risk of last-minute rush.

All this is strange enough when one remembers that Schumann was a great composer. But it becomes almost incredible when one also remembers that, only a short time before, he was, on his own admission, a crazily irresponsible spendthrift, throwing whatever money he had out of the window with both hands. By 1836, when he came into his inheritance, the miracle seems to have happened; for instead of going near the window, he began to husband his resources with sagacity.

Here is one of those rare instances of a badly spoiled child with sound latent qualities of character which develop and come into play on the disappearance of the spoiler. A silk purse evolves out of what had apparently been a sow's ear.

Schumann's mature personality had arrived. Erler [1] pays tribute to

[1] *Robert Schumanns Leben aus seinen Briefen,* Ries und Erler, 1887.

the boundless wealth of his inner being, the winning lovableness of
his character, true as gold. A noble presence . . . clean-hearted,
without envy, one who sets himself the highest standards . . . (incidentally revealing a touching modesty), he has consideration and
encouragement for the weaker . . . but is inexorable and condem-
natory toward even the famous, if they leave the strait and narrow
path and go in for empty show.

Not all writers on Schumann seem to have understood just
what was involved in this transformation of character and habit.
Apparently misconceiving the duties of a busy editor, Constantin
von Sternberg, a pupil of Wieck, says of Robert: "Quite aware
of his unfitness to brave the rough touch of the world, he cau-
tiously avoided contact with it." It is a somewhat peculiar
method of becoming an anchorite,

> The world forgetting, by the world forgot—

to found a polemic magazine, and for a decade to bear the whole
brunt of the necessary rough-and-tumble contact with contributors, printers, printers' devils, creditors, debtors, envious rivals,
and assorted enemies!

Sternberg says Schumann discovered, in his ivory tower, "that
intimate note which touches us so often in his works." But perhaps that tenderly intimate note is all the more poignantly
touching and consoling because it came, not from a sterile
Stylites, perched on his solitary pillar, but from a many-sided
genius who had flown to his brief solitude enriched by the warm
human contacts of the hurly-burly.

For a spendthrift—reformed or not—Schumann was remarkably
kind, thoughtful, and generous when it came to financial dealings with his publishers. One reason why he could be so sympathetic with their viewpoint was that he had so much publishing
blood in his own veins. Here is an instance. Some years later
Breitkopf and Härtel offered him a certain sum for the *Ritornelle,* Op. 65. He answered:

I cannot conscientiously ask as much as that, but only eight
Louis d'or. Don't think this affectation. The pieces are small—besides
which, stuff for men's chorus has only a limited public. So I beg of
you not to give me more than I said. I am *perfectly satisfied with it.*

If only I could once turn out something that would bring you in a substantial profit! [2]

This is Florestan at his clearest and most engaging.

For all his generosity, Robert was shrewd, and had a maliciously gleeful eye alert to enjoy the human comedy. For example, even as early as July 29th, 1834, he was far from blind to the less admirable aspect of Wieck, and could enjoy a laugh at his tricks and his manners. He wrote Henriette Voigt:

Wieck, with a whole Knigge [3] written on his countenance, was undecided who should get out of the wagon first when it reached the church door, the ladies or himself.—His good genius finally decided in favor of his own person.

With time, Robert's comments on his master took on acerbity. For example, four years later he informed Fischhof:

In the case of Wieck, everything is partisanship. If it weren't for the play of politics, he wouldn't bother in the least about you or me or the whole *Magazine*.

Anyone as creative as Robert would not have been human if he had not chafed at the way his editorial job hindered composition. For it was not long before the load of responsibility, so blithely assumed by the "five backs," had shifted its whole dead weight to Robert's single one. Sometimes he confessed that his gorge rose at having to write

about such paltry trifles of bad compositions. Then I seem to myself like a diamond that nobody has any use for except to cut common glass.

Such an emotional conflict naturally involves a nervous drain. His work on the *Magazine* was wearing and tearing him down and hastening his final collapse. But he was still young. And, for the first few years of its existence, he filled it with such a

[2] Here he anticipates the great-hearted way in which Johannes Brahms was to deal with his own favorite publisher, Simrock.

[3] Knigge, a combination of the Emily Post and the Dale Carnegie of those days, was the author of the standard book of etiquette, *Umgang mit Menschen,* or *Getting Along with People.*

sparkle of high spirits that the uninitiated might well have envied the carefree editor the fun he was having. Before or since, there never has been a musical magazine of such quality. And it was actually paying for itself. To literary work of this kind, the epigram which Robert got off about the interpretive musician might seem to apply: "The word *'play'* is very beautiful, since 'to play an instrument' must have the same meaning. He who does not play *with* the instrument does not play it."

Now, the play element was the most precious part of Schumann's writing; but years and accumulating cares crowded it out. The spontaneous frolicking of those playfully conceived characters, his two opposed selves, grew rarer and eventually ceased. Eusebius made his final bow in 1839, and Florestan, in 1842.

The first use Robert made of them in his published music was in the F Sharp Minor Piano Sonata, Op. 11, begun 1833, and finished two years later. Originally it bore the inscription

> Pianoforte Sonata
> Dedicated to Clara
> by Florestan and Eusebius
> Op. 11

The idea of leaving out his lady-love's last name—in fact, the whole inscription—was in those days as original as the music itself.

Then, in *Carnaval,* Op. 9, composed 1834-35, we meet Clara (Chiarina) squired again by Florestan and Eusebius. And these two latter make their last trip to the concert-stage in the highly original inscriptions which he placed above some of the *Davidsbündler Dances,* Op. 6, composed in 1837 and published the following year.

The musical regeneration of Leipzig, which Schumann and his friends had begun with the founding of the *Magazine* in 1834, went on with enthusiasm. They were to find a powerful ally in the very next year, 1835, when the hide-bound music world of the city was suddenly galvanized by the advent of a young musician named Felix Mendelssohn-Bartholdy. He made his debut as conductor of the Gewandhaus concerts, and introduced that startling novelty, the baton. Soon he aroused idolatrous enthusiasm, most of all in the generous Schumann, who reported:

In the first moment there flew to him a hundred hearts! . . . It was a joy to see how, with his eye, he shaded in advance the spiritual sinuosities of the compositions, from the most delicate to the strongest. How unlike the conductors one sometimes comes across, who threaten to beat up with their scepters the score, the orchestra, and the audience!

Gifted with a brilliant sense of established form, Mendelssohn was, underneath the thin Romanticist veneer, essentially a Classicist, born out of due time into an age of Romanticism. This and a stiff technical training in formal structure inclined him toward conservatism, and made him impatient of wayward novelty. Like Robert, he had begun as a pampered wonderchild. But, unlike Robert, he had been further spoiled by riches and unceasing adulation. So he was unable to appreciate anything so new, original, and unlike his own as the music of Schumann. He was not the man to turn an indulgent eye on the other's structural shortcomings, or to value properly the greater emotional vividness and power of this novel music. True, he performed it at the Gewandhaus, and forwarded it in various ways; but without inner conviction.

Personally he was correct to the adoring Schumann; but he never could get over the fact of Robert's being a writer on music—a genus for which he had a fierce and irrational hatred. Probably some writer had once criticized him adversely; and any sort of opposition roused him to rage. It was not what he was accustomed to. This was enough to damn the whole race of musical scribes forever. Then too, he had no use for amateurishness—a quality which, in undue measure, he imputed to Robert. All of which made the friendship somewhat lopsided. On the one hand was the ardent Robert, who late in 1835 wrote a friend, using his old diamond simile:

> Mendelssohn is a splendid chap,—a diamond straight from heaven. We like one another—I think. Besides, we have a lot to talk about.

By the following year, his admiration had risen, *crescendo:* "Mendelssohn is the one to whom I look up as to a lofty mountain. He is a real god."

Meanwhile the winds of recognition had begun to puff, though feebly, in Robert's direction. The summer of 1835 brought a review of his Opp. 1-5 by Gottfried Weber, in the *Cäcilia Magazine*. The gnarled style of this gentleman is an awe-inspiring example of German at its worst. In an involved and artificial lingo, anticipating Henry James, he praises simplicity and naturalness:

> I must not refuse the (as I repeatedly assume, *young*) composer the attestation that out of his productions—which are not so much unripe as ripened in the hothouse of premature striving after the extraordinary—so much genius nevertheless shows forth that one cannot be sure he will not, in his own good time, find his way out of the confusion of strange tone-products back to simplicity and naturalness, and from there to the summits of art.

"That refreshed me for once in a way," wrote Robert to Töpken.

It was stimulating, too, just then, to have Wieck sounding his praises in extravagant terms. The pedagogue was actually calling him "the second Beethoven," and "the German Chopin and Bach." [4] (One wonders what Wieck supposed Bach's nationality to be!)

But it gave Robert even more of an impetus to have the barely rising generation begin to look up to him with awe, and to play

[4] Walter Dahms, usually so level-headed, got mixed up, and stated that Schumann said these complimentary things about the uncreative Wieck. Which would have proved our hero already quite insane at twenty-five.

his music. A little urchin named Alfred Dörffel, so young that his tiny fingers could barely negotiate a stretch of a seventh, was crazy to hear Clara's concert on November 9th, 1835. But he had no money. However, on the advice of Günther, his teacher, he boldly called at Wieck's house, was admitted, and marched quaking up to the grim pedagogue.

"Please, sir, I am a piano student and I'm studying the *Papillons,* and I want to hear Clara's concert but I've got no money."

"Show here your hands!" growled Wieck.

The boy held them out, and the man shook his head over their size. "Come, let us hear you play."

Alfchen had to sit down at the square piano. "But this stool's too low for me."

"Never mind that; you play!"

Though Alfchen could not manage solid octaves, he had developed a nimble facility in breaking them. After the Introduction he hit up a vigorous pace, and managed to make a good fist of Number One. The grim Wieckian countenance relaxed and gave forth a brief but immense bark of laughter. The young lady behind the piano and the gentleman at the window (who turned out to be Clara and Herr Schumann) laughed until Alfchen feared they might do themselves an injury. He was puzzled; for he himself could find nothing funny in the situation.

"Good, good," growled Wieck. "Just show up at the stage door. You won't need a ticket."

Sure enough; on the great evening they let Alfchen in free; and he posted himself as near as he could get to Clara,—already another of her many adorers.

That was the beginning of his boyish career as regular Gewandhaus deadhead, page-turner, and universally beloved mascot, who was even allowed to turn for such great ones as Moscheles and Mendelssohn.

And that is the story of how the youngest Schumannite crashed the gate with *Butterflies,* and helped to build up his favorite composer's self-confidence. It was one child's advance payment for all the treasures which his idol was soon to shower upon the world of children.

A moment ago it gave this biographer a real thrill to open the Peters Edition and discover on the title-page:

ROB. SCHUMANN'S
WORKS
for Pianoforte Solo
revised by
ALFRED DÖRFFEL

CHAPTER 11

SWANS ARE REALLY LARGER GEESE

IT would be interesting to know in what month of 1834 Robert sent a certain letter to Clara. If one can believe his implied declaration that Ernestine had driven her out of his heart, it was probably written not long after that lady's appearance on the Leipzig scene; for Clara had recently been hustled away to Dresden. In it he makes very subtle love to the fourteen- or fifteen-year-old *Backfisch;* [1] but begins with a bit of teasing—in veiled allusion to that day, two years before, when she had confused ducks with geese.

My dear and honored Clara!
There are haters of beauty who claim that swans are really larger geese. One would be equally right in saying that distance is only an extended nearness. And it is, too; for, indeed, I talk with you daily (in a softer tone than usual), and know that you understand me.

He then went on about various fanciful plans he had hatched for their correspondence, such as filling his balloon with thoughts and dispatching them to her address by a favoring wind. Another fancy was to catch butterflies and press them into the service as messengers. Evidently the post-horn had just delighted him by announcing the arrival of a message from her, for—

Postillions, dear Clara, have the same magical effect on me as the very best champagne. When one hears them trumpeting so gaily to all the world, for sheer lightness of heart one thinks that he no longer has a head. . . . As I have intimated, the postillion's horn sent me out of my old dreams into new ones.

[1] An enthusiastic, sentimental girl of about fifteen. There is no equivalent in English for this word.

93

It took him a year, however, to be fully rid of Ernestine, and invite his first love back to her rightful place in his heart.

In April 1835, when Clara returned from five weary months of concert touring, Robert was the first caller; but it seemed to the girl that he gave her "scarcely so much as a casual greeting." With tears overflowing her eyes, she confided to a friend: "Oh, there's nobody I love so much as him; but he didn't even look at me!"

Clara was never more mistaken. The normally tongue-tied Robert was struck more than usually dumb by a complex of emotions induced by the miracle of her return. He was surprised and delighted at this sudden flowering of the awkward *Backfisch* into a beautiful young woman. And he was seized by a conviction of inconstancy and guilt when he remembered the affair with Ernestine.

However, he soon recovers poise enough to make his true sentiments clear. On August 28, 1835, he writes her from Zwickau of "an angel's head" which he constantly sees before him, and which looks "as much like a certain Clara of my acquaintance as one hair resembles another. . . . You know how I love you." And, in a P.S., the superstitious fellow calls attention to the lucky omen of this being written on Goethe's birthday.

That fall the much-adored Chopin stopped over in Leipzig and electrified the musical world. At once, Mendelssohn took him over to the Wiecks' to see Clara, who proceeded to play him Robert's F Sharp Minor Sonata. The Pole was polite about the ordeal, but liked Schumann's productions even less than Mendelssohn did. Somewhat later he was heard to say about *Carnaval* that he admired the charm of the engraving and general design of the piece, but could not regard it as music.

Then Clara played a couple of Chopin's Etudes and the finale of one of his concertos. The visitor was fervent in his praise of her; and evened the count by performing his best-known *Nocturne*, the one in E flat.

Level-headed Clara was not carried off her feet. That evening she confided to the diary that the little man was feeble. In order to make a robust tone, he had to get upon his feet and bring the weight of his whole body down upon the keys. She thought highly of his *pianissimo* (that elusive blue bird of pianism), but complained of his *rubato,* with its capricious exaggeration.

Mendelssohn, on the other hand, who the year before had censured Chopin's overdone "Parisian sensibility and despair," now found this performer "the perfect virtuoso." That night, at his own home, he held open house.

I had to play him my latest oratorio [*St. Paul*], and in the entr'actes he played me his new Etudes and the new concerto; while curious Leipzigers stole in to listen and to be able to boast that they had beheld Chopin.

As for Robert, who had been summoned to the Wiecks' almost as soon as the distinguished guests had arrived, his critical faculties were overwhelmed by heels-over-head enthusiasm. He let Eusebius write:

Chopin was here. Florestan simply fell upon him. I saw them arm in arm. They were floating rather than walking.

He never forgot that day. Its glories were heightened by the miracle taking place in his own heart. For, in his *Book of Life,* just after Chopin's name stands: "Clara's eyes and her love."

Yet the all-compelling wave of passionate love did not really engulf them in its foam until the day when Robert noted, in what he called his *Bridegroom's Book,* as Number One under the rubric

Difficult Partings

I. In November 1835, after the first kiss on the staircase of the Wieck house, as Clara was starting for Zwickau.

And Clara confessed later:

As you gave me the first kiss, I thought I was going to swoon. All went black before my eyes and I could barely hold the light which I was carrying to show you the way.

Clara was due to give a concert in Zwickau, and Robert came tumbling after. In his *Book* he inscribed the word, "Union."

Later, with such tenderness as is often found in his music, he reminded Clara of those ecstatic days:

Tomorrow it will be three years since that evening I kissed you in Zwickau. I shall never forget those kisses. That night you were simply too enchanting. And then, at the concert, you couldn't look me in the face, you Clara, in your blue dress.

On another occasion he confessed to her: "You are my first love. Ernestine had to come in order to unite us."

CHAPTER 12

STAY TRUE

LOVE and artistic triumphs had by now ripened Clara into what many of her contemporaries called "the most charming bud in all Leipzig." When the lovers returned to town, Robert set down in the *Book:* "Blissful evenings at the Wiecks' house in her arms." Under the delusion that Wieck had long ago begun forming Clara to be an ideal wife for him, Robert savored these evenings with a light heart. He was certain that, whenever he should ask, the pedagogue would eagerly accept him as a son-in-law. And the only thing which, for the moment, held him back was that his engagement with Ernestine had not yet been definitely canceled.

Poor Robert was lamentably mistaken. Clara's father had not the least intention of bestowing his gifted and valuable daughter upon any man, least of all upon an impecunious young musician of no matter what genius. For a skilled teacher of youth, he had been singularly blind to the romance rapidly blossoming under his nose; but as soon as his suspicions were aroused, Wieck and his wife made the atmosphere of the house impossible for Robert.

He read Clara a sharp lecture, forbidding her to correspond with the young man or receive his letters. And, on January 14th, 1836, he carried her off in all haste to Dresden. There he craftily arranged to have her caught up in a whirl of gaiety, besides making her give two concerts.

Robert's shocked and forlorn state may be imagined. And it was sadly aggravated on February 4th by an event already described in these pages—the death of the mother whom he loved

97

with the uncanny force of psychic fixation. She had always been his comfort, refuge and source of counsel whenever, as now, life had borne too hard upon him.

Not all his desperate filial devotion, however, could overcome his fear of facing death and funerals. This fear had recently made him retreat home from Leipzig to escape the imminent passing of his beloved friend Schunke. As has already been suggested, the tragedy of his beautiful sister's suicide when he was at the impressionable age of sixteen had perhaps given him an invincible horror of death and the dead. A little later, this horror may have been intensified by his father's death while Frau Schumann was away from home and could not shield her youngest from the cruder aspects of mortality. Three years before, in 1833, when his brother Julius died, Robert had refused to return home for the funeral in spite of passionate entreaties from his mother. His explanation, that he was too ill to do so, was undoubtedly true enough psychologically, if not physically. And now, it was the same story all over again. Robert could not force himself to go home and face a situation which might bring on another attack of nervous exhaustion. Instead, he went directly toward the woman who was in so many profound respects to take the place of his mother in his life. On February 7th he set out for Dresden and for Clara.

The lovers had ostensibly been obeying Wieck's interdict upon their meeting each other. Clara had even made a very prim entry in her diary for her father to see. But she and Robert had managed to keep in close touch with each other all the time, and he was aware that Wieck was going to be out of the city for a few days. This fortunate circumstance made it all the more feasible for Robert to turn southeast to his beloved instead of south to Zwickau and the home where his mother was lying dead.

Now, Clara had one quality rather rare in a great interpretive artist: she was extremely maternal. And, ever since the days of the stumbling-block stones in the path to Connewitz, Robert had been highly responsive to this side of her. Indeed, a motherly word which she let drop, about his sometimes seeming like a child to her, was presently to be the chief inspiration which produced one of his notable masterpieces, the *Scenes from Child-hood*.

In this dark crisis, bereft suddenly of his lifelong comfortress and spiritual support, had not Clara been there to turn to, he would indeed have been in a pitiable state. The final catastrophe of madness might have been anticipated by almost a generation, and Schumann would now be known to us merely as the composer of a handful of remarkable pieces for piano.

Those stolen days in Dresden were full of the deep satisfaction of reunion and the renewal of vows. When at last, Robert, to avoid Wieck's return, took post-chaise to iron out inheritance matters at Zwickau, there came another of the "difficult partings." On February 11th, 1838, Robert wrote Clara in retrospect:

Two years ago today I parted from you in Dresden. "Stay true to me," said I.—You gave a heavy-hearted little nod; and you have held true to your word.

The notation in the *Bridegroom's Book* ran: "Parting at the Dresden Post. Clara in little red hat. Long separation."

Soon she received from Zwickau the first of the love letters exchanged at this time, in which the ecstasy of their passion drowns out every voice of distress and sorrow.

> At the Post in Zwickau
> after ten at night.

My eyes have been heavy with sleep. For two hours now I have been waiting for the express coach. The roads are so badly torn up that I may not get started before two in the morning. How vividly you stand before me, my darling, darling Clara, ah, so near, it seems to me that I could grasp you. Once I could put into elegant words how strongly I was attracted to somebody. Now I can no longer do that. And if you, of yourself, did not know it, I could not manage to tell you. Only love me well, do you hear? I demand much, for I give much.

This has been a full day—my mother's will, accounts of her death. Beyond all the darkness, though, I see your radiant likeness, and it helps me to endure everything.

I may tell you, too, that my future is now much more assured. It is true that I shall not be in a position to fold my hands in my lap, and must toil tremendously to attain what you recognize when you happen to pass a mirror—but meanwhile you too will be glad to remain an artist and no Countess Rossi,[1] i.e. you will want to help shoulder the load, work with me, share my joys and sorrows. Write me about this.

In Leipzig, the first thing will be to order my outer affairs; my inner ones are already at peace. Perhaps, when I ask his blessing, your father will not withdraw his hand. On this subject I realize that there is much to consider and to straighten out. Meantime, I trust in our good genius. Fate meant us for one another. Long ago I realized that; but I was not so bold as to hope that I could tell you of it before, and be understood by you.

All this I am writing to you today briefly, in shreds and patches. Later I will more clearly explain it to you. After all, perhaps you will not be able to make out my writing, anyway. Know then just this one thing—that I love you clear beyond all words.

The room grows dark. Passengers near me are asleep. Outside it is snowing and drifting. But I will stow myself deep into a corner, burrow my head into a cushion, and think of nothing but you. Farewell, my Clara.

Your ROBERT

Suddenly the lover's innocent assumption that father Wieck would prove no real obstacle to marriage with Clara was brutally and thoroughly shattered. When Wieck heard—we do not know how—that Robert had been surreptitiously in Dresden, he turned into a raging demon. A molten rain of denunciations, insults, and threats beat down upon young, defenseless Clara. Father swore to shoot Robert on sight if the scoundrel ever again dared to have anything more to do with her. This terrified the girl so that she promised to return Robert's letters, demand her own back, and completely break off relations. The pedagogue then sent Robert a farrago of deadly insults, and felt that he had won the fight.

He reckoned, however, without the steely will and long-suffering persistence of purpose of August's son, which had already shown up to advantage in founding and maintaining the *New Magazine*. Like the two little men in the toy barometer,

[1] At the height of her career, the famous dramatic soprano, Henriette Sontag, secretly married the diplomat, Count Rossi, which led to a long retirement from the operatic stage.

210 63

who alternately back in and come out, Eusebius the dreamer retired to a temporary limbo, and a determined Florestan met the onslaught with a virility as powerful as Wieck's; but also with a self-controlled patience that never transgressed the limits of good breeding.

Indeed, in this period, his forbearance bent over backward. He wrote a contributor in Breslau not to be thrown off his balance if Wieck should talk badly about him, Schumann. "He is a man of honor, but an eccentric." How much of a man of honor, the poor young fellow was soon to find out!

It did not take long for these savage troubles to change Robert from boy to man. Long afterward he wrote Therese Schumann: "If he [Wieck] had known me better, he would have spared me a good deal of pain, and never sent me a letter which aged me by two years."

As his confidante, sister-in-law Therese had now taken his mother's place. He wrote her:

My stars are strangely mixed up. May God guide to a happy end. . . . I will tell you in person about the Wiecks and Clara. There I am in a critical situation and lack calmness and clear-sightedness to pull myself out of it. But, as things now stand, either I can never exchange another word with her, or she will be wholly my own.

No one can blame Wieck for not immediately giving Clara to an almost unknown composer with a lame finger and a slender income. Mr. Burk, indeed, argues that the pedagogue had one reason for opposing the union more cogent than all the others put together: the tendency toward invalidism and possible insanity which Robert had inherited. However, Wieck could not have been aware of this handicap, or, when things finally came to a showdown in court, he would most certainly have urged it in his indictment of Robert. But he never did.

What we blame and execrate Wieck for is not his refusal, but the revolting, peasantlike avarice, treachery, and brutality with which he fought the young couple, and his failure to see reason when the valid obstacles to which he objected gradually melted away.

Friedrich Wieck's life-story goes a long way toward explaining what manner of man he was. His entire training, first in theology, then as a teacher, had encouraged and flattered a naturally overbearing bent. Preachers and teachers are *ex officio* protected against back-talk. Hence they are apt to develop a feeling that critical traffic must be always one-way—must, in the nature of things, run from themselves to others. A dignitary laying down the "truth" in pulpit or classroom comes easily to believe that his word constitutes a natural law, any opposition to which is criminal and impious. Such a feeling comes more facilely to him than, say, to a lawyer, or soldier, or man of business, who can see both sides of a question and is less allergic to contradiction.

Wieck was born in 1795 in the mean little Saxon village of Pretzsch. This lay only about a dozen miles from the Wittenberg church doors upon which another equally determined fanatic, Martin Luther, had once nailed the theses that started the Reformation.

The lad of Pretzsch had miraculously pulled himself up by his own boot-straps and, like Robert's father, lived out a Horatio Alger success story. This was a self-made man; and on the whole, well-made. Lacking good teachers, he struggled against such dire poverty that he usually went hungry. With but meager formal schooling, he was forced, by the chance of winning a scholarship, into qualifying for the ministry, a profession which he disliked. He went through the theological seminary; but after preaching one sermon, felt he could no longer endure the life. Friedrich embraced the first profane job that presented itself, and became a tutor. Now, at that time and place, a tutor's social rank was little higher than a lackey's. But Wieck refused to be kept down in the servile and obscure position expected of the likes of him. He did the impossible, and finally managed to escape again, win a foothold as a piano teacher in Leipzig, and marry the granddaughter of the first flutist of the Gewandhaus. To crown all, he actually made of himself such a skillful and efficient pedagogue as to turn out two of the foremost pianists of the age. One was his own daughter, to whom, in a confidently prophetic mood, he had given the name Clara, which can be taken to mean "brilliant" or "famous." The other was Hans von Bülow.

Wieck was curiously like Jean Jacques Rousseau in having: studied in a religious seminary, been a private tutor, and despite inadequate technical equipment—a music teacher. If such experiences had been as bad for Wieck's character as they seem to have been for that famous blackguard, neither Clara nor Robert might have lived long enough to require biographers.[2]

Unfortunately the wretched poverty, privations, and humiliations from which he had escaped had left their brand on Wieck in the shape of a sharp fixation on money. When it came to finance, he was as fiercely avaricious as the most brutal peasant on the outskirts of his home village. We shall see how this fixation impelled him to defraud even Clara, the being whom he loved most. He was, as well, a great rationalizer. When this ex-theologian tried to break up Clara's concert tours by intrigue, and refused to give up her money and even her overcoat, he doubtless persuaded himself that he was acting for her own best good and *ad majorem Dei gloriam.* All this sounds somewhat mad. And, indeed, there was madness in the family; for his daughter Cäcilie died insane.

A further explanation of Wieck's bumptious aggressiveness and vanitous rage when opposed may be suggested by the way in which certain Anglo-Saxons mispronounce his name. Perhaps the aggressiveness was a symptom of a superiority complex. And perhaps this was built up as a defense against an inferiority complex resulting from a consciousness that he was in a weak

---

[2] Apart from the success of his daughter Clara, the chief event of Wieck's life was his visit to Beethoven, a year before the Master's death. He was introduced under false pretenses as an ear-specialist and a maker of hearing-machines, as well as a "tone-poet" and writer. They drank much red wine and the deaf Beethoven asked about the greatest variety of subjects. Wieck had to scribble like mad in the Conversation Books; but, halfway through, Beethoven would always divine the end of everything, and abruptly change the subject. The talk dealt with the iniquities of the Master's aged housekeeper, and of his brothers; with the stupidity of certain Viennese (here Beethoven rolled his eyes desperately, and grasped his head and hair); with the Gewandhaus, democracy, Napoleon, Italian opera versus German, and Wieck's own ideas about piano-playing. Then the Master improvised with a spontaneous flow "of the clearest and most charming melodies," and the exhausted Wieck tottered away, full of enthusiasm and red wine.

position. Though he had set himself up as a learned professor, he was forever haunted by the knowledge that he had little schooling and no diplomas to buttress his pretensions. Masterfully he propelled his pupils along the rocky road to virtuosity; but he himself had too little technic to demonstrate for them the more difficult passages. The unhappy man was no Leschetizky.[3]

He was gnawed by the secret consciousness of his inadequacy. His musical attainments and general culture were as full of holes as a colander; and he could never do that which, by some happy instinct, he so successfully directed others to do. If only he had, in early life, enjoyed reasonable advantages, he might have turned out to be a great musician and a really good fellow.

The depths made him mean and, in conjunction with the heights of success, they made him vain. He grew to believe that, besides himself, there were no other piano teachers worth mentioning. Once he actually said to Dorn: "Ten years ago I told Liszt that if he had had a proper teacher he would have become the foremost pianist in the world."

Wieck's avarice and his egotism had a mutually inflaming effect. Perhaps unconsciously, his pride must have been pinched when he was forced to look up to the creative ability of his ex-pupil Robert. And we can imagine how it infuriated him when that young sprig dared to face out his fulminations and refused to give up all hope of winning Clara.

Wieck must have made a difficult lord and master for the nineteen-year-old Marianne who was his first wife, and Clara's mother. While bearing five children in seven years, the amiable, easygoing girl was fiercely drilled by her fanatic of a husband, both as concert singer and as pianist. While pregnant she was made to toil many hours a day at the keyboard. She was forced to appear as Gewandhaus soloist in Mozart's *Requiem,* as well as in piano concertos by such immortal tone-poets as Field, Dussek, and Ries.

However, the poor woman finally revolted and left him. It is characteristic of Wieck's egocentricity that when he gave little

[3] Teacher of Paderewski, and a virtuoso in his own right.

Clara a diary and began it for her, with a few lines supposed to
start her life-story, on almost the first page he set down this dissonance: "[My mother] abandoned my father on May 12, 1824,
to go to Plauen and get a divorce." [4]

For a year and a half after Wieck's furious letter of interdict,
Robert and Clara were cut off from communication with one
another. And their love was under constant artillery and small-
arms fire from Wieck and his second wife. The unfortunate
Clara had to face a continuous barrage of gossip, insinuation,
insult, and downright slander directed against Robert and his
character. Wieck scorned no chance of discrediting Robert in
her eyes. And this kept on, whether Clara was on tour, or at
home. How was a girl of seventeen or eighteen to assert herself
against the parental authority of such a dominating tyrant?

At first she meekly bowed to the storm. But this slip of a thing
had in her not only the blood of her fanatical father, but also
that of a mother with tremendous endurance and a mind of her
own. Clara was at times blown rather flat; but she was never
entirely crushed to earth.

One dodge, however, almost succeeded. Wieck installed in
his home Robert's so-called "friend," Karl Banck. Ostensibly he
was to be assistant singing master and critic for Clara. The girl
played him her repertory and brought him her compositions.
When he saw that she had come to like him, Banck went to
work as delicately as a cat, with tales of Robert's unfaithfulness,
to oust him from her heart so as to occupy it himself.

Occasionally he would run to Robert with tales of Clara's
flirtatiousness and general frivolity, and of how she had forgotten him. In consequence, toward the end of 1836, though Robert
thought Clara still loved him, he came to believe that he had
lost her.

It was during this difficult summer that he wrote the *Fantasie*, Op. 17, and poured into the noble work his love and despair, his sorrow and longing. He began it as a contribution to

[4] She married Adolf Bargiel, a poor Berlin music-teacher; and their son
Woldemar became a well-known composer in the Schumann tradition.

a fund for erecting a statue to Beethoven in Bonn. He wished
to call the three movements either: *Ruins, Triumphal Arch,* and
Wreath of Stars, or simply, *Ruins, Trophies,* and *Palms.* But the
publisher objected to these as too fanciful. So he substituted as
motto a verse by Friedrich Schlegel:

> *Durch alle Töne tönet*
> *Im bunten Erdentraum*
> *Ein leiser Ton gezogen,*
> *Für den der heimlich lauschet.*

(Through all the tones in Earth's many-colored dream, there sounds
for the secret listener one soft, long-drawn note.)

Years after, he wrote her suggesting that she was the *Ton* in the
motto; that the work meant to him the miseries of that summer
of 1836 when he had given her up; and that he thought he had
never written "anything more impassioned than the first movement. It is a deep lament for you."

"In 1837," he reminded Clara some years later,

I had resigned myself; but then the old anguish burst forth again—
then I wrung my hands—then in the night I often cried to God:
"Only have patience and let this one thing happen without my going
mad!" (I thought at one time that I should find in the newspapers a
notice of your engagement.) Then something seized me by the neck
and forced me to the floor, so that I cried aloud. Then I longed to
cure myself. I wished to force myself with all violence to fall in love
with a woman who already had me half enmeshed.

That part about his neck sounds a bit queer; as if the mere re-
membrance of that agonizing crisis could again push him close
to the mental border-line.

Banck finally succeeded in shaking Clara's loyalty to the point
where she could entertain unworthy suspicions of Robert's goodwill towards her. The Wieck in her blood kept the girl from
comprehending the delicacy which forbade her lover to puff her
compositions over his own name in the *Magazine,* and led him
to have her piano concerto reviewed by another—mildly, at that
—while Robert heaped extravagant praise upon one by Sterndale
Bennett.

But what made her really angry was this: she felt that her lover, in a review of dance music by Chopin and others, had held her up to ridicule under the fancy name of Ambrosia. This supposition was made easier by the mention of De Knapp [5] as Ambrosia's "shawl-bearer." She was described as threshing rather than understanding a piece by Liszt, 'sweating visibly,' and smiling at Robert with 'love in her eyes.' Later she sat next to De Knapp, "partnerless, with trembling lips." And it was explained that 'she lacked a man because she was one herself.'

With her inherited strain of suspicion and jealousy, Clara took these things as insults directed against herself. And the more readily, because she realized that she was not only somewhat inclined to "thresh" the piano,[6] but also possessed, beneath her feminine exterior, a doughty gift of truly masculine determination and initiative. And the fact that Robert had probably not meant Ambrosia to represent Clara at all, but had instead identified her with another character called Beda, whom he had treated very well, did not materially lessen his guilt. For a person of his imaginative power, and his knowledge of Clara's weaknesses, should have seen at once the likelihood that she would misunderstand the review. In any case, Robert had represented himself in print as paying simultaneous attention to two girl pianists, and had claimed that one of them loved him. This reminds us of his gross lack of tact in dedicating those unfortunate Chamisso songs to Ernestine. In fact, it looks even queerer than his remark about his neck a few lines earlier. The trouble over Clara may have struck like flint on one of the sharp edges of his "diamond," and produced a tiny spark of momentary madness.

As a matter of fact, on the rebound from this incident, Clara nearly became engaged to Banck. It was touch-and-go.

Banck was the person whom Robert had been trying to injure in the dance-music article. He wanted revenge for the man's underhanded efforts to estrange him from Clara. He described De Knapp's face as looking like

[5] Substituting p for b, Knapp is approximately Banck spelled backward.
[6] It will be recalled that when she first came back from Paris, Robert said that she played like a hussar.

the open war-cry of scandal, not to speak of his baldness and the immoral cut of his nose. He is a pitiable snooper who hates me . . . in short, I can discover in myself a whole Shakespeareful of abusive words, just by thinking of him.

At the end of the article he hears De Knapp accusing him of "indecent behavior toward the daughter of the house," and at once challenges him to a duel with pistols. "N.B. Last night De Knapp made himself scarce."

This fanciful postscript was prophetic. As a result of the article, Banck was literally laughed out of Leipzig. He went the more readily because, just then, Wieck began to fear lest the assistant singing master was making too good progress, and withdrew from him the light of his own grim countenance.

It may be that these unpleasant incidents mark the point where young Clara's faint spark of humor was finally snuffed out. Thereafter she grew increasingly prone to entertain the suspicions and jealousies that were to temper the pure joy of her relations with Robert and his great successor, Brahms.

For the biographer no problem of the Schumanns is more difficult than the question of Clara. I have sincerely endeavored to handle with sympathy and justice the indisputable facts of the case. At the same time I am well aware that my interpretation is far from the sweet and conventional treatment which has made of this eminent artist and extraordinarily appealing woman a sort of musical Madonna. And I know that many things in the following chapters will shock and outrage many a reader brought up to heroine-worship by the very biographers whose idealizations of Clara I am forced to correct. After all, unless the present-day biographer can tell the whole truth as he sees it, without fear—if not without reproach—it would be scarcely worth his while to sharpen a pencil for page one.

CHAPTER 13

TREASURE TROVE

I N spite of all these tribulations, Robert's youth and vitality gave him occasional hours of mirth and high spirits. In one of these he was out room-hunting with his Man Friday, a doctor of medicine and ardent Davidite named Reuter, who did for Schumann what Schindler, and Zmeskall, "the Music Count," once did for Beethoven, from tending him in illness to supervising his laundry.

"Look there," cried Robert, pointing to a romantic-looking house in the Rothen Colleg near the Bookdealers' Exchange. "That room facing all those trees. I think I must have it."

"But," objected the doctor, "there's no To Let sign out."

"Never mind; something tells me it's letable."

Just then a woman appeared in one of the windows.

"And there, I think, must be the old girl herself."

Frau Johanna Devrient had reached that point of physical expansion where a bust changes from an asset into a liability. This morning something had moved her to have a look out of a second-floor window. Two attractive youths were gazing fixedly up at her kind face. They burst into laughter, waved their hands, and sauntered on.

She was still wondering about the strange couple, when the door-bell rang, and there they stood. One of them had his lips puckered as if about to whistle, while the other asked if there was not a room to let. The whistler burst into renewed laughter, which set the other off. Finally he managed to explain that her prompt appearance at that window, as if in response to a stage cue, had been so pat as to be funny.

For four years Frau Devrient and her daughter took kindly care of Schumann. Though they heard the commotion attending the birth-pangs of the *Fantasiestücke*, Op. 12, the *Kreisleriana*, and the *Scenes from Childhood*, they had no idea how mighty a man they were harboring. But one day when Mendelssohn began a series of often-repeated calls, the Devrients saw a great light. At long last they realized that their taciturn lodger must be a person of more than ordinary importance.

However, the kind landlady soon found it somewhat complicated to harbor even a genius, when he was as unstable in temperament as Robert. When she took him to task for staging a noisy party which had kept the whole house awake all night, he flared up, for he could not stand opposition:

After what you have written me, I cannot stay here a day longer. I will therefore quit; and the sooner the better. . . . The miserable weather and all my troubles are responsible for my rowdiness.

But next morning came reaction:

I permit myself to wish Madame Devrient an excellent good morning; and entreat her to believe me when I declare that nothing less than personal violence would persuade me to give up my rooms. My lucky star led me to her house, and I am much too grateful for all her loving care.

The habit of taciturnity was growing on Robert. His friend Klugkist testified that in their Heidelberg days he was as voluble as anyone. Even in 1837, Sterndale Bennett did not find him "a very silent man." But this was probably because Robert was so enthusiastic about Sterndale that he made special efforts to emerge from his shell of silence. For, in April of that same year, our hero wrote Zuccalmaglio:

I'll be heartily glad to see you here. However, there's nothing to be got out of me. I say almost nothing. More in the evening, and most while at the piano.

One cause of his taciturnity may have been the poor quality and meager volume of his voice. It was said of him that his talk was as illegible as his handwriting. The musician in him would naturally be sensitive about these vocal shortcomings, and seek through silence to betray them as little as possible.

Then too, he may have reasoned that the less you talk, the more you can think and feel. In 1837 he quoted to Goethe's son Jean Paul's aphorism, "You can recognize a friend by the fact that he doesn't make conversation on a walking trip"; which may possibly have moved Hazlitt to cry, "I can see no wit in walking and talking." [1]

To the end, Robert's love of stillness kept on growing. In 1845, Hiller and Concertmaster Schubert took Félicien David to call on Schumann. After greeting them cordially, he lapsed into a formidable and embarrassing silence. Hectically Schubert and Hiller made talk, upon which the other two bestowed their critical attention. Finally Schumann turned to Hiller and half whispered.

"David doesn't talk much?"

"Not much" [I answered].

"That's fine!" said Schumann, with a friendly smile.

At this period, it might well have been said of him, as it was of Uhland:

> Er spricht nur halb, wenn Andre schwatzen,
> Doch fühlt er ganz, wie Viele halb.

Which might be translated:

> Speaking but half where others babble,
> He feels twice more than all the rabble.

Franz Brendel, though, knew how to bring out another side of the Master:

If one considers him as invariably silent, one has a very false impression. In this he varied much at different ages. Schumann could be very voluble when the inner flames shot up; while at other times one couldn't get a word out of him for hours, and he sat there, sunk into himself.

It was not really a conversation that he would carry on. His remarks were always of a more fragmentary nature and came out by

---

[1] The title of Hazlitt's book, however, would not have appealed to Schumann. It was called *Table Talk*.

fits and starts. That was how he freed himself of what was agitating his spirit. . . . He could be extremely lively and excited, and again quite introverted, sunk in revery and apathetic, gruff, and peevish. Then again, *when he woke from his dream-world,* he could be a perfectly fascinating heart-winner, full of the most devoted amiability.

Such expansive moments, however, were rare, and grew progressively rarer.

The impairment of one of a man's five senses usually heightens the efficacy of some other sense, especially when the sufferer is creative. If the blindness of Bach and Milton, the deafness of Smetana and Beethoven, and even the club-foot of Byron and the stutter of Arnold Bennett helped them to write better, it is natural to suppose that Schumann's difficulty with speech was somewhat compensated by his amazing fluency in penning both words and notes.

His growing taciturnity was paced by his love of solitude, a preference which Herbert Bedford sneeringly calls "a twist in the mind." I wonder if that biographer knows about the habits of Sibelius; [2] or that Brahms once declared he could not even think about music, let alone write it, with anybody else in the room. Now, Schumann was never so extreme as this. But if he had been less ruthless in cutting down on sociability, we would have far less of his music to enjoy today. And who knows whether his end might not have been hastened by an attempt to combine more social life with the imperative necessity for working out his inspirations? There is deep wisdom in his youthful aphorism:

Like a Greek god, the artist should have friendly association with men and with life; and only when they dare to touch him should he vanish, leaving nothing but clouds behind.

In the fall of 1836, that delicate-minded editor Robert Schumann temporarily set aside his delicacy in the matter of self-actuated publicity. It strikes us as somewhat out of character that he asked Moscheles, his boyhood hero, whom he had met at the Wiecks', to review the F Sharp Minor Sonata in the *New*

[2] See *An Almanac for Music-Lovers,* by Elizabeth C. Moore, p. 252, Note. (1940, Henry Holt and Co.)

Felix Mendelssohn

Friedrich Wieck

Magazine. This the old virtuoso did in October. The year before, he had heard the work played from manuscript, and had found it "very labored, difficult, and somewhat confused, though interesting." As he did not care, in response to Robert's request, to write what he really thought, the article was a tissue of kindly banalities.

September 13, 1836, showed what stuff Clara was made of. It was the first birthday for a long time that Robert had not helped her to celebrate. Despite the occasion, Wieck made her give a concert in Naumburg. On the way to the hall, the carriage was overturned and she might easily have been killed. But she escaped with a damaged dress, severe contusions of head, arms, and legs, a fright, and a severe shock. In spite of all this, the heroic girl went through the concert with success, and even sang two songs. However, the following morning, her left hand was badly swollen; and for days after she was in much pain.

Early in February 1837, both father and daughter left on a three months' concert tour of North Germany. In Berlin Clara had the joy of a reunion with her real mother, Frau Bargiel. It could be damped but little by Wieck's absurdly pompous posturing on the threshold: "Here, Madame, I bring you your daughter." Both the women breathed easier when he refused to enter.

The celebrated Spontini and the rest of musical Berlin received Clara with marked enthusiasm. This was despite the lies of the famous critic Rellstab. His vitriolic pen blamed her, among other things, for playing "such nonsense as Chopin," and described her packed houses as "half full."

Clara has reaped great credit as a fearless pioneer of good taste and an innovating uplifter of fallen programs from the slough of Hünten and Herz; but, as a matter of fact, much of that credit belongs to her rascal of a father. In some ways, Wieck was a deplorable rotter; but at this time he was endowed with a ripe artistic understanding and appreciation well in advance of his age. And, as we shall see, Clara's own private musical taste did not reach maturity until after she had lived a good many years under Robert's kindly tutelage.

Of Bettina von Arnim, once the girl-friend of Beethoven and
Goethe, Wieck's diary remarks: "Very intelligent, fiery woman—
when it comes to music, nothing but false judgments. She brims
over with humor." Bettina turned out to have two faces. With
one of them she flatteringly cooed to Clara: "It is a real shame
that a seventeen-year-old girl is already so capable!" With the
other she informed her friends that Clara was:

one of the most insufferable feminine artists that I've ever come
across. With what pretension she sits down at the piano, and actually *without* notes! On the other hand, how modest Döhler is, with
the notes in front of him!

The trouble with Bettina was: in her younger years, she had
enjoyed such a monopoly of the center of the stage that now,
at fifty-two, she could not bear to be superseded by a mere chit.
To make matters worse, Clara had blossomed out so that her
expressive eyes, exquisitely cut features, and lovely arms won
all—or almost all—hearts.

Having cashed in substantially, Wieck denounced Berlin as
"a sink of iniquity," and took Clara on to Hamburg, Bremen,
Hanover, and Brunswick, towns which, as usual, she charmed
and he excoriated.

In May, soon after their return to Leipzig, Robert sent Clara
the now published F Sharp Minor Sonata which Florestan and
Eusebius had dedicated to her. Long afterwards he told her
that it represented "a single outcry of the heart for you in which
your theme appears in all possible shapes." (What he meant by
"your theme" will appear in the second part of this book.) He
was sadly disappointed to get back a cool acknowledgment.
His first bitter thought was: "Karl Banck must have been right
in telling me that Clara has forgotten our love! Well, if that is
so, I'm glad to be rid of her; for she's no good!"

But then, in reaction from this, came a second thought: "However, it's true that she's the last girl in the world to wear her
heart on her sleeve."

Clara then made his heart leap with a radiantly reassuring
message of thanks for the sonata, and of love for its composer.
It was couched not in words but in tones. After her two years'

silence in her home city, Wieck had arranged a Leipzig concert for her on August 13th. And there on the program stood:

> Three Etudes Symphoniques ⎱ R. Schumann,
> with previous theme ⎰ (Op. 13)

Now, only a few weeks before, Robert had resolved to go in and win Clara again; but at first her choice of this piece actually gave him pause. In the circumstances, how could she summon the nerve to sit up there and play a work by him? Why, such an ordeal would be enough to make a strong man quake! If she could manage that, surely she could not be in love with him any more. However, like the heroic creature she was, Clara went through with it; and the music sped with its divine reassurance from soul to soul.

Did it never occur to you [she wrote him later] that I played that piece because I knew no other way of showing you something of my inmost heart? I did not dare do that in secret, so I did it in public. Do you not think my heart trembled all the time?

This was the way in which the parted lovers were reunited. Clara's friend Ernst Becker had come from Freiberg for her concert. She told him how matters stood and begged him to go to Robert and ask him for those letters of his to her which Father had forced her to return in June 1836. Robert answered that she might have not old letters but new ones. And here is part of the first new one which he sent back by Becker, with a bouquet. It was endorsed on the outside: "These lines were written after long days of silence filled with pain, hope, and despair. May they be received with the old love. If that no longer exists, I beg that you will return this letter unopened."

On the 13th of August, 1837.

Are you still faithful and firm? Unshakably as I believe in you, still the strongest courage can waver when nothing is heard from the dearest person in the world. And you are that to me. A thousand times I have thought everything over, and everything tells me: it must come about if we will and act. If you are willing to hand your father a letter from me just on your birthday [September 13th], write me only a simple Yes. . . .

All this I mean with my whole soul, exactly as it stands, and sign it with my name

ROBERT SCHUMANN.

Message, bouquet, and letter bridged the gap that for the last year and a half had yawned between the two—and united them for life. The contraband correspondence and secret meetings resumed their course after Clara's answer:

Leipzig the 15th [3] of August, 1834.

Is a simple "yes" all you demand? Such a tiny little word—to be so important! Still—should not a heart so full of inexpressible love as mine whole-souledly be able to say this little word? I say it, and my innermost being whispers it to you eternally. . . .

Perhaps fate will soon let us talk together and then—. Your plan strikes me as risky; but a loving heart pays no great attention to dangers. So again I say "Yes!" . . . I too have long felt that "it must come about." Nothing in the world shall turn me aside; and I will show Father that a young [heart] can also be a steadfast one.

Your CLARA.

in great haste

On her birthday Clara handed Robert's eloquent letter to Father, together with a little message to herself, which the old man confiscated. Wieck wrote Robert a correct note:

You are a splendid man; but I know more splendid ones. I do not really know what I shall do with Clara; but it would not be fitting for me to do so now. [His very words.]

Whereupon Robert wrote Becker:

Wieck's answer was so confused, so uncertainly declining and agreeing, that now I really do not know what to start. . . . I am terribly depressed and unable to think.

Their personal meeting resulted in a draw. Wieck would say neither yes nor no. Robert wrote Clara:

September 18, 1837.

The interview with your father was terrible. This coldness, this lack of goodwill, this confusion, these contradictions. . . .

[3] A mistake for the 14th.

What now, my dear Clara? . . . My reason has gone to pieces and emotion will never accomplish anything with your father. What now, what now?

Above all, arm yourself, and *never let yourself be sold.* . . .

You will have to be very *strong,* stronger than you think. Your father himself gave me these terrible words: "Nothing can shake me!"

He goes on to the effect that, if all else fails, they must seek the support of the law. The solemn close of this letter is deeply affecting:

And today before I say goodbye to you, my beloved girl, swear to me again *on your hopes of Heaven* that you have courage bravely to surmount the ordeals that confront us, as I do at this moment, raising two fingers of my right hand in an oath. I will never forsake you. Trust me entirely!

So may God aid us, and I remain eternally *your*

ROBERT.

The six days during which he waited for a reply were the most panic-stricken of his life. He knew how cruelly the young thing was being torn by a divided allegiance. When the answer finally came, he noted on the paper: "Read on Sept. 26 with a thousand joys":

Still do you doubt me? I will forgive you that, for I am a weak girl! Yes, weak. But I have a strong soul—a heart firm and unalterable. Let this be sufficient to dispel all your doubts.

Up to now I have been very unhappy; but just write me a word of reassurance below these lines, and I will go forth into the wide world without a care. I have promised Father to be cheerful and to devote a few more years to art and the world. You will hear many a thing about me. Many a doubt will stir within you when you hear of this or that. But then just tell yourself—"She is doing all that for me!" Could your constancy ever waver?—if it did, you would break a heart that can love only once.

CLARA.

[Outside] *Open this, but send me back these lines. Do this for my peace of mind.*

And Robert wrote back:

One does not return such heavenly words. They are safe also with me. And now, not another word about the past; but let us calmly and steadfastly keep our eyes upon the goal of our lives. . . .

My last request before you go away from me—give me now what I have sometimes had from you in our hushed moments—the *Du* that unites us more intimately. For you are my ardently loved betrothed, and once later—one more kiss—Adieu

YOUR ROBERT.

What an exhilarating, infectious glow of vitality radiates from the letters of this young pair! This much they won from Father: they were allowed to see one another in public ("a spectacle for the whole world to gawk at!" the lover exclaimed bitterly), and to correspond in a friendly way (i.e., through the Wieckian censorship) when Clara was on tour. These poor privileges they of course supplemented, sub rosa.

Why did Wieck set himself up as a domestic tyrant? Because his yearning for superiority could not, on account of his meager artistic attainments, satisfy its appetite for world-wide authority and the larger leadership. He therefore needed a submissive family circle to gratify his lust for power. And he could not bear to lose from it the member who gratified it most because she was famous. At home, armed with all the sentimental and legal rights of a German father, he could at least enjoy the privileges of a tyrant in miniature. He confessed that "Clara with a perambulator" was "a hateful thought" to him. Among his other motives for despotism, the fixation on money was a strong second.

For the lovers, a pleasant surprise and lift over a time of anxious stress came in a review of three Schumann compositions in the Parisian *Gazette musicale* for November 12, 1837. Its author, Franz Liszt, was unknown to Robert.[4] This appreciation of the *Impromptus*, Op. 5, and the F Sharp Minor and F Minor Sonatas, Opp. 11 and 14, was more encouraging than any other review in the first decade of Schumann's professional life. Here are a few words of it:

[4] Indeed, the already famous virtuoso was still unknown to the world as a composer.

We direct the attention of musicians to the works of a young pianist, which among all the recent compositions we know—except the music of Chopin—are those in which we find the most individuality, novelty, and knowledge. . . .

The more one penetrates into Schumann's ideas, the more power and vitality one finds there. The more one studies them, the more one is surprised at the richness and the fertility which had at first escaped us.

Today, putting one thing with another, we may well doubt whether these praises were quite sincere. But at least they gave Robert a leg up over a difficult stile.

The *Davidsbündler Dances,* Op. 6, were dedicated to Goethe's son, who reported how they were born: "Schumann held his hands over the keys of his little grand in the Rothen Colleg, and . . . under them everything came alive—was plastically realized!" On September 11th, 1837, the composer was well advanced with the work when he wrote to this friend a delightful poetic remark: "I'm in the best of spirits, and am doing a lot of flying." And the following February he confessed to the old composer Spohr: "I have never written anything else . . . which has come so lightly from my heart."

On October 15th, Wieck against hustled Clara away from Robert on a seven months' concert tour to Dresden, Prague, and Vienna. But this time he found the eighteen-year-old Clara a very different person from the meek, docile creature of the trip to Berlin. Outwardly she was Wieck's daughter and pupil. Inwardly she was Robert's future bride. She had quietly begun picking at the fastenings of the paternal leading strings, resolved, if they would not yield, to cut them as Alexander once slashed the Gordian knot.

Naturally, as she was very human, her heart had its undulations. There were the usual lovers' misunderstandings and reconciliations. Sometimes Clara lent too filial an ear to the constant stream of innuendo and slander which Wieck directed to Robert's account. Once the girl came to fear that she would repent the marriage if, with their straitened means, they could not afford to give elaborate parties; and Robert had to shame her out of it.

On this trip, Clara's task was herculean in more than one sense. Vienna had long been considered the musical hub of the universe. Why, the Viennese themselves admitted it! She knew that in no part of the Austrian Empire could you swing a cat by the tail without desecrating a spot sacred to Haydn, Mozart, Beethoven, or Schubert. So she was all the more shocked and pained to find how frivolous the musical taste of the Viennese really was, and how sloppily down-at-heels were their orchestral performances. As a matter of record, her complaints on these scores sound like echoes of Beethoven's and anticipations of Brahms'.

All the more credit to the young girl for her courage. Most of her first public program was in the prevailing light bravura style with a little leavening of Chopin. In her second, she gave the startled Viennese a Bach fugue. What is more, she made them like and encore it, which established a new high for that stretch of the Danube. And in her third, she even managed to electrify the somewhat infantile minds and hearts of her audience with a novelty never yet heard in a public concert thereabouts from the days when it had been composed in the vicinity a third of a century before. It was the *"Appassionata";* and it caught on, and started the local fashion for giving Beethoven sonatas in public. In private she had furnished them another novelty by an almost unknown local music-maker, written a decade before— the E Flat Trio of Schubert. If Vienna insisted, thought Clara, on neglecting its own geniuses while they were alive, at least it should be made to love them posthumously.

Grillparzer, the famous poet who had, not eleven years before, written Beethoven's funeral oration, now published a poem on Clara's playing of the *"Appassionata."* And—though he made her a shepherdess who fished out of the ocean the key to unlock the magic casket of tone—the poem is really good. One proof of which is that it is nearly untranslatable.

By now, the Viennese were as enthusiastic about Clara as about their own little pet bravura virtuoso, Thalberg. And when Liszt arrived, she actually held her own against him in popular favor. Chopin's praises had made the gallant Franz so keen to know his young colleague that, promptly on arrival, he had flicked his visiting card through her open window.

There ensued lively sessions at the piano, Franz and Clara playing solos to, or duets with, each other. Though the charming young fellow was almost irresistible, her heart was no longer in the market; but she won Franz's liking for Robert's music—really genuine, this time—by playing him *Carnaval*. "That," shouted the Hungarian, "shows a mind back of it! It is one of the greatest works I know!" In retailing this to Robert she added, "You may imagine my delight!"

Liszt's enthusiasm was all the more welcome to the composer of the *Symphonic Etudes*, the F Sharp Minor Sonata, and the *Fantasie*, because the sluggish taste of a world that had not yet quite accepted Beethoven and Schubert was still far from beginning to comprehend a Schumann whose first published compositions were so much more originally independent of the past than those of his great predecessors.

Though Robert still paid exaggerated homage to Mendelssohn as "the best musician," and "a real god," that child of fortune had made even less progress toward condoning in Robert the 'ignominy' of being a writer on music [5] than he was ever to make in liking Robert's music and appreciating the rare quality of his originality. So the inspiring resonance that came from Liszt helped Schumann to go on, not only with composing, but also with reviewing the mediocre music which every critic has to get through, but which often irked him sorely. On December 4, 1837, he wrote his Viennese friend, Fischhof:

If you really knew with what disgust I set about criticizing such miserable compositions, you would sympathize with me. After cutting off their heads I usually get out my old Bach. He renews my strength for work and gives me zest for art and life.

[5] See Spitta's article on Schumann in *Grove's Dictionary*, 3rd Ed., p. 657; Niecks, p. 303; *Mendelssohns Briefe*, II, p. 116; and Hiller's *Felix Mendelssohn-Bartholdy*, 1878, p. 64.

Chapter 14

BRINGING RAPTURE

LATE in 1837 Robert consciously or unconsciously realized the precarious nature of his physical and mental inheritance; for he noted: "I often feel that I have not much longer to live." But early in 1838 he wrote a friend, "I am frequently overflowing just now; don't know where to stop." He was putting the finishing touches to the *Davidsbündler Dances,* Op. 6, and the *Fantasiestücke,* Op. 12. The latter work had simply gushed out of his pen, and he knew that it was a success. Of the former he wrote Clara: "There are many marriage thoughts in the *Dances*—they were created in the most joyful excitement that I can remember."

The next months were a period of adjustment on the part of both Robert and Clara to their new and always deepening vision of their future together. Often in the course of it there were small misunderstandings, differences, and discussions about Ernestine and finance and Father, what would you do, Clara, if he were to discover that we write to each other? Of course, in the last resort, you can always go and live with your mother, can't you?

The lovers' secret correspondence was made possible by the connivance of Clara's devoted maid, Nanny. It was a jolting set-back to their hopes when Wieck, who had not said much to his daughter of late, for fear of spoiling her Viennese concerts, boiled over to Nanny. And Nanny, of course, carried his words straight to her mistress: "If Clara marries Schumann, I would declare, on my deathbed, that she is unworthy to be called my daughter."

It would be hard to find a neater example than this of the pedagogue's blind vanity and power-obsession. It amounts to the claim that if the world's greatest woman pianist dared marry the genius whom Wieck himself had called "the second Beethoven," she would be unworthy to claim as father a music teacher who could not practice—nor play—what he preached.

Standing up at her bureau late in the night, alert to slip the writing materials into a drawer if warned by her sentry, Nanny, that Father was on the prowl, Clara scribbled heartfelt words to Robert. Such precautions were necessary because she was forbidden to lock her door. And as the inkstand was in the next room, and its removal might be spotted, every time the pen needed dipping, she had to steal there on tiptoe.

In the night I am simply beside myself when I hear my Father's voice raging, when his curses wake me and when I hear that they are aimed at my dearest one. Oh, God! I am no longer so fond of Father as I was. I can no longer be really fond of him, though I should so much like to be. That is my highest wish—. Perhaps that also may be granted, and then we shall be able to love each other untroubled. You ask if I will again let myself be frightened by my Father. My answer is—"No, never again!"

In one respect, Wieck's brutal treatment of Robert was all to the good. It forced that pampered young fellow to do some honest heart-searching, and this tended to correct the bad start given his character by a foolishly indulgent mother. The magnanimity with which he turned to the pedagogue the other cheek also tells volumes about the improvement already attained.

A man is apt to regard himself much as others regard him. After the way your father has used me, I am forced to ask myself—"Are you actually so bad, so base that you can be treated thus?" I have always been used to overcoming difficulties with ease. Love and happiness have continually surrounded me. Because I have been spoiled by having everything made easy for me, now I can hardly stand being rebuffed, offended and slandered. . . . [A clear-sighted and courageous bit of self-analysis.]

If I had ever injured your father, he would be justified in hating me; but I cannot fathom why he should abuse me without cause

and, as you yourself put it, hate me. But some day my turn will
come. Then you will see how much I love him and you. For I must
whisper into your ear that I love and honor your father for his many
fine and noble traits. No one besides yourself could venerate him as
I do. It is a special, inborn liking, a submission which I feel towards
all energetic characters. And when he will have nothing to do with
me, it doubles my pain. Well, perhaps now at long last we shall have
peace, and he will tell us—"take one another."

The strain of these anxious days was eased by the arrival of
an interesting person. Ludwig Spohr, the composer and violinist,
quitted his provincial Cassel for a short visit to Leipzig. Robert
was delighted to meet him, and improvised for his famous guest
a string quartet evening at the Rothen Colleg. No doubt Spohr
led some of those *quatuors brillants* of his which violate all the
democratic canons of chamber music because the first violin is
"a cook and a captain bold, and the mate of the *Nancy* brig,"
while the other players are merely among those who also sailed.
In his autobiography, Spohr said Schumann honored him with
great warmth, but otherwise was "very quiet and serious," and
pleased him by playing "several of his interesting *Fantasiestücke.*"

During this period Robert often had quartet mornings at
Frau Devrient's for the purpose of trying out the new literature
which had come to the magazine for review. The mornings were
enlivened with champagne and with his boyish talent for
mimicry. His imitations of famous virtuosos were especially
appreciated.

Those sessions led Robert to try his hand at composing a
string quartet; just as seventeen years later, the quartet evenings in Joachim's Düsseldorf rooms were to inspire Brahms to
compose some of those twenty works for four strings which he
burned before publishing his first. Schumann's attempt probably
had a similar fate, as it promptly vanished from mortal ken. By
it, he told Fischhof, he "was made entirely happy, although it
can count only as an experiment."

The rocky road of adjustment between the lovers was rough-
ened by distance. This kind of adjustment is never easy. And,

because artists have one skin fewer than ordinary folk, it was even harder for them. And they deserve more credit for trying. When Clara wrote of how she pitied her father's sadness at the thought of losing her, Robert feared she was wavering, and laid down the law. She must stop this, or else—return his ring. To which she retorted with some unfortunate teasing. And when she showed her jealous nature by a reference to that never-to-be-forgotten rival of hers, she flicked Robert's guilty soul really on the raw. The following letters show the vivid contrast between the feminine practicality of Clara and the poetry of Robert. She wrote:

You rely on the ring! Good heavens, that is only an external bond. Didn't you give Ernestine a ring, and, what is more important, your promise? And yet you have broken that bond. The ring is of no importance.

Against this charge the unhappy fellow defended himself as best he could, going on:

And now you think so little of my ring! Since yesterday I have ceased to care for yours, and now wear it no longer. . . . I had a dream of walking beside a deep pool. A fancy seized me and I cast the ring into it—then I passionately longed to cast myself in after it.

This is sheer stuff out of the deep and terrible springs of the unconscious; and more than that, a terrific foreshadowing of the end of a great mind and heart. Once in a long while a human being manages, perhaps unconsciously, to perceive the shadow of the future falling square across the present. In view of Schumann's final catastrophe there is about this passage the presentimental power of a prophecy, the spiritual terror of a true ghost story. "Then I passionately longed to cast myself in after it," Robert cries. Let the analysts, in the technical terms of their craft, say what they will—the terrible truth is that Schumann was never able to destroy that longing, and in the end, the dark dream was to destroy the man.

Craftily inspired by her father, Clara then made matters still worse by writing pessimistically about their financial future and her unwillingness to bury her art under a load of domestic worries. The quarrel was eventually patched up; but for the time it increased Robert's despair by robbing him of his musical inspiration.

Being engaged to Clara intensified both the manic and the depressive aspects of his temperament. In one of the manic phases, he wrote to his brothers on March 19, 1838:

> I'll tell you no more about my luck in possessing such a girl. Through art, kinship of spirit, the habit of yearlong association, and the deepest, holiest affection, our tendrils have quite interpenetrated and grown us together. My whole life now is joy and activity.

And to Therese Schumann he wrote announcing Clara's visit to her on the way back from the south:

> So, for my sake, welcome the high maiden [*das hohe Mädchen*] as she deserves. For, Therese, I cannot tell you what a being she is, all the qualities she unites in herself—and that I absolutely do not deserve her. But I will make her happy.—Let me keep silence about that. My feelings do not fit into words.

Being engaged, even though widely separated from Clara, seems to have been almost as good for Robert's creative work as marriage was to prove. Early in 1838 he produced in rapid succession the *Scenes from Childhood*, Op. 15, the *Novelletten*, Op. 21, and the *Kreisleriana*, Op. 16.

The first of these works ranks high among his most original pioneer achievements, and recalls the insight of his early aphorism: "In every child there lie wonderful depths." It was destined to be one of Schumann's best-loved compositions.

His love and comprehension of the little ones, which we have already seen standing him in good stead in the winning of Clara, now led him to be the first composer in history to produce easy masterpieces in tone, full of the authentic spirit of childhood. The *Scenes from Childhood* is the musical counterpart of that delightful bit of poetic pioneering, Stevenson's *A Child's Garden of Verses*. Too bad that the German Robert could not have lived to chuckle over the Scottish Robert's counterpart of *Glückes genug:*

> The world is so full of a number of things,
> I'm sure we should all be as happy as kings.

And how he would have relished the Stevensonian parallel
of *Kind im Einschlummern!*

> My bed is like a little boat;
>   Nurse helps me in when I embark;
> She girds me in my sailor's coat
>   And starts me in the dark.

Or that poetic *Träumerei, Escape at Bedtime:*

> The Dog, and the Plough, and the Hunter, and all,
>   And the star of the sailor, and Mars,
> These shone in the sky, and the pail by the wall
>   Would be half full of water and stars.
> They saw me at last, and they chased me with cries,
>   And they soon had me packed into bed;
> But the glory kept shining and bright in my eyes,
>   And the stars going round in my head.

That Spring Robert wrote Karl Kragen:

Often I feel such a compulsion to compose that, even if I were
on a lonely island in the middle of the sea, I couldn't stop. . . .
Sometimes the stream overflows so mightily that I simply don't know
where I shall come to the end. It makes me altogether happy, this
art.

And a buoyant word sped to Clara about a series of pieces "intimately bound together and written with love and zest":

Here in the last three weeks I've composed you so terribly much—
jocosities, tales from Egmont, family scenes with fathers, a wedding,
in a word, most charming stuff—and the whole business is called
Novellettes.

Without pause (or regard for numerical continuity), this Opus
21 led to Opus 16, which was hurled onto paper in a week's
inspired frenzy:

Fancy, since my last letter, I've done a whole book of things. I
want to call it *Kreisleriana.* You and one of your thoughts play the
leading role there, and I wish to dedicate it to you—yes, to you and
nobody else. You'll smile when you discover yourself there.[1]

[1] The Clara source-motive which runs through the sonatas and the

However, for some reason, the *Kreisleriana* were eventually inscribed to Chopin, who reciprocated with the dedication of his F Major *Ballade*.

These works of genius were so original, and the personality of their maker was so subtle, that the public did not in the least appreciate them. At this stage, even Clara caught but a dim notion of what sort of composer she loved. From his dizzy eminence, an idolized musician like Mendelssohn could patronize Robert and his works, without the faintest suspicion of how he was laying himself open to the smiles of posterity.

Both men were hypersensitive; and Mendelssohn was even more intolerant of any opposition than Schumann. In fact, one single sentence that rubbed him the wrong way was sufficient to turn Mendelssohn against a friend for life. So it is no wonder that, to the end, the relations between these two were not marked *molto tranquillo*. In 1838 Robert wrote to Clara:

> I have not often gone to Mendelssohn. . . . They say he is not sincere with regard to me. That would give me pain; for I am consciously loyal to him, and have proved it. . . . I know exactly how I compare with him as a musician, and for years to come I could learn from him. But he could also learn something from me. If I had grown up in circumstances like his, dedicated from childhood to music, I should outsoar you one and all—the vigor of my ideas tells me that.

Time has not only proved this comparison sound, but has also shown Schumann outsoaring Mendelssohn, despite the handicap of the provincial upbringing, the unmusical parents, the law school, and the late start.

The only aspect of the situation that very greatly exercised the unassuming Robert was his desire to be understood by Clara. So he sent her a somewhat nebulous attempt at self-revelation:

> My mind is at work. Musical ideas are turning into compositions. Nothing that goes on in the world—politics, literature, human beings —is foreign to my nature or fails to affect me. In my own way I mull

Fantasie (see p. 297 ff.), will be found, upright or inverted, in all the numbers of the *Kreisleriana* except the Seventh.

it all over, and somehow it gets turned into music. So many of my works are at times hard to grasp because their causes are remote. Now and then they are striking because remarkable events lay hold of me and must find their musical expression. [Comparing most contemporary compositions with his own] . . . The best of these do not reach what is the point of departure in my music. . . .

I cannot really speak of these things, and particularly about music one grows quite incoherent; though I think much about it. In a word, you will sometimes find me very grave, and will not know what to make of me. Then too, you must not watch me over much while I am writing music, for that would make me simply desperate. And I promise to reciprocate by listening very seldom at your door. All this should bring us a life full of poetry and blossoming; so that we will play and poetize together like angels, bringing rapture to mankind.

But I don't mind admitting that it would please me a lot if I could only manage, for once in a way, to write something that, interpreted by you, would make the public really lose their heads. After all, even when we have no reason to be, we composers are a vain lot.

Alas! it was to take longer than his brief lifetime for the delicate distillations of this rare spirit to be heartily appreciated by the masses. Creative artists who, like Mendelssohn, have had an immediate success with their contemporary audiences have usually taken this as an intimation of immortality. On the other hand, those who, like Schumann, have not at once appealed to a large public, have customarily consoled themselves with the assurance of posthumous fame. And how few have been right, as was Mendelssohn in the one class, and Schumann in the other!

On March 15th, 1839, Robert wrote in his happiest vein to Simonin de Sire of Dinant in Belgium, the man who had overjoyed him with the first letter of appreciation from abroad. (De Sire had mentioned some piano compositions of his own, written on three staves.)

The only objection to your way of writing is that people's eyes are not accustomed to it. As it is, they can scarcely manage two staves. Then too, if your system were adopted, Hünten and Czerny would be in despair; for they hardly have ideas enough for *one* stave. . . .

Perhaps you will agree with me that my own style keeps growing lighter and mellower. Once I reflected long. Now I strike out scarcely a note. Everything comes to me of itself and, indeed, sometimes it seems as if I could play on eternally and never come to the end. . . .

[He promises to send him his own portrait in lithograph.] But don't [hang it] between Beethoven and Weber, though in the vicinity, in order that I may learn from them as long as I live.

Despite his personal hostility, Wieck too liked Robert's music. He still appreciated and admired the young man's creative genius. And the last evidences of it had melted the ice in his breast so perceptibly that Clara plucked up heart and advanced to the assault. When Father gruffly admitted that he would allow Robert to visit the Leipzig house (though merely in the guise of a "friend of the family"), Clara announced with emphasis that she intended to marry him or nobody.

Her pleading—joined to the appeal of the music itself—finally wore Wieck down to the point where, when she brought him writing materials, he set down in the diary his first hedging and grudging semblance of a permission. Only, it was so undermined by ifs, ands, buts—and bad faith—as to be next to worthless. The young couple must not live in Leipzig. Father's ostensible reason for this was fear lest their noses be put out of joint by the superior luxury of the establishments maintained by Mendelssohn and Concertmaster David. His true reason may have been to escape a constant living reminder to himself and his friends that Wieck the infallible—his most blood-curdling vows to the contrary notwithstanding—had backed down over Clara's marriage. Or, it may have been because he was convinced that, as he openly declared, Schumann could never summon up the initiative needed to move himself and the *New Magazine* away from Leipzig. Or it may have been the calculation that, if Robert tried to establish himself anew where he was not known, it would be easier for Father to wreck his chances by secret intrigue and slander, than in Leipzig, where the young fellow had hosts of loyal friends. Wieck's other stipulation was more reasonable: his daughter must be given "more than two thousand thalers a year to spend."

Taking all this in good faith, Clara immediately thought of a plan.

CHAPTER 15

THE BEAUTIFUL BROWN DANUBE

CLARA had it all figured out. They would take the *New Magazine* under their arms and move to Vienna. The glamorous old Austrian capital would be a better place for musical journalism. She herself could earn far more there than in Leipzig, and she innocently believed that her lover's music would be better performed.

Robert would go anywhere to win his girl. He rejected that stipulation of Wieck's about calling "as a friend of the family," (1) because it was not true, and (2) because it might place him in an invidious position vis-à-vis Clara.

May 1838 saw the Wiecks back in their home. In the ecstasy of reunion, the lovers' sage resolutions to meet only once before Robert's projected trip were smashed to smithereens. The young man jokingly remarked that their kisses "had spared no house-vestibule on the way to the suburbs."

Wieck promptly lived up to his perfidious character. No sooner did Robert decide to start for Vienna than Father threatened to do everything in his power to prevent both the transplantation of the magazine and its editor's success there.

It is not known whether he ever made good these sportsman-like menaces. Robert may have been defeated solely by the exasperating character of the magic city which, a few years before, had turned good-natured young Beethoven into a bear and, a few years later, was to play the same trick on good-natured young Brahms.

Joseph Fischhof was Robert's closest Viennese friend. He wrote inviting the composer to be his guest on the Danube.

The refusal of this invitation throws light on Robert's modest appraisal of his own disposition: "You will come to know me yet, and will be happy to get rid of me."

That fall, shortly before setting out Viennawards, Robert wrote Moscheles that he felt his own musicianship was solid enough so that the south would not affect it. He was right. For, though he afterwards declared that his Viennese compositions were not of his best, they included such fine things as the *finale* of the G Minor Piano Sonata, the *Faschingsschwank aus Wien,* Op. 26, the *Three Romances,* Op. 28, and the *Humoreske,* Op. 20.

But the Austrian capital was a sore disappointment to this young idealist, who liked to look upon the bright side of things and people. All his life he had heard echoes of the (Vienna-instigated) claim that that city was the world's most important musical center. Now, he sadly wrote in the *New Magazine:*

Vienna is the city where Beethoven lived; and there is perhaps no place in the world where Beethoven is so little played and mentioned as Vienna. There they fear everything new, every departure from the lazy old rut.

And a few months later:

The clique here is a continuation of the same one that formerly hissed *Don Giovanni* and the *Leonore* overtures, a clique . . . as miserable, as ignorant, as incompetent in judgment and performance as any in Flachsenfingen.[1]

His high hopes of musical Vienna had been dashed. He found it full of nasty little coteries; and in writing his family about them and about the serpent's feet, he made an almost Hibernian bull: "To obtain a solid footing among them, I would need more of the serpent in my make-up than I think I possess."

In all justice it should be noted that he had come at a time when the Viennese public taste was unusually superficial. The favorite composers were Rossini and the waltz-magnates, Strauss and Lanner. Ideals of performance were typified by Thalberg and his curlicues. In the theater one heard "more clapping than

---

[1] A tiny principality in Jean Paul's *Hesperus.*

music." "Serious people," complained Robert, "are little sought after hereabouts, and little understood."

All the musicians were scrabbling about in the lighter sorts of music "like flies in buttermilk." He declared that he could not find any of them who were "entire people," and understood Shakespeare and Jean Paul; and that, while in the streets of Berlin you saw many folks carrying books, here what they had in their hands was food.

The local publishers, jealously hostile, were deaf to his proposals about the *New Magazine*. The Bureau of Censorship gave him some faint idea of how Austrian bureaucracy could shackle freedom of the press, and how interminably long even the shackling would take.

Here he found gossip and other small-town vices worse than at home in Zwickau. These things, with the tastelessness and the plague of officialdom, made him lonely, 'melancholy enough to shoot himself,' and led him by comparison to appreciate how much of a real metropolis Leipzig was.

The longer Robert struggled and ran from official to buck-passing official, the more convinced he became that he just did not belong in that city. "I doubt," he wrote, "whether all this talk about the good humor of the Viennese means anything more than agreeable faces."

In spite of the Burgtheater, with its consummate performances, and of those congenial friends Fischhof, Vesque von Püttlingen, Thalberg, and Mozart's son, he sometimes caught himself gasping like a fish on the sand. However, he loved the fresh picturesqueness of Vienna, and its beautiful forest environs with their stimulating effect on his creative powers. In the magazine he confessed:

Put together the pictures of the Danube, the tower of St. Stephen's, and the distant mountain ranges, cover them with the faint perfume of Catholic incense, and you have a portrait of Vienna. And when the charming landscape comes wholly alive for us, strings may be heard that otherwise might never have sounded within us.

With surprising frankness for an engaged man, he wrote the family in Zwickau about the temptations and dangers of "the

lovely sensual life" of Vienna; and described two jolly, lively
women in particular who had pleased him.

And he made other cheering discoveries. Going to worship at
the tombs of Beethoven and Schubert who, in those days, slept
three graves apart in the Währing Cemetery—

Just think what I found on Beethoven's corpse-stone [*Leichenstein*]:
a pen. What's more, it was made of steel. I took it as a good omen,
and will treasure it as a holy relic.

He did even better; for with this lucky pen [2] he was to write
his B Flat Symphony, and a review of another discovery, which
concerned the occupant of the other grave. For he had learned
that the late Franz Schubert's brother Ferdinand, a needy
schoolmaster-composer [3] with eight children, was living in Vienna; and that his whole property consisted of certain music
manuscripts. These yellowing sheets, though a drug on the
Viennese publishing market, were calculated to send any truly
intelligent publisher quite off his head with joy. For they were
unpublished masses, operas, and symphonies by Franz Schubert!

The sound critical sense of the young man from Zwickau
picked out of this lot the prize specimen, the great C Major
Symphony. He promptly arranged to have it performed by
Mendelssohn in the Gewandhaus, and published by Breitkopf
and Härtel. In his review of this master-work, Robert coined a
wingèd word destined to live, when he wrote of its "heavenly
length."

He was glad to place Breitkopf and Härtel under obligation
to him by sharing this momentous discovery with them; and was
quick to seize the favorable moment to advance his own interests. The letter of January 6th, 1839, in which he announces the
find, and assures them that Ferdinand Schubert will be content
with a modest recompense, closes with a plea for the immediate
publication of his own *Fantasie* and *Novelletten*.

[2] Which Sir George Grove mistakenly said Schumann had found on
Schubert's grave.

[3] A *Requiem* by Ferdinand Schubert was the last music Franz heard,
sixteen days before his death on November 19, 1828.

The publishers responded enthusiastically with a generous offer. Schumann then did one of those things which are unpardonable even in a genius. Although meanness and the advancement of his own interests were things which he sedulously avoided in the *Magazine,* and although he was often a generous friend of other musicians, especially contemporaries, on this occasion he acted in the worst traditions of both publishing and professional writing. It is hard to escape the conclusion that he did so for purely selfish reasons, though the business training in the economics of publishing, learned from August Schumann, may have had something to do with it. In any case, Robert went to Ferdinand Schubert, who desperately needed money, and talked him into accepting a miserable 180 florins for Franz's great work, and wrote Breitkopf and Härtel on March 29th that he had persuaded the schoolmaster to accept the smaller figure. Thus the shameful underpayment that had always been practiced upon Franz Schubert was continued, through the influence of his artistic heir, upon his material heir.

Within a few months Schumann's *Fantasie* and *Novelletten* were promptly published.

Shabby though Robert's dealings with the C Major Symphony were in a business way, his generosity as a critic was not affected. Writing to Becker from Leipzig in December 1839, he said of it:

In rehearsal today I heard part of the symphony of Franz Schubert. From that point all my life's ideals began to unfold. It is the greatest piece of instrumental music that has been written since Beethoven; Spohr and Mendelssohn themselves not excepted!

Indeed, the symphony made a profound and lasting impression upon him. Its influence will be noted in the discussion of his symphonic writing.

Another of Robert's activities at this time does not seem particularly worthy. He was intriguing for a doctorate from Leipzig University, in order to impress that monomaniac, Wieck, and as a counterpoise to Clara's recent title of Chamber Virtuoso to the Emperor of Austria. Leipzig refused; but Robert kept on fishing, and finally landed a Ph.D. from Jena. There is a striking contradiction between the crassness of such angling and his delicacy in scarcely allowing his own music to be mentioned in the *New Magazine*. But we cannot forbear a sympathetic smile with him when the honor is won and he writes Keferstein: "My girl is still a child, and will jump for joy to be a doctor's betrothed."

CHAPTER 16

THE MALICE OF FATHER WIECK

FATHER WIECK now began to show the sadism of a peasant with an inferiority complex. Enraged that Robert had disproved his wily calculations in actually going to Vienna, he cynically canceled all his promises and ordered Clara to forget that any such creature as Schumann had ever existed. Marrying him was quite out of the question.

By thus giving Clara bad faith for good, he was—if the madman had only realized it—effectively hurling her into Robert's arms. For even the most devoted filial love is not proof against treachery so crass as Wieck's. A new note of maturity, freedom, and self-reliance crept into her letters. And, from Vienna, Robert responded in kind:

When you wrote what your parent promised if you would give me up, I had to smile. The "happiest life" would be your lot. Dressed up in fine clothes, you would be taken about town and given oranges to eat. That is the so-called happy life.

I had it all nicely figured out. I was sure that your father would be convinced by this step of mine how dead serious I am about guaranteeing our future. I had thought he would let things run along in peace, and that if I made a position here for myself, he would in good faith let me have you. But now he is training upon me the most hostile and lethal weapons. Again I say to you this one thing, that you must leave him immediately. A little girl, without money or guile, should never have been treated thus—least of all, you, with your inexpressibly noble character. We have much too long endured it that he who is supposed to love you should hold you in so little respect as deliberately to wound and destroy you in the flower of your youth, for all the world to see. You cannot possibly belong to us both. You must give one of us up: him or me.

Farewell, act, act—
Unchangeably,
Your ROBERT.

Wieck's cruelty was not prompted by any sudden rush of hot-blooded rage. It was the hard, calculating cruelty which must have inspired the architect of Hell. It was even venomous and sinister enough to intrigue for the destruction of his own daughter's artistic and moral reputation—anything to ruin that marriage. Her devoted maid Nanny was dismissed. The lovers trembled for the very lives of their other kind go-betweens, Ernst Becker and Dr. Reuter. To Clara's further humiliation, her stepmother was sent to use physical violence in frisking the girl for clandestine correspondence. Fortunately, however, she found none.

Clara responded to this treatment as if she had, by infection, caught something of Robert's manic-depressive trouble. One moment, up in arms against Father, and full of valor, she would write Robert:

Rely on me when the time comes! I'll follow you to Vienna. It will be hard to part from Father. I shall be up against lots of difficulties; but love will find a way to strengthen me for everything. God in his Heaven will forgive me—it is only love!

In this heroic mood she defied the old man, and went alone on a concert trip to Paris. But once there, reaction set in. Sorely missing Wieck's managership, she lost courage and confidence, tried again to win Father over, and sent Robert almost despairing letters.

Now, half of Clara's personality, including her suspicious and jealous bent, was inherited from her Father. So that the unfortunate Robert had a Wieck-and-a-half to contend with. And at times this was almost too much. For example, when Clara had been for some time in Paris, she definitely repeated her promise to marry Robert the following Easter: "You are everything I have on earth, and you are eternally dear to me—I will do anything you desire, and at Easter I am yours."

But Clara was very young and her father was devilishly persuasive. No more than five days after this vow, she allowed the Wieck without and within to talk her around and fill her with secret doubt of Robert's assurance that he could so soon support her. She quite lost her head, went back on her solemn promise, and wrote him that they would have to wait a year or longer. Still more foolishly, she even gave countenance to an impertinent letter written Robert by her friend Emilie List. It urged him to give up the struggle, go into his dead brother's book business, and do his composing 'in his hours of leisure.' The drift of her ill-advised counsel was that, though the pen is mightier than the sword, penury is mightier than the pen. This epistle was closely followed up by a second, and still more brutal, letter from Clara.

Shocked, disappointed, and furious, Robert went wild. He tore these two letters from his girl to bits, and answered in such exasperated language that Clara caught fire too, and destroyed his message.[1] The attack upon his vocation turned the composer into a tiger whose cub was being threatened. This was the direst quarrel the lovers were ever to have. It left indelible scars, though patched up in the following lines:

Tell me, my good, beloved Robert, what shall I do to bring back your more tender feelings for me? Please tell me; I cannot be at peace when I know you are angry with me. You have misunderstood me; that was the whole trouble, and you doubted me—that you should not have done!

Kiss me with your old love, as I do you with love ever renewed. . . . What bitter tears you have cost me again!

And we are glad to find Robert replying with a new note of manly authority:

A few days ago I wanted to dispatch myself out of the world by the quickest route, but first awaited your letters. . . . Now the thought that I have you again! That I know you are again firm and determined! . . .

Ah, your second letter, so corpse-cold, so dissatisfied, so obstrep-

[1] The purport of these letters was learned and reported by Clara's biographer, Litzmann.

erous. . . . My days were frightful. . . . Let it be a warning to you,
my dear Clara, that in the future you should always treat me with
much forbearance. . . . I feared that your inner nature had been
changed into its opposite. Your letter, which I tore open with trembling, flung wide for me one gate of heaven after another. . . .

But now surely no more fears for our future will touch you. You
will promise me, will you not? to fall a prey to no more unnecessary anxieties, and to trust and obey me; for the man is above the
woman.[2] . . . One can harness me like a child to a cart; but I simply
will not allow myself to be beaten.

Robert acted with determination. On his birthday he sent
Clara the drafts of two letters. One was a final appeal to Father.
And, in case this was refused, the other was a formal petition
to the Court of Appeals for its authorization of their marriage.

The former was insultingly rejected, so, in September 1839,
Clara signed the latter, and wrote: "The instant when I signed
was the most important of my whole life. I set my name down
with firm resolution, and was boundlessly happy."

It would be interesting to know whether a certain indiscretion
of her lover's had helped persuade Clara to punish him by post-
poning the wedding and writing and abetting the cruel letters.
Robert always had an appreciative eye for feminine beauty; and
in September 1838, just before leaving Austria, he had rashly
written the jealous Clara this naïvely trusting confidence about
the pretty girls on the Danube:

I am one of the warmest admirers of beautiful women's and girls'
faces—when I see them I can, so to speak, really smirk and swim in
praise of your sex. So when we one day wander through the streets
of Vienna and something pretty meets us, so that I cry out: "Whew,
Clara! just have a look at this child of the gods!" and so on, don't be
alarmed and don't scold.

Surely a hazardous remark to make to a jealous fiancée, when
you are setting forth alone for a town like Vienna. Especially if
she, like Clara, has an elephant's memory for slights.

Naturally, the row had a fearful effect on Robert. It threw
him into a severe depressive phase, and for weeks paralyzed his

[2] Lucky for him that he did not write this to an Anglo-Saxon woman!

creative powers. Nor was this state helped by his brother Eduard's death while Robert was returning from Vienna to Leipzig. He wrote Clara that, at half past two in the morning, he had heard within his head a trombone chorale; and learned later that Eduard had passed away at that very time. "Everything affects me so frightfully," he went on. "I am quite bowed down and deadened by pain."

Torn between an obstinate adoration of her father and an imperishable love for her lover, Clara, almost up to the moment of her marriage, did a continual seesaw which exasperates us when we read of it a century after, but which must have been no less than maddening to both men. Such extremes of filial devotion, heightened no doubt by her modicum of the paternal mulishness, make one the more impatient with her when the lengths are recalled to which the raging Wieck went in those strenuous days.

He wrote to the dealers not to let her have pianos because she would ruin them. He strove to drive away her audiences by spreading reports that she was "shameless," "a miserable, demoralized girl." He said whatever he could against Schumann, even to such ridiculous charges as that he wrote an illegible hand and spoke in too soft a tone. And whenever he met Robert on the street, he spat demonstratively.

One is particularly impatient with Clara for swallowing such insults when it is realized that the stress induced by Wieck's savagery must have materially shortened the sensitive Robert's life.

And this Wieck was the man who made a special point of inculcating virtue in his pupils! The diary contains a gem of self-exhortation: "Let your highest goal be the forming of your charge into a good person." When, at fourteen, Clara received her first communion, she also received this paternal admonition:

More and more, at every opportunity, cultivate a taste for noble and unselfish actions, for doing good to people and being truly humane; and hold the practice of virtue for the—true religion.

It is amusing to find Marie, Wieck's daughter by a second marriage, defending the marital virtues of this most contrarious man by writing of Clara's mother that "she did not suit him on account of her spirit of contradiction"! [3]

Presently, in the usual bad faith, Wieck drew up a new set of stipulations for winning his consent to the marriage. Among others he insisted that:

1. The couple must not live in Saxony; but the *New Magazine* must earn as much as if they did.

2. He would withhold the 7000 thalers which Clara had earned in the last five years, paying 4% interest.

3. Robert's estimate of his income must be guaranteed by the court.

4. Robert must make no attempt to communicate with Wieck before the latter should give the word.

5. Clara must make no claim to inherit anything from himself.

Any means looked good to Wieck, if only it would help him vent his overpowering rage against the "thief" of his Clara. Schumann wrote despondently to the good Becker:

We have tried everything against this obstinacy—nothing was any good—on the contrary, from day to day he so surpassed himself in insolence that it became an impossible spectacle. You can imagine Clara's position: far off in the wide, wide world, in a strange country, living for years now in inner unrest and yearning to make an end of it. I fear it has seriously injured her health. My anxiety is terrible.

[3] Mr. Norman Hoyte suggests that Wieck's cruelty to Clara may have sprung in part from a desire to hurt this mother of hers, with whom the girl was on affectionate terms.

CHAPTER 17

BOOMERANG

W HERE should they live after the wedding? The lovers were uncertain. Vienna was highly doubtful. In Leipzig, so close to Wieck, they would be asking for more trouble. Perhaps they could commence life together in Zwickau. Robert toyed with this idea as he answered a lachrymose letter:

Aha, so you have been weeping. Didn't I forbid that? Supposing I should pay you a kiss for every tear, and tell you something pretty and amusing into the bargain, then would you cheer up? Well, here is a first kiss and then an amusing idea. Dear Clara, whenever I think of our first summer as married people in Zwickau, the world becomes a protecting arbor of roses; and there we sit among them, arm in arm, a young bridal couple, intent upon feasting and working. Think of that and of our wonderful happiness.

He plays on with the dream. Clara is to pick up cooking "between laughing and joking with Therese." [1] Their *ménage* will protect itself "against all tedious and nosey visitors." On their walks, Robert will point out all places where he once "wrestled with other boys." "How I would compose and how you would play!"

The middle of August 1839, Clara was relieved to turn her back on the Paris where she had been lonely and none too successful. She had to be present in a Leipzig Court of Justice for the first attempt at reconciliation. Wieck failing to appear, this came to nothing. Naturally the girl could not live in her hostile home; so she went to Berlin and stayed with her mother, Frau Bargiel, who had cordially signed consent to the marriage.

[1] Robert's sister-in-law.

143

"I never really enjoyed my childhod at all," Clara wrote to Robert.

You will make up to me for the loss of those youthful years. I was always a stranger in the world. Father loved me greatly, and I him; but I never enjoyed what a girl needs so terribly—mother-love; and consequently I was never wholly happy.

She was convinced that a real mother would have found a way to soften the harsh differences between herself and her father; whereas her stepmother, besides treating her with formidable coldness, only encouraged Wieck in his brutal despotism. The poor child had been made to feel like a stranger in her own home. So that, on reaching Berlin, it was an indescribable comfort and joy to feel about her the welcoming arms of her real mother.

The three days which she had spent with Robert in Saxony had been heavenly; but now began the anxieties of the bride-to-be, and she confessed to the diary:

One thought sometimes disturbs me—will I be able to hold Robert? His spirit is so immense; and there I cannot begin to come up to him, even though I wholly understand him. Perhaps this last circumstance may in some way compensate.

Then she went on sadly about how much she still loved her father; but mourned that, in his avarice, he had kept back all her hard-earned savings, so that she had not even a thaler towards a trousseau. Her own financial embarrassment was all the harder, as it kept her from alleviating the good Frau Bargiel's bitter struggle for existence. It was the first time that Clara had ever come face to face with real poverty; and this necessarily threw a shadow or two over the problematical future of the lovers.

Meanwhile, Robert's own outlook had not always been too rosy. The conflict was torture for nerves which were more sensitive than most men's—nerves which were growing more and more taut. On July third, he had written Clara: "*Dein Vater schüttelt sehr an unsren Blüthenbäumen* (Your father sorely shakes our brightly flowering fruit-trees)"—which, besides accidentally being a good line of verse, is good poetry.

Franz Liszt

Clara in 1840

Lawyer Einert of Leipzig was dispatched by the lovers as a plenipotentiary. When he sought to pacify Wieck, the pedagogue shouted that he would enforce his will, "though it meant the destruction of thirty people"—a truly Neronian touch.

"What a man!" commented Robert.

No wonder that this year the composer's health was shaky and his periods of depression deeper. In the warm, cordial atmosphere of the Bargiel home, where he appeared on September 13th as a surprise for Clara's birthday, he enjoyed some happy, buoyant days with her arms around him, but soon slumped from grace to be harried by thoughts of death and decay.

In passing, his morbidity infected Clara. On September 19th, her diary confessed: "I am in a sorry mood. I feel very unhappy, and my anxiety on Robert's account keeps on growing."

From these blue devils they were rescued by their art. If this pair could have foreseen the poetry of Edna St. Vincent Millay, how they would have endorsed her line:

> Music, my rampart and my only one!

On the 20th, Clara noted:

Robert's improvisation is heavenly. One could dissolve in his tones. His chords translate one wholly into another world. I would like to compare music to love! If it is too lovely and intimate, it hurts. That's the way it is with me. Sometimes it brings my heart near the bursting point.

Years later, Wasielewski once had the luck to arrive at Schumann's door and overhear him improvising to himself.

I stood still and harkened to the mystically veiled and fantastically clashing waves of sound. . . . Among them were tones and tunes so unique and sense-intoxicating as I had never before heard. . . . It was hardly piano-playing as we understand it; but more of a spirit-like floating and weaving in tone-waves of ether, a visionary sounding and ringing from the realms of faerie. [Remember that Schumann was the most advanced modernist of his time.] Often it sounded like aeolian harps breathed upon by sweet melancholy, a dreamlike interwoven phantasmagoria, from which, here and there, came flashes like the twinkling of colored lights.

And his friend Töpken, who also heard him improvise, remembered how

ideas flowed to him in inexhaustible abundance. Out of one thought, which he exhibited in all its aspects, everything else, as of its own volition, welled and gushed. And through it ran his own characteristic spirit with its depth and with all the magic of poesy, already marked by the clearly recognizable features of his musical personality, as well on the energetic, elemental side as on that of fragrantly tender musing and dreamy thoughts.

Wieck wrote Clara that he wished to break off legal proceedings and come to an agreement with her. But when they met, he gave her a perfunctory peck, and set up outrageous conditions. Far from receiving the dot which was then customary in well-to-do families, she must give her brothers two thousand thalers, and redeem her property and instruments with another thousand; and Robert must turn over to her two thirds of his capital. Also, he tried to persuade her to go with him on a three months' concert tour.

Her refusal made him so wild that, when the weather turned cold, and she sent the servant to get her winter overcoat, Wieck sent this gallant oral reply: "Who, then, is Mamsell Wieck? I know but two Fräulein Wiecks. They are my little daughters here. I do not know any other."

And he sought to wound Clara further by registering in public the most extravagant admiration for Camilla Pleyel, her competitor as a girl piano virtuoso. He even turned pages at her recital, and ostentatiously ogled her in the most absurd way. He well knew how to make any daughter of his suffer.

But Clara had still other cares. People did not take to Robert's work. To her diary she wailed:

I would gladly play it; but the public has no understanding of such music. How anxious it makes me when I think that Robert must one day see how little, in comparison with the insipid stuff of others, his compositions find favor. He is much too deep a spirit for this world. And on that account, must he be misjudged!? I believe the best thing for him would be to write for orchestra. . . . His compositions are all orchestral. . . . My highest wish is that he write for orchestra—there is his field!—May I succeed in bringing him to that point!

Poor Clara! She complained that the public did not understand Robert's music; but she herself was far from understanding it. How absurdly ignorant to call the *Davidsbündler Dances*, the *Fantasiestücke*, the *Scenes from Childhood*, the *Kreisleriana*, and the *Novelletten* "orchestral"! This was the girl who still preferred the *March* in the *Fantasie* to the other and better movements. She wanted Robert to write symphonies; but she would have liked to have them sound as nearly as possible like the popular Mendelssohn's. How true was the epigram that her lover put into Raro's mouth—"In an artist the extraordinary is not always recognized at once—to his advantage."

If Clara was sad in Berlin, Robert was sadder in Leipzig. His marriage troubles, and the death of his dear friend Henriette Voigt, brought him to the brink of another nervous breakdown. He was so fearfully depressed that his letters gave Clara more anxiety than pleasure. He complained of "a complete lack of ideas, especially at the piano," and of the "ferocious weakness" of his head.

When his nerves were ajangle, Robert easily took offense, even at Clara. But by this time she had made some progress in the art of handling him. When he acted hurt, she immediately assumed the role of the injured party. This at once brought Robert around by filling him with timorous compunction. And the odd thing is that, even though he was fully aware of the ruse,[2] it never failed.

In December 1839 Clara came to Leipzig for the second Court attempt at reconciliation. This time Wieck appeared, glared at her in horrible anger, and grew so passionately abusive that the judge had to shut him up. Robert's behavior, on the other hand, was exemplary.

Clara's entry for December 18th shows the fluctuations of a woman's heart. She wrote of Wieck:

This day has parted us forever, at least torn the delicate band between father and child. My heart, too, is, as it were, torn. . . . All

[2] As is shown by his letter to her, March 13, 1840.

my childish love for him [Wieck] has again been awakened and, in spite of everything, will always be alive in me.

One may imagine the emotions with which her lover read these no-yes lines!

In Court the pedagogue's objections were all thrown out, except the claim that Robert was a drunkard. The composer was ordered to bring proof to the contrary within six weeks and three days. Frau Devrient refused Wieck any help; and Robert's friends, including David, Mendelssohn, and Count Reuss, volunteered to testify in his behalf.

So the baffled Wieck sent Clara a letter in disguised handwriting, which he signed "Lehmann." This was full of insulting charges against Robert's character, and of warnings against him. It was timed to arrive just before her great Berlin recital, so as to upset her. Acting upon her suspicious nature, such a caddish trick might easily have proved disastrous had not Robert learned of the letter through his hero-worshiper, young Alwin Wieck, and thus been able to warn Clara that her father had written it. But even so, it was just as well that she hurt her hand and had to postpone the concert. This was only the first of a fusillade of scurrilous epistles by Wieck, attacking the moral character of the young couple and libeling them to their friends and supporters. The letters did small harm, however, to anyone but Wieck, whose shameful acts boomerang-ed back upon himself.

Robert's patience was at last exhausted, and he sent Clara this vigorous message: "If you perhaps believe that later on you will be able to reconcile me with your father, give up all hope of it. Your faintest wish of that sort would insult me."

In his desperate search for backing, Wieck turned hopefully to the girl whom Robert had jilted. But his fury grew almost insane when the sportsmanlike Ernestine foiled him by answering:

How is my good Clara? I have read a lot about her in the papers which, you may feel sure, has given my parents and me pleasure. Clara will never be happy without Schumann. Of this she assured me; for she loves him beyond words.

Under the strain of the conflict, Robert too was fast approaching the borderline of sanity. One day in Leipzig, a friend of Clara's named Frau Carl let drop a careless remark: "If only Wieck doesn't get around Clara once more!" And the tortured Robert rushed home to write his girl:

I certainly will not hold you back if you wish to return to your father. True, my reason might snap if you did—but, hold you back—certainly not.

Caught between the devil of her father's despotism and the deep sea of her lover's sensitiveness, Clara showed more courage and steadfast endurance than either of her men could muster. And in her stride she took many a smaller trouble: the injury to her hand, dizzy spells, illness, last-minute withdrawals of soloists from her concert, and the surprising news that the case could hardly be decided before the end of September 1840. Despite all this, and so ill that on the way to the hall she could scarcely hold up her head, and that several times during the evening all went black before her eyes, she kept up on champagne and, with trembling hands, played a program long and hard enough to tax a titan. And she played it so well that nobody found anything amiss. The concert was an immense success.

CHAPTER 18

THE YEAR OF SONG

T HE first intimation of a new period in Robert's creative life reached Clara at Berlin, early in 1840, when he wrote: "As always in February, I'm dreaming lots of music. You'll be astonished at the amount I've written in these days—no piano things. However, you're not to know it yet."

Soon he exultantly added that he had composed seven books of songs and one of vocal quartets.

I cannot tell you how easily all this has come and how happy it has made me. Usually I compose these songs standing or walking, not at the piano. This is really a quite different sort of music, that need not be first carried by the fingers—much more direct and melodious.

Sending her the *Liederkreis* with text by Heine, the first of his vocal works to see print, he wrote:

This is by way of being a modest reward for your last two letters. The songs are my first printed ones; so don't criticize them too severely. As I composed them, I was all wrapped up in you. Your eyes pursue me everywhere, romantic maiden that you are. And I frequently remember that, without such a betrothed, I could never write such music. In your particular honor I say it.

And to Keferstein, on February 19th: "I can scarcely express to you what a joy it is to write for the voice . . . and how it surges and storms inside me when I sit at work."

Few women in all history have received such gifts from their lovers as the manuscripts, fresh from the mint, of *Widmung*, the *Dichterliebe*, and the *Frauenliebe und Leben*.

150

Indeed, considering the stresses under which Robert had been laboring of late, this come-back was even more admirable than Clara's courage at her recent concert. The spontaneous impetus of his creative urgency had in it something miraculous. It can be compared only with that of a Bach, a Mozart, or a Schubert. On May 15th he confessed to Clara:

I have again composed so much that sometimes it seems to me altogether uncanny. Oh, I cannot help it, I would like to sing myself to death like a nightingale. Twelve Eichendorff songs. But I've already forgotten them, and started something new.

When, in the light of his subsequent history, others read those words about singing himself to death, they too have an uncanny feeling!

At the close of this remarkable year he told Zuccalmaglio: "Music still devours me. I must often tear myself from it by violence." To listen to the music that Schumann wrote in these anxious and glorious months is to feel the same exhilaration of luxuriant vitality that streams from the most exuberant canvases of Rubens. Coming after the long, bitter struggle with the Wieck-and-a-half, the good hope of winning his woman had banished any lingering doubts of his own creativeness, and turned on a magic inner gramophone which sang him, at his pleasure, the most delicious and original strains.

As swiftly as it had begun, Schumann's chief burst of song ended and made way for something larger. On May 10th, 1842, with the vocal year well behind him, he wrote Kahlert:

You speak of my future. I do not trust myself to promise more than I have already accomplished in the song line; and I am also satisfied with it.

That sounded, certainly, a trifle ominous. For, when an artist is satisfied with his achievement, he is usually ready for the six pine boards. In fact, the greatest creators have never been satisfied. Witness what Beethoven exclaimed just before the pine boards came for him: "It seems to me as though I had just begun to write."

Perhaps Schumann's chief fault was that he was sometimes too easily satisfied with his own work. True, he often rewrote, and left many alternative readings of doubtful passages. But he did not always proceed with sufficient thoroughness when he *did* rewrite. What a composer he would have made if, far more spontaneous and initially brilliant than Brahms, he had been as hard to satisfy!

However, in view of the fact that Schumann accomplished more in the Lied than anyone else but Schubert, he should not, in this instance, be grudged his meed of self-satisfaction. Besides, his complacency about the songs was short-lived. Not four months after the Kahlert letter, he wrote in answer to praise from Kossmaly:

As for your estimate of me, I trust that it may be justified in the sequel, where I hope to accomplish still more. In the path already trodden there are various things that please me; but they are as nothing compared with the far prospects that I glimpse here and there in occasional good hours.

Presently Franz Liszt, borne on the wings of his own private whirlwind, descended upon Leipzig. With his nobility and infectious charm he at once won Robert's heart for himself, though not for what he composed. The two spent their days together; and soon the visitor exclaimed: "It seems to me as if I'd known you these twenty years!" Robert reported to Clara that, in this short time, they had become intimate enough to give one another the rough side of their tongues; and that the Hungarian deserved it, for Vienna had spoiled him too much.

Clara replied:

I laughed a lot about your being rude to Liszt. You say he's spoiled; but aren't you also a bit spoiled? However, such matters can be taken care of, once you are my husband.

Alarums and excursions continued. Liszt made people furious by turning up his aristocratic nose at bourgeois Leipzig, and by increasing the price of his recital tickets after the sale had begun. Boycotted, he sulked in his tent; but was restored to general favor by the popular Mendelssohn, who gave his friend a tremendous concert, where the Hungarian shone with incomparable luster.

Then, at the elaborate banquet organized in his honor by Hiller, Liszt showed the quality of his capacious spirit. After the usual toast to Mendelssohn, he astounded the honest Leipzigers by eloquently praising Robert Schumann, not as writer on music, nor editor, but as a tremendous creative artist—a prophet without honor in his own country. This speech may have been a turning point in Robert's career. He wrote:

> For the last few days we have had nothing but suppers and dinners, music and champagne. He [Liszt] has turned our whole way of life topsy-turvy. We all love him tremendously; and yesterday in his concert he again played like a god. The clamorers and gabblers have been shut up.

Exhilarated by these festive days, Robert urged Clara to come and share the fun with him. She came and enjoyed it, though she felt the strain of consorting with that human dynamo from Hungary. However, she could well stand it for, as Robert explained, she possessed "the endurance of a man."

Liszt left. Again she walked with her lover on that path to Connewitz where, as a little girl, she had kept him from stumbling over the stones, only to do so herself. After all the tumult and the shouting, she looked her intended over, and was glad she had chosen him.

> I never feel so satisfied, so homey, as when I walk with him. He need not say a word. I like it so much when he is only thinking, and I wish I could overhear every one of his thoughts! And then, when once in a way he softly squeezes my hand, I am so deeply contented in my inmost being—then I wholly feel that I am his dearest.

> Today he showed me many of his songs. I had expected nothing like them. My admiration of him grows with my love. No one alive is musically so gifted as he.

On August 6th, just ten days before the banns were published for his marriage, a young pianist named Amalie Rieffel visited Schumann, and put down in her diary a sharply etched vignette of the man and his setting:

I went with Father to see Schumann, not without terror and heart-pounding; for how much depended on winning his favor! His outer man is not very prepossessing. He looks like an honest citizen. However, sometimes a sarcastic line flits about his mouth; his eyes grow dark—and then he becomes interesting. His nature, too, is like that, plain, quiet, so simple, as though one need not seek spiritual gifts or talents at his address. He speaks softly, in disconnected sentences. Furthermore, he has a friendly, winning smile, and often accompanies his words with a gentle nodding of the head.

As we entered, we were met by the most heavenly perfume of flowers. On the right stood the grand piano, over which hung portraits of Bach, Beethoven, and L. Schunke, as he was drawn on his death-bed. Under them was a sparkling likeness of Clara. My emotion on seeing her, whose friendship means so much to me, decidedly did not escape Schumann; for he took my hand and softly pressed it. By the door at the left stood a big, tall case full of music; farther up, a writing table with a great lot of fearful caricatures of the most famous musicians; [1] e.g., Liszt with four hands, Paganini caricatured with rolled-up sleeves, and strings hanging down, furiously contemplating the G string. He [Schumann] seemed to take enormous pleasure in these things; for we had hardly sat down and exchanged a few words before he began to call attention to them.

Schumann made Amalie play for him, which she did with fear and trembling. But he liked it so much that he drew nearer and nearer until both elbows rested on the music-rack. In the end he dedicated to her the *Scherzo, Gigue, Romanze and Fughette,* Op. 32. Once, when she played him *Des Abends,* he made a remark prophetic of the large-hearted way in which Brahms was to treat his pianistic interpreters: "Well, my conception of that is entirely different; but keep to your own way—I like it better."

[1] Dantan's statuette of Thalberg with ten fingers on each hand was a commentary on Schumann's wistful longing to have ten good fingers in all. And a Raphael Madonna, which he had stipulated for on renting the rooms, cast a sidelight on his mother-fixation. There is significance in a remark he made to Robena Laidlaw when they were discussing the Sistine painting of this subject, that the Madonna should be half child, half woman, like his favorite Murillo in the Louvre. This might suggest that he wanted his own mother-image to be half Clara, and half his own mother. Truhn found neither road nor path leading to his door; which suited his love of privacy and of unspoiled nature.

Thus do really spacious musical minds pay tribute to the universality of their art.

On July 7th, Robert and Clara were immensely cheered by the news of Wieck's having failed to furnish the required proofs that the young composer was a sot. In suspense they lived through the period of grace allowed him in which to file an appeal. And when these days were over, and nothing had happened, they jubilantly celebrated the incredible fact that Father, whose every missile had boomerang-ed back upon his own grim pate, had ignominiously folded up. Who could have blamed Robert if he had signalized the high occasion by getting drunk?

On Clara's name-day, August 12th, the Court formally sanctioned the marriage. The young people lost no further time. After the second banns were called, on the 23rd, Robert wrote Keferstein: "To hear this made me blessedly happy. Clara too, as you may well imagine. The trials of patience through which we went were simply too unworthy."

On September 12th, at Schönefeld near Leipzig, almost five stormy years after their first kiss, and the day before Clara's twenty-first birthday, they were quietly married by Prediger August Wildenhahn, one of Robert's old school friends. And we are glad to know that the faithful Becker and Reuter, who had so valiantly helped to bring about this happy consummation, were on hand.

In her diary, Clara sent up a prayer that she might keep her Robert

right long, long years— Ah! the thought that I might at last lose him, when that comes over me all my senses are at once confused. Heaven preserve me from such a calamity! I could not bear it. . . . This has been the loveliest and most important day of my life. . . . Now begins a new existence, a beautiful life, a life wrapped up in him whom I love more than myself and everything else. But heavy responsibilities also rest on me and heaven grant me strength to fulfill them faithfully, like a good woman!

The satisfaction of their friends in this union was expressed by none so well as by the felicitous—if somewhat flowery—Liszt:

In the world of art, no happier or more harmonious combination could be imagined than that of the inventive man with the interpretive wife. . . . The annals of art will in no way separate the memories of these two nor be able to utter their names apart from one another. The future will weave a golden shimmer about both their heads, and allow to shine over both brows but one single star.

It is curious what artistic blessings came to Robert from apparent misfortunes. His mother's dislike of a musical career for him, which was heartily shared by his brothers and his guardian, invested music with all the seduction of forbidden fruit. Hurting his finger made him a composer. Wieck's hateful hostility steeled his will, built up his energy, intensified his passion for the forbidden Clara, and—both before and after marriage—put him into the emotional state to do his best work.

If, at the first go-off, the pedagogue had patted him on the shoulder and cooed: "Charmed, my dear boy!" and Clara, unmoved by suspicion or jealousy, had fallen to his lot like a ripe cherry, without his even bothering to shake the tree, we might never have had the best of his piano pieces, songs, symphonies, and chamber music.

Robert's misfortunes, however, were far from blessing his nervous system. Of course, if all the storm and stress of the courtship had broken upon a mind more foursquare on its foundations, the results might well have been entirely good. But as it was, the strains of the conflict with the Wieck-and-a-half left a permanent mark on Schumann's mental stability.

One thing more. Robert often chafed in the shackles of the *New Magazine;* but without the difficulty the young couple experienced in getting married and launched, he would never have persisted in his editorship and in becoming the world's best composer-critic.

The marriage was a brilliant success. Naturally, many of Clara's admirers of both sexes mourned the transformation of her whom—despite Wieck's libels—they called the virgin-priestess of music, into a wife and mother who still sometimes kept on with her art. But they had no idea how much more interesting a person would result from the change.

The two were almost ideally suited to one another. Perhaps it was the profound contrast in their artistic abilities which prompted Raro to say: "Like powers cancel each other out; unlike powers intensify each other."

I sometimes wonder if there could perhaps have been an unconscious strengthening of their sympathy in the circumstance that they had cognate functional afflictions. For the first eight years of her life, Clara had been deaf; while Robert, from an early age, had more and more trouble with speech, until he grew almost dumb.

Clara's strongly maternal nature played a very important role in their affinity. For Robert's tie with his own mother, if not an actual complex, had at least been a very powerful fixation. And, when Clara was able to supplant his mother, as well as to give him the love of a devoted wife, marriage held for him a double satisfaction and stimulus. This explains why it did not in this case have the effect it so often has, of dulling the artist's creative edge, but sharpened it instead.

Naturally, no marriage is flawless; and it would be absurd to look for any such halcyon state between two nervous and highly strung artists. A difficulty arose because Clara must not practice while Robert was composing; and Robert composed nearly all the time. He, at least, could afford to be philosophical about the situation:

Clara understands that I must cultivate my talent, that my powers are at their height, and that I must make the most of my youth. Well, that's how it is in artist marriages—one cannot have everything at the same time; the chief thing is the happiness that remains, and we certainly are most happy to possess and understand one another—understand so fully and love so entirely.

And, on the 5th of December, Clara told her diary:

Today it is a quarter of a year since we were married. Perhaps the happiest year I have yet known. Every day I arise with fresh love for my Robert; and if I sometimes seem dejected and almost unfriendly, that only comes from anxieties which always spring from my love for him. . . . If anything can, for an instant, overshadow my joy, it is the thought of my Father, for whom I feel the most

profound pity because he cannot see our happiness; because heaven
has denied him a heart and he has no sympathy for a happiness like
ours. Now he has no joy, and has lost, by his actions, not only me,
but all his friends, of whom he did not have many. . . . I hope, my
tenderly loved Robert, that you will not be angry with me for feeling this pity. For once in a way [*sic!*] my childish feeling cannot be
entirely suppressed, and so you will even forgive me my sad thoughts
about my Father.

This subject was all the more ticklish because Robert's libel
suit against Wieck hung in the air,[2] and negotiations were then
being conducted by Major Serres for the restoration of Clara's
piano and other property, including the winter coat. But the
old man showed himself so niggling, avaricious, hateful, and
generally impossible that he actually drove Clara, for the moment, over to her husband's side. And when the libel case was
closed, all prospects of a reconciliation were temporarily
crushed.

Hope, however, sprang eternal in Clara's breast. On Wieck's
birthday, a few months later, the irrepressible daughter held out
another olive branch of appeasement. And on September 2nd,
1841, even Robert wooed him with the announcement of his
granddaughter Marie's birth. But the old ruffian remained insultingly irreconcilable.

In Clara's musical culture Robert found holes that were surprising when one considers her mastery of the keyboard and her
upbringing in a really musical household. It has already been
seen that the things she preferred among Robert's piano compositions were not always the most admirable, and that she was
wide of the mark in thinking them all orchestral. The two lovers
had not been married a fortnight before they began to analyze
together Bach's *Well-tempered Clavichord;* and Clara's ignorance of the very rudiments of form is shown in her surprised
entry: "Robert shows me the places where the subject comes
back again. Why, it's a really interesting study!" In other words,
theoretically speaking, she still did not know a duck from a
goose.

[2] Robert won it in the Spring of 1841.

But her taste rapidly improved. In July 1841, she wrote: "The less I play in public, the more I hate the wholly mechanized virtuoso stuff. I have quite come to turn against concert compositions like etudes of Henselt, fantasias of Thalberg, Liszt, etc."

Well, if she had quite turned against such things, and acquired good taste, it was a very recent development; for the program of her Gewandhaus concert of March 31, 1841, closed as follows:

Duo Concertante

for melophone and violoncello,

played by Messrs. Giulio Regondi and Joseph Lidel of London.

Fantasie on themes from Rossini's *Moses*

by Thalberg

Played by the concert-giver.

Mr. Dr. Felix Mendelssohn-Bartholdy has had the kindness to take over the direction of the orchestra.

Which shows that in March, Clara's ideals had a long upward journey still before them. A melophone, by the way, was a kind of concertina shaped like a bastard guitar or 'cello. One can imagine the sort of music it played.

Two years later, Clara admitted that string quartets (the loftiest and purest of all musical vehicles) had always bored her until Robert began to write them. Only then, she confessed, had she begun to enjoy them. Such a non-musical ground for musical enjoyment is indicative of the state of Clara's education at the moment. However able he may have been as a teacher, Father Wieck had certainly neglected his daughter's development in the field of music appreciation—but of course it might not have brought in the financial rewards that her performances did. Marriage also filled some of the other holes in her lop-sided culture by introducing her to such poets as Shakespeare—and Jean Paul.

Happy though this marriage was, it turned out scarcely an

unmixed blessing for Robert's creative gift. Many years elapsed before Clara was educated up to the point of understanding and appreciating the best in her man's music. And, in the meantime, her influence was sometimes positively detrimental. Even as late as April 4th, 1839, she had been capable of urging him to prostitute his gift by writing a pot-boiler. This letter suggests in undertone the influence of her money-loving father:

Listen, Robert, won't you, for a change, compose something brilliant, easy to understand, and with no titles . . . ? I'd so love to have something of yours to play in public that is suitable for the crowd. Naturally such a thing is humiliating to a genius; but policy sometimes demands it.

I do not think that Clara was ever successful in wheedling Robert into so crudely denaturing his genius. In fact, the following month, after a dispute about his criticism of her *Notturno*, he wrote her: "I believe that we are often wide apart in our judgments. If only this does not later bring us bitter hours!"

Her musical influence, however, was otherwise unfortunate. In *The Musician* for June 1910, Mr. Cuthbert Hadden wrote:

Schumann's marriage, helpful as it was in many ways, was yet restrictive of the manner of his thoughts, and tended to make his expression merely pianistic and within the appreciation and technical powers of his wife. Had either Robert or Clara been orchestral players or opera singers, [*sic!*] the outlook of the composer would probably have been wider, and the limitation arising from the association of the two would not have existed, or would have been of a different nature.

Yes, the association was restrictive; but not because Clara was no orchestral player or singer; nor because marriage "tended to make his expression merely pianistic,"—for after marriage he wrote for piano much less than before; and the merely pianistic passages in his other works are far fewer than many critics would have us believe. Clara was bad for Robert's art because she was a timid reactionary whose musical development lagged far behind her forward-looking husband's, while she possessed the stronger character, and so morally had the upper hand.

My friend, the late Hermann Hans Wetzler, was a well-known

composer and conductor who studied six years with Clara Schumann. He assured me that, in some ways, Clara's influence on Robert was bad. She was so conventionally minded, so intent on smoothness, so averse to boldness and ruggedness, and such a worshiper of their most famous contemporary, that her tendency was towards Mendelssohnizing Schumann. In his youth, Mother Johanna had openly fought a losing fight against the idea of Robert's becoming a musician. In his maturity, Johanna's successor, Clara, fought a covert and somewhat more successful fight against the unheard-of-originality which he showed in his early works.

Of course, she made this up to him in various ways: by throwing her influence towards conservatism in finance, thus toning down his spendthrift instincts; by letting him work at the expense of her own technic; and above all, by making him comfortable and happy.

To sum up: Schumann's marriage was wholly good for him as a man; but its effect on his creative life was mixed. Clara helped his genius by furnishing favorable living and working conditions, stimulating him sexually, and bringing him joy. She harmed it through her undeveloped musical taste, and by throwing her influence upon the side of timid conservatism.

CHAPTER 19

THE SYMPHONY YEAR

C LARA now faced a difficult situation. Here was a young girl whom the world's adulation had already done its best to spoil. She was far more famous than her husband; but she knew that she was only a talent,[1] while he was a genius. It is hard enough, in all conscience, for an ordinary person to live in close contact with the sensitivity, the unceasing special demands, and the consuming excitements generated by genius. But the feat becomes immensely complicated for a person like Clara. Her career soon bade fair to be hampered by the impossibility of practicing while Robert composed, and by the handicap of childbearing. For an artistic genius—though he were as deep in love as Tristan—his art must always come first. And it needed no little self-mastery on the part of the naturally jealous Clara to keep from showing resentment at the dominant hold of music on Robert's affections. The more so, as in her immaturity she had not yet begun to realize the immensity of her husband's gift.

Naturally there were times when inspiration burned so imperiously that all Robert wanted was to be left alone with his thoughts. And then Clara could not help jotting down a gentle complaint:

For some days, now, Robert has been cold to me. Of course, it is for a very joyful reason, and nobody can more sincerely sympathize

[1] Why such a critic as Sir Henry Hadow (*Studies in Modern Music*, Seeley, 1908) so far exceeded his usual British sobriety of judgment as to call Clara a "genius" is an enigma.

with everything he undertakes than I; but sometimes this coldness, which I least of all deserve, gives me pain.

And, no matter how ardently he loved her, Robert, who had long lived free as a bird, was naturally a little restive under the artificial restrictions of matrimony. Nietzsche was right: "Too brilliant men need marriage, and at the same time revolt against it as if it were an obnoxious medicine." It was at those moments —when the composer felt the new tie chafing his dearly beloved freedom—that Clara had to put forth her utmost in the way of tact, forbearance, and feminine magic.

Robert too had forbearance with Clara's somewhat crude musical taste, her suspicious nature,[2] and her intense filial piety. For—though scarcely credible—the fact is that, even after all the atrocious things that Wieck had done to them, ending with the unworthy squabble about Clara's property, the libel suit, and the insults after the birth of his granddaughter, she was still seeking a reconciliation with the old tyrant.

Another sore point was this: Robert, in his masculine pride, hated to think that Clara's interpretive fingers were helping his career. Hirschbach told Erler:

[2] Premonitions of Clara's growing bent toward suspicion have already been seen in the willing ear which she lent to the slanders of Karl Banck (see pp. 105-6), in the way she put the worst construction upon Robert's editorial treatment of her (see p. 106), and in the distrust of his financial assurances, which made her sanction Emilie List's outrageous letter and postpone the wedding (see p. 139). By the end of her life, this failing had grown on her to a painful degree. In reply to a torrent of unjust accusations against Brahms, who had for decades been her chief benefactor and friend, he wrote her:

In your letter you treat Wüllner and me, not like two honorable men and artists, who are in your opinion perhaps mistaken, yet who, according to their lights, are working for a dear and holy cause earnestly and with love. Far from that, you treat us as the exact opposite of all this. What is between the lines of your letter, what it really breathes out, is something into which I prefer not to go.

And a few days later he added:

It is hard, after forty years of faithful service (or whatever you wish to call my relationship to you), to be nothing else than "one more bad experience." Well, that must be borne.

I still remember the evening when Assessor H., an old acquaintance of Schumann's, remarked to him that Clara had helped a great deal to smooth his path as a composer and obtain a public hearing for his works. Highly insulted, Schumann sprang up, and called to me: "Come on, Hirschbach!" With that our sitting at Poppe's was ended for the evening.

However, both Clara and Robert had large natures. They made concessions, met each other halfway, and built one of the most successful marriages that two artists have ever managed. It is seldom that a man shows such delicate appreciation of marital sacrifices as Robert did when he wrote:

Too often she must pay for my Lieder with silence and invisibility. That is the way it goes in an artist marriage; but, if people love one another, it's still good enough.

What a beautiful love story is that of Robert and Clara! One is struck each time by the dignity and delight of the letters which Schumann wrote after he found himself and, in the finding, knew that it was Clara he loved. How different from the romantic balderdash he wrote about other women in his earlier years! And it is remarkable that after they were married these two people made less to-do over the fact that each was gifted and famous in his or her way than almost any modern couple could have done. Even though their later years were not so perfect as those in which they were finding each other, the whole story is a noble one.

Unsatisfied desire usually has a happier effect upon creative work than its opposite. Not so with Robert. Fulfilled longing brought no let-down in his creativeness. One reason for this may be that the practical Clara was the same girl whom we found happily busy in the kitchen cleaning the knives, a few minutes after returning home from a long concert tour. She probably gave Robert a better material environment for work, and for keeping in trim for work, than he had ever before known.

Another cause may have lain in the fact that Clara's richly maternal nature answered Robert's mother-fixation. A factor such as this causes a man's desire to be less easily satiated, and more quickly renewed. The fixation may perhaps account for the fact that the passion which abounds in Schumann's music is never voluptuous, and that he took so little pleasure in Wagner's frankly sensual pages.

Yes, as marriages go, this was a model of felicity. In February 1841, Clara wrote in their common diary: "We enjoy such happiness as I have never before known. My Father always made fun of so-called *domestic bliss*. How I pity those who do not know it! They are only half alive!"

These words were set down in thanks for those which Robert wrote there when he had finished the First Symphony.

Clara began the entries for January 17–23, 1841, with:

The Symphony will soon be done. True, I've heard nothing of it as yet; but I am most happy that Robert has at last entered the field where he and his imagination belong.

Jan. 25

Today Robert has pretty well finished his symphony. . . . My poor Robert has spent several sleepless nights over it.

She went on to exult that the whole thing was sketched in four days; to exclaim that she never would have believed he had such facility, and to confess that he continually gave her new respect for him.

Halfway through the instrumentation, Robert returned to the diary, after five weeks of silence—five weeks of creative bliss and torture:

The symphony has brought me many happy hours. . . . I thank the good spirit that let me hit upon such a sizable work so easily and in such a short time. . . . But now, after many sleepless nights, exhaustion comes too. My state might be compared to that of a young mother who has just been delivered—so light and happy, and yet sick and sore. My Clara knows that too, and cuddles up to me with double tenderness which, some day, I will make up to her. After all, if I should undertake to tell of all the love which Clara showed me during this time, and with such a willing heart, I should never get through. I would not find one in a million who would give me so much attention and so much indulgence.

On February 20th, the instrumentation was finished; and the *"Spring"* Symphony, Op. 38, was conducted on March 31st by

Mendelssohn, in Clara's Gewandhaus concert. It was an immense success. Robert thought that no symphony since Beethoven had been so warmly received. In the diary he exulted:

So then, with God, farther along this road! At present my spirit is so cheerful that I believe I shall bring various things to light which may gladden men's hearts.

And Wenzel received this outburst of joy: "Just think, a whole symphony—and moreover, a Spring symphony. I can't believe, myself, that it's done."

Writing to Spohr, however, on November 23rd, 1842, he carefully disclaimed any idea that this title meant he had written program music:

I finished the symphony in 1841, at the end of winter and, if I may say so, under that vernal impulse which sweeps all men along, even the most agèd, and every year carries them away anew.[3] My purpose was not to describe or to paint.[4] I am convinced, however, that the season in which the symphony was composed influenced its formation and helped make it exactly what it is.

To Wilhelm Taubert he developed in some detail what Opus 38 came to mean to him after he had written it. And let us remember that music is a thing of such amplitude that any reader of this book has just as much right as Schumann had to apply his own imagery to the B Flat Symphony.

If you could breathe into your orchestra, as it plays, some Spring yearning [though *Frühlingssehnsucht* is intranslatable!], that is what I chiefly had as I wrote it in February 1841. Right at the first trumpet entrance I'd like to have it sound as if from on high, like a call to awake.

In the following part of the Introduction, I could then put in how it begins to grow green everywhere, perhaps a butterfly [5] floats up,

[3] All this about the vernal impulse of a Saxon January may seem a little strange, until one remembers that the grimmest of winters may breed in the imagination of genius a more authentic Spring than ever blossomed in April.

[4] In writing the *Pastoral* Symphony, Beethoven set down as his ideal, "More expression of feeling than tone-painting." The younger composer—even though a leading Romantic—was far truer to this ideal than the older.

[5] Note that, ever since the *Papillons*, Op. 2, emerged from the chrysalis,

and in the *Allegro,* how little by little everything comes together that belongs to Spring. However, these are imaginings which came to me *after* the work was finished.

That incredibly fertile Spring saw as well the birth of an adagioless little symphony, the *Overture, Scherzo and Finale,* Op. 52, about which Robert informed Hofmeister the publisher: "The whole has a light, friendly character. I wrote it in a really gay mood." He also did a *Fantasie for Piano and Orchestra,* which was destined, later on, to become the first movement of the great A Minor Piano Concerto, Op. 54.

As a composer Schumann now felt himself to be on a new plane. And some years later he tried to express this feeling to Van Bruyck:

I wish that you might have an opportunity to hear my larger com positions for orchestra. For though . . . I work as seriously in the smaller forms as in the larger, one gathers his strength together in a quite different way when one is dealing with masses.

Towards the end of May, Schumann began to sketch the D Minor Symphony. This was really his Second; but when it was performed, it did not satisfy him, or the audience, either. So he put it away. Ten years later it was taken out, revised, and numbered the Fourth.

After this remarkable work had been swiftly sketched, the married lovers went on a picnic to their favorite Connewitz; and returned, according to Clara's entry, "cheerful and content with ourselves and with heaven."

Two days later, Clara had as yet heard nothing of the new work except "D minor occasionally sounding wildly out of the distance"—

so that already I know in advance that this is another composition born of his deepest soul. Heaven surely must mean well by us. Robert cannot be happier in creating than I am when he shows me such a work. . . . I think he can look back with zest upon the past year

the word "butterfly" has been a sort of leit-motif for Robert. On page 93 he proposed to use butterflies as aerial messengers to Clara. They also figure in his last essay, the one heralding Brahms. The butterfly was used on Beethoven's tomb as a symbol of immortality.

and upon himself. One sees that, in spite of everything, marriage has been good for him. One so often says it kills the spirit, robs it of its youthful freshness! But my Robert provides the clearest disproof of that.

Which was, with a vengeance, reasoning from the particular to the general.

When Marie, who was Robert's and Clara's first child, born on September 1st, 1841, was christened,[6] Schumann gave his wife the newly printed *Twelve Songs*, Op. 37, which they had written together, the parts of the "*Spring*" Symphony, still wet from the press, and the manuscript of the D Minor Symphony. The christening took place on Clara's twenty-second birthday, September 13th, and Schumann, deeply and blissfully in love, wrote of the joy which he felt:

I had quietly finished. What else could I offer her but my artistic endeavors, and how lovingly she sympathizes with them! . . . One thing makes me happy: the consciousness that I am still far from my goal, and then the feeling that I have the strength to attain it. So then, my Clara, courage and forward march at my side!

Not a bad note on which to end the first year of that perilous adventure, a marriage of artists.

[6] Clara may have named the child after her half sister in another effort to appease Father.

CHAPTER 20

THE YEAR OF CHAMBER MUSIC

A GOOD deal has been written in the foregoing pages of what Clara thought about Robert. Here is the way he struck a more impersonal observer during that hectic summer. On August 4th, David, the famous concertmaster of the Gewandhaus, wrote Mendelssohn:

Schumann came to me yesterday, and remained without speaking for a whole hour. From which I gathered that he would not be averse to hearing his symphony once more in public. I hinted that it would be better for him to hear the horns rehearse; on which he made it clear by signs that he would willingly pay for a rehearsal to make the work go thoroughly well. After this he smoked two cigars, rubbed his mouth twice, as if to prevent a single syllable from coming out, took his hat, forgot his glove, nodded his head, tried the wrong door, and at last got away through the right one.

While Schumann was fathoms deep in the D Minor Symphony, a part of his mind could still attain enough detachment to consider the future. Plans for turning two Calderón plays into operas were mulled over and laid aside. Then he toyed with the idea of a secular oratorio, and informed the diary: "Now Th. Moore's *Paradise and Peri* has made me entirely happy. Perhaps something beautiful can be won out of it for music." But the symphonic impulse was too strong. After finishing the D Minor, he started a small symphony in C Minor, and his first composition for chorus and orchestra, based on Heine's *Tragedy*. Both were shelved unfinished.

Recovering from childbirth, Clara went to Weimar with Robert, where his B Flat Symphony and her playing were

cordially received. This whetted her appetite for more of the
same. On December 6th she gave a Gewandhaus concert in collaboration with Liszt. His bravura playing "stole the show" and
left but little of the public's favor to spare for herself, or for
Robert's D Minor Symphony, and *Overture, Scherzo and Finale*.
Both on her own account and Robert's, Clara was indignant that
Liszt should have walked away with the honors, and from that
evening onward her estrangement from the young Hungarian
began to grow. Unable, for the moment, to attack his playing,
she took her feelings out upon his compositions, which she
stamped upon as

a chaos of the rawest dissonances, a continuous muttering simultaneously in the deepest bass and the highest treble, boring introductions. . . . As a composer I could almost hate him.

Having done her wifely duty in bearing a child, and having
suffered a professional set-back at the hands of the mighty
Hungarian, Clara was wild to burst forth and reconquer the
world. A Russian tour had to be put off because she (rightly)
feared the competition of Liszt. But, early in 1842, the couple
were invited to repeat their Weimar performances in Bremen
and Hamburg.

So, for five weeks, Robert tore himself from his duties with
the *New Magazine,* and in the middle of February they set out.
The close of Robert's entry about the Bremen concert throws a
diverting light upon the absentmindedness that was rapidly
gaining on him:

The [First] Symphony (under Riem's direction) went better than
I thought it would after only one rehearsal. The Bremenites are stingy
with applause. . . . On the toneless grand, Clara played as beautifully as ever she could. [And of the evening concert:] My poor little
Clara wasn't allowed to leave the piano. After the Mendelssohn fugue
in C major, my thoughts were so carried away that I heartily applauded with the others, such was the beauty of Clara's performance.

During a side trip to Oldenburg, Robert had the first of many
occasions to savor the sweetness of being less famous than his
wife. After Clara's recital, she alone was invited to Court, which
her husband very properly took as an insult to himself. All the

same, she went, and returned very much pleased with herself. This hurt Robert still more; and he wrote: "The thought of my unworthy position in such circumstances, however, killed all my happiness." Truly a painful experience for one who, during his whole spoiled, provincial youth in Zwickau and Heidelberg, had had everything his own way as cock of the musical walk!

In Hamburg the public were kinder to him. But hardly had his spirits risen in response, when they suffered another fall. Clara was urgently invited on a concert-tour to Copenhagen. Robert could not go along; for the *Magazine* needed him. Besides, he was sick of playing second fiddle to Clara's first; and he dreaded more insults like the Oldenburg invitation.

As for Clara, she wanted to earn money for the household (though this was a matter that must never be breathed to the morbidly sensitive Robert!). And even more she wanted to win her own independence as an artist, by establishing a precedent for the future. She felt herself to be a personality in her own right, and secretly longed to call her apron-strings her own.

So Robert turned south and Clara north. But the parting broke her up to such an extent that she was unable to give the concert which had been arranged in Kiel, and had to pay expenses of 45 marks out of her own pocket. When, on March 19th, she at last embarked on "the so long dreaded but glorious ship *Christian the Eighth*," she confessed:

I was in a terrible state of mind as we left the land. How I sighed for Robert and the little one! And I almost believed that I should never again set foot on the solid earth.

Which access of nerves reminds one of Robert's worse depressive moods. What a fuss about a ferry trip! And this was the same girl that had played a successful concert an hour after being injured in a formidable accident!

In Copenhagen Clara scored an agreeable success; though she reported that the public was mad about Italian opera, even when badly given. The terrible orchestra was made up of nothing but artisans. And she attended a performance of Mendelssohn's *Hymn of Praise* where, after four different conductors had led the four rehearsals, a fifth directed the concert.

Meanwhile Robert languished at home, too depressed to compose, and was driven to the study of counterpoint and fugue. "A miserable life!" he groaned. Here is his entry for March 14th:

The parting has made me poignantly feel my strange and difficult position. Shall I neglect my talent in order to serve you as traveling companion? Have you—should you—let your talent lie unused because I am tied to the magazine and the piano? Now, when you are young, and at the height of your powers? We found the solution. You took a female companion. I returned to the child and my work. But what will the *world* say? That's the way my thoughts torture me. Yes, it is absolutely necessary that we find out how to use and develop our talents side by side.[1]

Note the passing access of philistinism in "what will the *world* say?" Had his wife's timid conventionality already made a fleeting impression upon the radical bohemian who had founded the Davidites?

Clara wrote him that everybody in Denmark knew his magazine and his name; though they were not yet familiar with his compositions. And it cannot have assuaged his gloom to hear that, though she was introducing the Danes to copious Chopin, she was offering them precious little Schumann.

While she was amassing 100 louis d'or, he was finding what solace he could in the study of Haydn and Mozart quartet scores, in reading, going to the theater where he enjoyed Schröder-Devrient, and in his own peculiarly mute form of conversation. The diary for April 18th notes: "Richard Wagner, who came from Paris."

Such periods as these, together with the financial worries, the inevitable wear and tear of marriage and fatherhood, and the anxieties caused by dubious health, were taking some of the sparkle from Robert's youthful high spirits, and tempering his enthusiasms. At the same time, they were deepening and ennobling his character towards the point where he could one day

[1] One seriously considered solution was a two-year concert tour to America. On March 6th, 1842, however, Robert wrote Töpken: "But the abyss is just too monstrous that would separate one there from the homeland." Beethoven and Brahms shared with him this terror of going overseas. It may have been founded on the instinctive feeling that the violent change of scene might harm their creative work.

write the profoundly noble *adagios* of the C Major Symphony
and D Minor Trio, the *Manfred* Overture, the "funeral march"
of the Quintet, and the "*Cathedral Scene*" of the "*Rhenish*" Symphony. Some imaginative person once put these words into the
mouth of Walt Whitman: "Whatever tastes sweet to the most
perfect person, that is finally right." Musically speaking, Schumann was "the most perfect person" of his day; and long afterward he proved to be "finally right."

On April 25th, Robert went to meet the returning Clara at
Magdeburg, "like a bridegroom, at once happy and anxious."
And the next day he brought her home. In the diary she re-
ported:

> Such a reunion makes up for all the pains of yearning I have suf-
> fered. Robert, too, seemed very happy, and led me to our house
> where I found everything garlanded. Moreover, Robert gave me a
> lovely carpet. But the most beautiful was his dear look . . . and
> the little red cheeks of my small angel that I could once more kiss.

Under these words her husband prophetically scribbled: "Now
better days are coming again."

As early as 1838, Robert had written Clara that he thought
of composing string quartets:

> The thought of the quartets gives me pleasure. The piano is get-
> ting too narrow for me. In composing now I often hear a lot of things
> that I can barely suggest. For instance, it is remarkable how I invent
> almost everything canonically, and never discover the imitative voices
> until afterwards; often too, end for end, in inverted rhythms, etc. As
> you doubtless have noticed, I take enormous pains with the melody.
> In that field as well much can be gained by industry and observa-
> tion. But by melody I mean, of course, something different from
> the Italian kind, that now seems to me like bird-song, agreeable to
> hear, but empty and devoid of thought.

The following year, 1839, he "began two quartets—I can
assure you they're as good as Haydn." But it was not until
Clara's return from Copenhagen, bringing him a new and
powerful access of creative energy, that Schumann String
Quartets, Inc., became a really viable concern. Presently he
exulted, in the diary: "I have been busy in a new field, and have

nearly finished and written out two string quartets in A minor and F major."

Before the end of June, another, in A major, was added, completing Opus 41 in the amazingly brief span of five weeks. Whereupon, at their own table, a friend proposed a neat toast to the "three children, scarcely born, and already perfect and beautiful."

For Clara's birthday, Robert arranged a private home performance of all three. She wrote:

My respect for his genius, for his intellect, altogether for the whole composer, grows with each work. . . . Here everything is new and at the same time lucid, finely worked out and always in quartet idiom.

Unfortunately she was wrong in this last qualification. There are pages in all three quartets which are far from idiomatic writing for strings. The truth is, she did not know what she was talking about, any more than when she pronounced all of Robert's piano music orchestral. We have already seen that, up to this moment, she had considered most quartet music ugly and boring, so she could not have understood it.

One of the first musical authorities of the day was the violinist and conductor Moritz Hauptmann, who that very year took Bach's old post as Cantor of the Thomasschule in Leipzig. To his master Spohr, he wrote:

At David's I heard three quartets by Schumann. His first, which delighted me immensely, made me marvel at his talent, which I had thought far from so remarkable. I had previously judged it from his earlier piano pieces, things so aphoristic and fragmentary, sheer revelings in strangeness. Here, too, there is no dearth of the unusual in content and structure; but it is cleverly conceived and held together, and—a great deal of it is very beautiful.

And, on October 15th, 1842, Robert, who seldom showed any great exhilaration over his own music, could not help writing to publisher Härtel:

This last summer I worked with much ardor at three quartets for violin, etc. We played them several times at David's, and they ap-

parently pleased both players and listeners, Mendelssohn in particular. [Presumably, however, he was only being polite.] I do not
care to say any more about them. But you may be sure that I have
spared no pains to compose something really good; indeed, I sometimes think, my best.

And five years later he wrote to the same firm:

My quartets which you brought out have regained fresh significance for me through the death of Mendelssohn, to whom they are
dedicated. I still regard them as my best work of the earlier days,
and Mendelssohn often spoke to me in the same sense.

This opinion was then, however, far from unanimous. And
one feels ruefulness between the lines of a letter he bravely
wrote to these publishers on August 17th, 1844. It had come to
his ears that the Müller Quartet of Brunswick had returned
Opus 41 to a local dealer with the remark, "Wretched stuff!"
But Schumann stoutly added: "I don't believe it. The whole
story is probably nothing but gossip."

The smooth and rapid creation of the quartets was all the
more remarkable because, at the same time, Robert was having
his editorial tribulations. A certain Gustav Schilling brought out
a textbook of harmony called *Polyphonomos;* and it proved to
be a shameful plagiarism of Logier's *Musikwissenschaft.* Now
Robert had inherited his publisher father's contempt for such
practices. In no uncertain terms he had Schilling branded in the
New Magazine as "a bumptious plagiarist, an arrogant, con-
ceited ignoramus and botcher." He may have delivered this
punch with all the more zest because, at Stuttgart in 1839, Clara
had almost fallen into Schilling's clutches. The botcher brought
suit for libel; and Schumann was sentenced to a modest fine of
25 Neugroschen, or a day in prison.[2]

One would think that such a fecund outpouring of symphonic
and chamber music would have exhausted any composer of
thrice Robert's nervous stamina. But no! In the last four months

[2] Poetic justice eventually caught up with the false Schilling. Robert
made Stuttgart too hot for him, just as he had once made Leipzig too hot
for Karl Banck. He was hunted to New York, and from there to Montreal
and Nebraska, where he died.

of 1842 he produced three more notable works: the great Piano Quintet in E flat, Op. 44, the Quartet in the same key for piano and strings, Op. 47, and the charming, intimate Piano Trio, Op. 88, which he afterwards called by his favorite title of *Fantasiestücke*.

In the end he had to stand and deliver the price of all this mental and emotional dissipation, an attack of what he called "nerve-weakness." Perhaps the reason for the frantic activity may have been an unconscious premonition that his career was to have an untimely end. In the light of our knowledge, it brings a lump into the throat when we read these words at the close of a letter to his friend Kossmaly, of October 28th, 1841: "Time presses and night begins to fall."

A vacation in Karlsbad and Marienbad did him some good, and brought the young pair the personal acquaintance of Prince Metternich, who affably promised his support and assistance in case they ever visited Vienna.

Robert's experience of the light-hearted capital, however, had taught him to take the friendly promises of its inhabitants, as well as its much-vaunted musical taste, with a grain of salt. Only a few months before, he had written to Dr. Alfred Becker: "I know Vienna. It will be hard to influence the general Viennese taste; but individual souls may perhaps be saved."

Relief of Robert and Clara Schumann

Richard Wagner

CHAPTER 21

DANGER SIGNALS

THE next two years of Schumann's life were crowded with events and ominous with shadows of the future. In January 1843, Mendelssohn founded the Leipzig Conservatory of Music, and installed Schumann as teacher of piano and composition. To this task the new professor brought the same absent-minded dreaminess and taciturnity that were to make him impossible as a conductor. Wasielewski played in a trio at one of Schumann's lessons. It proved to be a lesson in name only; for, "as a sheep before her shearers is dumb," so the master opened not his mouth—or scarcely opened it during the whole session, despite a host of matters that cried aloud for criticism.

On April 25th, the second Schumann child, Elise, saw the light, a few weeks before the completion of *The Paradise and the Peri*. On May 5th Robert had written Kossmaly: "At the moment I am engaged on a large piece of work, the largest that I have yet undertaken—it is no opera—I almost believe it is a new sort of thing for the concert hall." And on June 2nd, he begged Dr. Krüger:

Forgive the handwriting—I soon will have wholly forgotten how to write letters of the alphabet. But let me tell you too that I've written many 100,000 notes of late, and that, exactly on Ascension Day, I finished a big opus . . . an oratorio—not for the hall of prayer, but for gay people—and sometimes a voice whispered to me as I wrote, "This that you are doing is not wholly in vain."

However, as so often happened to Robert, he was mistaken in thinking that he had actually finished on Ascension Day; for

177

later, on June 19th, he wrote Verhulst: "I finished my *Paradise and the Peri* last Friday, my largest piece of work and I hope also my best."

It was poetic justice that Richard Wagner, the man who upset Schumann's cherished plan for an opera to be called *Lohengrin,* should have suffered a disappointment with Moore's poem. He informed Robert:

I confess that you have pleased me by the mere mention of your composition. Not only am I familiar with this wonderful poem, but it has already passed through my musical sense. However, I could find no form in which to set the poem, and so I wish you only luck in having discovered the right one. You are right: the concert-hall, when fitted out as you people have done in Leipzig, may well become the sole place of refuge and of musical cultivation.

Truly a remarkable utterance from an arch-egotist of Wagner's esthetic principles!

Though they both apparently tried to be fair, between these composers there was never much admiration or love lost. Presently, when Robert was seeing something of Richard the Great in Dresden, he could not conceal the fact that the vociferous maker of music-drama rubbed him the wrong way. The man, he complained,

has an enormous gift of the gab, is as full as he can stick of thoughts that threaten to suffocate him. One can't listen long to him. . . . He has a poetic and moreover a clever head; but in his musical judgments he always seeks to shoot beyond the purely musical.

After they had walked together, Schumann was vexed because the other had simply talked his head off; while Wagner took it amiss that Schumann had never once opened his puckered lips. Nevertheless the dramatist tried hard, though vainly, to sever the congenial ties that incongruously united this forward-looking Davidite to the staid Mendelssohn, and win Robert over to his own revolutionary party. In his autobiography, he called him "a profound, energetic musician" whose work appealed very much to him, and whose preternatural awkwardness in conducting the *Peri* aroused his pity. "Decided well-wishing, friendly intimacy prevailed between us."

Shortly after the score of *Tannhäuser* was published, Wagner hastened to give it to Schumann, who thereupon wrote Mendelssohn:

> Truly he can scarcely think out and set down four good measures in a row, to say nothing of beautiful measures. And now the whole score lies before us finely printed—with all its fifths and octaves— and now he'd like to revise and erase—too late!— The music is not a hair better than *Rienzi*, if anything, more turbid and forced!

But on hearing this opera performed, he changed his mind and candidly admitted to the same correspondent:

> I'll have to take back some of what I wrote you after reading the score. From the stage everything gives you a very different impression. Much of it moved me profoundly.

However, probably from association with Clara, that incurable reactionary to whom everything Wagnerian always remained anathema, even this mild degree of admiration was destined to cool. Moreover, quite apart from Clara's influence, Robert felt his own ideas of music opposed on every page of Wagner's books and scores. And opposition was something that Robert had not yet learned to take. Indeed, until almost the end of his days, he was never to learn openness of mind or patience with people who contravened or criticized his work. When he encountered criticism or contradiction, he would either fling out of the room without a word, or fly into a rage and denounce the contradictor.

He often reacted badly to adverse criticism. For instance, when a young sprig wrote him a bit of kindly meant advice about Romanticism, he received this stinging facer:

> I must object to your letter which, in view of our respective positions, is presumptuous. You, who have given no proof of ability as a critic, send to a man who has, at any rate, shown some evidence of capacity, advice fit to offer a beginner. Did you not think of that? Thirty years ago your ideas were old to me, and a decade back, I taught them to my pupils.

On December 4th, 1843, the *Peri's* première in the Gewandhaus scored a notable success. The oratorio soon became known
to the musical world, did much for Schumann's fame, and even
brought a polite note from Mendelssohn.

The year 1843 saw the completion of the *Andante and Variations* for two pianos, Op. 46. It was scored originally (in both
senses!) for two pianos, two 'cellos, and a horn. But in March,
when the music was tried out at the Härtels', difficulties of
execution and problems of balance led Robert to rescore it for
the two pianos alone. In this form, on August 19th, it had a
public debut at the hands of Clara and Mendelssohn.

In May, Schumann, now at the height of his powers, confessed
to Kossmaly: "That Bach and Jean Paul had the greatest influence over me in earlier years is a fact which you could deduce
for yourself without my saying so. *Now* I have become more independent." No sooner had he written this than he conceived
and began to press the idea of a complete edition of J. S. Bach's
works. The carrying out by the Bachgesellschaft of this grandi-
ose project, which began in 1850, a century after the Master's
death, led to the Bach renaissance that is even today still gaining momentum; and for this Schumann must have equal credit
with Mendelssohn.

Wieck, though he had never believed that Robert would
amount to much in the eyes of the world, had by now been
taught a bitter lesson. To his chagrin he learned that his ignoble
treatment of the young pair had cost him nearly all of his
friends, and much of his musical authority. So, when Robert
falsified his predictions by slowly making an important name
for himself, Father concluded that the time had come for a
right-about-face. As his eyes were always focused so intently
on the main chance, the hurt to his pride counted less than the
advantage of basking in son-in-law's reflected glory. So, in
February 1843, he made up with Clara. And in December, after
the resounding success of the *Peri* in Leipzig, and eight days
before its Dresden première, he wrote his daughter enclosing
a note which began with the common misquotation of a familiar
Latin motto:

Dear Schumann—
>   *Tempora mutantur et nos mutamur in eis.*
[Times have a habit of changing, and we, of changing within them.]

Taking Clara and the world into account, we two can no longer be estranged. Also, you are now the father of a family—why long explanations?

In artistic matters we always saw eye to eye [*sic!*]—indeed, I was your teacher—my expression of opinion was decisive for your present career. My sympathy for your talent and your true and beautiful endeavors is a thing of which I need not assure you.

With joy there awaits you in Dresden
>   Your father
>   FR. WIECK

Wieck was like the sort of statesman who will stab any friend in the back to secure an advantage, and leap upon the bandwagon only when he thinks that he is guaranteed an absolutely sure thing. Because they could never wholly trust Father, Robert, and even Clara, could not help feeling his less admirable traits to an extent which precluded the re-established relationship from ever being as spontaneous and close as it had originally been. None the less, the couple did spend Christmas at the Wiecks'.

On January 25th, 1844, they deposited the babies at brother Carl's, and set forth on that conquest of Russia which they had so often planned for the relief of the family purse. The route led through Berlin, where Mendelssohn pleased Clara with the dedication of six *Songs Without Words*.

The girl's extraordinary resistance to the hardships and fatigues of travel spills out between the lines of a letter from Tilsit to her father: "I played a lot; although after the concert last evening in Königsberg, I packed half the night, got up at five, and traveled all day."

By way of Riga, where they suffered annoying hardships, and through forests full of wolves, they reached the city then known as St. Petersburg, and Moscow. Clara was glad to be resuming her career as a virtuoso, even though handicapped by having started the trip too late in the season. In spite of this, she was cordially received, and made money.

Robert, however, suffered from ill health and impossible conditions for creative work. He was annoyed by a cloister service in Moscow where the monks sang the same composition, full of the fifths and octaves he loathed, for two hours on end. But most of all he suffered from having to play second fiddle to the more famous Clara.

He was somewhat mollified when those excellent amateur musicians, the Wielhorskys, arranged a private concert in which he could conduct the "*Spring*" Symphony, and where he and Clara were shown great kindness by the Henselts, and by the Prince and Princess of Oldenburg.[1] All during the trip the Quintet was much played and appreciated.

In May, at St. Petersburg, the Grand Duchess Hélène held long discussions with the Schumanns about the feasibility of founding a conservatory there and, as its nucleus, keeping the talented couple in Russia.[2]

They reached home May 30th, 1844; and Robert then gave up for good and all the burden of editorial duties. After a few days he wrote Verhulst: "I have wholly turned over the *New Magazine* for the present year to Lorenz, and scarcely think I shall ever again take it up.[3] I should like to live entirely for creative work. . . . Happy the man who is comfortable within his four walls, score-paper before him, and painting into it splendid compositions."

The middle of August, Robert's health failed seriously. He took advantage of a temporary improvement to finish the *Faust* music up to the final chorus; but only, as the joint diary says, "by sacrificing the last of his strength." Then, as in 1833, he went badly to pieces, in "a complete nervous exhaustion that made all work impossible." This condition was not helped by the dis-

[1] Probably they were belatedly trying to redress Robert's old grievance. See p. 170.

[2] Four years earlier, many hundred versts eastward towards the Ural Mountains, in the province of Vyatka, a baby had been born who, at the age of 23, became one of the first pupils in the newly realized dream of a St. Petersburg Conservatory. He was destined to be the chief glory of that institution. His name was Peter Iljitch Tchaikovsky.

[3] The following year the magazine passed into Brendel's hands.

appointment of having the Gewandhaus choose as its new director not himself but Gade.

In September, a trip to the Harz Mountains was so far from bringing relief that, on his return, he took to bed, and "could scarcely walk across the room without the utmost exertion." They tried a visit to Dresden; but Clara noted: "The trip was fearful. Robert thought he would never survive it."

Partly as a result of Father Wieck's stupid attempts to tear Robert "out of himself by violence," the patient grew steadily worse. As Clara described the situation,

Robert could not sleep a single night. His imagination painted him the most fearful pictures. Early in the morning I usually found him bathed in tears. He quite gave himself up.

However, the middle of October showed a temporary improvement; and, on the impulse of the moment, with the uncertain judgment of illness, they moved to Dresden for good.

November brought a farewell visit to Leipzig. Härtel gave them a party at which a Hungarian boy of fourteen performed on the violin. Clara sniffed at the lad's playing, which she found too cold. His name was Joseph Joachim. She was soon to change her mind and to become one of his closest friends.

With Mendelssohn she did some of the *Midsummer Night's Dream* music for four hands; and the composer took the scherzo so fast that she confessed she 'didn't know where she was.'

The Gewandhaus audience received her performance of the *"Emperor"* Concerto with an enthusiasm that touched her. Finally the Schumanns gave a last musicale, offering Robert's Piano Quartet and Beethoven's *"Waldstein"* Sonata. At the parting from so many old friends, their tears flowed.

Back in Dresden, Schumann was in no state for composition; but so exigent was inspiration that he simply could not let the harmful work alone. He might well have said to his art what the Roman poet Martial said to his difficult mistress:

There is no living with thee or without thee!

His physician, Dr. Helbig, reported that as soon as he fell to writing, his feet grew cold, he weakened and began to tremble.

A pitiable fear of death was shown by his terror of high places, of metal dishes and tools, and of medicines, all of which he suspected of being poisonous. As he would always discover excellent reasons for not taking the remedies, Dr. Helbig was driven to prescribing cold showers and intellectual work other than music. Robert chose, now natural history, now physics, etc. But in one or two days he was always back again at his music.

He developed still further what he had a decade before described as "virtuosity in clinging to unhappy thoughts." "Melancholy bats," he called them; and from these he was destined never again to be entirely free.

Just before leaving Leipzig, he had written to Dr. Krüger:

Perhaps you have no idea how very ill I have been with a nervous trouble that attacked me a quarter of a year ago, so that the doctor forbade me all exertion, even mental. Now I am somewhat better. Life begins to look up. Bit by bit, hope and confidence are returning. I think I had taken too large a dose of music—had of late sunk too deep in my music to Goethe's *Faust*—so that, in the end, mind and body went on strike. . . . For a while I could not stand listening to music. It cut into my nerves like knives.

This breakdown of 1844 was caused, in the first place, by Schumann's bad nervous inheritance; in the second, by the intensive toil and excitement of the year of song, the year of symphony, and the year of chamber music. All this was aggravated by money troubles, the new experiences of fatherhood, the Conservatory job, for which he was wretchedly fitted, and the strenuous Russian adventure. Also, the *New Magazine* had, for a decade, been a steady drag upon his strength. Then too, he never had much idea how to keep himself in physical condition. After using himself up all day in the most exhausting kind of creative work, he would sit in a café, drinking beer or wine. Beyond a little walking, a little dancing, a very little skating, and a few student attempts at fencing, which disgusted him, he seems to have taken no exercise. If only he had worked his body half as regularly as he worked his mind, he might have kept his health and reason much longer. This bad regimen came on top of the strain of a protracted and trying engagement, and of being newly and passionately married. In these conditions, if Schumann had not broken down he would have been a superman.

Robert Schumann's youth was over, and the forces which were to compass his overthrow were already in motion. Sometimes even he himself seemed to have an inkling of this fact. There was to be much in these future, less happy, years of the blissful, triumphant and creative. But from here on the dark moments were to be on the increase.

CHAPTER 22

KETTLEDRUMS AND TRUMPETS

IN 1845, Dresden was an aristocratic Court city of 80,000; while Leipzig, half its size, was both the center of the German book-trade and the musical capital of Europe. The former was known as "a small big town," the latter, as "a big small town." Painting was Dresden's esthetic specialty; although its exercise was sadly handicapped by the arbitrary authority of the Court crowd, who imagined that they had inherited the divine right to lay down the law about all artistic activities. On the other hand, there was almost no music in Dresden except opera; and even this hybrid form of art was constantly prejudiced by the interference of the Court know-it-alls.

To make such a place congenial to himself after having enjoyed the advantages of Leipzig, an absolute musician would need the physical vitality, the despotic, commanding will, the infectious charm, and rhinoceros hide of George Frederick Handel, the man who lifted English music by the sheer force of a tremendous personality.

Robert, alas! had few or none of these qualifications. Perhaps when he changed cities he was moved by some passing pique against Leipzig, for all its love of books and music. He may have been under the spell of such an illusion as dupes the bicyclist, who always imagines that the other side of the road would make smoother going. Or, in his secret heart, could he have hoped that Clara's reactionary influence on his writing would be less potent, once she was removed from the neighborhood of Mendelssohn, and of all the other too-conservative musicians among whom she had grown up? He knew that while the music which he had composed since marriage was good, somehow he missed in it the full originality of his bachelor days.

Even so, one would think that if Robert's judgment had not been upset by illness, he would never have left the musical center of the continent, hoping to find more congenial conditions for composition amid the stuffy and snobbish intrigues of a crassly unmusical provincial Court town.

On September 25th, 1845, he wrote Mendelssohn, hitting upon a neat hirsute figure of speech for the local unprogressive spirit:

They want to get up subscription concerts; but I doubt if that can be managed. Nothing can be done with the orchestra; also nothing without it. Here the powdered pigtail still hangs mightily down people's backs.

After these concerts had been organized, with Hiller and Schumann as conductors, the latter sent another report to the same address. It was compounded of triumph and homesickness:

One Beethoven symphony a year, and at that with decorative curlicues by the orchestra *ad libitum*—this is now a thing of the past Will the Leipzigers sometimes lend us their support? We count on it very much; we hope for it tremendously.

As a forward-looking modern composer, Schumann could have taken but meager satisfaction in directing these moss-backed Dresdeners who, as he afterward complained with rueful mirth, bit into every new composition "as if it were a sour apple." The concerts were doomed to a miserable existence and a mercifully quick end.

Robert's "nerve-weakness" lasted through much of 1845. When the magnitude of his *Faust* sketches and of his opera plans filled him with the impotent fury of discouragement, Clara tactfully proposed that they should each solve a daily problem in counterpoint. She realized that her own attempts were worthless; but Robert's gave him much the same distraction and amusement that a crossword puzzle now gives John Doe. On his better days, he applied himself with fiery joy to these contrapuntal studies. Also with unchanging modesty he cried: "In my opinion, Bach is simply not to be equaled. He is incommensurable (*inkommensurabel*)."

And here is the published result of these attempts to gain lightness of touch in handling the difficult old polyphonic forms:

> Opp. 56 and 58. *Studies and Sketches for the Pedalier.*[1]
> Op. 60. *Six Fugues on the Name of Bach, for Organ.*
> Op. 72. *Four Fugues for Piano.*

To Schumann at the height of his career, such exercises were mere play. While diverting him, they used up so little of his true creative power that, with the approach of warm weather, he was able to throw himself into making two of his chief masterpieces: the Piano Concerto and the C Major Symphony.

Meanwhile Father Wieck, that other newcomer to Dresden, who had turned speciously genial for (business) purposes of reconciliation, reverted to type. He showed his real nature to such a repellent extent that the new cordiality rapidly lost its sparkle. A second estrangement from Robert, and in part from Clara, set in, this time to stay.

The low musical standards of Dresden seem to have infected Wieck's formerly shrewd judgment. With a loud flourish of trumpets he brought out his daughter Marie and other pupils, long before they were prepared. When the Schumanns remonstrated, he became violent and abused them with a peasant's rough-and-ready vocabulary.

In 1846, when all three of them were in Vienna, Robert and Clara thought to do him a kindness by having a favorite pupil of his appear at one of their private evening concerts "before all the leading musical authorities." But Wieck rudely declined the invitation. Pontifically he declared that he knew of but two musical authorities in the world: Nicolai and Meyerbeer. The former had already come out in favor of his pupil; the latter would soon do so.

This was scarcely calculated to please Robert; for if there was a musician on earth that he despised and hated, it was this same Meyerbeer, whose later operas he had roundly attacked in the

---

[1] This was a pedal-piano, for whose popularity Schumann entertained high but unfounded hopes.

New Magazine. The friction grew until, in 1848, Wieck forbade Marie and his pupil Minna Schulz to attend the rehearsals of the choral union which Robert conducted.[2]

By May 1845, Robert's contrapuntal diversions had refreshed him to the point where he was again ready for genuine creative work. In 1841 he had written a piano piece which he called *Fantasie,* and tried to sell. But the publishers were not interested, and it always came home to roost. That series of rejections turned out to be one of the most fortunate in the whole history of the arts. For, one fine May morning, Robert began to revise the piece, and made it so much better that he took fire, added a slow movement and a finale of equal value, and a concerto had come into being—a new kind of Romantic concerto that tended to reduce vulgar exhibitionism to a minimum, and was somewhat more like a symphony with piano obligato than like the tinsel tribe of show pieces by Kalkbrenner, Thalberg, Henselt and Co. These now appeared to Clara as flashy things "with passages tedious, patchy, and unnecessarily difficult." On New Year's Day, 1846, at the Gewandhaus, she played the première of the A Minor Piano Concerto. And soon it was on its triumphant way to become one of the best-beloved pieces in the entire concerto repertory. Again, as on the path to Connewitz: "the stone which the builders rejected" became "the headstone of the corner."

Four years earlier, publisher Simrock had committed a somewhat less happy rejection. When Schumann had offered him the unimportant duets, Opus 43, and a group of ballads, he had taken the former and declined the latter. But one of the ballads, *The Two Grenadiers,* Op. 49, No. 1, afterward turned out to be an inexhaustible gold-mine. And Simrock must have been as rueful as those American publishers who many years later were to reject the manuscripts of *David Harum* and *The Story of San*

[2] Marie, by the way, must have inherited her father's crassness and love of self-advertisement. In her autobiography, *Aus dem Kreise Wieck-Schumann* (Dresden, Pierson, 1912), she stated that Robert never was "as good a pianist as Wieck's daughters Clara and Marie," and actually added this modest self-estimate: "Marie, who still lives among us, is a pianist of the first rank." Clara, however, was of a different opinion. She found Marie's playing cold and machine-like.

Michele. He must have felt like Emerson, to whom the "hypocritic Days" offered "diadems and fagots . . . bread, kingdoms, stars and sky." Whereupon the poet confessed:

> I . . . hastily
> Took a few herbs and apples, and the Day
> Turned and departed silent. I, too late,
> Under her solemn fillet saw the scorn.

Clara exulted over the new concerto: "I am very glad about it; for I have always wanted a large bravura [*sic!*] piece by him. . . . When I think of playing it with orchestra, I am as happy as a king."

At high summer, Schumann had reached the full tide of creativeness, and wrote Mendelssohn:

> For the last few days it has mightily kettledrummed and trumpeted within me (Trombe in C). I don't know what will come of it.

What, indeed, should come of all this interior commotion but the C Major Symphony? It was sketched between December 12th and 28th, when the composer was still fighting his "nerve-weakness." He declared:

> I sketched it while I was still in bad shape physically. Indeed, I can perhaps say that it was the resisting power of the spirit that here had a visible influence, and through which I sought to help my bodily condition. The first movement is full of this fight, and its character is very capricious and refractory.

It was called the Second Symphony, though it was really the Third. After its performance at Hamburg, he wrote Otten, the director there:

> I wrote the symphony in December 1845, when I was still ailing; and it seems to me that this must be evident in the music. Only when I reached the last movement did I again begin to feel like myself. Not until the end of the work was I actually a lot better. But, apart from that, it is a souvenir of a dark period.

That autumn his health had indeed been through a difficult time. In September he wrote Mendelssohn:

All writing is a severe strain on me. . . . I itch and twitch every day in a hundred different places. A mysterious complaint—whenever the doctor tries to put his finger on the thing, it seems to take wings. But better times will come again; and to look at my wife and children is joy enough.

In February 1846 his ears developed a continual ringing and roaring, so that he had to interrupt the instrumentation of the C Major Symphony and go for a rest to nearby Maxen. But this was an unfortunate choice, and Clara should have known better than to sanction it. For they settled down within full and ominous view of an insane asylum, which drove Robert frantic. Finally they fled to the seacoast at Norderney. There he recovered and finished the symphony.

In his *Jugendleben*, Ludwig Meinardus described the interior of the Schumann home at this period. There was just room enough in the study for a stove, a few chairs and bookcases, and a grand piano in the middle.

The furnishing of the reception room showed simple but choice taste. True, one could no more discover a trace of heavy silken window-curtains and fashionable gloom than of soft carpets covering the whole floor, as in Mendelssohn's apartment. [Slight though it was, Robert's experience as a 'cellist had probably given him a horror of such things.] But to make up for this, valuable prints adorned the walls.

From which we may gather that, in his ideas of interior decoration as well as of music, Schumann was more modern and forward-looking than Mendelssohn.

On February 23rd, 1846, Robert began a *Small Book of Memories of Our Children*. Here are the thumbnail vignettes of the two oldest, who were not yet five and three:

Marie: Cheerful, of a vivacious disposition, not too willful, easily led by kindness; pliant, with a warm heart and very affectionate. Fine memory for the tiniest happenings of her little life. Easily teased. Apparently likes music; gives no signs of any unusual gift. Has started knitting; seems quite to lean towards the domestic and practical. Has a lot to say—sometimes continuously.

Elise: In many ways just the opposite of Marie: obstinate, highly disobedient, frequently has to be switched, a hearty eater and drinker. Is capable of showing extremely high spirits; has a better sense of humor than Marie, is also pensive, as if meditating on things. [Here we have Florestan and Eusebius cropping out in the temperament of the next generation, just as Marie took after her mother in being easily teased.] A too indulgent nurse spoiled her in infancy. If thwarted, struggles with hands and feet.

This is the sort of lovingly minute and sympathetic observation which we would naturally expect from the composer of the *Scenes from Childhood* and the *Album for the Young*. Playing with his little ones must have been a prime means of relaxation and restoration for Schumann, especially when grappling simultaneously with great works and illness.

On November 5th, 1846, when Mendelssohn conducted the première of the C Major Symphony in the Gewandhaus, there was some small friction between the two men. It began at rehearsal, when Schumann ventured certain criticisms of the orchestra, which were taken in somewhat bad part. The performance went well; but Schumann was disgruntled because the symphony was placed at the end of a long and taxing program, and because Mendelssohn was so doubly thoughtless as to repeat, for an encore, the whole of the long *William Tell Overture*, so that people were too tired to appreciate Robert's music properly. Despite these handicaps, however, the work was received with gratifying approval.

Quite uninfluenced by Schumann, the *Leipziger Tageblatt* upbraided Mendelssohn for his thoughtlessness, which made for more tension. This grew when, "after various excellent revisions," the symphony was repeated at the concert of November 16th. Mendelssohn's state of irritation did not help his conducting; and the poor performance left on the one hand a sense of guilt, and on the other, a sense of injury which took some little time to evaporate.

Clara was becoming a better musician. On her programs bravura was finally being pushed into second place in favor of Bach and Beethoven. She was now one of the foremost pianists of the age. Her musical development, however, was far from complete. As late as 1849, while her husband was putting the finishing touches to the romances and ballads, Opp. 67, 75, and 141—works considerably below his average in quality—she went into such ecstasies of *Schwärmerei* over them as would have befitted the advent of the *Scenes from Childhood*, the String Quartets, the Piano Concerto, or the Second Symphony:

Ah, what a lucky man he is! What a blissful feeling it must be to have such an inexhaustible imagination transport one forever into a higher sphere of living!

In spite of the zealous pains which her husband took with her musical education, Clara's taste and understanding still left much to be desired; though it is only fair to remember that Robert was notably poor as a teacher. And judgments become so blurred when one adores the creator of a work as Clara adored Robert. Besides, if she had been more of an artist, her feet might not have been so firmly on the ground, and Robert's physical well-being might have suffered.

In 1847 he assumed the leadership of a men's singing society, the *Liedertafel;* and for this he wrote the choruses Opp. 62 and 65. Leading it pleased him. It brought back the old illusion that he could conduct—a talent which he thought he had lost through what he described as "nervous hypochondria." He now felt quite at home with the baton.

This *Liedertafel* pleasure, though, was fleeting. The men had "too little real musical ambition." And finally he confessed: "When one has made music all day for himself, one cannot savor these eternal six-four chords of the men's chorus style."

In April 1847 the *Faust* music was completed; though a new version of the final chorus supervened in July. On Clara's birthday, September 13th, he surprised her with the finished manuscript of his First Trio, in D minor, Op. 63. It was tried that same evening; and Clara wrote:

It sounds as if composed by one from whom there is still much to expect, it is so strong and full of youthful energy and at the same time worked out so masterfully. . . . The first movement is to my mind one of the loveliest that I know.

And the following year, when Robert sent it to Reinecke in published form, he seemed of Clara's opinion: "It will please me if you like parts of it. I almost believe that of the first movement." Neither of the Schumanns seemed to realize that the main blemish of the work is the too thickly scored piano part of this same first movement.

In July, Zwickau got up a charming festival in honor of its greatest son. For the occasion, Robert wrote a choral piece with small orchestra, *Song to be Sung at Parting*. He directed the C Major Symphony. Clara played the Piano Concerto and some solo pieces. The pair were given a torchlight procession and serenade, for which Herr Music Director Klitzsch had composed a *Hymn of Homage*, to be sung by a chorus with orchestral accompaniment. The text of this was presented to Robert by his proudly beaming old teacher, Herr Kuntsch.

On Sunday afternoon, when the Schumanns went a little way out of town to a concert at the Burgkeller, they enjoyed much the same experience that Goethe's Faust had during his Easter walk with his *famulus* Wagner beyond the city gate. They were greeted with a triple flourish of trumpets, and the acclamations of thousands. Clara was not too well pleased when old flames of Robert's put in an appearance, together with the daughters of old flames. But, on the whole, the occasion was happy and delightful, and filled her with a proud new sense of her husband's rising importance.

This outing was a useful diversion; for inspiration still pressed Robert hard, and the Second Trio, in F major, Op. 80, was written between August and October. Clara "loved it passionately, and wanted to play it again and again." Robert wrote to Reinecke: "It is of a quite different character from the one in D [Minor]—and has a friendlier and more immediate effect." Many of us today, however, cannot enter very fully into Clara's raptures, and prefer the First and the Third.

Robert's growing taciturnity and seriousness by no means affected his sense of humor. On December 22nd, 1847, he informed Whistling, the publisher who was often dilatory in correspondence:

You'll never get into heaven! When St. Peter makes to open the gate, you will still contrive all sorts of excuses for not going in; e.g. that you forgot to bring along your handkerchief from the Earth. In short, you will start back—and later it will be too late.

And Reinecke [3] tells of another case in point, a few years after. To help Schumann out, he coached a tenor from the ms. of *The Pilgrimage of the Rose*. Afterwards, at the railroad station, he sang him the parts with which Schumann was not satisfied. When the singer expressed surprise that Reinecke already knew the music, Schumann smiled and murmured: "Oh, *he* already has my stuff by heart before I have composed it." Which suggests that Brahms inherited from his discoverer certain traits not only of musicianship, but of humor as well. He was Schumannian, for example, when he told an interpreter: "You made that piece sound better than I composed it."

With Clara, however, laughter was less and less at home. As she grew older, better-looking, more reactionary, more jealous, and deeper in love with her husband, she lost every vestige of that inestimable gift which she had in her youth. As more and more love flew in at the window, more and more humor stole out at the door.

But love was not alone responsible. As they grow famous, flattered, and sought after, it is natural for interpretive artists to take themselves and the world with a crescendo of seriousness. The hard conditions of Clara's life may also have tended to suppress mirth. It had been her lot to fight her adored father-teacher, tackle the world alone, defiantly marry a somewhat sickly and almost unknown composer (who would not write potboilers even when she begged him), bear the absent-minded genius children on all possible occasions, and get ahead with her career as a virtuoso—although she could not practice much for fear of disturbing him. Such great keepers of the flame deserve a deal of sympathetic consideration.

Clara's mixed feelings toward her father may also have tended to kill laughter in her. While half of her heart was still fixed on

[3] In his reminiscences, *Und manche Schatten steigen auf.*

him, the other half hated his cruelty. And, as Wieck had a pronounced sense of humor, she may have unconsciously come to identify this faculty with the side of him which she loathed. The deep congeniality which she later felt for Joachim may have flourished all the more luxuriantly because the great violinist had little humor, and was as jealous as Clara herself.

It is certain that she grew to relish Robert's risible side less and less. Reinecke tells of two instances when she was far from amused:

At breakfast [Schumann] told me, with a highly roguish expression, that his Clara had achieved phenomenal success in teaching the little children the theory of music. They were sitting over their morning milk at a tiny table by themselves. Then he began to put them through a serious examination. But when they soon came to the end of their wisdom, and their teacher-mother grew angry, he almost died laughing.

In the second instance the composer asked Reinecke to play the piano part in the Quintet, while Clara turned pages. At the end she said, in a somewhat irritated tone: "Robert, tell me why you allow Reinecke to take the tempo so fast, while you always insist on my playing slowly?" Schumann winked at his friend. "You see, Clara, a man generally plays the fast parts fast; but a woman all too often plays the slow parts fast." Poor Clara did not relish the joke; and her eyes filled with tears of mortification.

Reinecke, it is true, tells of one occasion when Clara actually did laugh; but it was at a different sort of humor. Once at supper Schumann grew so merry that he insisted on dancing, cleared out the tables and chairs, and waltzed "with the most unbridled abandon." Then he insisted on Reinecke's dancing, while he spelled him at the piano. The young fellow protested that he did not know how, but was overruled. Robert promised to play slowly. The beginner made a few "grave and solemn steps." Then the music struck into a vigorous *accelerando*, the pair whirled madly, until Reinecke grew so dizzy that he steered wrong, and they collapsed over a sofa. "Clara became almost convulsed with laughter."

The longer she lived, the more difficult the great woman became. She had a chip on her shoulder that was a chip of the old block, and her fancy was always on the alert for slights. When the (then) well-known composer Félicien David visited Dresden to conduct his own works, Clara requested his autograph for her album. David, with no idea of either her meaning or her fame, thought she wanted a testimonial, and sent her one couched in fairly restrained terms. Whereupon Clara, who could see nothing funny in the situation, blazed away:

> Madame Schumann, n'ayant pas demandée [*sic*] une attestation pour son album, remercie Monsieur David pour sa bonne volonté et prie du reste d'accepter l'assurance de sa parfaite estime.

Clara had her faults. But with them all, what a woman she was, and what a marvelous wife for Robert! No wonder that he wrote of her to Mendelssohn (on October 22nd, 1845): "She deserves all possible love and encouragement as an ever industrious, ever aspiring artist; and then as a woman—altogether she is a gift from above."

CHAPTER 23

BUT HE LOVES ME

T HE last of November 1846 saw the Schumanns setting out on a concert tour, with Vienna the first stop. Their hopes were high. There, nine years before, as a young girl, Clara had won fame, ducats, and a title. And though, the year after that, Robert's visit had not enjoyed much success, everything ought to be quite different, now that he was a well-known composer. Hadn't the *"Spring"* Symphony been heartily applauded in the Gewandhaus; and hadn't the *Peri* begun to take on in the most gratifying way?

Alas! it was always dangerous to reckon on that delightful, superficial, charming, sensuous, and most fickle of towns. In all these years it had not changed a bit. If Clara had fed it the same sort of bravura trash as on her first visit, Vienna might (or might not) have received her with its easy effusiveness. But here she came featuring the serious, "heavy" music of that taciturn and rather solemn husband of hers—'a fellow nobody ever heard of.' Besides, Meyerbeer and Flotow had come to town. Now *there* were geniuses who wrote the sort of music that the folk of Vienna could comprehend and enjoy.

Though it offered but little music by Robert, Clara's first concert made only a few gulden. The next brought the Quintet, and the *Variations,* Op. 46, in which Anton Rubinstein, aged sixteen, played one of the pianos. In spite of that, expenses just balanced receipts. The third, which gave the B Flat Symphony and the Piano Concerto, with Robert swinging the baton, cost one hundred gulden in cash—a new and shocking experience for the leading woman pianist. The favor of the public was in exact

198

ratio to its dwindling numbers. Of this concert Hanslick, the famous critic, noted:

> The size of the audience was very moderate, the applause cool, and obviously meant for Clara alone. The piano concerto and the symphony did not take well.

Otherwise, those heathen the critics furiously raged together. Father Wieck, intent on bringing out his pupil, Minna Schulz, sniped at his children in his old way, from ambush. True to her suspicious nature, Clara thought everybody in Vienna her enemy, and would have liked to renounce professional music for ever. Robert sought to comfort her with: "All this will be very different in ten years."

The fourth concert was packed to suffocation. It paid for their trip, and 300 thalers over. The public was wild with enthusiasm. But—this was all because their dear old friend Jenny Lind took a hand. She had arrived in time for the third concert, had sat there seething with indignation against the Viennese, and had insisted on sharing their final appearance. The Schumanns' success was embittered through the knowledge that a song by the "Swedish Nightingale" could madden a town which had turned an icy shoulder upon the best that they had to offer.

The bitterness lasted. In 1848 Robert wrote Nottebohm.

> As you yourself say, Vienna and Berlin are no abodes for the musician. . . . [Vienna] always was an ominous place for the good musician, if he was not at the same time something of a charlatan or a millionaire.

And a few months before the final catastrophe of his life, he was to write the poet Hebbel his valedictory to Vienna:

> There, so far as I know, there is no real musical spirit. [Which was going, of course, too far!] Everything drains away into parties and cliques; and one feels the lack of a master who would gather excellence about himself. Then too, in that place one must often hear bad music, and that is the worst.

Johannes Brahms, a lad of thirteen at the time of the Schumanns' visit, was destined to supply Vienna with such a master.

But his complaints about conditions there turned out to be
strikingly like those of Schumann a generation, of Beethoven a
half-century, and of Mozart a century, before. In the face of all
this, however, Brahms could have echoed what Schumann
wrote to Van Bruyck in 1852:

> But in spite of everything, one is always drawn back there, as if
> the spirits of the departed great masters were yet visible, and as if it
> were the real musical homeland of Germany.

Besides this feeling, the Danube offered them other compen-
sations in the devoted services of their true friend Fischhof, and
association with the poets Grillparzer and Eichendorff. Of
course, there had been the kind of embarrassing and farcical
episode which was always happening to the Schumanns. Clara
had, by invitation, been playing at Court, and at the conclusion
of her concert, a princely ignoramus had asked her: "Is your
husband also musical?"

On the way home, the cordial and intelligent enthusiasm of
Prague almost made up for the stupid indifference of Vienna.
At the first concert, the Quintet was received with heartening
applause. The second, on February 2nd, 1847, stirred up a
furore. Clara wrote:

> Robert's concerto gave extraordinary pleasure. I succeeded very
> well in it. The orchestra accompanied, and Robert conducted, *con
> amore*. And he was called out. This amused me a lot. For, when the
> public would not stop clamoring, I almost had to shove him out
> upon the stage, and the way he comported himself there was just
> too funny. [This was the sort of comedy which Clara was capable of
> appreciating.]

Young Smetana brought one of his own compositions for
criticism; but Schumann did not like the thing. He felt that it
smacked too strongly of Berlioz.

The couple reached home on February 4th. In six days they
were again on the concert path. The hard-shelled old Singakademie in Berlin had, as an enormous concession to modernity, decided to take the *Peri* into its repertoire.

On the 20th, there was a performance in the presence of the

King. It was terrible. The orchestra consisted of amateurs. The chorus did not know what to make of such an unconventional thing as a secular oratorio. And the tenor and soprano soloists, who had treacherously backed out at the last minute, had been replaced by dilettantes hardly capable of hitting their notes. In Part III, the first three soloists got entirely out; so that the pianist had to play their parts until they could find their way back into the fold. The entire affair was reminiscent of some of Beethoven's lamentable first performances in Vienna. The disgusted Robert gave up any idea which he had had of settling in Berlin.

During these months, Schumann was eagerly searching for an opera libretto. He considered and rejected the most varied material:

> Till Eulenspiegel
> Calderón's El galan
> The Nibelungenlied
> The Contest of Song in the Wartburg
> Abélard and Héloïse
> The False Prophet (from Lalla Rookh)
> Chateaubriand's Atala
> Byron's Corsair, and Sardanapalus
> Maria Stuart
> Sakuntala
> The Smith of Gretna Green

Finally he settled on the (alas!) undramatic story of *Genoveva*, and wrote its author, Hebbel, for permission to set it, modestly introducing himself with the words, "I am a musician."

The ordinary opera-text simply goes against my grain. I do not know how to find music for such tirades, and do not like them.

Hebbel visited him; and Schumann wrote of what a great honor had befallen him in entertaining "the greatest genius of our day." But the negotiations came to nothing; and the composer then collaborated with the poet Reinick in putting together a text based on the books of Hebbel and Tieck. "His undramatic eye," wrote Dahms, "overlooked the weaknesses of action and of motivation." To his taste, the libretto was a gem.

Richard Wagner realized Robert's danger and sought to counsel him; but the advice went unheeded. Afterwards Wagner once related:

No objection of mine could induce Schumann to discard the unlucky, foolish third act of his version. He grew angry and thought that, by my dissuasion, I was trying to ruin his greatest effects.

Thereupon Robert, in Clara's best style, called Wagner's music "paltry, downright amateurish, formless, and repellent."[1]

Though Schumann's view of Wagner was one of his few glaring failures as a critic, such a misjudgment need surprise nobody. It is unfair to expect great creators to be judicious critics. Not everybody can be everything. Mendelssohn was cool to Schumann's music. Tchaikovsky, Wolf, and Wagner were deaf to the merits of Brahms; and Brahms, to those of Tchaikovsky and Bruckner.

A creative artist is a person intensely concentrated upon his own particular—and necessarily limited—point of view. Why expect him to possess an unbiased, well-balanced, and catholic judgment? That Schumann had this for the work of all the great composers except Wagner makes him well-nigh unique among the world's best music-makers. It had been developed by his years with the *New Magazine*.

While Schumann idolized Mendelssohn and all his works, the brilliant Berliner had little interest to spare for Schumann or his music. And the C Major Symphony—Robert's greatest—he positively disliked. It is pathetic to find Robert wooing him, on November 18th, 1845, with this wistful request and happy thought:

After all, couldn't we write to each other from time to time, even without any adequate reason for doing so? If our friendship were wine, this would already be a good vintage.

And he reminded him that they had first met one another a decade before.

[1] Towards the end of his life he modified this harsh judgment. May 8th, 1853, he wrote Van Bruyck: "If you heard many passages from his [Wagner's] operas on the stage, you would certainly not be able to defend yourself against a deep excitement."

But no! To write "without adequate reason" was a thing which Mendelssohn never did. As Litzmann observed: "He who gives to so many can spare but little for any one person." He was always correct in his public attitude towards Robert's music, and always polite and kindly in rendering the pair personal services. Though he was much too swift and imaginative in taking offense, there was never any truth in the venomous reports of the Schumannites that Mendelssohn was professionally jealous.[2] For the idol of society and of the conservative musical world felt himself too immeasurably superior to be jealous of anyone so awkward as, in his irritation, he considered Robert. (How shocked and angry he would have been if, suddenly endowed with clairvoyance, he could have foreseen their relative standing a century thence!)

Like the hero of Browning's poem, *Time's Revenges*, Mendelssohn could have said of Schumann:

> I like him, but he loves me.

The one liked the other with his cool head. The other loved the one with his warm heart.

Mendelssohn was an extrovert with an immense social gift. Schumann was an intravert with no social gift whatsoever. Virtually the only things the two had in common were a love of music, and that hatred of contradiction or of any other opposition which they had acquired in their spoiled youth.

However, Mendelssohn must have had a high regard for Schumann's artistic integrity. And, in his Olympian indifference to the other's music, he made one exception. Once when Joachim came for a lesson, Mendelssohn announced: "No work today. There's a fine concert that we simply must not miss." And they went to a performance of *The Paradise and the Peri*.

It was a sad pity that relations between the two composers could not have remained friendly up to the last. But these were

[2] But, after Mendelssohn's death, his family was very probably jealous of Schumann's growing, and relatively larger, fame. That may have been the reason why, in their biographical books, they so unjustly suppressed all correspondence between the two, and even went so far as to cut out every mention of Schumann's name.

the years when central European music was convulsed by rabid partisanship. The Mendelssohnians and the Schumannites, disregarding Wagner's threat against the pre-eminence of their respective heroes, sought to pluck each other bald. They were almost as hostile as were, a generation later, the Brahmins and the Wagner-Brucknerites.

The Schumannites began hostilities with a vigorous attack on Mendelssohn's music, into which the *New Magazine* was also drawn. Now Mendelssohn, as we have seen, hated and despised all writing about music, especially that by Schumann. He assumed that his friend was behind this attack, although Robert had had nothing whatever to do with it. Considering the latter's worship of Mendelssohn and his music, that would be beyond belief. The irritation of the darling of fortune may be deduced from the offensive tone of toplofty patronage at the end of the following letter to Carl Klingemann:

Leipzig, 31 Jan., 1847.

I shall not be able to give you a letter to Madame Schumann: Her husband has been behaving very equivocally (or more than equivocally) to me, and has worked up an ugly business for me here [Leipzig] about which I shall not waste a word; but which has most damnably cooled down my former keenness to help him along and be obliging to him. More by word of mouth, if you think it worth the trouble.

When that interview took place, it is a pity that there was no one behind the arras to overhear and record those words of mouth!

While the trouble between the two composers was at its height it came to a sudden and tragic conclusion. On November 4th, 1847, Mendelssohn died of nervous apoplexy. This was a severe blow to Robert; but he was able to find a little comfort in composing on the spot the touching piano piece, *Erinnerung*, which afterwards found its way into the *Album for the Young*. In addition to his personal grief, he suffered from a feverish and crazy fear of succumbing to the same disease. He was like so many of us who, if we read a medical book, immediately feel all the symptoms there described.

Here are some of his notes about the trip to the funeral in Leipzig:

To Mendelssohn's house—his children below playing with dolls—the noble dead—the forehead—the mouth—the smile about it—he looked like a glorious warrior—like a conqueror—some twenty years older than in life—two highly swollen veins on his head—the laurel wreaths and palms.

Sunday the 7th, mild day, like Spring—overflowing memories of Mendelssohn—R. Franz from Halle—the decorated coffin—his friends, all—Moscheles, Gade and I on the right, Hauptmann, David and Rietz on the left of the coffin, besides Joachim and many others behind—procession too long to see all of it—beautiful funeral service, the E minor March from the 5th Book of the *Songs without Words* played on the way—in the church the choir—chorale from *St. Paul* (in F minor) *Wir preisen selig*— Closing chorus in C minor from the *Passion Music* of S. Bach.

With Gade plucked laurel-leaves from the coffin— Evening, the old acquaintances.

Yes, it was a bitter blow. Yet we cannot follow Mr. Burk in saying that Schumann had lost his "dearest friend." For such words imply a mutual feeling, and do not fit Mendelssohn's cool liking for Schumann, mingled as it was with pity, patronizing condescension, and a trace of contempt for his silence, his awkwardness, and his scribbling.

Back in Dresden life jogged on again as usual. Robert conducted the Singakademie, in his dreamy, listless, and inefficient style. And he never noticed that Clara, at the piano, was the real conductor, marking the entrances more sharply with her head than he with the baton.

That was but one of the many ways in which she became an intermediary between her man and the world. Whenever possible, she spared him contact with the practical side of life. This was good for the rehearsals, but bad for Robert, because it hastened the paralysis of his will to live in the world. Progressively he took less interest in his fellow-creatures, musical or unmusical, and grew more sensitive, irritable, and silent. His unfitness as teacher and conductor grew.

In his own broad, sympathetic, and constructive attitude toward young composers, Schumann was the complete antithesis of Mendelssohn and of those Dresden musicians who bit into new music as into a sour apple. Witness his charming advice to the somewhat reminiscent young Carl Reinecke, on January 22nd, 1846:

The fact that you cannot yet yield a product *entirely your own*, that memories of your models often come through, must not disconcert you. In such young years as yours, all creation is more or less reproduction. And the ore must pass through many a washing before it becomes pure metal.

Which—considering the purity of Schumann's own metal, from the *Papillons,* Op. 2, on—was surely great-hearted counsel.

But Schumann might well have taken a little more to heart the first half of another bit of advice which, on April 9th, 1848, after words of genial encouragement, he gave Emil Büchner:

. . . But here and there one also notices the piano-*player* too much. Him you, and every composer, must wholly cast into the fire if you would attain more than temporary effect and importance. Nothing but what comes from the heart, nothing but what is created and sung out of one's innermost being, has stability and triumphs over time.

To another embryo music-maker he wrote:

Be sure to get into the way of *imagining* your music in your own mind without recourse to the piano. That is the only way in which you will ever find free expression for the fountainhead of your emotions. One cannot write much about this; but the great thing is that the composer should *keep open the ear of his mind.*

In the midst of his orgy of chamber music, on August 4th, 1842, he wrote to Johann Herzog:

Also *read* much music. This, more than anything else, sharpens the inner ear. Do not play any piece before you have heard it accurately *inside your head* . . .

But do not do too much at one time, and always finish everything you have begun . . . even though you may not be quite satisfied with it.

On September 16th, 1848, he advised Ludwig Meinardus to:

keep turning and twisting the melodic principal themes in your head until you can say to yourself: "Now it's all right." One does not succeed every day in catching the right thing as it were in the flight of an instant—and the sketch-books of great artists, such as Beethoven's, bear witness how long, how painstakingly they polished and worked away at a small melody.

CHAPTER 24

ALARUMS AND EXCURSIONS

DURING the five Dresden years no fewer than four more children were added to the Schumann family: Julie, March 11th, 1845, Emil, February 8th, 1846, Ludwig, January 20th, 1848, and Ferdinand, July 16th, 1849. Three of these lived. Only Emil, born a scant eleven months after little Julie, died in infancy.

But Clara's resilience was extraordinary. Only two months after Ludwig's birth she was performing Bach in public. On April 6th, at the last Gewandhaus concert of the season, she had a brilliant success with her husband's concerto. And the following evening, in a party at publisher Härtel's, the dauntless and masterful woman held up her end of the D Minor Trio (with fiddlers David and Grabau trying—probably in vain—to hold up their own). Almost on the day of Ludwig's advent, Clara had the additional anguish of seeing Robert break down under the strain of working on the ill-starred *Genoveva*, an undertaking that was to bring so much further unhappiness.

In the autumn of 1848 Schumann wrote to his friend Verhulst:

I completed my *Genoveva* last August and, coming in sight of the end, I felt joyfully convinced that much of it had been successfully accomplished. Now I want to see and hear it; but owing to the tempestuous look of the political world, I have as yet done nothing about it.

From January 10th to 23rd, 1848, he orchestrated the first act. Then his nerves gave out. After a rest of a month, the creative fever recurred and he attacked it again. And so on, in alterna-

208

The Mature Schumann

Robert and Clara Schumann
Lithograph by Höfelich

tions of furious toil and painful prostration, until on the 4th of August it was finished. Here were exemplified the words of Hugo Wolf, who was to share Schumann's terrible fate, about the slow, agonizing suicide of the creative artist. This suicide had now been going on for a long time; and in the drawing which Höfelich made of the couple as early as 1847, it is noticeable that Robert already looks somewhat abnormal.

Glancing at his last years from 1845 on, one is lost in amazed admiration at the spiritual energy and the heroic will that triumphed over a weak body equipped with ragged nerves, and kept him true to the destiny of singing himself to death. Like Kundry in *Parsifal,* or like a conscientious physician who has fewer patients the more he cures, Robert was obliged to strive against his own salvation by creating the music that was killing him. In his stilted professional language, Dr. Richarz, Schumann's last physician, declared that his last fatal illness

was not a primary, specific insanity. It consisted more of a slow but ceaseless degeneration of the organization and powers of the entire nervous system, of which the psychic alienation was only a partial phenomenon. Apart from a germ of sickness in his original organization, such as indeed everyone carries within himself, this illness, as always, was caused by overexertion which brought about a wasting and disappearance of the substance of the psychically functioning central portion of the nervous system. This wasting progressed faster than the pace of recovery. An unmeasured spiritual and chiefly artistic productiveness must be considered as the chief source of this fearful disease which defied all attempts at cure.

In view of this diagnosis, Clara's innocent rejoicings over her husband's imaginative fertility are pathetic.

Having been scorched in the frying-pan of that unfortunate musical form, opera, Schumann now leaped into the fire of a form in some ways still worse. The combination much used in *Manfred* of music with the spoken word is known as "melodrama." Although this has an appropriately sinister sound, perhaps a more descriptive word—if it be permissible to coin one— would be "melocution."

Schumann may have been so strongly impelled to compose

Manfred because he felt himself closely akin in character and agonizing fate to the hero of that morbid and melodramatic poem. Perhaps also because, as a veteran writer of vocal music, he had a subconscious intimation of the wrongs he had done to the delicate word-melody of poetry, and an equally subconscious feeling that if he now sinned against music in the same way, two wrongs would make a right. For he may have had some dim realization that the spoken word can destroy music as effectually as music can destroy the ethereal textures of word-melody.

In the diary, Clara reveals that Byron's poem inspired Robert "to an extraordinary degree." He tinkered at translations by Posgarn and Böttger, and hoped that the resulting book would be suitable for stage presentation. In this he ran counter to the wishes of Byron himself, who was so disgusted with what the theaters had done to his plays, and had such a bitter contempt for Drury Lane, that he declared his intention to make *Manfred* utterly impossible for the boards. In this contest Byron beat Schumann. Though *Manfred* has occasionally been given in the theater, it does not belong there.

By November 23rd, 1848, the overture—one of his finest works —and the fifteen other numbers were finished. Taken by itself, the music was splendid; and to celebrate its completion he brought home a bottle of champagne.

The year 1848 was a revolutionary one in European history. It was to have as liberating an effect upon the human spirit as Schumann and his Davidites had had upon the art of music. Once again, as they had more than half a century before, the people of Europe were stirring, and their ferment was to have profound consequences. But of this political unrest Schumann was not a part. The creative drive in his own spirit occupied him almost to the exclusion of the outer world. This 1848, he told Verhulst, was the most fruitful year of his life; and he mentioned with especial satisfaction *Genoveva* and the *Album for the Young*, Op. 68.

I've composed 40-50 piano pieces for young people which I think will give pleasure also to you. When I wrote them I felt so fresh that I could have turned right around and done as many more again.

About this same work he had written on October 4th and 6th to Reinecke:

I think the *Album*, especially from about Number 8 on, will sometimes win a smile from you. I don't know when I've been in such a good musical mood as when I wrote the pieces. It simply streamed to me.— . . .

I composed the first things in the *Album* for the birthday of our eldest child; and so one after the other followed along. I felt as if I were beginning once more from the very start to write music. And also here and there you'll find something of the old humor.

He explained that the *Album* was written from a child's-eye viewpoint, as contrasted with the grown-up memories of the *Scenes from Childhood*. The delightful *Musical House- and Life-Rules* [1] were originally intended as an appendix to the *Album*.

On May 3rd, 1849, the revolution reached the city of Dresden. It found Schumann so deep in his growing introversion that he paid but slight heed to the violent rush of events. Clara, poor woman, was almost seven months gone in a new pregnancy. Leaving the cares of the universe to her, Robert buried himself above the ears in his art.

This was, of course, none too lionlike of him; but at least he cut a somewhat more virile figure than Goethe who, in the Napoleonic wars, had buried himself trembling under the bed-clothes, and left to his mistress the slight detail of denying the foe the door. If Clara had not in many ways been so feminine, and if Robert had not in many ways been so masculine, one would be tempted to think that she was more of a man than he.

The King driven out of town. Barricades in the streets. Citizens defending them with scythes. On the fourth, Clara and Robert took a walk and, in the courtyard of the Clinic, saw fourteen corpses. On the fifth, a home guard was formed, and came to insist that Robert—of all warriors!—join up. Upset as he was by the recent death of his brother Carl, this was not the moment for him to have such a brutal experience.

Twice Clara denied that he was at home. When they sullenly threatened to search the house she took Robert and Marie,

[1] They will be noticed further, on p. 273 ff.

and escaped by the back garden, leaving three other children behind with the servants. And this, though Henriette, one of the maids, was seriously sick—for all Clara knew, with an infectious illness. After being searched for weapons by men armed with scythes, they made their way to the Bohemian Railway Station, and from there to the villa of their friend, Major Serres, at Maxen.

At three on the morning of the seventh, Clara returned with another woman to Dresden. Robert was left behind for fear that the insurgents might force him to join them. Non-stop cannon thundered. And when forty scythe-men advanced upon her, Clara thought the game was up. But, summoning all her dignity and resolution, she kept calmly on. And the heroic personality which had so often carried the day on the concert stage prevailed even in war. Like the Red Sea before Moses, the waves of warriors respectfully withdrew to left and right, and let her through unscythed.

She found her children still asleep, tore them out of bed, and in a trice had them dressed. This diary passage about the sick maid contains a bit of unconscious self-revelation:

> Henriette, who was already ill when I left, I found still in that condition. She lay in one spot and took no interest in anything. It upset me very much that this should happen right now, when I needed her so badly.

Not a word of sympathy or help for the patient herself, nor of remorse for having abandoned her small children for two days in an embattled city, and in the same house with a very sick woman. In Maxen, on the ninth, she learned that Henriette's trouble was smallpox.

On the tenth she returned again to town, leaving the one-year-old Ludwig "right unwell," which made her "uneasy"—as well it might, considering the infection to which he had been exposed. She would have sent the sick Henriette away, and moved the children back, if the doctor had not forbidden it.

The air was full of atrocity stories: twenty-six students found hidden in a single room, taken out one after the other, and shot; dozens of people thrown out of third- and fourth-story windows.

But when Robert came, he would not hear a word about such things. Clara noted:

They say that Conductor Wagner has also played a role with the republicans. Made speeches from the Town Hall to the throngs below, designed barricades for them to build, and so on!

Presently there came word that a warrant was out for Wagner's arrest, and that he had fled the country. Clara did not mind.

Robert, unlike Richard the Great, had never been more tranquilly immersed in creation. On May 13th, he finished the *Songs for Young People,* Op. 79, and Clara noted:

It seems extraordinary to me how the terrible things going on in the world so paradoxically awaken his inner poetic feelings. Over all the songs there hangs a breath of the most utter peacefulness. Everything in them seems like Spring, laughing like the blossoms.[2]

There followed the songs from *Wilhelm Meister,* Op. 98a, and Op. 137 for male chorus with horns *ad lib.* The fact that Schumann's spirit was able to remain so long aloof from the passionate intensity of the time, immersed in the joys of cultivating his own esthetic garden, shows that his withdrawal from the world had progressed very far.

But the next work, a motet for men's voices, *Despair Not in the Vale of Anguish,* Op. 93, seemed more in tune with current events. And with the four military *Marches,* Op. 76, finished May 15th, the violent character of the present seems at last to have percolated to Robert's remote consciousness, though not at all to the advantage of the music.

Liszt praised these atrocious marches—said they were "carved upon boulders"—which was a sad commentary on either his taste or his honesty. Clara also impugned the worth of her critical judgment by calling them "most brilliant and original. They are folk-marches that make a magnificent effect."

The fact is that Schumann was anything but a man of the hour. He could no longer react favorably to stimuli from the outer world. When, on June 15th, from the midst of the revolu-

[2] One is reminded of Beethoven during the siege of Vienna, writing the happy music of his A Major 'Cello Sonata.

tionary alarums and excursions, he wrote the mistaken Brendel, agreeing with him "how strongly my music strikes roots into the present," he had little idea that precisely those military *Marches* which, alone of all his works, directly reflected the hideous present were his feeblest efforts, and that his best pages were

not of an age, but for all time.

CHAPTER 25

AS LONG AS DAYLIGHT LASTS

SCHUMANN'S political convictions, so far as he seriously entertained any, came out in a walk which he once took with Count Baudissin. To his own complete satisfaction, the Count proved that constitutional monarchy was the best of all possible forms of government. Silent as usual, Schumann listened in apparent agreement; for he nodded from time to time. But he must have been simply agreeing with his own inner musical thoughts; for when the Count asked him point-blank if he were now a convinced monarchist, the reply was: "All the same, the republic remains the best form of government."

Of course, Schumann may only have been putting on an act, and pulling the monarchist's leg. For, though health might be deserting him, his strong sense of humor never ceased functioning. Frau Lindemann, who helped the family celebrate the Christmas of 1849, tells with what exquisite drollery Robert played the *Bear's Dance* out of the new *Four-hand Piano Pieces*, Op. 85, smiling roguishly, while his hands became clumsy bear-paws.

Nor did his goodness of heart ever call a halt. Not long after, in visiting Leipzig, he arranged to have Clara, David, and Grabau play Reinecke's C Minor Trio in a large and important gathering of musicians. The idea was to get his young friend's music better known. In addition, he soon found the Trio a publisher. Presently he was to do all this and more for the youthful Brahms.

His benignity enthusiastically took in the animal kingdom. Reinecke tells of walking with him and some other musicians

215

when the nightingales were singing. One of these was so lost in its own *bel canto* that it let them come up quite close. Someone remarked that the nightingale must be a precious stupid bird. But Schumann, almost in anger, cried: "On the contrary, it has the soul of an artist!"

When we look back a few years to Robert as a selfish, spoiled, young poseur, and see him now as a lovable, noble, great-hearted man, we are conscious of a miraculous transformation. How was this accomplished? Not necessarily through composing lofty music. Wagner composed that while remaining personally obnoxious. Perhaps it was done by the power of his lofty love, combined with the fortunate chance that a youth upset by a fixation on his mother had found in her successor both a mother and a wife to satisfy his most fundamental instincts, and make him happy.

This, however, is not saying that Schumann was an easy person to get on with. In his nature, there was no element of the "joiner" or of the "royal good fellow." He would not have fitted congenially into a Pullman smoking compartment. When Brendel invited him into a newly founded music society, he answered:

Excuse me, dear Brendel, from joining your association. As you know, I have always loved freedom and independence, have never joined any sort of society, and what's more—never will.

In saying this he quite forgot the pirates' band, the literary society of his boyhood, and the Davidites; though perhaps he reckoned that this last did not count, as its chief members were only aspects of his own personality.

When his admirers were rash enough to try pulling him into the general conversation, they were often heartily rebuffed. On one occasion Weber's son publicly asked his opinion of Cimarosa's *Secret Marriage*, then playing at the Opera House. Schumann suddenly grew scarlet. His eyes gleamed as from an overdose of adrenalin, and he roared: "Leave me in peace with the canary-bird music and the bag-wig melodies!" [1]

Such irascibility was, of course, somewhat pathological. The

[1] How this would have irritated the contemporary French painter, Delacroix, who put Cimarosa far above Beethoven!

previous year, it had almost led to a rupture with the sunny-tempered and self-restrained Liszt during his sudden visit to Leipzig. Their previous meeting had left none too cordial memories; and Robert's attitude towards his old friend may be partly gauged by the fact that, in 1846, he had made the following note: "Mendelssohn on Liszt's way of life, a continual alternation between scandal and apotheosis."

The Hungarian man of the world laid himself out to be charming, and asked to hear Robert's D Minor Trio. Clara scurried around, secured fiddlers, rehearsed with them; and all was ready at the appointed hour. But no Liszt! Finally they decided to while away the time with Beethoven's "Geister" Trio. At the final page of the finale, Liszt stormed in, two hours late.

This heightened the explosive quality of Schumann's already sufficiently irritable mood. And when Liszt, after praising the Trio, heard the Quintet and called it "too Leipzig-like," Robert nobly fought down an eruption of rage. Liszt's epithet was based on what he considered Leipzig's regularity and conservatism. But it may have been prompted by jealousy arising from the virtuoso's (probably unconscious) realization that he himself, the musical innovator *par excellence,* was powerless to create anything like this Quintet, that bade fair to outlast the drums and tramplings of esthetic conquests. The unconscious, too, may have led him on to commit further indiscretions. This episode marks one of the blots on Liszt's admirable character, but one for which, in his own handsome style, he promptly atoned.

After supper, as Clara told the diary, Liszt "played so shamefully badly that I was downright ashamed of having to stand there beside him and of not being able to leave the room at once." However, one must take all of Clara's pronunciamentos, especially on rival pianists and composers, with an understanding of how jealousy, suspicion, lack of humor, and strong reactionary feeling were wont to color her musical judgments. It should be borne in mind, for example, that she could see nothing in Wagner but disgusting rubbish.

Liszt was none too well pleased with the cool reception given his music. And when the company began to speak adoringly of the late Mendelssohn, he could no longer restrain his love

of mischief. So he began praising Meyerbeer at the expense of
the other. This was, of course, less than tactful of him. As a
reader of the *New Magazine*, he knew Robert's violent contempt
for Meyerbeer and his hero-worship of Mendelssohn. Liszt's
words pulled the pin out of the grenade. When Robert heard
the name of his great hero, who had been dead scarcely a year,
maltreated, he forgot that he was the host. Surging to his feet,
he grasped Liszt by the shoulders, and bellowed:

Sir, who are *you* that you dare to speak thus of a musician like
Mendelssohn? Compared with him, Meyerbeer is a miserable creature. Mendelssohn is an artist whose labors have blessed, not only
Leipzig, but the whole world. As for you, you had better hold your
tongue!

Then he rushed to his bedroom and slammed the door.

Complete gentleman that he was, Liszt showed his admirable
nature. He tried to pass the incident off lightly. But, meeting
only hostile eyes, he gracefully eased himself out of that grim
atmosphere, merely stopping to murmur to Clara: "Please tell
your husband that there is but one person on earth from whom
I would so calmly take such words as he has just offered me."

Clara wrote in the diary: "That wound went too deep for
Robert ever to forget it." And she added: "I am through with
him for all eternity."

Robert, however, was not so furiously irreconcilable as his
steel-cored wife. He knew that his manner had been far from
correct. And when, a year later, Liszt great-heartedly wrote to
ask if he might use the *Faust* music for the Weimar centenary
celebration of Goethe's birth, Schumann answered pleasantly.
He made an allusion to the delightful scene in that drama, between Mephistopheles and the Freshman, where Leipzig is called
a "little Paris." Note, however, that while, this time, his manner
was urbane, he still upheld his original position:

But, dear friend, might you not perhaps find the composition
[*Faust*] too Leipzig-like? Or do you perhaps regard Leipzig as a
little Paris, in which place also something might be accomplished?
Seriously, I would not have expected a man like you, who know so
many of my compositions, to deliver *such* a verdict, condemning a

whole artistic culture in a lump. If you will look more closely at my works, you will necessarily find there a considerable variety of viewpoints. For in each of my compositions I have always striven to bring out something different, and I do not mean in form alone. And truly the Leipzig crowd wasn't so bad—Mendelssohn, Hiller, Bennett, etc.—we could stand comparison with the Parisians, Viennese, and Berliners. If there are certain similarities in what we composed—call it philistinizing, or what you will—you will find the same thing in all the different epochs of art, and in 100 passages, Bach, Händel, Gluck, later Mozart, Haydn, Beethoven resemble each other to a hair (though I except the last works of Beethoven, despite the fact that they point back again to Bach). Nobody is *entirely original*. So much for your remark, which was an unjust and insulting one. For the rest, let us forget that evening—a word is no arrow—and striving ahead is the important thing.

Liszt took this like a thoroughbred and answered, as might have been expected, in his large and gracious manner:

Above all, allow me to repeat a thing that, for a long time now, you should have realized almost as well as I do, namely that nobody admires and honors you more sincerely than my unworthy self. To be sure, we ought to be able to have an occasional friendly discussion about the significance of a work, a man, or a city.

This was calculated to heal the breach. But then, in the best-meant way in the world, Liszt spoiled it all again with a little joke. He offered to come to Dresden for the approaching première of *Genoveva,* and be "a claqueur." It is probable that Clara first took this the wrong way, as a prediction by Liszt that the opera would fall through if it lacked the artificial stimulus of paid applause; and that she then convinced Robert, who was in a morbidly sensitive state, that his old friend had again insulted him.

So when Liszt actually did come on for that première, and afterwards sat down with the Schumanns to a celebration supper, there was a distinct tang of frost in the atmosphere.

Everybody laughed when Liszt broke a string in reading from the ms. of the *Album,* then pulled a long face and declared: "Look here, such a thing has never before happened to me!"

But, though the ice was broken, the summery warmth of real friendship never returned.

From that time on, Clara and the Schumannites, mildly abetted by Robert, took every opportunity of ridiculing the good Abbé and his works.[2] The magnanimous Hungarian, however, realizing that he had to do with a sick man and his followers, continued to take no offense. Indeed, so long as he lived, he never lost a chance to make glowing propaganda for Robert's works and Clara's playing.

The labor on *Genoveva* had got Schumann's nerves into a sad state. He confessed to his friend, Professor Kahlert: "I lost every melody again as soon as I had thought of it. What I heard inside my head took too much out of me."

He suffered from terrible headaches. The old obsessing fear of mental hospitals came back to plague him. He wrote to Hiller, who was resigning as music director at Düsseldorf and urging Schumann to be his successor:

Recently I looked up Düsseldorf in an old Geography, and found listed under the sights: three nunneries and an insane asylum. I don't mind the former; but the latter made quite unpleasant reading for me. . . .

I must take care to avoid all melancholy impressions of that sort. And if we musicians live so often on sunny heights, the disaster of reality cuts all the deeper for that, when it appears so nakedly before our eyes. At least, that's the way it goes with me and my lively imagination. . . .

In these years I have been very industrious. . . . One must work as long as daylight lasts.

And there is another touching premonition of doom in a letter to Härtel, written at this time. It concerns his wish to succeed Rietz as director of the Gewandhaus:

As unforgettable as recent years will be to me, who have been able to live exclusively for composition; and much as I know that such

---

[2] How that fanatical lady would have snorted had she been able to peer forward through the generations and discover these words in Isadora Duncan's autobiography: "I often danced . . . the inspired and holy music of Liszt."!

fruitful and, in this respect, happy years will not so quickly come again, still I feel the urge toward an active occupation.

As all truly wise musicians since King David have been, Schumann was a practitioner of musical therapy. He discovered the music cure, and practiced it with success on himself. For this purpose his Choral Union came in handy; and he made it sing the very music for his complaint: "There I heal myself with Palestrina and Bach and other things that one does not otherwise get to hear."

The music cure, however, could not do much against the terrible lethargy which, like an octopus, would seize him in its black arms and, for weeks on end, hold him powerless. The unshakable persistence with which Schumann kept on writing during every hour that illness allowed him constitutes one of the most inspiring exhibitions of good sportsmanship [3] in the history of the arts. The wonder is not that he wrote so much poor and indifferent stuff during these pitiable years, but that he was still sometimes able to defy "the fell clutch of circumstance," and turn out a masterpiece.

As for Clara, she differentiated almost as little among Robert's works as she did among Wagner's. She was enchanted with everything her man composed. She had not yet nibbled enough apples from the tree of musical knowledge to enable her to tell a golden hawk from a rusty handsaw. Apparently she received the same thrill from the worst of the weak *Romances and Ballades*, Opp. 67 and 75, over which she raved, the mediocre *Stücke im Volkston* for 'cello and piano, Op. 102, which she found "of a freshness and originality that quite ravished" her, and the fine *Songs*, and *Requiem of Mignon*, Op. 98, which "moved" her "most deeply."

On August 29th, 1849, the second day of the Goethe centenary celebration, Robert had the satisfaction of three premières of as much of his *Faust* music as was then finished.[4] They took

[3] This word covers a whole code of ethics, which includes: never-say-die courage, honesty, good winning, and good losing.

[4] The first performance of the complete work was given by Hiller, January 14th, 1862, at a Gürzenich concert in Cologne.

place in Dresden, Weimar, and Leipzig. The first two were highly successful. Beforehand Robert wrote Härtel:

> I only wish I could have Faust's mantle for that day, in order to be everywhere and hear everything. How strange, the piece lay five years in the desk. Nobody knew anything about it, and I myself had almost forgotten its existence—and now in this unusual celebration it has to come to light!

For a good while, Schumann and his wife had felt growing discomfort in the stiff, unmusical Court atmosphere of Dresden. The bureaucrats contemptuously rebuffed his attempts to organize a memorial service for Chopin, who had died in October, and insultingly refused his polite request for a seat at the Opera. Worst of all, he received no creative response from the people of Dresden. There was no spiritual repercussion to stimulate his pen to fresh efforts. So Hiller's suggestion that Robert succeed him in Düsseldorf was timely, and fell upon well-prepared ground.

During the five Dresden years, despite uncongenial surroundings and much bad health, he had made progress. He had written his greatest symphony and one of the supreme piano concertos. His music had begun to be internationally loved and to win the recognition it so richly deserved. Not long before he had been cheered by the news that the American Musical Institute of New York was preparing the American première of the *Peri*.

For all that, Dresden was too wet a blanket. And on November 26th, 1849, a wistful note sounded in his letter to Ehlert: "After strenuous work one now and then needs a little applause. Otherwise the strongest will weaken."

CHAPTER 26

WELCOME TO THE RHINE

FOR the Schumanns the early part of 1850 was a period of painful uncertainty. To celebrate Robert's fortieth birthday, there was a concert at the Preussers'. The *Minnespiel* was sung by a quartet, and the not too inspired *Stücke im Volkston* were played by Grabau. At the cool reception given the latter, Clara, who was naturally prejudiced in their favor, took offense.

Düsseldorf was now pressing for a decision. When the Dresdeners got wind of this fact, they seemed to wake with a start to some realization of what they might be losing. Hopes were held out of the second conductor's post at the Opera, which had been vacated by the flight from arrest of that revolutionist Richard Wagner. But Clara decided that Wagner's leavings would be unworthy of her husband's dignity. And anyway, the position was offered, not to him, but to a gentleman named C. Krebs.

As early as June 1849, Robert had been summoned to Leipzig to help prepare the production of *Genoveva,* which had been accepted the year before. The usual exasperating delays had intervened, until the late Spring of 1850 was settled on. Robert groaned to Härtel: "Who goes to the theater in May and June, rather than out into the green world?" But he need not have worried. On arrival in February, he found, to his inexpressible rage, that he had been elbowed further along the schedule by —of all people—his *bête noir*, Meyerbeer; and *Genoveva* must yield to the obnoxious *Prophet.*

The Schumanns filled in the period of waiting with a concert

223

trip to Bremen and Hamburg. In the former their success was spoiled by the intrigues of Herr Eggers, a local dignitary who felt that he had once been slighted by them. Hamburg, however, received the pair with jubilation. The Quintet, the Piano Concerto, the Variations for two pianos, and the *Genoveva* Overture all created a sensation.

Unfortunately, Robert's nervous irritability could not help casting a shadow upon the Hamburg ovation. After the second concert, Schuberth, Grädener, and a few other friends took them to an oyster cellar for an impromptu supper. Following generous rounds of wine, a toast was drunk to the eminent composer. Whereupon—wonder of wonders—Robert arose and, in his weak, unsonorous voice, called attention to the fact that this, the 21st of March, was the birthday of two of Germany's mightiest geniuses: Johann Sebastian Bach and—Jean Paul Richter. To this pair he proposed a toast, which went down with a will. But Grädener, the head of the local Singakademie, had already drunk to such purpose that he was at the disputatious stage. He arose and cried: "To Bach, yes, will I drink; but not to Jean Paul, who is unworthy of mention in the same breath."

Robert turned as purple as he had two years before when Liszt had played Meyerbeer off against Mendelssohn. Springing to his feet, he shouted at Grädener: "You are a shameless fellow!" Then he stalked out into the night, followed by Clara and Schuberth, leaving the rest to stare hollow-eyed at one another. This was the final antic of that spoiled child to whom a too doting mother had foolishly allowed his own way without opposition. The next morning, Grädener was magnanimous enough to call, apologize, and make up. The outbreak seems all the more extraordinary because, seven years before, Robert had written Kossmaly that both of the men toasted in the oyster cellar had even then begun to mean less to him.[1]

Jenny Lind brought a welcome surprise by suddenly appearing as she had in Vienna, giving concerts with Clara, and singing Robert's songs to the delight of all, including their maker.

By the middle of May it was time to begin rehearsing *Geno-*

[1] See p. 180.

veva. And in the highest state of agitation the pair reached Leipzig. On this occasion, Robert Friese, who had not seen his old friend for several years, testified that he was more taciturn and withdrawn than formerly, besides having put on flesh and being noticeably bloated in the face.

The Mendelssohn clique, vigorously intriguing against the new opera, caused some annoyance. But at the long-awaited opening, the Schumannites made a brave showing. There were Hiller, Gade, Spohr, Reinecke, and Moscheles. Despite Robert's displeasure at the "claqueur" joke, Liszt had come all the way from Budapest. The composer's old teacher Kuntsch of Zwickau was there in his proud glory. And Grädener had been amiable enough to make the journey from Hamburg.

Here is the report which a trembling Clara wrote into the diary:

> The singers took all sorts of pains. The first two acts went very well; but in the third, Wiedemann (Golo) had the bad luck to forget the letter for Siegfried. Both ran desperately about, and this scene went quite for nothing. The singers themselves were so upset by this that the last two acts went less well. And another handicap lay in the poor furnishings of the magic chamber. Still, the public was very attentive, and at the end loud applause twice made the singers and Robert appear.

Clara fulfilled her usual function of propelling the confused and frightened Robert from the wings onto the stage where he stood blinking like an owl at high noon. He had absent-mindedly left his dress-suit behind in Dresden, and had to issue forth in a frock-coat and striped trousers. To complete his disorganization, a laurel wreath was hurled at him, which the prima donna balanced upon his back hair, while his lips puckered themselves in tremendous silent whistlings.

There were three performances, each better than the preceding. The applause was unstinted and, in his innocence, Robert supposed that he was made as an operatic composer. Alas! he had only scored a *succès d'estime.* Nor could it have been otherwise. Both the libretto and the composer of *Genoveva* were too hopelessly undramatic.

One more instance of Clara's unsound critical judgment was her opinion of this work: "The music quite filled me with bliss. What dramatic vitality, what instrumentation!" She unerringly picked out as the object of her raptures the opera's most unfortunate defects. *Genoveva* is none too well instrumentated, and dramatic vitality is conspicuous by its absence.

In this connection it is worth noting that, four months before, Clara had brought out one of Robert's worst productions, the *Introduction and Allegro Appassionato*, Op. 92, and had been vexed with the public for not paying homage to what she described as "the beautiful concert piece."

It took a year for Robert to awake from his fond illusion of operatic success, and to face the prospect that this work would never set the Rhine afire. On August 2nd, 1851, he wrote to publisher Peters, who had sportingly printed *Genoveva* in advance of production:

I begin to worry whether you are going to get back your large investment in the opera. But it will not be the fault of my work if it does not become so quickly profitable to you. That would assuredly be owing to the terribly degenerated taste of the theatrical public.

This is a remarkable case of rationalization by a mind whose past musical judgments had on the whole been consistently sound. As for Clara, it was natural for her to attribute the failure to nothing but the malice of envious friends and the insidious machinations of enemies, known and unknown. Her wishful thinking was stimulated by her great love.

Before deciding to accept the princely sum of 700 thalers a year for directing the musical destinies of the provincial town of Düsseldorf, Robert asked some searching questions about the orchestra; for Mendelssohn, a former incumbent, had told him that it was pretty bad. But Hiller reassured him that it might be a good deal worse. And Robert signed the contract.

While shaking Dresden's dust from her feet, Clara took deep satisfaction in again giving vent to her long-accumulated grievance against that city.

It is really as though the people here had no blood, and could not pump up a bit of enthusiasm for anything.

I must say that I leave here with pleasure, and am glad that
nothing binds Robert to stay. What a position that would place him
in! These gossipy, false people in the orchestra who would go any
length to preserve their sloppiness. They constitute a beautiful, a
worthy gang . . . people who prodigally toss about "dear colleague,"
and "my treasure," after which they would like to scratch each other's
eyes out. . . .

And now just have a look at the sort of audience they have here,
at a symphony by Mendelssohn! Like lumps of wood they sit there.
In those blighted faces, not the tiniest spark of life to be seen—with
hands and feet I'd like to leap into their midst and cry: "Isn't there,
then, one single drop of blood in the lot of you?"

Litzmann thought that the Wieckian zest with which Clara,
at this particular moment, baptized Dresden from the vials of
her wrath, was born of the fact that the male members of
Robert's Choral Union, disheartened by his poor conducting,
had recently been playing hookey from the rehearsals, which
touched her pride on the raw. But, if so, she was hardly consistent; for, only in May, she had admitted that their performance of the cathedral scene from the *Faust* music was "inspired."

Yes, life had proved none too congenial in Dresden. All the
same, Robert had made notable progress there in his art and in
his fame. And it was with high hopes that the distinguished
couple pulled up stakes and, with children and household gods,
set out for the Rhine.

On September 2nd they arrived in Düsseldorf, which, as Clara
noted:

lies in an unexpectedly friendly situation, and is even surrounded
by a small mountain ridge. We were met by Hiller and the board of
directors of the concerts. The latter welcomed Robert in a most
friendly way with a speech.

That evening the *Liedertafel* gave them a serenade. These
vivacious Rhinelanders, with their love of wine, woman, and
song, stood out in grateful contrast to the "bloodless" crew of
Court-hypnotized Dresdeners whom Clara had come to think of
as fossils.

There followed a sort of honeymoon period of pleasure in

their new lot, darkened only by the difficulty of finding a congenial home. The first they chose, after painful search, was too
noisy, and soon they had to try again.

The evening of September 4th brought another serenade, this
time by the orchestra which Robert had come to lead. They
played so well that he had high hopes of them.

Agreeable and interesting people made advances. Soon they
began to form a stimulating circle of friends, prominent among
whom were Hildebrandt the painter, and Schadow, head of the
Academy of Fine Arts. But the difficult Clara could not at all
put up with the democracy of what she called "the lower classes
of people," and complained that they were "uniformly rough,
pretentious and impertinent. They regard themselves as our
equals." (In this snobbish utterance, there is a dim echo of
Father Wieck's superiority complex.)

On the 5th, the concert committee arrived, wearing dress-
suits in broad daylight, as Germans do when they want to be
elegantly ceremonious, and invited the newcomers for the 7th to
a concert, banquet, and ball in their honor. The all-Schumann
concert consisted of the *Genoveva* Overture, the songs: *Widmung, Die Lotosblume,* and *Wanderlied,* and the second part of
Peri, all of which went encouragingly well.

About the banquet which followed, Clara somewhat acidu-
lously commented in the diary: "There was wretchedly little to
eat. Consequently each course was always greeted with a hurrah, which struck us as awfully funny."

She complained that the principal speaker's toast to Robert
began back at the creation of the world. A few days later, at a
supper after the first subscription concert, Schumann was still
more dissatisfied with another toast. When Hiller drank to Clara
instead of to himself, he was so annoyed that, as Clara's entry
bears witness, he "was almost at the point of standing up and
leaving. It was highly unpleasant for me, and put us both quite
out of humor."

The Rhenish honeymoon soon showed signs of eclipse. The
newcomers began to realize that the Rhinelanders' youthful
effervescence, enthusiasm, and friendly sociability had an ob-
verse side of superficiality and disinclination to be serious, in-

dustrious, persevering, or thorough; and that they could be effectively led and managed by none but a hail-fellow-well-met. Otherwise they were likely to turn suddenly rough, crude, surly, and even violent.

For their part, the Düsseldorfers soon came to learn that Clara, though in theory a most democratic person, was in practice a bit too aristocratically minded to suit them. Moreover, Robert was not jovial enough; and anyway, he was not fitted to be an orchestral conductor. He lacked the necessary initiative, alertness, strength, decision, persuasiveness, tact, presence of mind, and ability to communicate his ideas. Robert scarcely bothered to listen to the orchestra under his direction, as if he were privately conducting to himself scores heard with his inner ear. The man was incredibly removed from the physical world. Like his often awkward personal contacts, his relations with orchestras were marked by an almost complete withdrawal.

This at least, however, may be said for his leadership. Unlike certain other weak conductors, he did not gobble like a turkey in the fortissimos, nor go through a course of setting-up exercises. Those baton-wielders who depend largely on calisthenics for the registering of emotion make one suspect that they try to compensate by bobbing their heads for an inability to bob their hearts.

Niecks gives some striking instances of Robert's strange technic with the baton:

Once at a mass he went on conducting after the movement was finished and the priest had begun to intone. At a choir practice the sopranos were singing several high A's and the effect was such that it aroused laughter; the sopranos stopped singing and the other parts gradually followed suit until Tausch was left playing the pianoforte alone. Schumann noticed nothing and went on beating time; and Tausch, thinking it was no use going on by himself, stopped too. Schumann beckoned him to come, and Tausch expected a reproof for having broken off. But no—Schumann showed him a passage in the score and said: "Look, this bar is beautiful."

Once when Schumann was rehearsing Joachim's *Hamlet* Overture in the presence of the composer, the horns missed a certain passage. Instead of hauling them over the coals, he turned with wistful sadness to Joachim and murmured: "They didn't come in!" And at a rehearsal of *Peri*, Clara, who was accompanying, rose from the keyboard and announced: "My husband says he would like this passage *piano*." Whereupon Robert, up there on the podium, nodded his head gratefully.

So far did Robert's absorption in the score and his oblivion of the orchestra as a group of real living human beings go that, if in rehearsal he was dissatisfied with anything, he would never say why, but would simply take the part over again. And if, in several repetitions, the players could not divine what was wrong, he would silently close the score and go on to the next number.

In his reminiscences, Reinecke tells of being summoned from Cologne by Schumann at a moment's notice, to act as pinch-hitter in the piano part of Beethoven's *Choral Phantasie*. The rehearsal "was a most painful and exhausting one; for Schumann could not adjust himself quickly enough to the frequently changing *tempi*, and it had to be eternally repeated; until at last the concertmaster and I myself took over the leadership behind Schumann's back." This was almost exactly what happened in certain concerts when Beethoven tried to lead. There the trouble was deafness; here, incipient dumbness, complicated by natural incapacity and faint, early symptoms of insanity—a combination certainly unpromising enough for the podium.

No, the essentials of conducting cannot be learned, but are a special gift from on high. When Schumann led *Peri*, he aroused Wagner's special sympathy by his awkwardness on the stage, where he was "above all Romanticist, sensitive creature of moods, dreamer, and enthusiast."

However, Schumann's tips to Spohr and Taubert about rehearsing his *"Spring"* Symphony show that, at least mentally, he was not so slipshod a leader as he seemed. In fact, it would not harm some of our contemporary prima donnas of the baton to study his warnings about various pitfalls in that charming work.

As time passed, the Düsseldorf situation grew more painful and impossible. Owing to sound drilling under that solid conductor, Hiller, which had lent them a certain momentum, the orchestra and chorus did not noticeably begin to go down-hill until nearly the end of the first season, when an anonymous newspaper article attacked Schumann's capacity for leadership. Clara was, of course, furious, took this as a piece of impertinence, and suspected that it had been treacherously written by a member of the committee.

From that point, the situation steadily deteriorated, until two parties opposed one another, each convinced of being in the right. On the one hand were Clara and Robert, both innocently unaware that he was not a born leader. On the other was the orchestra committee, under growing pressure from a public disgusted by the rapid falling-off in the quality of the concerts. They were anxious to treat the genius in their midst with all the homage he deserved. But they realized that he was unfit to conduct, and that Hiller had been guilty of gross irresponsibility in recommending him for the post. Their duty was to their subscribers rather than to their leader; and with heavy hearts they finally performed it.

Without going into all of the unpleasant details of the squabble, it is enough to say that, with Clara storming mightily, Schumann's contract was cancelled, in the fall of 1853, by his angry self.

CHAPTER 27

"RHENISH" SYMPHONY

DESPITE all these troubles, the move to the Rhine brought Schumann fresh creative inspiration. The 'Cello Concerto, Op. 129, took form in October 1850; and between November 2nd and December 9th, the *"Rhenish"* Symphony in E Flat, Op. 97—known as the Third, but actually the Fourth—was completed. Around the turn of the year, the overtures to *The Bride of Messina* and *Julius Caesar* were written, and he began work on the gigantic oratorio, *Luther,* that never was finished.

In April and May there followed a light choral work, *The Pilgrimage of the Rose,* Op. 112. On May 6th, 1852, a choral ballad, *The King's Son,* was brought out; and the composer naïvely thought that it would be "the most effective" of all his works. It found an early death. The four-hand *Ballscenen,* Op. 109, appeared next.

Robert's days followed a stereotyped program. He would compose until noon, then take a walk with Clara or some friend like Albert Dietrich or Wasielewski, whom he had lured from Leipzig to be concertmaster of the orchestra. After dinner he worked again until late afternoon, read the papers in a café over a glass of wine or beer, smoking those favorite strong cigars which he smilingly called his "little devils," and spent the evening quietly at home, or in some friendly house.

But this does not mean that he had much of anything to say in the friendly house. Taciturnity was constantly growing upon him. Wasielewski, who at this time had rare opportunities for observation, testified:

He simply did not know how to talk about matters of everyday living; for empty forms of speech disgusted him, and about things that interested him intensely he let himself go but seldom and, as it were, under protest. One had to watch for a favorable moment. When this arrived, Schumann, in his own way, could be as loquacious as others. He surprised one then by significant and intellectually distinguished remarks that, at least from one angle, sharply lit up the subject in hand.

In June he was suffering so much from nervous troubles that Radecke's organ-playing very nearly gave him a fainting spell. So travel was indicated. At once he felt better. In nearby Bonn, the lighthearted students with their songs, the beauty of the Rhine which had always inspired him (and was yet to play such a role in his life), and no doubt the pervading spirit of Ludwig van Beethoven, combined to lift his spirits up to vacation level.

This level he maintained in Heidelberg, with its memories of the mythical Countess von Abegg and the days when he had dedicated himself for good and all to the service of music. There followed Baden-Baden, where, long afterwards, Clara was to bring the children for their summers; Basel, sacred to the younger Holbein, and Geneva and Chamonix, where, from their hotel window, they could watch the purple shadows pursuing one another across the dazzling glaciers of Mont Blanc. Then a long jump to Antwerp, where Robert had rashly agreed to sit on the jury of a song competition. But not even listening to men's choruses giving out "the worst stuff" for twelve hours on end could get him down again.

No sooner had they returned home refreshed than the meteoric Liszt descended, bringing along his lady love, Princess Wittgenstein, and his own unique kind of non-stop uproar. Clara groaned in the diary:

Wherever Liszt comes, all domestic order is instantly turned topsy-turvy. He plunges one into a never-ending excitement. . . .
We made lots of music: Second Symphony of Robert (for 8 hands), *Springbrunnen* and *Kroatenmarsch* out of the *Album*,[1] then the whole *Kinderball*; and for the wind-up he played a new concert-piece and a

[1] They were out of the *Twelve Fourhand Piano Pieces*, Op. 85.

few "*Harmonies.*" As always, he played with a truly demonic bravura, he really mastered the piano like a devil; but alas! the compositions! they were simply too fearful stuff.

That remained Clara's verdict on Liszt's best composition, the B Minor Piano Sonata.[2]

Robert's summer and fall were full of important work: the *Three Fantasiestücke,* Op. 111, for piano, the two sonatas for violin and piano, in A Minor, Op. 105, and in D Minor, Op. 121, and the splendid G Minor Trio, Op. 110. To finish the year, he orchestrated *The Pilgrimage of the Rose,* re-orchestrated the D Minor Symphony, and wrote the overture to *Hermann and Dorothea* "with much zest in few hours." In the diary, Clara registered her *Schwärmerei:*

When I consider what a happy woman I am, happy above millions of others, a burning anxiety often overcomes me; and then I frequently ask Heaven if the happiness is not even too great. What are all the seamy sides of material existence as compared with the joys and the hours of ecstasy that I enjoy through the love and music of my Robert!

And particularly about the completion of the Trio she exulted:

How glorious it is in the company of such a restlessly creative spirit, how fortunate I can call myself that Heaven has given me understanding and heart enough to grasp this mind and spirit thus, so entirely.

It was fortunate for Clara that she did not realize how far she yet was from making good this boast.

Early in 1852, Liszt mightily cheered Robert by proposing to attempt a first performance of *Manfred* in the Spring. It was, however, postponed until June 8th, when illness kept the composer from attending.

Schumann's most ambitious attempts at religious music, the *Mass,* Op. 147, and the *Requiem,* Op. 148—perhaps because composed in 1852, at a time of enfeebled creative and critical power—need not detain us. He was not a religious man in the

---

[2] Dedicated to Robert Schumann. This shows how much Liszt thought of him.

sense that he believed in dogma. It is true that he had remarked
in a letter to Strackerjahn: "To spend one's strength on religious
music remains perhaps the loftiest aim of the artist." But seeing
that he had always been the absolute musician par excellence,
who had consistently placed the worth of the music itself above
that of any literary program with which it happened to be associated, one is inclined to suspect that these words had been written in a period of mental let-down.

It was during such a time that he grew enthusiastic about the
works of Elisabeth Kulmann, a mediocre lyric poet. The lady's
looks and works fascinated him. He set many of her poems, hung
her portrait over his writing table, and even crowned it with
laurel. One wonders with what eyes Clara regarded this performance.

In March, a Schumann Week was organized in Leipzig, and
such good friends as Liszt and Joachim met the couple there.
But the celebration fell flat. The Leipzigers had not yet learned
the worth of the prophet from their own country. Even the devoted band of Schumannites had no adequate idea what a world
figure had attracted their allegiance.

At the close of the *"Rhenish"* Symphony, Clara thought she
detected "real enthusiasm"; but that was wishful thinking. In
1851 Schumann had written Richard Pohl resignedly: "At a first
hearing I am used to having my compositions, especially the
better and deeper ones, not understood by the greatest part of
the public."

All the same, the larger audience outside of Saxony was growing; so that, the following year, Robert could write Van Bruyck:

My music is spreading more and more, also outside Germany, especially in Holland and England; and for an artist to see such things is
always a joy. For it is not the praise that lifts him up, but joy in finding that what he has felt resounds back harmoniously from the hearts
of men.

CHAPTER 28

CALM BEFORE STORM

I N the early part of 1852, the bitter was well mingled for the Schumanns with the sweet. They had to move again; and the new home proved noisy. On one side was an English family. Their piano backed up to the party-wall and, day and night, was manhandled—or rather, child-handled. All appeals to show mercy and move the instrument to another room were roughly denied. On the other side were loud building operations. In front, the pavement was being repaired. Clara seemed to have a genius for choosing impossible dwellings.

All this may have had its own unfortunate effect on the religious music mentioned in the last chapter. It is significant that, in the midst of these alarms, Schumann orchestrated his motet, *Despair not in the vale of anguish*. It must have been done with special conviction. The poor man needed some person like the good Frau Truxa who, years after, by her diplomatic guile, was to clap a silencer upon Brahms' noisy pianist neighbor, so that he might work undistracted.[1] It may be that Schumann approached his English tormentors with much the same direct forcefulness that Brahms was to show in dealing with this Frau Ronchetti, whom he christened "the female piano-beast." For Robert could be very abrupt and thoughtless, even with his beloved Clara.

One of his best friends in Düsseldorf was the celebrated painter Bendemann, who even dared, on occasion, to run the risk of reprimanding the supersensitive composer. Niecks tells how,

[1] See my *The Unknown Brahms*, pp. 228-9.

at a party given by the Bendemanns, Schumann sat the whole evening by himself in one of the inner rooms. . . . The pianoforte was in another room, and after playing, Clara joined her husband, who asked, "Who was playing?" "I." "Really?" And she wept. . . . Clara . . . later went to him and said, "I feel unwell, shall we not go?" "But why should we go? It is so nice here." And they remained. At last Bendemann said to Schumann: "Although it is very impolite of a host to say so to a guest, I cannot help saying that you should have taken your wife home before now." Schumann said nothing but was angry. Next day Bendemann received a letter in which Schumann said in an irritated way that he did not need to be told of his wife's excellences, that he was well aware of them. Bendemann apologized, and the friendship was restored. On another occasion Bendemann called to take Schumann out and found him dressing. After fumbling with his tie for some time he called out, "Clara, my waistcoat." And she brought it, and afterwards his coat. Bendemann reproved him for this without convincing him.

Introversion had carried him far indeed in his withdrawal from the amenities and other realities of life. Here is a vignette made by Strackerjahn in Leipzig, 1852, of Robert hearing Liszt and Clara playing together. He

sat in the adjoining room quite alone, and listened. . . . I can still see the quietly smiling happy face, and how he pressed his upper lip with the fingers of his right hand.

Even when no audible notes were to be heard, he had the appearance of one who continually hearkened to an interior concert.

His absence of mind grew apace. When the two well-known violinists, Langhans and Japha, called upon him, they were shown into a darkened room. After a long wait, Schumann opened the door, peered at them, closed it again, and vanished. After a tedious interval, the fiddlers made inquiries and found that the Master had long since left the house.

Towards the end of his life, this absence of mind extended even to his correspondence. Writing to Strackerjahn on January 17th, 1854, he expressed a wish to be enveloped in Faust's mantle of invisibility, and ten lines below he said the same thing over again.

On the street he would even fail to recognize his own little
ones; although, being fond of children, he would stop and speak
kindly to them; which must have had a curious effect upon his
daughters. Eugenie, the youngest, states that this was only make-
believe, in fun; but at the time she was too young to distinguish.

While he was conducting, Schumann's absence of mind went
so far that he would lose touch with his baton and send it flying
among the fiddlers, to the peril of bridges and bows, glasses and
eyes. One day before rehearsal, looking and sounding very much
pleased, he showed an acquaintance a string tied at one end to
a baton, and at the other to his right wrist. With a simplicity as
delightful as that of *Glückes Genug* in the *Scenes from Childhood,* he said: "Look—now it can't drop again!"

In 1853 he finished the *Faust* music by scoring the overture.
He had approached this music with deep trepidation. Eight
years before, when it was partly done, he wrote Mendelssohn:

The scene from *Faust* reposes in my desk. I am absolutely afraid
to look at it again. The lofty poetry, especially of the final part, moved
me so deeply that I ventured to begin. I have no idea whether I shall
ever publish it.

Of a private hearing of parts of it in 1848, he wrote to Nottebohm: "It gave me pleasure. The whole thing impressed me as
stronger than the music of the *Peri*—doubtless because the poem
is grander." And at the same time he confessed to Brendel: "I
often feared the reproach: 'Why add music to such perfect
poetry?' "

From the esthetic standpoint, this conscientious and intelligent misgiving does the poetry-lover and absolute musician in
him great credit. It sets him in a class apart from nearly all other
composers for the voice. And this, though he proceeded in the
next line of the letter to rationalize away his well-founded fear.

On September 12th, 1853, the pair celebrated their thirteenth
wedding anniversary. Pulling a long face, Robert announced that
his present would arrive a day too late. At noon, with Dietrich
and other friends, they started for a picnic at Benrath. When at
five they reached their Bilkerstrasse home, the wondering Clara
saw two ladies and two gentlemen grouped about a new grand

piano decorated with flowers. The moment she came in, they began to sing the poem which her husband had written her thirteen years before (when he had given her the first grand piano) and which he had set to music for this occasion. Even then it took her some time longer to realize that this was not an instrument rented to accompany the singers, but was her very own.

Besides the piano, Robert's presents to her included the manuscripts of two new works: the *Concert Allegro with Introduction,* for piano and orchestra, Op. 134, written for her, the *Fantasie* for violin and orchestra, Op. 131, written for Joachim, and the score, as well as arrangements for two and four hands, of the *Faust* Overture.

Without a misgiving about the terrible immediate future, and far too uncritically ecstatic to realize that two-thirds of these compositions were quite unworthy of her husband's genius, Clara found an outlet for her joy in the diary:

> Could a wedding anniversary possibly be lovelier than with a loved and loving husband at one's side and six lively, well-formed children about us! My heart is filled with gratitude for all the rich blessing— may Heaven long preserve this fortune for us! . . .
>
> Perhaps you will think me in too high spirits if I say it, but still is it not true, am I not the luckiest woman on earth?

That evening, after bidding their guests farewell, they sat together and played the new things through. Litzmann finely remarked that one of the lines in the *Faust,* whose overture they did, is:

> *Eherner Füsse Rauschen vernehm ich!*
> (I hear the clashing of brazen footsteps!)

But these two happy mortals did not hear them.

On the 14th, Schumann wrote Joachim:

> How we wished yesterday to have you among us! It was a day of joy, the birthday of my wife. I fooled her with a grand piano, and then with a few compositions . . . and a *Fantasie for Violin and Orchestra,* in writing which I thought more of you. I send it along. It is my first attempt. Let me know what in it is perhaps not practicable. Also I beg you to write into the ms. the bowings of the arpeggios and other passages.

Perhaps these enormous pains which Robert took to delight Clara on their anniversary were in response to unconscious promptings that he was doing her a wrong by his too great marital assiduity—and absentmindedness. For, at the close of the month, she again found herself pregnant, and saw the so often deferred English tour brought again to nothing. And to the diary she groaned: "My last good years are slipping away, my strength too—certainly reason enough to be depressed. . . . I am more discouraged than I can say." In condonation of Robert's thoughtlessness it should be borne in mind that in the Germany of those days large families were customary; and that birth control had not yet been invented.

Early in 1853, Schumann developed a sudden obsessing interest in Spiritualism. This should not be regarded as a symptom of mental weakness. He may well have possessed some mediumistic power; but its exercise must have been bad for his already overstrained nervous system. On April 25th he wrote to Hiller, who was in Paris:

Yesterday for the first time we tipped tables. A wonderful force! Just think, I asked it how the rhythm of the first two measures of the C Minor Symphony went. It hesitated longer than usual before answering—at last it began ♪ ♩♩ ♩ —but at first rather slow. When I told it: "But, dear table, the tempo is faster [a remark contrary to the rules of the game], it hastened to rap in the right tempo. I also asked it if it could give me the number that I was thinking of, and it correctly gave *three*. We were all beside ourselves with astonishment, as if surrounded by wonders.

April 29

We have repeated our magnetic experiments. It is as though one were surrounded by wonders.[2] When you are here, perhaps you too will take part in these things.

Another avocation which must have been bad for his nerves was an attempt to put together an anthology of writings about music. With Teutonic thoroughness he began with the ancients. For this he had to refurbish the slight classical education of his

---

[2] Note the absent-minded repetition of this remark. Such *da capos* grew more frequent towards the end of his life.

Joseph Joachim

Johannes Brahms
Silverpoint by J. J. B. Laurens

youth. With an enormous expenditure of effort, he went through the original text of many Greek and Latin authors in search of their ideas about the art. *The Poet's Garden* was what he planned to call the collection.

On September 30th, 1853, Robert made a momentous entry in the diary: "Herr Brahms from Hamburg." This was the first of a series of jottings on the same subject:

1 Oct. Visit from Brahms (a genius).
2 Oct. Much with Brahms.
4 Oct. Music at home. Fantasie by Brahms.
5 Oct. Songs by Brahms and Sonata for violin and pianoforte.
7 Oct. Much with Brahms. Quartet by him.
8 Oct. Clara played Brahms my F Minor Sonata.
9 Oct. Began essay about Brahms.

And so the diary went on in an organ-point built upon the fundamental note "Brahms."

This episode, so momentously important in the lives of the Schumanns and of Johannes, was engineered by Joachim. The violinist had insisted that the young composer, in his walking tour down the Rhine, should call upon the Master. Now Johannes had a prejudice against Schumann, and doubted whether he would present Joachim's letter of introduction. But on the way he happened upon some Schumann scores and grew enthusiastic over them. This accident brought him to Düsseldorf.

That day Schumann chanced to be less absent-minded than usual; but when he asked the young guest to play, his manner was so withdrawn that Johannes' heart sank as he seated himself at the piano and began one of his early sonatas. However, after a few measures a remarkable change came over the Master's impassive features. His eyes grew animated. He edged forward on his chair and his lips puckered themselves in tremendous silent whistlings. Abruptly he sprang to his feet and held up one hand over the boy's blond head.

"*Aber bitte*," he cried, "would you wait a moment? Clara—" He rushed to the foot of the stairs and called: "Clara—come here at once!"

Clara hurried down anxiously. "Is anything the matter?"

Robert was laughing with excitement and pleasure. He pushed her into a chair: "My love, you must hear this. Such music as you have never before listened to! Young man, start again!"

They made Brahms play one of his works after another, and grew steadily more enthusiastic. Johannes was quite overwhelmed when the great man stroked him upon the shoulder and murmured: "Young fellow, you are the one I have been waiting for. We two understand one another!"

They kept him to dinner, and he made friends with the six children exactly as Robert had, long before, captured the hearts of the little Wiecks. Not many minutes passed before Johannes, for the first time, felt himself a part of real home life in a cultured, well-ordered environment. His early struggles in the depraved slums of Hamburg had been too strenuous to allow for anything like that.

When he returned, however, to the back room of the lowly tavern where he lodged, reaction set in. He was overcome with shame at his presumption, and with terror at the feelings which the beautiful and gracious Frau Schumann had awakened in his heart. So he resolved to stay away from the earthly paradise. And not until Clara had in person investigated the local hotels and lodging houses and dragged him back, insisting that he take all his meals at the Schumanns', did he capitulate.

It has already been remarked how difficult it is for composers to understand and appreciate their living colleagues. Although Beethoven relished Cherubini, Liszt appreciated Wagner and Schumann, and Brahms liked Dvořák—Beethoven once declared: "If I want to listen to good contemporary music, I will listen to my own." Liszt was not a great composer; but he was such a sympathetic soul that he would smack his lips over everything, good, bad, and indifferent. And against Brahms' relish for Dvořák we must pit his utter detestation and contempt for Tchaikovsky and Bruckner.

Robert Schumann, while discriminating, had the most catholic taste of any great composer that ever lived. He loved everything there was to love in Mendelssohn, Berlioz, and Loewe. It will be recalled that at the outset of his career he exclaimed of the debutant Chopin: "Hats off, gentlemen—a genius!" And at the other end of his life he became "the voice of one crying in the wilderness" when he discovered Johannes Brahms, and told the world: "This is he that should come!"

On the 19th the good times with Brahms were interrupted by a terse jotting: "Conference. Shameless people," which denoted that the harassed orchestra committee had been trying, more or less diplomatically, to squeeze him out of his post. Before reaching Robert, the gentlemen had to run the gauntlet of the formidable Clara. She noted that she had denounced their mission as an "infamous intrigue and an insult to Robert," and "a piece of insolence." "I cannot express what a towering rage it threw me into."

Robert's entry for October 9 shows how deeply he was moved by the encounter with "the young eagle," as he called Johannes. After many years of journalistic inactivity, he again wrote an article, his last, for the magazine which he had founded. It was entitled *New Paths*, and was couched in a curious reversion to the high-flown, lush, Jean-Paulian style of his early days. For example, it compared his young friend to a splendid river

like the Niagara at its best, when as a waterfall it rushes down from the heights, bearing rainbows upon its waves, with butterflies playing upon its banks and accompanied by the voices of nightingales.

The article tactlessly hailed Johannes as the coming man, at the expense of various other living composers such as Gade, Bargiel, and Franz, who were mentioned by name, and who naturally became furious and revengeful. While it made the musical world intensely curious about the unknown composer,[3] this article, on the whole, did Brahms more harm than good by arousing extravagant expectations and bitter opposition. Rumors of Schumann's sad condition had spread; and some anonymous libeler in the *Süddeutsche Musikzeitung* even went so far as to accuse the young man of having taken advantage of the Master's

[3] Mr. Burk makes Brahms' musical origin somewhat more humble than it really was, by calling his teacher, Marxsen, "only an unknown provincial musician"; whereas Marxsen then enjoyed a national reputation. And Hamburg, far from being provincial, was one of Germany's largest cities, with a symphony orchestra and a respectable musical life of its own.

mental disorder to wheedle this puff out of him, thus craftily making "a name for himself before he was officially in the least entitled to it." But Johannes bore all this in silence. He once declared that he would not reply to a newspaper attack, even if it should make him out a parricide.

Schumann, Brahms, and Dietrich now zestfully threw themselves into a musical lark. In collaboration they wrote a violin-and-piano sonata for their absent friend, the great violinist. The germ motive that ran through the piece was FAE. This was Joachim's motto. It stood for *"Frei aber einsam"*—"free but lonely." When Joachim arrived, the ms. was presented to him, concealed in a basket of flowers; and without hesitation he correctly guessed the authorship of each movement. The congenial good times with Brahms and Joachim and Dietrich which followed must have proved dangerously exhausting for the senior member of the company.

His meeting with the Schumanns was one of the key events in Johannes' career. He promptly fell in love with Robert's music —and with his wife. It was Robert who understood the boy, encouraged him, introduced him to the world, and secured him as publisher the ancient and honorable house of Breitkopf and Härtel. He also gave him discreet financial assistance. I think, however, that Moser goes too far in asserting that Brahms would have starved but for Schumann and Joachim.[4] The lad's marked ability as accompanist and concert pianist was a financial asset. He could have continued his hack-writing under the pen-name of Marks. And, if worst came to worst, he could have gone back to playing in dance-halls.

To the end Schumann had Brahms and his future career on his heart. One of his last letters, written on January 6th, 1854, was to Joachim:

Well now, where is Johannes? Is he with you? Then greet him from me. Does he fly high—or only under flowers? Does he still let no trumpets and kettledrums resound? Let him always remember the beginnings of the Beethoven symphonies; he should try to make

[4] *Joseph Joachim,* by Andreas Moser, 1910, v. II, p. 78.

something similar. The beginning is the main thing. When you have started, then the end comes, as if of itself, to meet you.

I always get into good humor when I write you. You are a physician for me.

Adieu!

Having been placed in a position where he felt obliged to break the Düsseldorf contract, Schumann did so, and began to look about for another post as conductor. Meanwhile, he and Clara toured in Holland. They were received with warm enthusiasm by the public, and with cold stuffiness by the Court. There the same old incident recurred. Prince Frederick graciously asked Robert: "Are you, too, musical?" and followed this up by wanting to know "upon which instrument?" This time Robert did not mind. No matter how ignorant and tactless such princelings as Frederick might be, he knew by now that the fame of his music was secure.

After the Rotterdam concert, a vast throng assembled in the icy blast before their hotel. Through it a torchlight procession wound its way. Led by Verhulst, a choir of 100 with orchestra performed the *Forest Chorus* and the *Birthday March* from the *Rose*. Robert was finally pushed out upon the balcony to stammer a few words of thanks.

Near the end of this tour, an incident occurred which proved that not all the changes which time was working upon Robert were for the worse. The old intolerance of any criticism or contradiction was giving way to a new personal humility, and a recognition that his friends might, on occasion, help him to avoid a mistake. From Amsterdam, December 20th, 1853, he wrote Verhulst to inquire about a portfolio (which he presently found that he had not lost after all); and to send him a small composition entitled *Parting Farewell*, asking him, if he liked it, to pass it on to the Dutch musical magazine, *Cäcilia*. Verhulst had the courage to advise Schumann not to publish the piece, on the grounds that it was insipid and unworthy of him. For less than this we have more than once seen Schumann fly into a passion. But this time he turned the other cheek also:

Dear Verhulst,

. . . I am pleased that you tell me such a powerful truth about the *Farewell*. Ordinarily my strong point does not lie in insipidity. What I was trying to do was to be *simple*. But you are right. . . .

Farewell, dear Verhulst! You are a good man!

What more could be asked for in the way of sportsmanship?

Christmas was spent at home in Düsseldorf. In the middle of January 1854 they went to Hanover for a fling with their friends Joachim, Brahms, and Julius Otto Grimm. Clara played the *"Emperor"* Concerto. Joachim conducted this, along with Robert's D Minor Symphony. Then, exchanging bow for baton, he performed the new violin *Fantasie*.

"The young eagle" must have found Schumann's vocal manner infectious; for Clara noted:

Brahms is conspicuous for his taciturnity. He says almost nothing. Or if, now and then, he does speak, it happens so softly that I cannot understand him. He surely has his own secret inner world—he absorbs everything beautiful and lives it inside himself.

Perhaps the boy feared that if he said anything, his voice would betray that terrific first love which was seething within.

Clara noted: "Very jolly, much champagne consumed." Nobody dreamed that this was the final farewell to the good days.

CHAPTER 29

THE RING AND THE RIVER

THOUGH Robert had written no music since November 1853, he had been happily at work compiling *The Poet's Garden*. The only upset to his health had been a brief aural attack in Holland. "Unnatural noises" inside his head frightened him so that he could not sleep. Nor could the sympathetic Clara. The cessation of these noises brought the hope that they were gone for good; but their silence was in reality no more than the pause between the overture and the opera itself.

On February 6th Schumann wrote his last letter to Joachim. These words have for us a poignant aura of meaning.

I have often written to you in sympathetic ink; and also between the present lines there is a secret writing that will later emerge.

And I have dreamed of you, dear Joachim. . . . Your hands were full of heron-feathers, and out of them flowed champagne. . . .

The music is silent now—at least outwardly. . . .

Now I will end. Already it grows dark.

For some years now, Schumann had suffered occasional auditory troubles, amounting at times almost to hallucination; with speech inhibitions, difficulty in making up his mind about tempi and in following fast ones, and attacks of morbid apathy, alternating with morbid irritability.

On February 10th, 1854, the illness which led up to the tragic catastrophe seventeen days later began with what he noted as a "pronounced and painful auditory affection." He was kept awake by hearing a single maddening tone, occasionally spelled off by one other.

247

The tones passed, but came back the next night. On the morning of the 12th, he employed a two-hour respite to write this remarkable letter to Julius Stern. Note the pun on the name Stern, which means star. See also how intelligent Schumann could be, even after the start of the final collapse:

I often live in lovely spheres, where I like it very much. Then, when I enter among human activities, and such a Star does not answer my letters, I am often thrown off the track. So do not let your last letter be really the last. I have sounded the tonic and third; now do you add the fifth to it.[1]

Then I will write you about my present situation in which there is also no outstanding harmony, a good deal like the first chord in the *finale* of the Ninth Symphony.

Farewell and let us drink together of Lethe.

What masterly understatement about the harmony, and what a prophetic good-by!

At ten that morning, every noise he heard was transmuted into music so glorious, and played on such wonderful-sounding instruments as no one else had yet heard on Earth. The sleepless nights were terrible for both Robert and Clara; but sometimes by day he enjoyed whole pieces played from start to finish by a full orchestra. However, that pleasure exhausted him terribly.

The doctors could do nothing to help. During the next days of alternate manic and depressive delusions, he grew steadily worse. On the 17th, he suddenly rose in the middle of the night to note down a melody which he said the angels had sung to him.

[1] Robert Browning, who prided himself more on his musical than on his poetic ability, may possibly have read this letter before writing his musical poem, *Abt Vogler*. Note in the following stanza his use of the triad and the star. It makes proud reading for a musician.

> But here is the finger of God, a flash of the will that can,
>   Existent behind all laws, that made them and, lo, they are!
> And I know not if, save in this, such gift be allowed to man,
>   That out of three sounds he frame, not a fourth sound, but a star.
> Consider it well: each tone of our scale in itself is naught:
>   It is everywhere in the world—loud, soft, and all is said:
> Give it to me to use! I mix it with two in my thought:
>   And there! Ye have heard and seen: consider and bow the head!

Next morning the angelic voices underwent an appalling change into those of demons. Accompanied by the most shockingly ugly music, they convicted him of deadly sin, and threatened to cast him instantly into hell fire. He fell into nervous paroxysms, and shrieked with anguish; for the angels now showed themselves as hyenas and tigers that hurled themselves upon him. He grew violent; and, for half an hour, two doctors who had been frantically summoned had all they could do to master him. Then friendlier voices breathed back a little courage into the tortured soul.

After resting, he actually arose and made some corrections in his 'Cello Concerto. This relieved him by somewhat muffling the eternal subjective voices. But the evil spirits soon returned to torture him again. When Clara labored to disprove their existence, he would answer piteously: "But, my dear Clara, surely you will believe that I am telling you no untruths!" Insane though he was, he kept true to form in hating contradiction; but the mellowing which his character had recently undergone was also carried across the mental Rubicon; so that Clara's opposition no longer made him angry.

The 20th he spent at his desk, listening to the angelic voices, and sometimes jotting down a word or two of the texts which they sang. In the next days, amid the visitations of the good and evil spirits, he managed to win enough clarity of mind to begin composing variations on the angelic theme which he had noted down a few nights previously. Often he begged Clara to leave him, for fear he might do her some injury. How many madmen are spiritually strong enough to recognize that they are mad, and to protect their dear ones against themselves? Character has been called "what a man is in the dark." A truer test of character would be what a man is in the mental dark.

On the evening of the 26th, Robert played Dietrich a sonata by young Martin Cohn, working himself into such a state of exaltation that the perspiration streamed down his forehead. Then he ate heavily and "in fearful haste." At half-past nine he suddenly got up and called for his clothes, saying that he must go at once to the insane asylum—an almost miraculous victory of mind over derangement. Then, with apparently unclouded intelligence, he laid out everything needed for the dreadful journey. When Clara objected: "Robert, do you want to leave your wife and children?" he gently answered: "It is not really for long. Soon I will come back quite well."

The doctor persuaded him to go to bed; but Robert would not let Clara stay with him, and insisted on having a guard. The next morning he was sunk in ghastly melancholy; and to all his wife's attempts at comfort and reassurance, he would only reply: "Clara, I am not worthy of your love!"

He made a clean copy of the variations, and was on the last one when Clara was called away for a moment, leaving Marie on watch. Clara said later that this was the first time in ten days that she had left his side; but this is contradicted by other statements of hers. Then Robert rose with a sigh, and wandered into the bedroom. Marie thought he would come back at once; but he did not. Instead, in slippers, and partly dressed, he ran out into a violent rainstorm.

It was some time before the family discovered that he had left the house. When Berthe the maid rushed in wild-eyed with the news of his disappearance, Clara thought her heart would literally stop beating. Dr. Hasenclever, Dietrich, and almost everybody in the house hastened forth to seek him; but without success.

Alone in his bedroom, Robert composed and left for his wife this note: "Dear Clara, I shall cast my wedding ring into the Rhine. Do you do the same. Then the two rings will be united." [2]

That done, he hurried down to the Rhine Bridge, through a gay Carnival throng that was as little deterred from its preoccupations by the weather as he himself. At the toll-gate he found he had no money, but gave the keeper his handkerchief instead.

When he came to the middle of the bridge, he paused and cast the golden ring into the Rhine. Did his bewildered spirit have some confused idea about the ring of the Nibelungs which was returned to the same river in the final catastrophe of the epic story? This may well be for, as will be recalled, Schumann an-

[2] It will be recalled that, sixteen years before, during the troubled days of courtship, he had dreamed of casting his engagement ring into a deep pool.

ticipated Wagner in considering the musical use of this saga.
Throwing his arms wide, the Master leaped after the ring.

Down in those green depths he heard beautiful music, of
which he afterward spoke with rapture mingled with bitter
regret that he could not set down on paper the elusive strains.
Perhaps, in his bewilderment, he thought he heard the singing
of the Rhine Maidens and of the Lorelei.

Some fishermen saw him leap, rowed hard to the spot, and
pulled him into the boat, from which the disappointed Master
made one more attempt at suicide before they reached land.

Eight men half-carried him home while, in despair, he covered
his face with his hands. In its motley costumes, the Carnival
crowd crowed with delight when they saw the fantastic group,
enjoying it as a well-acted part of their celebration. Thus Schumann's final catastrophe poetically synthesized the alpha and
omega of his art, which nearly began with the *Carnaval,* and
nearly ended with the *"Rhenish"* Symphony. It also symbolized
his life, which began with a merry childhood of fond make-
believe, and ended in the second childhood of insanity.

Out of consideration for Clara's pregnant condition, she was
not allowed to see Robert. The doctors told her that he had
again asked to be sent to an asylum; and they recommended a
private one at Endenich, near Bonn. Later she wrote: "He, my
glorious Robert, in an asylum! How could I possibly stand it?
And there I was, forbidden even to press him once more to my
heart."

It hurt her unspeakably to think that she, who in the good
days had not failed him, must now at his time of most dire need,
appear to do so. Describing what happened on the 4th of March,
she wrote:

Oh, God! now the carriage stood at our door. Robert, having dressed
in great haste, entered the carriage with Dr. Hasenclever and two
warders, without a word of inquiry about me or the children. And I
sat . . . in dazed stupefaction and thought—now I must die! . . . I
had slipped Dr. Hasenclever a bouquet for him, and this was passed
along during the drive. He held it long in his hand without noticing
it; then he smelled it, smiled, and pressed Dr. Hasenclever's hand!
Later he gave a flower to everyone in the carriage. Dr. Hasenclever
brought me his. I kept it, but my heart bled!

CHAPTER 30

SCHUMANNDÄMMERUNG

S O now the stricken Robert had to share the exclusive place he had until recently held in Clara's heart, with another musical genius, a conservative of far less disturbing originality but nevertheless of even more essential greatness. When Brahms heard of the tragedy at the Schumanns', he hastened to move to Düsseldorf, arriving on March 3rd so that, in this crisis, he could stand by the woman he loved. Like Robert, Johannes had a mother-fixation, which fiercely intensified his passion for the maternal Clara. Perhaps a predisposition for such a fixation was inherited; for Brahms' father had married a motherly woman seventeen years older than himself; and Clara was fourteen years older than Johannes.

However, even the most devoted adoration and the most appealing crisis of need could not manage to keep a brusque, impatient nature like Johannes' and a jealous, suspicious nature like Clara's amiable enough to make perpetual harmony. Perhaps she discovered girls making eyes at him, and let him feel the weight of her possessiveness; for as early as March 26th she complained in her diary:

Just now Brahms was not very nice to me; and, generally speaking, it seems to me that he has been spoiled by the fearful adoration of the other young people; for often he expresses himself about things in such a manner as, for instance, I have never heard from my Robert.

This was the first intimation of what was to be a lifelong disappointment. Clara never succeeded in getting the strong and independent Johannes tied to her apron-strings as she had tied Robert.

But soon, both the Endenich news and Johannes' disposition improved, and Clara was notably cheered. On April 10th, Dr. Hasenclever brought her word direct from the asylum that the patient had made the first step toward recovery. And Clara wrote:

> O God, how I thank thee for this glimpse of light in my misfortune! . . . The good Brahms keeps on showing himself as a really deep-feeling friend. He does not express it much; but one sees in his features and his eloquent eye how he mourns with me for the loved one whom he so highly honors.

On June 11th, Clara, surrounded by love, but unhappy, gave birth to her eighth child, Felix. And on July 21st she was cheered by a bouquet of flowers which she called: "the first sign of love in five months from him, from my Robert." To obtain a reasonable picture of Clara's emotional state after Robert's catastrophe, one must balance the statements which she entered in the diary about her grief for Robert, and the protestations of innocence she wrote to her children many years afterwards, with the mutually fervid love-letters that passed at this time between her and Brahms. Not all of them have survived, because Brahms later cast a large bundle of them into the Rhine. But even in those which it was considered discreet to preserve and publish, he who runs may read a very swift and violent flare-up of intimacy and passion, followed by a long cooling-off, comparable to the afterglow beyond a Norwegian fjord.

Most biographers of Brahms and the Schumanns have stoutly denied any extreme intimacy between Clara and Johannes; but for argument they have been forced to fall back upon that letter to her children in which she denied the truth of the scandal which most of her world affirmed. While there is no sure affirmative evidence beyond the fact of their week's walking trip up the Rhine together at the height of the affair, these are strong probabilities: (1) That, while Robert was in the asylum, Clara and Johannes had a liaison; [1] (2) that, owing to Johannes' psychic

[1] Some years ago, a book was published in Germany with the object of

handicaps [2] and to the consequences of Clara's excessive maternity, this liaison was not a brilliant success; and (3) that it soon cooled down into a platonic friendship.

Mr. Burk categorically states that Brahms was deterred from a liaison by his respect for her "superiority . . . in the knowledge of experience," and for "her sanctity as the wife of Robert Schumann." But Johannes, in his mighty, young creativeness, undoubtedly knew himself far superior to Clara as a musician, even though he might not play the piano quite so well. As for poor Schumann, he was mad and out of the running. Not long before, the depressed and discouraged Clara had complained that her last good years were being eaten up by eternal pregnancies. (See p. 240.) Now suddenly she found herself reprieved and presented with a new lease of life. Here she was, lonely and in love with Johannes, who was wild about her and was giving her for the first time the youth she had missed under the stern rule of Father Wieck.

To life in the Endenich asylum Robert adapted himself with amazing smoothness. And soon there was a temporary improvement, so that he was permitted an almost daily pilgrimage to salute the Beethoven monument in Bonn, that very monument which had once played its part in inspiring the piano *Fantasie*.

On September 18th, 1854, he wrote Clara:

Now I should like to beg something of you, that you would write to Dr. Peters and ask him to give me sometimes what money I want, and then repay him. Poor people often beg from me, and then I feel sorry. Apart from this, my life is not as active as formerly. How quite different that used to be!

In their childlike simplicity, these last words are heart-rending.

All his thoughts were now of the past. His wounded mind shrank from the future. Sometimes he corresponded a little with his publishers, and even improvised at the piano. Or, reverting to the task begun in his youth, he tried to harmonize the

proving that Felix, Clara's youngest child, was the son of Brahms. It is unobtainable, having been bought up and suppressed by the Schumann family. Felix wrote the text of one of Brahms' best songs, *Meine Liebe ist grün*.

[2] See *The Unknown Brahms*, p. 252 ff. Also there probably was a physical handicap, due to pituitary insufficiency.

Caprices of Paganini. He said he hated to be inactive for "as little as a quarter of an hour."

Geheimrat Oebeke, the nephew of Dr. Richarz, often saw him walking in the asylum garden:

He would frequently stand still, and occasionally would tell himself aloud: "That is not true; that is a lie!" My uncle told me that these remarks were in answer to inner voices which denounced his compositions as plagiarisms.

He enjoyed the visits of Brahms and Joachim. The latter wrote:

Three times I visited Schumann in Endenich. The first time I received comforting impressions. It was really his old friendly glance, the richly affectionate true-blue eye just as it shines out at us, dreaming of lovely worlds, from so many ranks of his notes. He talked much and hastily, asked about friends and musical happenings, and showed me lists of the names of cities, arranged alphabetically, which he had zealously compiled.

When I was about to leave, he took me with great secrecy into a corner (although we were unobserved) and told me that he longed to get away from that place; for the people did not understand him at all, nor what he stood for, or wanted.

The mind that had created the *Fantasie*, the Quintet, the Quartets, and the C Major Symphony, was now ardently occupying itself with the sort of exercise that ordinary men and women might use at night to induce slumber. For Schumann the golden day was done, the imagination was dimmed, the radiance dying in the west. These bedtime routines of the mind were its preparation for the longest sleep of all. When not engaged in them, he would often sit simply inert, his right hand holding a handkerchief to his lips.

Medical opinion seems on the whole to be that Schumann's trouble was a manic-depressive inheritance. This was aggravated by his being spoiled in childhood, and thus unfitted for a smooth contact with life; further, by the sabotage to his nervous system of the long and chaste engagement and the savage struggle with Wieck and with the Wieckian side of Clara herself, during which his creativeness was, to a certain extent, dammed back. When this mighty force was released by eventual triumph and marriage with a woman who gratified his mother-fixation, it proved uncontrollable, and ended by crushing him. The final result was not, as some have thought, progressive paralysis. The fears, depressions, and strange habits, such as walking on tiptoe and puckering the lips, the dizziness and fear of high places and of edged tools, the suspicions, the trouble with speech, the aural delusions, the slow loss of intellect—all these, progressing by fits and starts, proclaimed the gradual approach of that dread foe of genius, dementia præcox.

There are passages in Schumann's Endenich letters that make one think of the charming children whom he remembered in the *Scenes from Childhood.* For example, that of September 18th, 1854, gave the same importance to the news that the new baby was born, that Marie and Elise had played pieces from *Bilder aus Osten,* and that Johannes had moved to Düsseldorf.

This lack of perspective is made all the more touching by various extremely lucid intervals. One of them is reflected in his fine, just appreciation of the new Brahms Ballades, Op. 10. Of the third of these he wrote, on January 6, 1855:

> Demonic—wholly splendid, and how it grows always more secret after the *pp* in the Trio; the latter quite transfigured, and the recapitulation and close. Has this Ballade, dear Clara, perhaps made the same impression on you? . . . Now, forward to overtures and symphonies! . . . A symphony or opera which arouses enthusiasm and makes a sensation gets a composer and also his other compositions ahead the fastest. He must! [3]
>
> Now greet Johannes heartily, and the children, and you, my heart's best love, remember with the old love your devoted
>
> ROBERT

Clara, however, was of a quite different mind about the third Ballade. In the part that Robert found "demonic" she saw angels winging their way through the azure heavens. And, though Brahms himself, and most other musicians from that day to this, have endorsed Schumann's view, the adjective "demonic" made her very apprehensive. In fact, she had been on the point of

[3] This last was a message to Brahms.

releasing Robert from captivity; but this about the Ballade—perhaps the most lucid page in all of his letters from the asylum—seemed to her so crazy that, on wrong grounds, she made the right decision to leave him where he was. What irony that the insane Robert's musical judgment should have proved sounder than the sane Clara's; and that he had to die before he had wholly completed the education of that musical taste and intelligence of hers which had been so rudimentary when they were married!

Clara's lot was not easy. Though a large purse was made up for her by wealthy Leipzigers, and Paul Mendelssohn sent her a substantial draft in memory of his brother Felix, she took to the concert stage in order to repay the Leipzigers as soon as possible, and she put the draft away to be cashed only in case of dire need.

Her courage, however, was mingled with relief that the tremendous handicap of childbearing was done with; that she could now practise as much as she liked without fear of disturbing a sensitive composer; and that, after all the years of thwarted ambition, she could now give free rein to her passion for concert-giving. At the same time, she could act as propagandist for Robert's music, and could get in general missionary work on the public taste. Living with Robert fourteen years had eventually brought her so far along the right road that she could genuinely despise mechanical bravura, and give programs of really good music from start to finish. She had even attained that degree of mastery where she could make an audience listen to every note of the redoubtable *Hammerklavier* Sonata of Beethoven, and like it.

As is usual in á difficult situation like hers, she had to cope with the half-baked advice of well-meaning friends, each with a different idea about curing Robert; and with others who earnestly strove to bring her to Jesus.

That masterful egotist Bettina von Arnim was the worst of all. She visited Schumann, and wrote Clara that his trouble was merely a passing attack of nerves, that the head physician, Dr. Richarz, was a hypochondriac, that Endenich was no place for him, and that she must get him home at once. Of course this excited and upset Clara terribly, and she dispatched Joachim post-haste to Endenich. After a thorough survey, however, her level-headed friend was able to convince her that the hasty and officious Bettina had been wholly wrong on every count.

Just in time for Johannes' birthday, May 7th, 1855, came the last letter which Clara was to receive from her husband:

DEAR CLARA:

On the first of May I sent you a Spring messenger; but the following days were very agitated; more you will learn from my letter which you will get no later than the day after tomorrow. Over it broods a shadow; but the rest of it, my lovely, will rejoice you.

I did not know about the birthday of the one we love; so I must put on wings so that the score may arrive tomorrow.

I have enclosed a drawing of Felix Mendelssohn for you to put into the album. An inestimable memento!

Fare well, you dear!

Your

ROBERT.

Robert had sent direct to Johannes the original ms. score of the *Bride of Messina* Overture, with a few affectionate words.

Despite Clara's distress over the ominous phrase in this letter about the "shadow," she greatly enjoyed Johannes' birthday celebration in her own home. She wrote:

He savored it to the full in the gayest of moods, so that I really seemed younger to myself; for he drew me along into the whirlpool of his humor; and since Robert's illness I have never known such a jolly day.

On the morrow, however, came bad news from Robert's physician. He was suffering from agitation and insomnia, and again complained of hearing voices.

At this time Clara cannot have been too easy to get on with. She quarreled with her dear old friend and benefactress, Jenny Lind, because the singer did not like Brahms' music. When Liszt came, as chivalrous, noble, and sportsmanlike as ever, and wished to compliment and please her by playing with her the four-hand arrangement of the *Genoveva* Overture, followed by some Bach solos, her diary treated him as roughly as if he had been the most miserable botcher of a pupil. According to Clara, her illustrious rival played "horribly." She felt these "hallowed rooms" so "profaned" that, as she put it, "I could ease my heart only through tears." And with naïve egotism she ended that though Liszt

had, on the one hand, taken from me all pleasure in making music today, yet I now felt the irresistible urge to hear a healthy tone and to end more worthily with Robert's *Symphonic Etudes*, which I played better than almost ever before.

Leaving on June 15th for an engagement at the tiny Court of Detmold (where she was afterwards to be instrumental in securing a long engagement for Brahms), she wrote: "Bad day . . . how difficult the parting from Johannes is for me! How I hang with my whole soul upon the friend! How mightily I always feel it when I must separate myself from him!"

Joachim was twice bidden to come and play with her there; and the second time she parted from him with tears.

At Ems she was met by Brahms. In Coblenz he stuffed their combined baggage into his rucksack. Taking along Berthe, the maid, as a gesture toward convention, they started on a tramp five heavenly days long up the sunny Rhine, through the Niederwald, to Frankfort. Even then they could not bear to part; and the idyl continued until they could dream, hand in hand, on the ruins of the romantic castle of Heidelberg. "What one lives through on such a day in one's innermost being," she wrote, "is past description!"

When Clara went alone for a further vacation on the Kieler Bucht, she felt thoroughly upset. Her biographer Litzmann says that

she tortured herself and her friend [Brahms] with all sorts of scruples and reproaches that were objectively unfounded and that, when she realized their unfairness, filled her with bitter remorse.

"At length a dear letter from Johannes," she noted on August 21st, "that lifts me up a little. If only I had not yesterday written him so reproachfully!" (This was a foretaste of the painful scene that she was soon to make in Göttingen, when she began to suspect that he was falling in love with Agathe von Siebold.) On September 10th she was again cast down by a letter from Dr. Richarz definitely announcing that she must give up all hope of her husband's complete recovery.

Early in 1856, Clara gave five concerts in Vienna. She approached that charming place with gloomy forebodings engendered by the indifference which, nine years before, Robert's music had encountered. But there must have been a little leaven at work; for this time the whole Viennese lump appeared miraculously leavened, so that it was hard to tell if people were more enthusiastic for Schumann's music or for its interpreter.

However, to the serious musician, Vienna is never quite all beer and skittles. Clara lamentably complained about the slipshod character of a Mozart festival which suffered atrociously from the local curse of *Schlampigkeit*. And when she had to play at "a fearful soiree" in the house of Liszt's Hungarian friend, Countess Bánffy, and protested to her old rival that her pieces were much too good for such an unmusical rabble, the everchivalrous Liszt suggested, with his otherwise irresistible smile: "Well, why not play 'em a couple of bad pieces by Liszt? They'd just suit this gang." And the humorless but forthright Clara made answer: "You are right. But that is a thing I could not do."

April 8th saw her started on the often deferred tour to England, a country which she disliked, and which she disciplined for its own good. One evening at Lady Overstone's the guests talked during the music. Clara took her hands from the keys and announced that she was not used to playing while conversation went on. The admonition was exactly what the English society of that day needed.

In barely three months, she played twenty-six times in public, made a few good friends, laid the foundations of her future immense popularity in Great Britain, and began to love the land.

Homecoming was bitter; on the day of her first London concert, she had learned that Robert's condition was desperate and that his illness had reached its final stages. On July 6th she arrived at Düsseldorf, and was shocked by a dispatch from Endenich saying that if she wanted to see Robert alive she must come at once. With Brahms she hastened there; but on reaching the asylum, learned that the crisis was temporarily past. She noted:

Johannes saw him and, together with the doctor, begged me not to go to him, put it in the light of a duty to my children not to upset myself thus, etc. So I traveled back without having seen him. But I could not stand it long, the pain, the longing for him, ah, to have only a glance from him, to let him feel my nearness—I had to go, and on Sunday the 27th I traveled there again with Johannes. Between 6 and 7 that evening I saw him. He smiled at me, and with a great exertion —for he could no longer control his limbs—put his arm about me—I will never forget it. That embrace I would not trade for all treasures. My Robert, that was the way in which we had to see one another again; with what difficulty I had to find my way to your beloved features; what an anguished look!

Torn from me more than two and a half years ago, without a farewell, how much I had on my heart. And now I lay quietly at his feet, hardly daring to breathe, and only now and then receiving a glance, clouded indeed, but so unspeakably mild.

Everything about him was so sacred to me, the air which he, the noble man, shared with me. It seemed that he kept talking much with spirits, could not long stand anybody about him, which made him uneasy; but one could no longer understand him. Only once did I catch "my." Surely he wished to say "Clara," for at the same time he gave me a friendly glance; then once more, "I know"—probably "you."

The following day Clara offered him wine. It spilled and ran over her hand, and Robert, "with the happiest expression and real haste," licked it from her fingers.

On Tuesday, July 29th, 1856, Robert Schumann died. He was quite alone. Not expecting the end so soon, Clara and Johannes had gone away somewhere. Two days later he was buried in Bonn. Five young plane trees surrounded the new grave. Beethoven's town had planted them in prevision of the passing of Beethoven's successor.

The honorary pallbearers were Brahms, Joachim, and Dietrich, the young trio who had been so dear to the Master. Brass instruments intoned ancient chorales. Grillparzer, the poet whose words had conveyed Beethoven and Schubert to rest, spoke here as well. Clara and the friends cast earth upon the coffin.

"Dust to dust."

Over the open grave Ferdinand Hiller spoke these beautiful words:

Your weary spirit! You had asked too much from it. The divine flame which may descend in a hallowed hour upon the grateful recipient, you demanded every instant as your right. Long it willingly appeared at your call—and who can say how it came to leave you? Ah, perhaps it was only a brief coolness such as comes between the best of friends, that seemed like dissension merely to our feeble vision. And now you two are again on the best of terms, and smile at all we say of you here, and smile indulgently and forgive us!

Those things that Robert Schumann had all his life feared and hoped had come to pass. He had finally encountered the dreaded heart of darkness, and it had laid his too-young body to molder beneath the young plane trees of Bonn.

On the other hand, as he had wistfully hoped it would, his music was taking on a manifold life. It had now begun reaching out towards all humanity in ever-widening circles—like those rings made in the waters of the Rhine by the fall of a golden circlet, or the death-plunge of a desperate sufferer. And young composers in Germany and Scandinavia, France and Russia were falling more and more under the spell of its influence.

Another event was taking place which he had neither hoped nor feared. One of his chief creations had been the taste and artistic intelligence of the loved woman who had inspired his noblest works. And from now on, as long as she should live, this woman with the Schumann-given taste and intelligence was to be the most potent of all the forces that furthered her husband's work, and was to pass on the torch by inspiring the best music of Robert Schumann's greatest successor.

INTERMEZZO

THE MAN OF LETTERS

*The artist's vocation—to send light
into the depths of the human heart.*

ROBERT SCHUMANN

THE MAN OF LETTERS

M ANY illustrious musicians have excelled at writing words as well as notes. Philipp Emanuel Bach, Rameau, Weber, Berlioz, Liszt, and Wagner had critical and literary ability. But among them all Robert Schumann was easily the best critic and man of letters. He was drawn toward the field of criticism by the lofty ideals of a reformer. And writing was in Robert's blood, inherited from the father who had ruined his health by finishing seven novels within a year and a half, and thereby earning not only the girl he loved, but also the amazing sum of a thousand thalers.

Apart from contemporary instances [wrote Sir Henry Hadow],[1] it is only in Schumann that we find a musician who unites the highest creative power with the true breadth and tolerance of a critic.

Besides steering German criticism away from the silly methods of Rochlitz and his colleagues, who wrote of music in terms of the poetic images which a performance happened to suggest to them, and besides elevating the deplorable taste of the day, the generous Schumann did invaluable service in encouraging those composers who deserved encouragement. He furthered the art as much by discovering and acclaiming such contemporaries as Chopin, Berlioz, and Brahms, as he did by writing his original music. His exploit in unearthing the forgotten Schubert manuscripts would alone have earned him the gratitude of mankind. And he discovered more than contemporary musicians. In his

[1] *Studies in Modern Music* (essay on Berlioz). New York, 1893-95, Macmillan.

degenerate day he was almost the only one to recognize and proclaim the greatness of Johann Sebastian Bach,[2] Mozart, Beethoven, and Schubert.

"The ideal critic," writes Ernest Newman,

would be he whose Raro alone spoke in public, after his Florestan and Eusebius had fully threshed out their views before him in the quiet of his own chamber. When Schumann speaks in his own person, it is usually after some such internal hearing of both sides. Hence the general rightness of his judgments. One's first impression is that he was uncritically lenient toward work that we now see to have been of the second class. But if we read carefully his remarks upon people like Sterndale Bennett, for example, we see that, while kindly enthusiastic about the best elements in their work, he says against it practically all that can be said today. . . .

It is the critics, perhaps, who should think most warmly of the master, for it was in his critical work that he had the greatest difficulties to face, and that he most unmistakably broke ground.

Here is an almost unparalleled phenomenon—a creative composer who was at the same time a creative critic and a selflessly greathearted appreciator of the best in his colleagues—no matter how vastly their popularity might exceed his own. In this man's reviews one looks in vain for the Kalliwoda-is-not-Beethoven sort of censure which has, throughout the ages, infested criticism. Schumann would have heartily endorsed such a saying as Van Gogh's: "Admire as many things as you can. *Most* people do not admire enough things."

He could actually admire musicians whose theories he combated. The following quotation will show that his philosophy as an absolute musician was antipodally opposed to that of Berlioz, the programmatist. Commenting upon an essay in which Hagen accused that Frenchman of formlessness, Schumann wrote:

---

[2] Here he should share equal honors with Mendelssohn (see p. 180), another master whose fame he did much to spread. How it must have startled the musical world when Schumann wrote: "The deeply combining poetic and humorous elements of the new music stem chiefly from Bach. The so-called Romantics are far closer to Bach than to Mozart. As for me, I confess daily to this high one, and seek through him to purify and strengthen myself."

We have not been able to find so much formlessness in the music, but rather the contrary, too often form without content. All the more do we agree [with Hagen] that it is a bad sign when a budding composer does not above all wish to make music, pure and simple, but desires instead to depict all sorts of things by means of music, and to use this art as only a servant or messenger.

Yet, despite this fundamental antinomy, Schumann could appreciate Berlioz in a big way. In his review of the overture to *Les Francs-Juges,* after pointing out its "uncouth Polyphemic" quality, he continued:

However, in the firm conviction that certain school-desk theorists have done far more damage than our practical heaven-stormer, and that the protection of pitiable mediocrity is a good deal more destructive than the honoring of such poetic extravagance, we once for all charge posterity to certify as follows. When it comes to the compositions of Berlioz, we have not done the usual thing and applied our critical wisdom ten years too late, but announce in advance that in this Frenchman there is something of genius.

When Chopin's Opus 2 came out, Schumann was the first to declare that he too was a genius, and to write of his music with delicate discrimination. Consider this about the *Nocturnes,* Op. 37:

They differ essentially from his earlier ones in simpler ornamentation, in a more tranquil grace. One is familiar with Chopin's former style, sown thick with gold baubles, tinsel, and pearls. Now he has aged and developed. He still loves ornamentation; but it is more thoughtful, and through it the nobility of poesy shimmers all the more lovably. Yes, one cannot deny him taste—taste of the finest. Of course this sort of thing is not in the thoroughbassists' line; they are alert only for parallel fifths, and every one of these can arouse them to fury. But they could learn a number of things from Chopin, and above all how to make fifths.

See the exquisite discernment with which Schumann analyzes the Italian ingredient in the music of his friend. He is dealing with the first movement of Chopin's B Flat Minor Sonata, Op. 35:

The first part of this work brings us lovely song. Indeed, as time goes on, the Polish national flavor of most of the former Chopin melodies seems progressively to vanish, as if he were often approaching Italy (via Germany). One knows that Bellini and Chopin were friends, that they often showed one another their compositions, and that each probably influenced the other's art. But . . . it is only a gentle leaning toward the style of the south. Directly the song is done, the whole Sarmatian,[3] in his defiant originality, again flashes out of the music. Bellini, at least, never dared nor could dare make such an interlacing of chords as we find at the close of the second portion of the first movement. . . . So, too, the close of the whole movement smacks little of the Italian—which reminds me of Liszt's apposite word: Rossini and his consorts always close with a *'votre très humble serviteur'*; —how different from Chopin, whose endings express more the contrary.

Consider as well this graceful appreciation of an Italian composer whom one would have thought far outside the sympathetic orbit of the mind that conceived *Carnaval,* the *Scenes from Childhood,* the quartets, and the Piano Concerto:

Now comes Cherubini, an artist grown gray in the highest aristocracy of art and in his own esthetic views, who at a great age is still the chief harmonist of our world, the learned, accomplished, interesting Italian who, in his austere seclusion and strength of character, I am sometimes tempted to compare to Dante.

Wagner is often praised as having been the first to recognize the true worth of Beethoven's last quartets. His book on L. v. B., with its rhapsodical poetic program for the C Sharp Minor, appeared in 1870. But the following review was published thirty-two years before that, in 1838. Schumann is speaking of "those treasures of the first magnitude," the Quartets in E Flat, Op. 127, and in C Sharp Minor, Op. 131:

for whose greatness we can find no words. Along with certain choruses and original works of Seb. Bach, they seem to me to stand at the uttermost limits which man's art and imagination have yet attained. [And in a note he continues:] Scarcely anything more wonderful can be offered the human spirit than those creations which, in

[3] Sarmatia is the old name for Poland and western Russia.

their profound fashioning, their flight of ideas outsoaring all earthly statutes, can in no wise be compared . . . with other, more recent, music.

To a man of Schumann's capacity for sympathetic appreciation and hatred of arrogant philistinism, it was second nature to attack the small-calibered critics of his day. His favorite bullet was the aphorism:

They reduce the proud oak to sawdust.
The music that moves the nightingale to a love-song moves the pug dog to yap.
Sour grapes, bad wine.
The equipped eye sees stars, where the unequipped can discern nothing but cloud-shadows.

A true poet and original thinker speaks from nearly every page of his two generous and fascinating volumes of *Gesammelte Schriften* (*Collected Writings*). His pen sparkles with vitality and imagination, as when it deals with Berlioz's *Symphonie fantastique:*

A first glimpse of the symphony cast me into an extraordinary frame of mind. Even as a child I often set pieces of music upside down on the rack in order to enjoy the strangely tortuous note-edifices —just as I later enjoyed the reflections of Venetian palaces capsized in the water. Right-side-up the symphony resembles such topsy-turvy music.

And of a great oratorio he exclaimed: "If you listen long enough to Haydn's *Creation*, you will finally come to hear the grass growing!"

Poetic figures and brilliant reflections (usually right-side-up) besieged him in such numbers that once in a fit of delightful exasperation he paraphrased the old saying about not seeing the wood for the trees: "I can't see the main issue for the thoughts!" And in all his writings one discerns the composer's finely discriminating ear, as when he calls "the eternal music" of the Italian language "a long-drawn-out A minor chord," and likens the name Moscow to the music of deep bells.

The distinctive creatively-esthetic feature of his music [asserts Tessmer] [4] is also the determining element of his writings about music, and at the same time their greatest merit. . . . The music criticism in his writings is an integral expression of the totality of his esthetic intuitions and demands.

To Schumann's way of thinking, the best criticism must "of itself leave an impression like that produced by the original work of art which called it forth."

He compared his *Magazine* to a river craft, on board which

we rich wanderers, sped by the current, fly swiftly down between the most fertile banks of the present and, if Heaven wills, attain the high seas and a fair destination.

When music aroused his antipathy, Schumann could be formidably severe. Few composers have ever suffered sounder castigations than his pen gave the commercially minded gentleman named Beer who changed his name to Meyerbeer. And after hearing one particularly detested opera, Schumann entered this eloquently laconic note in his *Little Book of the Theater:*

"Prophet" by Giac. Meyerbeer.

(Feb. 2, 1850)

†

Toward lesser offenders his severity was usually spiced with humor, as when he remarked of Loewe's repetitious Piano Sonata, Op. 33:

Heavens, thought I . . . to tell a person four times hand-running that you have little to tell seems to me a bit too much.

With one tiny spark of wit he could illuminate the quality of another's musical judgment, as when he observed that Becker felt himself the equal of Bach, or when he confided to De Sire that Czerny did not have ideas enough to fill one stave, let alone three. Of the editor of the *Stuttgarter Nationalzeitung* he said:

[4] Hans Tessmer, *Der klingende Weg.* Regensburg, 1923, Bosse.

"On the musical side he's feeble; but he knows how to blow his own trombone."

As a prime example of Schumann's imaginatively humorous writing one should read his essay *Der Psychometer*, in *Collected Writings*, I, 101. The psychometer is a clever invention of Florestan's. Though antedating our modern lie-detector by almost a century, it far surpasses that machine in every way. The thing is indispensable to the music critic; for all he need do is to shovel the review copies into its maw, and out comes an absolutely trustworthy analysis of the composers' faults and excellences, without odium to the reviewer.

Even in gauging the effectiveness of his own music, Schumann did not often allow wishful thinking to cloud his clear judgment. Few composers have ever been in a position to write of a favorite child as, in 1838, he wrote to Clara about the *Symphonic Etudes:*

> You have done well not to play my Etudes. They are not suitable for the public, and it would be silly if I should complain of their not understanding what was not intended for their approval but exists solely for its own sake.

But what damning evidence of the bad public taste of his times!

This man had none of the arrogance of the little tin gods of criticism. No infallible Wagnerian ukases fulminated from his direction, for he possessed the humility of true greatness, and this humility extended to his work as an editor.

> We still [he wrote] require a magazine devoted to "the music of the future." In its editorial chair we naturally need only such men as the former blind cantor of St. Thomas's School, and the deaf *Kapellmeister* who reposes in Vienna.

Here, however, Schumann did himself an injustice. He was better equipped for such a post than either of the giants mentioned. What Beethoven's music-pen started among the pedantic theorists of his time in the way of wig-scratching, head-shaking, and anathema-launching, Schumann's critical writings accomplished among the backward-looking estheticians of his own day. And the deaf *Kapellmeister's* inspiration for forward-looking youth was possibly no more potent than that of the half-dumb composer-editor.

Schumann had the modesty of the great critic.

The riper the judgment, the more unassuming and simple its expression. He alone who has pursued phenomena through studies ten times repeated, through conscientious comparison in long-continued self-denial, knows how meagerly our knowledge accretes, how slowly our judgment purifies itself, and how correspondingly cautious our statements should be. Somewhere I read: "Without the most varied experiences and funds of guiding information we confront a work of art open-eyed but blind."

This quality made Schumann one of the first great musicians to recognize the invaluable function of the musical amateur.

Be careful, Eusebius, not to value too lightly the worth of that better sort of amateurism which is an integral part of the life of art; for the catch-word, "no artist, no connoisseur," must be held as a half-truth until one can point out a period in which art has flourished without the mutual inspiration of artist and amateur.

—RARO

How felicitously this poet-musician could express himself, even in so unliterary a form as a catalogue! Here is his list of desiderata for musical performance:

Just think what factors must be united if beauty is to appear in its entire nobility and glory. To this end we must have: (1) great, deep intentions and idealism in the work of art, (2) enthusiasm in its interpretation, (3) virtuosity in performance, harmonious ensemble, as from one soul, (4) inner desire and need of giver and receiver, favorable mood of the moment (on the part of both hearer and performer), (5) the happiest constellation of time-elements, and special factors of spatial [acoustical] and other minor conditions, (6) communication and direction of impressions, emotions, points of view—reflection of the joy of art in the eyes of others. Is not such coincidence a throw, with six dice, of six times six?

—EUSEBIUS

In contrast with this elaborate program he summed up in a word the viewpoint of the creator: "The most beautiful music is where the Faust-mantle of fantasy envelops powerful forms."

Wordsworth's memorable definition of poetry as "emotion recollected in tranquillity" would have appealed to the Schumann who declared:

A frenzied Roland could make no poem; a wildly loving heart would be the last to express itself adequately. The phantasmagoria of Franz Liszt's music would take on form if he should begin to recognize this truth. In its light the most remarkable secrets of creation should be studied. In order to move something, one must not stand upon it. Let us take warning from the crass materialism of those medieval figures from whose mouths hang great placards with explanatory captions.

No survey of Schumann's literary contribution should close without mention of a little work which has done more to educate musicians than any other book on music. Here are a few bits of wisdom from the *Musical House- and Life-Rules:*

Always play as if a master were listening.

When you grow older, play nothing that is purely fashionable. Time is precious. One would need a hundred lives to become acquainted with all the good music in existence.

Everything merely fashionable will go out of fashion, and if you keep on with it until you grow up, you will be a simpleton whom nobody respects.

If everyone wanted to play first violin, we could get no orchestra together. So honor each musician in his own place.

When you are bigger, associate more with scores than with virtuosos.

Seek out those among your comrades who know more than you.

Behind the mountains there are also people. Be modest! As yet you have thought and invented nothing that others before you have not already thought and invented. And even if you have, look on it as a gift from above that you must share with others.

But what does it mean to be *musical?* You're *not* if, with eyes anxiously glued to the notes, you labor through the piece. You're *not* if, when someone turns two leaves at once, you are stuck. You *are* musical, however, if in a new piece you somehow have an anticipatory instinct for what is coming. And if you know a familiar piece by heart. In a word, if you have music, not alone in your fingers, but also in your head and your heart.

Honor the old highly, but bring a warm heart to the new. Harbor no prejudice against unknown names.

Look well about you in life as well as in other arts and sciences.[5] The laws of morality are also those of art.

Without enthusiasm nothing worth-while is brought to pass in art.

Not until the form is clear to you will the spirit be wholly clear to you.

Perhaps none but the genius wholly understands the genius.

There is no end to learning.

If he had never uttered a note of music, Schumann's aphorisms, letters, and essays would alone constitute a priceless legacy to mankind.

[5] He once wrote to Clara: "Everything that goes on in the world affects me"—which echoes Terence's "I am a man, and nothing human is foreign to me."

PART II

THE MUSIC

Their works do follow them.

REVELATION, XIV, 13

Apart from the complete piano works, only the more important music of Schumann will be considered here.

CHAPTER 1

MUSIC FOR PIANO

NO other great composer had quite such a single-track mind as Schumann. During the nine years from Opus 1 to Opus 23 he wrote piano music exclusively. Then, for a year, he composed little but songs. Thereafter his product was more mixed; but it falls roughly into three periods, devoted respectively to symphonies, chamber music, and choral works.

To find the earliest ancestors of Schumann's piano pieces, we must go back to sixteenth-century England, where, in such compositions as *A Toye, His Dream,* and *Nobody's Gigge,* the Farnabys, father and son, worked out an expressive technic for that brave new instrument, the virginal. From them the line descends through Martin Pearson's *The Fall of the Leafe,* and Couperin's harpsichord pieces,[1] through the *Bagatelles* of Beethoven and the short pieces of Schubert, to Schumann.

While the little tone-poems that Schumann first wrote had their distant prototypes, they showed a freshness of creative inspiration which made them virtually a new phenomenon in the world of music. Short-winded, crude, and awkwardly proportioned though they sometimes were, they were unique in their comparative independence of earlier models, in variety, enthusiasm, fullness of life, boundlessly resourceful invention, self-renewing verve, novelty of harmony, rhythm and melody, and in spontaneous, pellucid mirroring of every facet of a personality richly fanciful and compelling in its intimate charm.

Hearing this delightful spontaneity, we could paraphrase a

[1] Especially *Les Folies françaises ou les Dominos,* which may have inspired *Carnaval.*

word of Keats' and say that if music comes not as naturally as leaves to a tree it had better not come at all. But then, in the next breath, we recall the struggles of a Beethoven in hammering out immortal beauty from crude ingots, and realize that we must allow every artist to get to heaven in his own natural way.

The world had never before known a Minerva-like composer, born so fully equipped.[2] Nor had it ever possessed a tone-poet whose creations, though without a hint of the erotic, were so mysteriously exciting.

Op. 1. The *"Abegg"* Variations

Schumann's first published work, composed when he was twenty, is a souvenir of his Heidelberg days which were critical in one sense, and uncritical in the other. The choice of music as his life-work then hung in the balance; and he had not yet developed that extraordinary self-critical perception which, from Opus 2 on, helped him to be one of the most original composers who ever lived.

Opus 1 has this in its favor: at a time when most variations were founded on opera melodies, its theme was original.[2a]

And, instead of following the fashion and simply overlaying the tune with ornamentation, Schumann made some attempt at the psychological approach which rings changes on the spirit of the music rather than on its letter. Moreover, the syncopations and cross-accents of the finale anticipated some of the ripe composer's characteristic rhythmical tricks.

[2] With Schumann, the quality of his earliest opuses more nearly approached his best quality than was the case with even Mozart or Schubert.

[2a] Remember that, in German, B stands for B flat.

However, in order to satisfy his taste for musical anagrams, Schumann invented a somewhat banal waltz tune as his theme. And, yielding to the repetitive impulse which was occasionally to sadden his admirers, he began by stating his germ of melody eight times running; and then, in mechanical reverse, repeated it eight times more.

The first two variations start auspiciously enough with harbingers of the future Schumann peering at us around this corner and that. But the very young are always dazzled by the exhibitionism of virtuosity. And Schumann succumbed to the then current rage for show. We catch echoes of the more mechanical passage-work, not only of Hummel, Moscheles, and Weber, but even—as a ridiculous bit of irony—of those fashionable nincompoops, Herz and Hünten, against whom Robert, his Davidites, and the *New Magazine* were shortly to launch a holy crusade. If these vulgar echoes had been confined to one variation, they could be taken for parody; but, extensive as they are, we must smile at them as youthful indiscretions. It should be said for the *"Abegg"* Variations that they are much more important than the first opuses of most other composers, and give us more of the personality of their creator.

Op. 2. *Papillons*

This group of pieces, all startlingly brief for those days, marks a long step forward. It is a curious fantasy inspired by the *Larventanz* [3] which ends Jean Paul's *Flegeljahre*. The last page of the finale bears a direction which shows what must have been in the composer's mind all through these twelve pieces: "The noise of the carnival is stilled.[4] The clock in the tower strikes six." Happily, music is a thing of such infinitude that any literary program which a composer may force upon his notes can no more exhaust their possible connotations than one suck of a medicine dropper can exhaust the sea.

[3] This is a pun, meaning either *Dance of the Larvae*, or *Dance of the Masks*.

[4] On reading these words, one cannot help thinking how, twenty-one years later, the noise of the carnival was stilled for him by his plunge into the Rhine.

Perhaps Jean Paul's book did all it could for music when it put dreams into the head of the young composer, who told Rellstab:

Often I turned over the last page. For the close struck me as a new start.—Almost without knowing how, I found myself at the piano: and that was how one "Papillon" after another came into being.

This graceful, convincing suite was written by a youth equipped with but little of the science underlying his art. He himself declared that, at this stage, Jean Paul had taught him more counterpoint than Marpurg (a well-known theoretical writer of the preceding century).

The *Papillons* show one of the composer's most winning qualities—a thing rarely found in any artist's equipment: he knew when to stop. Each number leaves us wishing that it were longer.

The simple melody of the rising and falling scale which opens No. 1

[Ex. 2]

must have held much significance for Schumann, because we find it again in the finale, and later on in the *Florestan* part of *Carnaval*. The stamping rhythm of No. 8

[Ex. 3]

and of No. 10

[Ex. 4]

is characteristic of the dance music of the German and Austrian peasants. At Grundlsee in the Salzkammergut I once danced with them to the clapping and stamping accompaniment of just such strains.

Schumann originally composed No. 8 in D minor, and fooled Töpken into thinking that it was by Schubert.[5] Another parody that strikes somewhat farther from the original comes in the third part of No. 10. It is a languishing waltz that guardedly sticks out its tongue at Weber's *Invitation to the Dance*.

No. 11 is a polonaise bubbling over with more boyish exuberance and pure delight in life than is to be found in all the polonaises of Chopin put together.

[Ex. 5]

The finale is a rough model for the corresponding movement of *Carnaval*. Both emphasize the *Granddaddy Dance*, a seventeenth-century tune

[Ex. 6]

[5] M. Basch was mistaken in giving No. 4 as the Schubert imitation.

with which Schumann liked to typify the old dry-as-dust formal-
ists and reactionaries—the same sort of gentry of whom Beethoven had once exclaimed with a chuckle of malicious glee:
"*I'll* shake the powder out of their perukes!" And between the
repetitions of this is sandwiched a fragment of an ancient folk-
tune which Papa Johann Sebastian Bach had used in his uproarious *Peasant Cantata.*

[Ex. 7] Schumann

[Ex. 8] Bach
Hey ding ǎ ding ǎ ding ǎ ding ǎ ding, Sweet lov-ers love the spring.

The words to the Bach quotation rhyme well with the gay,
youthful spirit of Schumann's finale. This *Peasant Cantata* opens
with a song in broad Saxon dialect about beer that goes to the
head (*das steigt in's Heet*). Perhaps Schumann's introduction of
this musical quotation may have been a subtle way of indicating
that those old-timers, the granddaddies, were already under the
table, and youth might now hold undisputed sway.

Much is made of the citation from No. 1 (Ex. 2). Six times
the tower clock strikes high A, and this original music gradually
fades to nothing.

Op. 3. *Studien für das Pianof. nach Capricen von Paganini*

Op. 10. *6 Etudes de Concert d'après des Caprices de Paganini pour le Pianof.*

These headings are taken from Schumann's own *Thematic
Catalogue;* and it is interesting to observe his rapid switch from
German to French.

He hated the desiccation of the Czerny–Clementi–Hummel–Kalkbrenner etudes so much that he decided to enrich the pianist's study repertory with something really interesting.[6] Young Schumann keenly felt his own ignorance, and wrote ex-teacher Dorn that he missed Dorn's help with the harmonizing; but was saving his bacon by the cultivation of extreme simplicity. The job was a useful exercise in self-education.

The six studies of Op. 3 are clever but literal transcriptions. In the second six he allowed his own imaginative personality freer rein. But today we cannot find much Schumann there, except in the somewhat Mendelssohnian No. 3 of the first series, and the slightly Chopinesque No. 2 of the second. Note that Op. 10, No. 1

Allegro molto

[Ex. 9]

is the music to which the *Paganini* movement of *Carnaval* alludes.

In a popular sense, these transcriptions were never very effective. There was in Schumann so little of the Paganinesque show-man that when Liszt, the arch-Paganini, came along with his own brilliant and knock-down versions of the same *Capriccios,* he cast Schumann's studies quite into the shade.

Op. 4. *Intermezzi*

Here Schumann launched out along novel lines full of significance, not alone for his own future, but also for that of many another music-maker to come. The *Papillons* used dance forms. The *Intermezzi* are in song-form with Trio.[7] They are foretastes

[6] Just as, a year later, young Chopin was to decide.

[7] Which Schumann here calls *"Alternativo";* though that term properly applies only to the older dance music.

of finer things of this character, by Schumann and his followers.
Opus 4 is the good-looking father of stronger, wiser and more
beautiful sons and grandsons. There are places where the
counterpoint sounds somewhat self-conscious and seems ostentatiously featured. Which reminds us that, in this department of
musical knowledge, the young fellow from Zwickau was still a
nouveau riche.

The work bristles with reminders of the past as well as of the
future. No. 1 starts with a dotted figure that was to become
characteristic of Schumann.

Allegro quasi maestoso

[Ex. 10]

It has the rhythm of the scherzo of Beethoven's E Flat Quartet,
Op. 127. Also, in a way, it is a condensed reminder of how Schubert's G Major Quartet starts, after the Introduction. And an
echo of the same master's *Erl King* jumps out of the 4th measure
of No. 4. No. 3 smacks of Beethoven, and No. 6, of Mendelssohn,
especially in the somewhat trivial *Alternativo.* At the first *a
tempo,* No. 5 looks forward to the opening movement of Brahms'
F Minor Sonata for piano. And in the midst of the *Alternativo*
we find a typical Brahmsian "ladder" theme, with rungs mounting at intervals of a fourth.[8] Taken as a whole, this No. 5, in its
purity, intimacy and plaintive nostalgia, gives earnest of the
great Schumann shortly to emerge.

Although these *Intermezzi* are only forerunners, they have
been unjustly neglected.

Op. 5. *Impromptus on a Theme by Clara Wieck*

As compared with Opus 1, these represent a phenomenal
advance. All traces of the old mechanical passage-work of

[8] See my *The Unknown Brahms,* p. 306.

Hünten and Herz have vanished. The young composer has made a step upward toward his future variation masterpiece, the *Symphonic Etudes*. The *Impromptus* were patterned after what Schumann then considered the supreme set of variations, Beethoven's Opus 35, which served as a model for the finale of the *Eroica*. The charming little theme of Clara's is preceded, *à la* Beethoven, by a ground bass, which starts with a quotation from Haydn's *"Quinten"* Quartet (marked by a bracket).

[Ex. 11]

We shall find this Haydn source-motive, here C F G C, running like a refrain through much of Schumann's music. I suspect that in his love of subtle allusion he always meant it as a private greeting to Clara.[9]

What Robert called his "herculean" labors on the Paganini material was of assistance to him in composing the *Intermezzi* and *Impromptus*. And these, in turn, helped him toward creating such incomparably greater works as *Carnaval*, the *Davidsbündler Dances*, the *Fantasiestücke*, *Scenes from Childhood*, *Kreisleriana*, and *Novelletten*.

Op. 6. The *Davidsbündler Dances*

This title is a misnomer, for there is scarcely a dance in the lot. To the general listener the nature of the suite would have been clearer if it had been called instead: *Eighteen Studies in the Psychology of Autobiography*. For the idea that stirred in the composer's mind was a series of dialogues between go-getter Florestan and dreamer Eusebius, that should bring out their antagonisms, congenialities, and reactions to the crude, ugly world of Philistia. All these reactions were, of course, heightened by the strenuous conflict with Wieck, in which Clara was the prize.[10]

[9] See pp. 337, 344, 473, and 482.
[10] For years, the opus number of this work puzzled me. Why should it be only Opus 6? It was composed in 1837 and published in 1838; while

In the original edition Schumann emphasized the programmatic nature of Op. 6 by setting "F" (for Florestan) or "E" (for Eusebius) after each *Dance;* and by writing in two stage-directions. After No. 8 stood: "Herewith Florestan made an end, and his lips quivered painfully." And before No. 18: "Quite superfluously Eusebius remarked as follows; but all the time great bliss spoke from his eyes."

The suite had no dearth of mottoes. Under the title stood an old saying:

> *In all' und jeder Zeit*
> *Verknüpft sich Lust und Leid:*
> *Bleibt fromm in Lust und seyd*
> *Dem Leid mit Muth bereit.*

Which might be freely translated:

> Delight is linked with pain
> Forever and forever:
> In joy, devout remain;
> In woe, lose courage never.

The first two measures of *Dance* No. 1

[Ex. 12]

the *Symphonic Etudes,* composed in 1834 and published in 1837, are Opus 13. A solution is suggested by the quotation from Clara's *Soirées Musicales,* Opus 6, which starts the first *Dance.* It is possible that Robert had been saving the 6th place in his opus list for the G Minor Sonata, which was begun in 1833, the year Op. 5 was written and published. But since the new finale of this sonata had not yet been finished by the time the *Dances* were ready for publication in 1838, Schumann may have given them the 6th place which he had saved for the sonata, so that he and Clara might be one, even to the opus number of the work quoting and the work quoted. And perhaps this is why the G Minor Sonata, when published at last in 1839, became Opus 22.

consist of the motto from Clara's Opus 6. Florestan and Eusebius
proceeded to make it as much their own as they were later to
make its composer. Before the last *Im Tempo* of this delightful
collaborative effort, note the breadth and modernity of the
harmony:

[Ex. 13]

which must have been as a cinder in the eye of the contemporary
pedant. And do not pass over the interesting dynamics in No. 7,
with the right hand loud while the left is a mere whisper; nor
the mischievous rhythm of No. 10, where ⁶⁄₈ time is made to
sound with ³⁄₄:

[Ex. 14]

In No. 2, a Eusebian dream of beauty marked with the characteristic designation *Innig*, notice the new sort of polyphony
which Schumann was creating for the piano.

[Ex. 15]

It employs no definite number of voices, but forms a shimmering web of tone in which the voices imperceptibly melt into one another, like the colors of iridescent silk. No. 2 must have had some special significance in the mind of the composer; for it i repeated at the end of No. 17, the piece which is charmingly marked "As if from the distance." [11]

No. 12, "With humor," is one of the many pages of his earlie works where Schumann simply could not help writing balle music.

Mit Humor

[Ex. 16]

The alternation of humor and revery, of high spirits and quie dreams of love that marks these *Dances*, was identified in Schu mann's mind with the festive doings on the eve before a wed ding, which the Germans call a *Polterabend*. In the finale, as i that of the *Papillons*, the clock strikes to wind up the gaiety There it announced six in the morning; but here, more discreetly twelve low C's mark midnight.

Robert wrote Clara:

[11] In the slumber song of the *Magelonen Lieder*, Brahms was to echo th start of No. 17.

In the *Dances* there are many marriage thoughts. They originated in the most joyful excitement that I can ever recall. . . . If ever I was happy at the piano, it was while composing these.

He declared that Opus 6 compared to *Carnaval* "as faces to masks." And while the modern taste rightly disagrees with him there, it is true that the *Davidsbündler Dances* have been neglected in public far more unjustly than the *Intermezzi*. Perhaps their enormous length may be responsible for the reluctance of pianists to exploit their wealth of humor, beauty, and high spirits. In the history of music Opus 6 holds an important place. And Reissmann was justified in calling it "the first finished work of the new movement."

Op. 7. *Toccata*

This is a virtuoso's finger exercise in sonata-form, that has been enriched and ennobled by the accolade of Schumann's genius.

 *[Ex. 17]*

Conceived in 1830 at Heidelberg, it was revised three years later. Schumann transposed it from D to C and, as he wrote Töpken, it came out of the process "no longer so wild, but much better-behaved."

Clara's half sister, Marie Wieck, tells how she once went to visit Smetana and heard him at the piano, slowly and conscientiously practising this *Toccata*, like one of her own good pupils. But, as soon as she stuck her head inside the door, Smetana laughed and suddenly quadrupled the tempo, so that

the mighty work roared to meet me with a power and verve which one could not have expected from the Master's physical fragility. What a welcome greeting!

Op. 8. *Allegro*

This represents a conscious effort of Schumann's to break away from short pieces and launch forth into a monumental piano style. But the attempt was premature. Here is "made" music. It came not from the heart but from higher up. There are hints of Chopin, and of rather sugary Mendelssohn, but very few of the real Schumann. It was dedicated to poor Ernestine; and Schumann remarked that "the composer is worth more than this work, but less than the dedicatee."

Op. 9. *Carnaval. Scènes mignonnes sur 4 Notes*

In *Carnaval,* however, he paid Ernestine an immortal tribute, after making a curious discovery that tickled his fancy for musico-literary anagrams. The name of Ernestine's home town, Asch, was composed of none but musical letters. And—weird coincidence—these are the only musical letters in the name Schumann. This would not, of course, hold true in English; but in German As is A flat, Es (or S) is E flat, and H is B natural.

Carnaval (as the composer arbitrarily spelled it) is a loose set of variations on these letters. Schumann called it *"Little Scenes on 4 Notes."* And the mystification is heightened by the said four notes' deferring their appearance until the fifth measure of No. 2, and not invariably showing their heads in every subsequent number.

In the midst of the suite we run across what Schumann labeled *"Sphinxes,"* which afford hints of the permutations and combinations of these key letters:

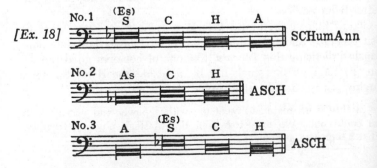

With these *"Sphinxes"* we come upon Schumann's first use of the germ-motive.[13]

In the *"ABEGG"* Variations we have already seen this anagram idea (p. 278, Ex. 1). Later in life, Schumann did the same sort of thing in his *Six Organ Fugues on the Name "Bach."* [14] Thrice he played with the name of his Danish composer friend Gade, in whose album he set to music the words *"Auf Wiedersehn,"* the bass spelling out "G-A-D-E, A-D-E" ("Gade, farewell"). The *Northern Song* in the *Album* gives the friend's name again.[15]

The cleverest trick of all comes in his breezy article on Gade in the *New Magazine*:

As if the accident of a name had pointed his way towards music— just as it did in Bach's case—the four letters of his name, strangely enough, stand for the four open strings of the violin. Let nobody brush aside this small token of grace from on high. Nor this other token: that, by means of four clefs his name may be written with a *single* note. Adepts at the cabala will easily solve this puzzle.[16]

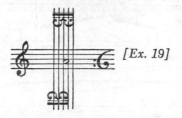 *[Ex. 19]*

[13] See p. 51, Note.

[14] I once discovered that, in paying this tribute to the father of music, Schumann had been anticipated by Beethoven's E Minor Quartet. See my *Beethoven*, p. 185, Ex. 62.

[15] See p. 353, Ex. 99.

[16] A hint: start with the tenor clef, and read clockwise. Schumann's love of name anagrams descended to Brahms. Witness the FAE Sonata (see p. 244), and the Agathe theme of the G Major Sextet. I have just discovered that all the musical letters of Brahms' own name are found in the first measure of his A Flat Minor Organ Fugue. Remember that our B flat is B in German. On the organ, C flat is B natural (which the Germans call H), and B double-flat is A.

Brahms Ab Min. Fugue

 *[Ex. 20]*

With the exception of the *Symphonic Etudes,* finished the year in which *Carnaval* was begun, *Carnaval* was the first work in which Schumann's genius blazed forth with full power. In the course of a century it has become one of his most popular compositions. Opus 9 is a sort of *Papillons* de luxe.

This suite shows Robert technically ripe as a composer for the piano. Here is an amazing harmonic and rhythmic versatility. Here is humor, and an apparently inexhaustible resourcefulness in luring out of four rather unpromising notes more rich variety in the way of unforced, lovely melody than a magician can lure out of a hat in the way of ribbon-paper, flowers, and white rabbits.

On this variety stage Robert's boyish gift for musical mimicry and portraiture comes to full fruition. He gives us as good Chopin (No. 12) as Chopin himself could furnish:

[Ex. 21]

and better Paganini (No. 17) than Paganini could.[17] He even characterizes himself in as fine portraits of the vigorous Florestan and the poet-dreamer Eusebius as we could hope ever to find. And No. 9 goes even further, to mimic one of his own pieces, the *Papillons.*

[17] The latter, which makes the last note of one measure sound like the first of the next, is a neat example of Schumann's zest in rhythmical trickery.

The reader who remembers Robert's appalling gaucherie in dedicating Opus 31 to the jilted and then widowed Ernestine will not be surprised at another piece of tactlessness which he showed her in *Carnaval*. Remember that this piece was written for her, on a theme giving the name of her home town significantly intertwined with his own. But here he not only introduces her rival, Clara, as *Chiarina,* but gives her precedence over Ernestine, whom he calls *Estrella.* To make matters worse, the musical quality of *Estrella's* number corresponds with the quality of *Estrella's* talent. That is to say, it is one of the poorest of the twenty-one; while *Chiarina's* has in it much of the authentic Schumann. How both girls must have secretly resented Robert's lack of diplomacy in thus publicly forcing them together!

Like most sound musicians, Schumann felt that the musicality of program music is questionable. He insisted that whenever he baptized his pieces with literary titles, he thought them up only after finishing the music. However, in the case of *Carnaval* at least, the notes match the names so well that we wonder if he did not revise the music to conform with them.

Certainly his characters which are chosen from the old Italian Comedy are melodically, harmonically, and rhythmically painted with utter appropriateness. So far as music, the vague and infinite, can depict, we find *Pantalon, Columbine, Harlequin* and *Pierrot* truly depicted, down to every traditional gesture and grimace, every furbelow and glide and leap. We are rejoiced when Pierrot nobly stalks a few pompous steps, falls over his own feet, gives a sheepish laugh, suddenly recovers his wobbly dignity, and so on, *da capo.*

Pierrot

Moderato

[Ex. 22]

And music could hardly be more sensitively descriptive than the
Lettres dansantes, the *Valse noble,* and the provocative *Coquette*
who ogles you while lisping ASCH, and underlines these terp-
sichorean letters with a sudden, vigorous stamp of each tiny
foot.

Eusebius

and *Florestan*

are vivid fragments of autobiographic characterization and confession in notes.

In the grand concluding *March of the Davidsbündler against
the Philistines,*[18] the mossbacked reactionaries, as typified in the
Granddaddy Dance, are crushed again, and yet more decisively
than they were in the *Papillons,* by the noble Band of David.
Such a finale could scarcely have been written in just this way
if, from the start of the suite, there had not been in the composer's mind a fairly definite program. Or perhaps, from just
after the start. For the *Préambule,* that majestically sets the ball
in motion with its lusciously satisfying chains of heavy chords,
is in itself not necessarily programmatic.

[18] For its start, see p. 73.

Quasi Maestoso

[Ex. 25]

This opening movement is given solid thematic unity through the same elementary germ-motive which locks together the parts of Beethoven's *"Kreutzer"* Sonata.[19] It is the two-note phrase

[Ex. 26]

which rises or falls the interval of a second. Aside from a repetition of the same note, simplicity could go no farther. Nevertheless, Schumann has made his *Préambule* as rich and varied as the banquet board of a Lucullus.

In this *Préambule* there is a four-note phrase (bracketed in the following example)

[Ex. 27]

which recurs in *Pause*, and which is almost literally echoed in the final *March*. It comes back a number of times in Schumann's later works, sometimes prefixed by the first two notes of Ex. 27, and will be known as the Carnaval source-motive.

[19] See my *Beethoven*, pp. 536-38.

CHAPTER 2

THE PIANO SONATAS AND *FANTASIE*

W HEN the musical ideas of Schumann's youth turned into such "long, long thoughts" that they threatened to burst the trim bounds of those suites of little pieces which were his first vehicles of expression, he instinctively gravitated toward the sonata. This was all the more natural, because sonata-form, like his own personality, came into being as the battleground of two opposing forces. In the case of the form, we call these forces the masculine and the feminine subjects.[1] In the case of Schumann, we call them his two contrasting natures: Florestan and Eusebius, or his manic and his depressive sides.

Sonata-form had been developed by Philipp Emanuel Bach and the Mannheim School, and gradually perfected by Haydn and Beethoven. But Schumann's originality had already placed him among the leading pioneers of the new era of Romanticism. Nobody could expect him to take over an old form and wear the thing uncritically, like a second-hand coat. It would have been strange if he had not made something brilliantly new out of the time-honored pattern. As Schubert had done before him, Schumann took Beethoven's sonata, played exuberantly with it, and remolded the thing "nearer" to his own "heart's desire."

It is fascinating to watch the fiery youngster seizing upon a form which had always been a bulwark of Classicism, and instantly making it so characteristic of himself, and of the spirit of the new age, as to transform it into a stronghold of Romanticism. To those who shortsightedly condemn his sonatas, trios,

[1] See Appendix, p. 512: SONATA-FORM.

quartets, and symphonies [2] for their departure from the conventional norm, should ask themselves: Whatever he wrote, how could Schumann possibly have been anybody but his own novel self? And would we have cared as much for him if he *had* been able to perform any such sterile miracle?

We have already remarked Schumann's fondness for insinuating subtle allusions into his scores. He now conceived a musical tribute to Clara that was subtler, better concealed, and on a much larger scale than any ABEGG, or ASCH, or GADE. Never before had any woman been honored with such a tremendous musical compliment as Robert paid Clara through the first four works which he published in a larger form. And how well he knew, in his love of secrecy and of the mysteriously allusive, the art of concealing from the uninitiated this vast compliment!

For many years I had studied the three piano sonatas and the *Fantasie* before coming to realize with astonishment that they are all bound together into a larger unity by the consistent use of a single germ- and source-motive:

[Ex. 28]

which, under one disguise or another, occurs in the thematic material of each of their fifteen movements. This melodic formula and guiding motto first gives interior unity to each work, and then unifies the whole group of works. It is derived from a melody of Clara's that, to cap the climax of compliment, Robert varied as the slow movement of the F Minor Sonata, Op. 14, which he called his Third. (See p. 310, Ex. 43.)

In *Carnaval* one marvels at the melodic variety which he dug out of ASCH. But what shall we think of a wizardry that could use the same motive in the themes of fifteen sonata movements and, by fertility of invention, succeed so well in disguising the identity that, to this day, no critic has ever remarked it?

Of course, the use of germ- and source-motives was nothing new in 1835. It began with J. S. Bach, and came down through

[2] Trios, quartets, etc., are only sonatas for three, four, or more instruments.

Stamitz, Haydn, and Mozart to Beethoven, who carried it much further, as in the germ-motives of the *Pathétique* and the *Eroica*, and the source-motive which binds together a hundred and fifty of his works.[3] But Schumann was not far behind in his use of these devices, and passed the technic on to Brahms.

It is significant that nearly all of these masters were mightily adept at the art of improvisation. This talent must have helped them enormously, both in placing and in camouflaging such cohesive material. For, without camouflage, germ- and source-motives must necessarily yield, not variety in unity, but the unity of flat monotony. So their identity must be disguised by inversion, turning end-for-end, changes of tempo, the interpolation of passing notes, and all manner of rhythmic and harmonic devices.

Op. 11. First Sonata, F Sharp Minor

The reader will recall that the original title-page read: "Dedicated to Clara by Florestan and Eusebius."

Since Beethoven's revolutionary dealings with the sonata, from Opus 101 on, this old form had sunk back into staid conventionality. Schumann's crisp, zestful approach to it is refreshing. We have only to compare Opus 11 with one of the machine-cut-and-dried products of Hummel, Moscheles, or Spohr to see how originally Robert Florestanized and Eusebianized the sonata, and how jarringly his astonishing departures shocked—and still shock—the old guard.

The three-page Introduction opens loud and bold with a lion of a tune, first in the treble, then louder in the bass.[4] It starts:

[Ex. 29]

---

[3] See my *Beethoven*, pp. 53 ff., 126 ff., and 578 ff.
[4] M. Basch was guilty of absolute bosh when he called it *"une Introduction en forme de berceuse et dont le contour mélodique et le modelé harmonique s'apparentent aux* Romances sans Paroles." Likewise when he de-

Anton Bruckner may have been inspired by it when he began his Eighth Symphony.

The closing portion of this passionate Introduction's second theme twice uses the cohesive phrase described above. We shall call it the Clara germ- and source-motive. In the examples that follow from the sonatas and *Fantasie*, this motive is marked by a bracket.

[Ex. 30]

clared that the first movement is in the style of Mendelssohn's music to *A Midsummer Night's Dream*!

The smaller bracket shows another germ-motive, the simple one
of the *Kreutzer* Sonata and of the *Carnaval Préambule*.[5] On
these two motives and their inversions this entire sonata is based;
but it would be tedious to trace the smaller one further.

The *Allegro vivace* is heralded by three of our composer's
characteristic descending fifths, and at once we again find the
Clara source-motive:

[Ex. 31]

Schumann gallantly informed Clara that the whole of Op. 11
was "a single cry of the heart" for her. But the internal evidence
of the music shows that his heart was by no means exclusively
occupied in yearning. It found plenty of gay things to chuckle
about; and our spirits rise to the infectious jollity of the last

[5] See p. 295.

example, and of the Scherzo, with its burlesque interlude. As for the exuberant finale and its trick rhythms, it exhilarates one like a hearty laugh.

The *Allegro vivace,* with its insistence on the brief phrases of Ex. 31, would be monotonous if it were not harmonically and rhythmically so interesting. Even in his first sonata, the irrepressible Schumann cannot refrain from bursting into ballet music, as we find him doing in the excitable, high-kicking episode in E flat minor.

With the tender second subject

[Ex. 32]

he seems suddenly to recollect that he is in love; and fills it with Clara's motive and its inversion.

This first movement has two novelties of form: (1) Starting with the B major section, most of the development is repeated. (2) The recapitulation, instead of echoing the whole exposition, is condensed to about one-fourth the length of the latter.[6] Thus the revolutionary Schumann shifts a long repeat from the third to the second section of sonata form.

With keen thrills of recognition, we find the lionlike first theme of the Introduction (Ex. 29) in the bass of the development. And we find the closing part of the Introduction's second theme (Ex. 30) near the start of the tender, song-like slow movement, which begins:

[6] The curtailed recapitulation of the first movement of Beethoven's D Minor Sonata, Op. 31, No. 2, which caused a sensation in its day, was still three-fourths as long as the exposition.

[Ex. 33]

Yearning is again forgotten in the wild fun of the Scherzo:

[Ex. 34]

but not the Clara source-motive, both topsy-turvy and right side up. In the bass of the Trio, listen to the bell-like quality of Robert's favorite fifths. Contrary to the traditional nature of Trios, this section is marked *Più Allegro*.

The *Intermezzo* of this movement is a droll bit of caricature. It is one of the funniest that Schumann ever perpetrated since those early days when his urchin pals stood about the keyboard, doubled up with howls of mirth as their leader Robinson took off in tones the idiosyncrasies of some member of that robber band. In polonaise rhythm, it deliberately invents one of the emptiest and most banal tunes imaginable:

[Ex. 35]

This vignette-in-tones of a stuffed shirt is a worthy companion-piece to the *Carnaval* sketch of the pompous *Pierrot* (p. 293, Ex. 22). Its closing recitative exquisitely parodies the more ludicrous aspects of the contemporary Italian opera, the kind which Brahms once described as consisting wholly of cadences. Beethoven hit off this sort of opera in the two *scherzoso* inter-mezzos with which he enlivened the finale of the *"Thunder-storm"* string quintet, Op. 29. And here Schumann has gone him one better. The part marked "quasi Oboe" is irresistible when that instrument snickers up the scale, staccato, with its hand over its mouth.[7]

The kaleidoscopic jollity and rainbow color of the rondo that

[7] I have heard pianists perform this page with the earnestness of a priest intoning the Litany.

The wit of Shostakovich's *Polka* from *The Golden Age*, which turns cur-rent harmonic fashions into a chromo of a sot far gone in liquor, stems from Schumann's gift for musical caricature.

serves as finale might'well have been inspired less by the humor-
less Clara than by some exuberant get-together of the clan of
Davidites, with now and then a tender but fleeting thought of
Robert's love.

The principal theme embodies a most diverting opposition of
metrical stress and motive stress. While written in ¾ time, it
also sounds like ²⁄₄. The accents above and below the next example are my own. The short brackets mark the apparent ²⁄₄ beat,
while the longer ones show the inevitable Clara source-motive.

[Ex. 36]

This infectious rondo, gathering momentum, culminates in an
exciting coda where, with a final exhibition of rhythmic sleight-
of-hand, ⁶⁄₈ time is made to sound with the prescribed ¾.

Florestan and Eusebius have had their tremendous say; but
the former has paid far more attention to those jolly good fellows, the Davidites, than the latter has paid to Clara.

Op. 22. Second Sonata, G Minor

This is my favorite among the three sonatas. Though both
sides of Schumann's nature are liberally represented in the first

two, No. 1 was created more under the aegis of that enthusiastic
and uproarious fellow, Florestan; while No. 2 is more contem-
platively subdued. As a counterpoise to the F Sharp Minor's
effervescent gaiety and humor, the G Minor has a haunting,
mystic beauty that makes it specially fit to be one of the choicer
treasures of a good musical memory. The vivid freshness and
spontaneity of this music remind one of the inexhaustible invention of a Schubert.

The G Minor is little more than half as long as either of the
others. Its form is more obvious and presents a sharper profile.
The work compares with the luxuriance of its brothers as Beethoven's concentrated F Minor Quartet compares with the
abundant, tropical glory of those dedicated to Count Rasoumow-
sky. It keeps closer to classical models than No. 1, and, in the
development of the opening movement, even brings a distant
echo of the second subject to cope with the first.

The principal subject of this movement at once announces the
presence of Clara:

This is the famous occasion on which Schumann directs the performer to play "As fast as possible"; but, when he comes to the exciting coda, absentmindedly urges, "Faster," and then, "Still faster."

As in the First Sonata, the slow movement is one of his early unpublished songs transfigured into absolute music.[8]

Here we have the composer at his most intimate and tender.

The tiny and wholly original Scherzo is as pregnant as that of the Beethoven quartet just mentioned. After four bars of dotted quasi-introduction, comes a novel strain that starts:

[8] The first three brackets in Ex. 38 mark another source-motive that is highly characteristic of Schumann's style. It might be called the "Bracketing" source motive; because, like a naval gun, it "brackets" the target, i.e., shoots first above it, then below, or vice versa, in order to find the mark on the third shot. In the first case of this procedure shown in Ex. 38, he first hits F sharp, then A, in order to strike G the third time. Note also, in measures 5 and 7-9, the characteristic rhythm of 2 against 3.

[Ex. 39]

One secret of its fresh effect is that the three phrases of which it is made up are respectively of 5, 3, and 4 beats, yet balance perfectly.

Schumann discarded his first attempt at a finale (which, by the way, also contains the Clara source-motive), and was not satisfied until three years later he wrote the fine rondo that begins:

[Ex. 40]

Rondo
Presto

In the memorable second subject, his tenderness and passion have full sway:

Etwas langsamer

[Ex. 41]

Notice the beloved rising and falling fifths.

In a brilliant *Quasi Cadenza, prestissimo,* Florestan's youthful zest in life sweeps away any lingering Eusebian vapors.

Op. 14. Third Sonata, F Minor

This the publisher originally called *"Concert sans Orchestre."* It is inferior to the other two, and is almost never found on concert programs. But when people manage to hear it, they are agreeably surprised to find how full it is of bits of the very best

Schumann. The variations on that charming melody of Clara's
may hold up their heads even among such proud folk as the
Symphonic Etudes and the two-piano *Andante*. The Scherzo is
above Schumann's scherzo average. And the wild momentum
and passion of the first movement, if they had been consistently
sustained, would have made it a masterpiece. Compare his use
of the Clara source-motive in the four movements: [9]

[9] In Ex. 44 this motive is varied by the addition of a passing note (in
parentheses).

[Ex. 44]

These examples by no means cover Schumann's use in Opus 14 of the compliment to Clara.

It may well be that the added strain of trying, for the third time on a large scale, to work with the same motive was just enough to take Schumann's spontaneity off the boil, and make the F Minor one of those tantalizing products that miss greatness by a hair—or, shall we say, by a germ-motive.

The following year, however, when for the fourth time he employed it in the *Fantasie*, his technic had improved to a point where creativeness was not hampered but stimulated by the difficulty of the problem.

Op. 17. *Fantasie*

If this *Fantasie* is not Schumann's chief masterpiece, it is very near it. The work tells of the gigantic strides which young Robert had suddenly made in the field of musical architecture. It shows him taking a classical form such as that of the fantasy-sonata of Beethoven's day, and altering it into full conformity with the novel content of his own forward-looking soul.

Mr. Herbert Bedford imputes insincerity and contradiction to Schumann on the ground that the titles which he originally thought of for the different movements were inconsistent with his assurance to Clara that the opening movement was "the most impassioned" one which he had ever written. "You can understand it only if you imagine the state of my feelings in that unhappy summer when I resigned myself to losing you." But Mr. Bedford quotes these tentative titles incorrectly, mixing up two alternative sets (both of which were soon discarded). For my part, I can find nothing contradictory or insincere in Schumann's idea of calling this first movement "Ruins"; for, during that depressive period, the poor fellow's hopes lay indeed in ruins.

When Clara was restored to him, there followed that march of manic joy for which the suggested "Triumphal Arch" would have been a perfect title. Along with the finale of the C Major Symphony,[10] this is the most triumphant music that he ever wrote. He assured Clara that every note of the *Fantasie* was full of her. So he must have been pretty sure of winning his girl at the time he composed the march. For the happy Eusebian pipe-dreams which close the work, what title could be more fitting than "Wreath of Stars"?

Mr. Bedford sees additional grounds for complaining of Schumann's insincerity in the fact that he was, in the first place, moved to begin the *Fantasie* in order to contribute the proceeds to the fund for a Beethoven monument at Bonn. But this argument also fails to convince. Why should not Robert's love for Clara have helped to express his love for Ludwig the Great, whose exponent she was?

After even a single hearing, who can forget the lofty passion of that opening subject, borne on a tempest of sound conjured up by the left hand? Here is the rhythmically doubled-up form of its restatement:

[10] See p. 409, Ex. 154.

This melody is wholly made up of the Kreutzer germ-motive [11]

 *[Ex. 26]*

which we shall not trace through the three movements.

The nadir of Schumann's depression is reached in the tragic C minor section, *In the Style of a Legend,* a dark tale in tone such as he often wrote when the black fit was on him; but never more grimly bleak and convincing than here. Then the great, passionate first subject comes back *fortissimo,* and leads to one of the most consummate movement endings in the whole realm of music. This memorable close elaborates on a fragment of tune which had put in a fugitive appearance a few pages earlier. It is a melody that Schumann was destined to use in more than one later work, and so effectively as to make it a significant source-motive.

Adagio

[Ex. 46]

Compare this with the last form of the closing subject of the C Major Symphony's finale:

[11] See p. 295.

and with part of the second subject of the F Major Quartet's closing movement:

and with the finale of the *"Rhenish"* Symphony (first subject).[12]

With one consent, writers on Schumann have attributed the paternity of this fine tune to a song by Beethoven, written twenty years before the *Fantasie*. It ends the cycle, *To the Distant Beloved:*

But they should have gone farther back, to the *Adagio* of the Viola Quintet in B Flat (K. 174) which Mozart had written sixty-three years before:

And from this they should have continued still farther back to the courante in Johann Hermann Schein's *Banchetto musicale*, published two hundred and eighteen years before.

[Ex. 51]

Let us call this the Schein source-motive.

12 See p. 414, Ex. 161.

The *Maestoso* march has already been mentioned.

[Ex. 52]

This virtuoso piece, of famously formidable difficulty, consistently maintains its jubilant excitement, except for some of the development in dotted rhythm, when it temporarily becomes a bit dry. Schumann loved dotted rhythms so well that he was often tempted to overwork them without sufficient contrast, as in the first movement of the C Major Symphony, the *Overture, Scherzo and Finale,* the finale of the A Major Quartet, and the Scherzo of the D Minor Trio. Note how in this march, at *poco animato,* he is up to his favorite rhythmical mischief, misleading the hearer about the prescribed beat by means of heavy accents on the weak parts of the measure.

The finale begins with the Clara source-motive in a 'cello tune.

[Ex. 53]

In these last two movements there are four cadences that have
a prophetic quality. One of them is at *rit.*, a page from the close
of the work.

These cadences have such a dewy, innocent, childlike quality
that they seem to look forward two years to the coming of the
Scenes from Childhood.

The second theme of the finale also contains a prophecy. Its
first measure

anticipates the three-note waltz in the Fifth *Novellette*: [13]

The young passion which informs this superb *Fantasie* is remarkable as much for its chastity as for its intensity. It gives
forth the sort of virginal fire which one would expect in a youth

[13] See pp. 337-8, Ex. 82.

long obsessed by a mother-fixation, who has come to find a mother-substitute in a highly maternal sweetheart.

Fourteen years after Opus 17 was composed, Franz Liszt, to whom it was dedicated, wrote his best-known *Liebestraum* (*A Dream of Love*). As a tribute to the dedicator of the *Fantasie*, he may have intended it as a dream of the love of Robert and Clara; for it sounds as though inspired by the first *Tempo I* of the *Fantasie's* finale. But its vivid sensuality offers a marked contrast to the chaste quality of Robert's music. This quality made the lines of Friedrich Schlegel which appear on the title-page, more appropriate than most mottoes for music:

> *Durch alle Töne tönet*
> *Im bunten Erdentraum*
> *Ein leiser Ton gezogen*
> *Für den der heimlich lauschet.*

> (Through all the tones
> In Earth's bright-colored dream
> One gentle note is threaded
> For him who hears in secret.)

Robert gave Clara to understand that she was the "note" in the motto.

CHAPTER 3

MORE PIANO MUSIC

Op. 12. *Fantasiestücke*

THIS series is a perfect expression of the contrasting natures of Florestan and Eusebius. They alternate in composing the first four pieces (though without affixing any visible signatures), and collaborate in each of the last four.

Eusebius begins with *Des Abends,* which seems to reveal to us, through the iridescent strands of gossamer veils, such sights

as youthful poets dream
On summer eves, by haunted stream.

Here again we find the composer at his rhythmic sport, making ⅜ time sound with ⅖.

[Ex. 56]

Aufschwung swings Florestan into action, and he appears at his most virile.

318

[Ex. 57]

Energetic determination is stamped across nearly every measure. He is poised to fight, to conquer, and to enjoy. Nobody is going to make a cage for *him* out of these steely bars! *Sursum corda*, with the sky the limit!—or somewhat similar sentiments.

In *Warum?* the gentle Eusebius, who seems to have been slightly nauseated by the unnecessary vigor and the somewhat crass display of force in the foregoing, is sicklied o'er with the pale cast of skepticism, and wants to know "*Why?*" Among the thousands of possible interpretations, it has been suggested that Robert asks, "Why not get married?" Clara wistfully replies, and Wieck dips his gruff oar into the bass.

Now we plunge into the swift action and healthy atmosphere of *Crillen* (*Whims*), although the direction *With Humor* puzzles me, as Schumann so often does when he uses this word. Perhaps the mysterious superscription may in certain cases have originated in a fit of subjective amusement which he absentmindedly forgot to project into the music. These rich, solemn harmonies

[Ex. 58]

seem more appropriate for some Gothic cathedral nave than for the bar-room of the Players Club in New York City with the actors and authors exchanging quips. Here is a certain gaiety, yes, but where is the humor? However, a sprightly style and a grave content fuse attractively. Who was it remarked that "gravity of matter and gaiety of manner form the glittering crown of art"?

Note the rhythmical subtlety with which the eight-bar periods are at first divided into phrases of three, three, and two bars each.

The Trio of *Grillen* is, if anything, even better fitted for that Gothic nave than the start. Savor the opulent, dusky coloring of the harmony. This sort of thing is one of Schumann's specialties, and we shall soon encounter it again in the first *Novellette*, and frequently thereafter. I wonder if he caught the idea from the divided-'cello opening of the *William Tell Overture,* and from the slow movement of the *Appassionata.* At any rate, he passed it along to the Tchaikovsky of the *1812 Overture,* and the Brahms of the A Major Serenade and the B Flat Sextet.

It is fortunate that Schumann wrote his pieces first, and fashioned titles for them second. The opposite procedure might easily have played havoc with the quality of the music—as witness Beethoven's regrettable storm in the *Pastoral* Symphony *In der Nacht (In the Night)* is typical of the sort of passionate wordless ballade in the minor, full of rapidly running figures, which was another of Schumann's many specialties.

[Ex. 59]

For this piece he thought up, *ex post facto,* not only a title but also a program: the tale of Hero and Leander. With Gallic vehemence, M. Basch declares that this does not fit at all, and that the true program is a storm at sea interrupted by the song of a siren. What I feel is that music never can be limited to any one "true" program. If only he has sufficient self-mastery to keep him from forcing them down the throats of others, the hearer may justly apply either or both of these ideas to *In der Nacht.* And not these two alone, but a million ideas of similar emotional content are also valid. Why not Arctic explorers interrupting their fight with a blizzard to enjoy a short rest in a hut of ice? Or the Battle of Malaya, with 'everything stopping for tea'? Or an airplane struggling against a gale and making a temporary landing in a blossoming oasis?

This *In der Nacht* represents perhaps the highest point in a notably well-sustained group. There would be no "perhaps" about it if the *cantabile* tune in the middle were less Mendelssohnian.

For me, *Fabel* contains a good deal more humor than *Grillen;* but others will find in it something far different from my private vision of a hustling, rustling go-getter, merrily mocking the impractical, helpless vagaries of his bespectacled friend up there in the ivory tower. It would be a terrible thing if others did not; for then music would be shorn of its chief glory—its infinitude.[1]

The title of *Traumes Wirren (Dream Tangles)* is perfect for a piece of music, because its amplitude gives imagination the widest possible play. (It reminds me of the patent short-story title, *The Trouble in the Family,* invented by Robert Underwood Johnson; he was proud of it because it would fit almost any short story.) *Traumes Wirren* illustrates one of Schumann's failings, a leaning towards rhythmic monotony. But here it flashes by before one has quite wearied of that sixteenth-note figure, so incessantly repeated.

Ende vom Lied (Song's End) opens with three of Schumann's characteristic descending fifths in a row; although the second of them is disguised by lowering the B flat two octaves.

[1] For *Fabel's* source-motive, see p. 483, Ex. 247.

Except for the coda, this charming piece would have made a fitting close for the *Scenes from Childhood*. Most of it has the bright freshness and innocence of early youth. I am devoted to *Ende vom Lied*. It is interesting to read what the composer wrote about it to Clara:

> At the time I thought: well, in the end it all resolves itself into a jolly wedding. But at the close my painful anxiety about you returned; so that it sounds like wedding- and funeral-bells commingled.

Note the bracketed *Carnaval* source-motive that begins the *Etwas lebhafter*:

These *Fantasiestücke* are earmarked for immortality.

Op. 13. *Symphonic Etudes*

Here is a composition of many names. In April 1836, Schumann let it be known that there were coming from the combined pens of Florestan and Eusebius "*Twelve Davidsbündleretuden.*" This title was shortly modified to "*Etudes in Orchestral Character*" by the same team of composers. The following year they were published, under Schumann's own name, as "*Études en forme de Variations,*" or "*XII Études symphoniques.*" We shall call them the *Symphonic Etudes.*

These 12 Etudes were actually composed in 1834, a year after Chopin had published his first group of 12 Etudes, Op. 10. Schumann may have been trying to go Chopin one better; and, in my opinion, he succeeded in creating the most ideal form of study then known.

Opus 13 is the most brilliant of his piano works of permanent value, though here he got entirely away from the mechanical bravura then fashionable. If these variations bore a motto it should be not "The playing's the thing," but "The music's the thing." However, by surprisingly original uses of the pedal, and by wide stretches, he added several important stones to the edifice of piano style.

This splendid work was a new kind of variation. It became the progenitor of such masterpieces as Brahms' variations on themes by Handel, Paganini, and Haydn. Sometimes, as in Etudes III and VII, we can detect neither hide nor hair of the theme. However, the music is so inspiring that we trouble no more over its absence from home than we object when a great oil portrait is not a photographic likeness of the sitter.[2]

Perhaps Schumann was all the more inclined to play hookey from the theme because it was none of his. It had been composed in a moment of authentic inspiration by Ernestine's adoptive father for his own flute. This is the way it starts:

---

[2] The nomenclature of Op. 13 seems unnecessarily complicated. Some of the numbers are called simply "Etudes." Others are called both "Variations" and "Etudes" at the same time, but with different numbers, as "Variation VIII (Etude X)."

[Ex. 62]

The quality of these delightfully contrasted variations is notably sustained. Whether they strike one as ghostly or elfin dances, love songs, martial strains, polyphonic tours de force, or those rarest of phenomena, deeply poetic bravura pieces, it is difficult to choose among them. The talented violist and musicologist Egon Kenton, better known as Egon Kornstein, writes me:

The variations are portraits of the same character, by different artistic temperaments. There are portraits by Florestan, Eusebius, Raro and some more Davidsbündler. And Schumann had indeed the genius's right to compose variations in which the Beckmessers are unable to detect any technical connection with the theme.

Note how the Clara source-motive [3] appears a dozen times in Var. VII (Etude VIII); and how, in Var. IX (Etude XI), its presence is rhythmically emphasized by coming as a quintuplet. Var. VII (Etude VIII) shows a curious, characteristic figure which we we shall call the Swirling Source-Motive.[4]

[Ex. 63]

sempre marcatissimo

[3] See p. 297.
[4] See p. 485.

In his boyish enthusiasm and love both of musico-literary allusion and of his friend, the English composer Sterndale Bennett, Schumann started the rondo finale with a new tune that begins with a very rough inversion of the theme. It is a quotation from Marschner's Ivanhoe opera, *Templar and Jewess,* introduced as a hail to the chivalrous spirit of Bennett's land:

Allegro brillante

[Ex. 64]

This was like what he did in the finales of *Papillons* and of *Carnaval,* where he brought in the *Granddaddy Dance* for an equally literary reason. But from this remote outpost he gradually works back to the real theme. And when the variations close, they miraculously leave a sense of unity.

Op. 15. *Kinderscenen (Scenes from Childhood)*

In a letter to Clara, Robert strikingly contrasted two of his best works:

> Play my *Kreisleriana* occasionally. In some passages there is to be found an utterly wild love, and your life and mine, and many of your looks. The *Scenes from Childhood* are the opposite—peaceful, tender and happy, like our future. . . .

In another letter he confessed that a stray word of hers about his sometimes seeming to her like a child had (in spirit) again clad him in the frilled frock of his infancy. Thus incongruously arrayed, he had composed

> around thirty droll little things, of which I picked out a dozen or so and called them *Scenes from Childhood*. You'll enjoy them; but of course you'll have to forget that you're a virtuoso.

When they appeared, Rellstab of the *Vossische Zeitung* showed how low music criticism had fallen. This was the writer who, fourteen years before, had made a sensation with an account of his visit to Beethoven. He was the miscreant who had pasted upon that master's Opus 27, No. 2 the fancy title *"Moonlight"* Sonata, and who actually preferred Field to Chopin. Rellstab wrote that, in composing Opus 15, Schumann had set upon his piano a howling child, and sought to give a realistic imitation of its tones. Schumann rightly protested to Dorn: "I've seldom come across anything more incapable and feebleminded than that!"

Mr. Bedford again accuses Schumann of inconsistency, if not of downright dishonesty, in stating (1) that these *Scenes* are maturity's recollections of youth for the mature, and (2) that he thought of the titles after finishing the music. But actually these propositions are not mutually inconsistent. Before beginning this engaging series he had been able, in a general way, to

recapture

That first, fine, careless rapture

of life's dawn. He had succeeded in taking the advice once given to old Nicodemus, and becoming again "as a little child"; all the while, moreover, maintaining the child's point of view in humorous contrast with the grown-up's. Then, not until after these tiny products of the unconscious stood finished, and he tried them over, did they suggest to his conscious mind the titles which he gave as "delicate hints on approach and interpretation."

In the entire field of music, I know of nothing more tenderly simple, unsullied, fresh, and humorously comprehending than these thirteen easy little pieces. Schumann's literary ideas about them are as happy as any of the thousands of possible interpretations. In his imagination youth skims strange wonderlands full of odd happenings (1)

[Ex. 65]

and mighty deeds of derring-do (6),

[Ex. 66]

crosses the frontier of the *Almost Too Serious* (10) to arrive with agreeable goose-flesh in the land where "the Gobble-uns'll git you ef you don't watch out" (11).

[Ex. 67]

Youth plunges into such sports as *Blind Man's Buff* and *Hobby-horse* [5] (3, 9), teases for jelly doughnuts, which it savors before the crackling log fire (4, 5, 8), there to hover deliciously beside the Sandman until engulfed in *Träumerei (Dreaming)*,

[Ex. 68]

that dream where all beauty is rolled up into one compact ball within a tight little fist (12, 7). Then *The Poet Speaks*—the poet of tone, that soul rich and profound and clairvoyant enough to reach out beyond the isolating pale of maturity, and share wholeheartedly in the tiny sorrows and joys of those to whom these are still all the world. And the Poet, that kindly cross between Santa Claus and the *Herrgott*, breathes his simple, serene and lofty blessing over the closed eyes in the flushed face.

[5] This title, *Ritter von Steckenpferd*, may be an allusive parody to remind his "high girl" of a pleasant incident that happened the year before. Herr Ritter von Ritterstein ("Ritter von Rittersberg" Clara's diary rechristened him) made a pilgrimage to hear Clara play; but did not want anything of Schumann's "because he expected the composer himself to play them much better." After a few days, he returned with his tail between his legs, to beg for something by Schumann because that gentleman had referred him to Clara.

[Ex. 69]

One understands how the music maker, who here for the first time had laid aside the technic of the accomplished pianist to create these radiant commentaries on the world of innocence and true beauty, could write:

In my compositions I myself have grown gayer, mellower, more melodious. Perhaps you have already found this out in the *Scenes from Childhood.*

After hearing a stupid, repetitious sermon, Delacroix once cried in disgust: *"Vive le frein!* (Long life to the brake!)" On hearing the masterly conciseness of the *Scenes from Childhood,* we echo this sentiment, but in the opposite spirit of admiration. One does not know which to admire more: the delicate distinction of the melodic line, the magic which combines rhythmical subtlety and variety with the elemental tang of the folk-tune, the originality of the tone-color, or the pure, intimate, limpid simplicity and restraint of the whole.

Among all of Schumann's works, this one may enter the most persuasive bid for immortality.[5a]

Op. 16. *Kreisleriana*

On March 15th, 1839, in reply to his first foreign "fan-letter," Schumann wrote of Opus 16 to Simonin de Sire:

The title can be understood by Germans only. Kreisler is a creation of E. T. A. Hoffmann's, an eccentric, wild, clever conductor. You will like much about him.

[5a] Debussy's *Children's Corner* descends in the direct line from the *Scenes from Childhood.* So docs Prokofiev's *Peter and the Wolf,* with its humor and its comprehension of the child's viewpoint.

As a matter of fact, for purposes of this volume of autobiographical confessions in tone, Kreisler becomes none other than Robert himself. Here that young fellow's romantic fantasy has free play. The *Kreisleriana* are akin to the *Davidsbündler Dances* in revealing the deeper strata of their creator's nature, as it functions there far beneath the surface, almost untouched by exterior reality. They bring us close to his sudden and startling manic-depressive alternations and contrasts: desperate, brooding melancholy, wild exaltation, a frantic soul straining to flee from itself, the joy of a delighted child, the querulousness of a spoiled boy who cannot brook contradiction. In Opus 16 we find the dreamer with his foot on the pedal while the harmonies mingle and blur one another like rainbowed films of oil on flowing water. We find the youth who is fixed on his mother, the ardent lover who has found a mother-substitute in the lovely young mate of his mind and heart and body; the miserable wretch condemned to lose this paragon. We hear chuckles and groans, cries of bliss and of anguish, tears of grief and tears of laughter. Here are visions of a youth conquering the world for his love. We see him floating with her in gondolas and through the nurseries of Heaven, with gay greetings waved to *Davidsbündler* who are smiling from the palace windows. That is to say—we may sit in a concert and hear and see all these things in the *Kreisleriana,* while rubbing elbows with someone who hears and sees there a thousand quite different matters.

It is easy to appreciate the remark which Robert made to Clara, on April 13th, 1838, after finishing this suite: "My music now seems to me so wonderfully complicated, for all its simplicity, so eloquent from the heart."

In truth, Opus 16 opened new expressive possibilities for the subtle art of harmony, and offered to the discerning quite unheard of innovations and hints of the future.

How full of Schumannian charm is No. 2! It begins with a faint suggestion of the youthful freshness of the *Papillons* and the wit of the first *Intermezzo*, Op. 4. Note the *Carnaval* source-motive under the bracket.

Sehr innig und nicht zu rasch

[Ex. 70]

No. 4 commences in the mood of Beethoven's deeper introductions, but changes to that of a *Scene from Childhood* for older youngsters,

Bewegter

[Ex. 71]

a mood which reappears in the first part of the sprightly No. 5. No. 6 is the Schumannian lay of a gondolier who sings his graceful craft an obligato through the mystic canals of some supernal Venice of the soul.

Sehr langsam

[Ex. 72]

Presently the music takes on the motions of great fish making
Swirling source-motives in the depths, or breaking water in a
brilliant rush. But then the *etwas bewegter* carries matters beyond the intellectual depth of any mortal gondolier. The taran-
telle-like theme of No. 8

[Ex. 73]

must have borne some very special connotation to its composer;
for three years later he introduced it, under a slight rhythmic
disguise, in the finale of his *"Spring"* Symphony. It turns out to
be another of the old amorous folk-songs which Bach quoted in
the *Peasant Cantata*.[6]

Op. 18. *Arabeske.*

Op. 19. *Blumenstück*

Schumann wrote slightingly of these pieces to Frau Voigt.
On another occasion, he declared in fun that he had composed
them in order to make himself beloved by the ladies of Vienna.
(But Clara did not see the joke.) In this object he succeeded; for

[6] See pp. 402-3, Ex. 144.

the music exemplifies the sentimental salon piece at its best. The English adored the *Arabeske* so much that Clara had to play it to them on all occasions. There is something very tender and intimate about its principal theme, which starts:

Leicht und zart

[Ex. 74]

A dozen bars from the end, note the premonition of *Widmung*.

Op. 20. *Humoreske*

This is a delightful collection of untitled pieces, to be played through without a break. Provided with the key of inner significance which we lack, Schumann may possibly have felt that they were all funny enough to justify the title; though, after finishing Opus 20, he wrote a friend that it certainly was "rather melancholy." Perhaps he meant *Humoreske* in the old sense of a moody, or capricious, piece.

We can all appreciate the fun of that choice caricature of a stuffed shirt in the section inscribed, *With a Certain Pomposity*. And Sir Arthur Sullivan must have found laughter in *Zum Beschluss;*

for he appropriated it almost literally for that jolly hit in *Pinafore*, "Never Mind the Why or Wherefore." [7] As for the rest, it strikes most of us as another series like *Carnaval*, with rare but less even quality, and lacking quite the freshness, spontaneity, and effervescent gaiety of the earlier music. But, to make up, we encounter many a flash of more mature excellence.

Perhaps Vienna, where he wrote Opus 20, may have taken too much out of Schumann to let him give music-paper his creative best. It was always exhausting for an accurate, prompt, conscientious northerner to try to do business with southerners like the Viennese, who were so light-hearted in practical matters. And, on this his first visit, Robert was vainly trying to do business with these elusive, exasperating charmers. However, it seems that he gave Opus 20 all he had. On March 11th, 1839, he wrote Clara:

> This livelong week I've sat at the piano and composed and written and laughed and cried all together. All this you will find beautifully depicted in my Opus 20, the "great Humoreske," which is already in the engraver's hands.

Op. 21. *Novelletten*

Probably in July 1839, Schumann wrote to Hirschbach:

> Four volumes of *Novellettes* by me have appeared. They are intimately interrelated, were written with enormous zest, are by and large gay and superficial, with the exception of places where I got right down to fundamentals.

[7] As Augusta Scheiber points out.

They are the first cousins of the *Fantasiestücke*, Op. 12. The popular favorite, No. 1, is by no means the best of the lot, despite the vigorous, exciting march with which it opens, suffused with that delicious dusky golden color which we have noted in *Grillen* as a Schumannian specialty:

[Ex. 76]

For the Trio, though bars 10-14 bring another prophecy of the great song, *Widmung*, is too sweetly Mendelssohnian to suit the real Schumann-lover.

No. 2 maintains the excitement. The powerful, opulent, interesting basses remind one that César Franck, the bass specialist, may have learned much from this sort of music. Jansen thinks that the weird *Intermezzo* may be the piece which the composer once played to Truhn with the ink still wet. And when Truhn asked about it, the taciturn Schumann emitted the one word, "Macbeth," then seized his hat. The theory gains color from the fact that this *Intermezzo* first appeared in the *New Magazine* with the motto:

> When shall we three meet again,
> In thunder, lightning, or in rain?

No 3 is a delicious bit of light farce.

[Ex. 77]

This example shows a source-motive and a half. The first two brackets ape the one we call Haydn with its halves slightly separated, and the third is the *Carnaval* source-motive upside down and end for end. The second page

[Ex. 78]

anticipates the playful second theme of the A Major Quartet's rondo finale:

[Ex. 79]

The fooling is interrupted and set off by the lamentations of the *Intermezzo*, a typical lightning change of mood.

No. 4 is marked "In the Spirit of a Ball." An infectious waltz takes one back again to the *Papillons* and *Carnaval*. Tchaikovsky was another composer who liked to produce waltzes on the slightest provocation; but he did it in season and out. Schumann had more sense of the fitness of things; and his love in three-quarter time nearly always has refined distinction. This particular waltz is characterized by an extreme simplicity and economy of material which was an extraordinarily new thing in that day, but which has since then been so much imitated that it now sounds banal in our ears:

[Ex. 80]

Ballmässig. Sehr munter

This number is a light curtain-raiser for the grand ball-scene of No. 5, which begins with a stirringly festive polonaise. Into the opening bars, Schumann packed three of his favorite idioms. The brackets show (a) the "Bracketing," (b) the Haydn source-motive, and (c) a third which will be discussed on p. 361.

Rauschend und festlich

[Ex. 81]

This is every whit as fine a polonaise as No. 11 of the *Papillons*. It makes up in pomp, circumstance, and momentum what may be lacking in youthful ebullience. Savor the composer's own dusky coloring in the first and fourth contrasting sections; and in the third, at *Sehr lebhaft*, the imposing harmony and exciting rhythmical monotony.

The second contrasting section, a waltz melody on three notes, is an echo of the *Poco più animato* in the finale of the *Fantasie*.[8]

[Ex. 82]

[8] See p. 316, Ex. 55. It also gives a foretaste of the first song in the *Frauenliebe* cycle.

Both of these tunes show how much Schumann had learned about economy of materials from such music as the Trio of the Scherzo of Beethoven's Fourth Symphony—an art which he was soon to exemplify in the first Scherzo Trio of his own First Symphony. This effect, as noted above, sounds commonplace to us; but in that day its stark simplicity must have struck the musical world with the impact of a stupendous novelty.

No. 6, marked: "Very lively, with much humor," begins

Sehr lebhaft, mit viel Humor

[Ex. 83]

with the German city-dwelling composer incongruously breaking into a Bohemian peasant dance. But the "humor" is somewhat extrinsically registered by means of sudden, startling dynamic contrasts, grace-notes, and a constantly increasing pace. The number has such a marked Czech flavor that it might have been tossed off, in an exceptionally happy hour, by the Dvořák of the *Slavonic Dances*. Which reminds us that Walter Dahms claimed for Schumann an important admixture of the blood of the Wends, the aboriginal Slavonic inhabitants of Saxony. Dahms also calls this *Novellette* "burschikos"; but that untranslatable word is over-Teutonic for such a Czechish piece.

No. 7 is a short, highly animated scherzo, planned to skip along "as fast as possible." The Trio is full of Chopin, but Chopin of a very high quality.

No. 8, the last, longest, and best of the *Novelletten*, is almost

a suite in itself. In this rich and vividly varied collection one
glimpses many of the facets of Schumann's genius. It begins with
one of his specialties, the strong, virile, exciting ballade-like
piece of high momentum—

[Ex. 84]

the sort of thing that was later to thrill all the world in *The Two
Grenadiers,* and inspire Brahms to write *Edward* and the C
Minor *Rhapsody.*

The two Trios take us back to Schumann's early masterpieces.
With the first ("Still livelier") our legs twitch to the danceable
strains of *Carnaval.* With the second ("Bright and jolly"),

[Ex. 85]

we vibrate to enlivening strains akin to the Marschner fanfares
of the *Symphonic Etudes* finale, and hope he is going to end the
piece with this triumphant idea. Now, however, a mystic "Voice
out of the Distance" is heard. It sings descending scales; but
manages to make them curiously touching. And this elemental

material is then, at "Simple and songful," transmuted into a lovely Lied:

[Ex. 86]

At "merry, not too fast," Schumann then gets a new inspiration: a broadly modeled scherzo

[Ex. 87]

even more satisfying than the Marschner-like theme, especially
when it comes back as the ending. Through the shadowy *legato*
section with its subtle, opulent, and deliciously satisfying harmonies, and the *nach und nach lebhafter*,[9] and a return of the
"Voice out of the Distance," our interest and enthusiasm grow
to the last tremendous chord. Schumann has finally made good
his word about getting down to fundamentals.

[9] With the insistent

rhythm which was soon to be inherited by the *Allegro* of the *Faschingsschwank aus Wien.*

CHAPTER 4

THE LAST PIANO MUSIC

Op. 23. *Night Pieces*

WHILE he was writing most of these pieces, Schumann must have suffered from one of his most depressive phases. His inner man kept seeing "funerals, coffins, miserable desperate folk," and hearing "someone sighing deeply from a heavy heart: 'O God!'" For no reason that he knew of, tears poured from his eyes. He proposed to call the series: *1. Funeral Procession. 2. Strange Company. 3. Nocturnal Carouse. 4. Round with Solo Voices.*

Then he received a letter which showed that his dark feelings had been in the nature of presentiments; for his dear brother Eduard lay dying. The first three of these pieces have all but perished from the repertory, despite the luscious, dark colorscheme with which No. 1 begins, and the charming start of No. 2, and the spirited and exciting opening of No. 3. I think this is largely because each contains a contrasting section disappointingly unworthy of its context.

But No. 4 is a different story, and has remained one of Schumann's most beloved inspirations. After all the foregoing depression, its arpeggios represent a phase of the purest, most ethereal beauty and beatitude.

[Ex. 88]

Op. 26. *Faschingsschwank aus Wien (Carnival Joke from Vienna)*

While Schumann was working in the Austrian capital on this exuberant suite, he called it "a great romantic sonata." But not long after, he toned the ambitious program down into "a romantic show-piece." The carefree gaiety, "folksy" light-heartedness, dancing quality, and delightful part-writing of the first, third, and fifth movements suit the pre-Lenten season, as it madly and merrily sang, tripped, flirted, and made love in old Vienna.

The first movement has a natural affinity with the *Préambule* of *Carnaval*, and with the *Papillons*, not only in its exuberance and bustling enterprise, but also in its abundance of

and

rhythms. But Op. 26 is as much more animated than Opp. 2 and 9, as Vienna then surpassed Leipzig in charm, enthusiasm, and mischievous, irresponsible merriment. It begins:

[Ex. 89]

In the third measure we can hear the characteristic stamping foot-technic of the "folk," dancing where a green bush over a doorway in Grinzing heralds the new wine within.

This *Allegro* has five contrasting portions—*Quasi Trios* they might have been called. In the third of these the composer repeatedly brings in the (bracketed) Haydn source-motive,

[Ex. 90]

preceded and followed by other descending fifths. The surmise has already been ventured that whenever Robert brought in this motive, it was as a secret greeting to Clara; because it first came into his mind when he was creating the *Impromptus,* his first essay at varying a theme by the girl he loved. What would be more pleasantly in line with his fondness for the allusive, the hidden, and the mysterious than such a secret musical greeting? It may be significant that, without apparently realizing the existence of this source-motive, Dahms calls the passage "an ardently sentimental act of homage to a lady." Its use would be especially appropriate in this particular movement. For into the next Quasi Trio Robert smuggled another allusion, a fragment of the *Marseillaise,* the song which Metternich had sternly proscribed in Austria. Robert disguised it with such wit that the angry authorities were impotent.[1]

[Ex. 91]

The fifth, and last, Quasi Trio plays a fast-and-loose, cup-and-ball game with high and low chords, after the manner of Beethoven.[2]

[Ex. 92]

The vivid coda ends in a veritable hurrah-boys.

The wisp of *Romanze,* with its engaging modulation from B flat to C, is pure Schumann. Homesickness for Clara might well have been responsible for its wistful beauty.

[1] He was to quote the famous tune again in *The Two Grenadiers,* and in the *Herrmann and Dorothea* Overture.

[2] Cf. the Trio of the Minuet of his E Flat Piano Sonata, Op. 31, No. 3. Saint-Saëns wrote his *Variations,* for two pianos, Op. 35, on this Beethoven theme.

On the other hand, the jolly *Scherzino* is pure Viennese prole-
tariat; but its sophisticated end prophesies the coda that, three
years later, was to wind up the A Major Quartet. Such a little
package of "unbuttoned" revelry might appropriately bear a title
à la Scenes from Childhood, such as *Feet off the Floor.*

Then comes the *Intermezzo,* like the *Romanze,* a bit of un-
alloyed Schumann, created in a depressive phase, but less somber. Here is the energetic manner of *In der Nacht,* or the start
of the eighth *Novellette.*

Sorrow and sighing are gustily swept away in the "most lively"
rush of the finale. We have a musical counterpart of the gay
frenzy of carnival-convulsed Vienna at its best. And, with no
hint of any extraneous Mendelssohn or Chopin influence, the
cantabile

[Ex. 93]

is satisfying provender to store up in memory against a rainy day. As is very meet and right, the *Faschingsschwank* ends with a *presto* fanfare.

Op. 28. *Three Romances*

In 1843 the composer listed these pieces with the *Kreisleriana*, the *Fantasiestücke*, and the *Novelletten*, as his best piano works. They are happy examples of how transparent his style, and how rich his polyphony, can sound.

The first is full of the true Schumannian quality. The start shows what he could do with extreme melodic simplicity.

The second is the justly popular favorite in F Sharp Major. The luscious 'cello melody, embedded in a harp-like filigree, and tenderly answered as if by the voices of violins, makes a piece of an *Innigkeit* unusual even for Schumann.

[Ex. 94]

The use of three staves may have resulted from the composer's jocular correspondence with his foreign "fan," De Sire, about this method of notation; for Op. 28 was written the same year as the letter.[3]

The third *Romance,* with its two intermezzi, is longer and more elaborate, but less deeply satisfying than its brothers.

[3] See p. 129.

Op. 32. *Four Piano Pieces*

These end Schumann's great period of piano composition. He wrote the first three of them, the *Scherzo, Gigue,* and *Romanze,* in Vienna. It must have been at a time when that alluring place had sucked dry the well of his vitality; for these pieces are on the "made" side. The *Fughette,* which he wrote in 1839 after returning to Leipzig, is an experiment in a daring new form, the harmonic fugue. Here he tried to do with harmonic masses what Bach had done with single voices. But though the younger master wrote Fischhof that this *Fughette* had given him "much joy," in the end he must have considered the attempt just as complete a failure as we do today; for he never again tried this experiment.

FUGAL WRITING

When Dorn cast him off as a pupil, Schumann carried on by himself. On July 27th, 1832, he wrote home to his first master, Kuntsch:

A few months ago I finished my theoretical studies with Dorn as far as canon, which I have studied all alone according to Marpurg. . . . Otherwise Sebastian Bach's *Well-tempered Clavichord* is my grammar, and what is more, the best of grammars. Down to the minutest details I have analyzed the fugues in their order. This procedure is very useful and, as it were, has a morally invigorating effect on one's entire being. For Bach—take him for all in all—was a man. Nothing of him is half done or morbid. Everything is written as if for eternity.

Eight years later he told Keferstein of Bach: "Daily I confess to this lofty one, and through him try to purify and strengthen myself." The same day he avowed to Henriette Voigt that J. S. B. was the refuge from which he loved to draw "joy and strength to work and to live."

Schumann must have felt in his bones that fugal writing was not in his line; for not until 1839 did he compose his first published attempt, that unsuccessful experiment, the *Fughette,* Op. 32, No. 4. He gave out nothing more of the sort until the nervous

collapse of 1845, during which he wrote works that look passing
strange in a catalogue of his music:

Op. 56. *Studies for Pedal-pianoforte.*[4] Book I, *Six Pieces in Canon Form.* Also for pianoforte for 3 or 4 hands.

Of these *Studies* I especially like the sweetly touching and
melodious fourth one in A Flat. This shows Schumann, by exception, remaining true to his own personality, even in the strictest of contrapuntal forms. As befitted a piece written for Clara
and himself, he liberally bestrewed it with the Clara source-
motive.

Op. 58. *Sketches for Pedal-pianoforte* (may also be per-formed on the pianoforte by 2 players)

Of these I prefer the last, the delightful *Allegretto* in D Flat,
with its gay *scherzando* spirit. This too is authentic Schumann.

Op. 60. *Six Fugues on the name "Bach."* [5] For organ or pedal-pianoforte

Op. 72. *Four Fugues for Pianoforte*

Eight years later he added a last member to this strange
group:

Op. 126. *Seven Pieces in Fughetta Form*

The composer's nervous collapse had been aggravated by the
too intense labor and excitement of his years of song, symphony,
and chamber music. One suspects that when, as he wrote Mendelssohn on July 17th, 1845, "an onslaught of terrifying thoughts"
had brought him "to the verge of despair," the tactful Clara had
coaxed him to try his hand at fugal writing, very much as we of
today would cajole a nervous invalid into doing crossword puz-

---

[4] A piano provided with a set of organ-pedals. In his innocence, Schumann predicted for this now forgotten hybrid a brilliant future.

[5] Our B flat is B in German, and our B is H.

zles, to take his mind from his troubles. The very fact that Schumann's intensely subjective nature made it almost impossible for him to give of his best in this formal, objective style allowed him to play with these contrapuntal forms without expending too much energy.

The first three numbers of Opus 126 have their exalted moments. The last two are not to be taken seriously.

Op. 68. *Album for the Young*

If some cataclysm should wipe out all of Schumann's music, letters, and other writings, leaving only the titles of the pieces in Opus 68, the New Zealanders of the future could, from these alone, tell much about this composer. That he had humor, tenderness, sympathy, understanding of children, and imagination, they would know from the following:

> Soldiers' March (Cheerful and at attention)
> Poor Orphan Child
> Little Hunter's Song (Fresh and merry)
> Wild Rider
> Happy Farmer Coming back from Work
> Knecht Ruprecht (a sort of Santa Claus)
> Little Morning-wanderer (Fresh and strong)
> Little Harvest Song (With joyful expression)
> Strange Man
> After-echoes from the Theater (Somewhat agitated)

There are 43 of these small pieces. No. 1, *Melody*, makes a perfect start for such a collection. No. 2 gives a juvenile echo of the scherzo of Beethoven's *"Spring"* Violin Sonata in F.[6] To counterbalance this loan, No. 9 (*Little Folk Song*) may have given Grieg the beginning of *Aases Tod* in the *Peer Gynt* music. Perhaps Grieg was attracted to this piece because its middle section sounds Norwegian.

I like the winning pathos of No. 6, and the blitheness of *The Happy Farmer* (the most popular item in the collection), and the Santa Clausian joviality of No. 12, which never fails to entrance every child.

[6] Schumann later recalled the first movement of this same sonata in the *Kinderball*. See p. 368, Ex. 120.

Who is not touched by the dewy simplicity and innocence of Nos. 13, 15, 16, 18, 22, 24, and 43? When other composers attempt this difficult sort of writing, they usually fade out and disappear, like a raindrop on a blotter; but Schumann showed his rare quality, no matter how much he simplified.

Perhaps those two martial strains, Nos. 2 and 31, were memories of Robert's Napoleonic childhood in Zwickau.

Little Romance, No. 19

[Ex. 95]

is often played as a sort of Trio with *Träumerei* in the *Scenes from Childhood;* [7] for the two tiny masterpieces go perfectly together. In its tender intimacy, the untitled No. 21 is highly characteristic of Schumann.

Langsam und mit Ausdruck zu spielen

[Ex. 96]

[7] See p. 328, Ex. 68.

So is No. 26.

With its horsemen realistically appearing and disappearing, *Rider Piece*, No. 23, is an example of the sort of literal program music which Schumann almost never wrote. *After-echoes from the Theater*, No. 25, shows his subtle humor and his ability to enter completely into the child's universe.

No. 27 is a delicious introduction to that world of canon which American children know best as *Three Blind Mice*. *Memory*, No. 28, was written on the day that Mendelssohn died; but for all that it is authentic Schumann. There is excellent child psychology in *Strange Man*, No. 29, with something strong and terrifying alternating with futile attempts on the part of the grown-ups to soothe away the little one's fears.

The very beautiful No. 30 really belongs in the *Scenes from Childhood*; for it suggests an adult's impression of the touching loveliness that can surround early youth.

Sheherezade, No. 32, is delicious both in melody and in harmony.[8] No. 36 is a fit companion for Beethoven's *Turkish March*. The *Sailor's Song*, No. 37, a favorite of mine, is a highly imaginative piece, with a certain ballad-like quality.

No. 38 shows how much may be accomplished by obstinately repeating the same motive. At *Ein wenig langsamer* in No. 39, it is pleasant to find again the same jolly pair of quotations which we found in the finale of the *Papillons:* the old folk-tune which Bach had smuggled into the *Peasant Cantata,* and the *Granddaddy Dance.*[9]

Kleine Fuge, No. 40, is a better fugue than any that Schumann wrote in the weeks of study described a few pages ago. And he actually made it wholly Schumannian. Not a trace of Bach! *Northern Song,* No. 41, as mentioned on p. 291 in connection with *Carnaval,* brings an anagrammatical greeting to friend Gade:

The melody of the *Figured Chorale,* No. 42, was once used by Bach; but Schumann, by the harmony of his original figuration, wrote his name upon it.

---

[8] For *Theme*, No. 34, see p. 481, Ex. 246.
[9] See pp. 281-2, Exs. 6, 7 and 8.

All through the series, notice how adorable in their limpid childish beauty and simplicity are the final cadences.

Neither before nor since Schumann has anybody made the children such a gorgeous musical gift as the *Album for the Young*.[9a]

Op. 76. *Four Marches*

These represent Schumann's reaction to the fighting at Dresden in 1849—once he began to take cognizance of it. This was the same revolution in which Wagner took such an aggressive part that he had to flee the country. The adjective that best expresses the quality of these marches is "ratty." Incredibly banal to come from the pen of a Schumann, they are glaring examples of war's effect upon the arts. But at least they are not quite so bad as Chopin's *Polonaise Brillante*, Op. 3, for 'cello, or that other *Polonaise*, Op. 89, which Beethoven manufactured for the Empress of Russia at the Congress of Vienna in 1814.

Op. 82. *Forest Scenes*

These pieces of moderate technical difficulty were composed in 1848-49, following the *Album*, of which they were the aftermath.[10] Of an admirable simplicity, they attain a maximum of effect with a minimum of mechanism.

The first piece, *Entrance*, immediately strikes a folksy, elemental note that is intensified in *Lonely Flowers* (No. 3),[11] and persists through the collection. No. 2, *Hunter in Ambush*, is an amusing example of Schumann's ignorance in the department of sport. Any piece of this name would naturally be breathlessly

[9a] Mussorgsky's piano pieces: *Memories of Childhood, Kinderscherz*, and *Souvenir d'enfance* are among the myriad offspring of Opus 68, just as his *Pictures at an Exhibition* are among those of *Carnaval* and *Bilder aus Osten*. Mr. Arthur P. Schmidt, the music publisher, says he wishes that Schumann had never invented juvenile music, because composers are constantly submitting children's pieces to him with the remark: "These are better than the *Album for the Young*." The trouble is, they never are!

[10] The title and tenor of this music may have inspired MacDowell's *Woodland Sketches*.

[11] Note that this piece begins with an echo of Schubert's song, *Frühlingsglauben*.

soft, and rhythmically as near static as any music can bring itself
to be. If any slight movement were indulged in, it would be
gradual and stealthy, for fear of rustling the dead leaves or stepping upon a dry stick. But here the true woodsman is startled
to find Schumann's music marked "Most lively." The hunter, by
hypothesis "in ambush," sets forth at a reckless pace through the
underbrush, with his corybantic dogs yapping and cavorting
around him in triplets. By the tenth measure the expedition has
reached *forte*, and all the game throughout that neck of the
woods has flown in wild terror. This bit of tenderfoot naïveté
reminds one of the third of the *Four Marches* just discussed. It
is labeled *Camp Scene*. The composer filled it with a portentous
bustle of marching and countermarching, because he did not
know that, in camp, soldiers do as little marching as possible.

In *Tabooed Spot* (No. 4), Schumann's true style seems
cramped, in a way unusual for him, by his morbid program.
Here he must have thought of the title first. The realistic imitations of *Prophet Bird* (No. 7) are more successful, and have made
it a favorite with concert pianists—though not with this writer.

The homey *Inn*, No. 6, is full of Schumann's intimate charm: [12]

[Ex. 100]

Notes 3-8 are a subtle greeting to Eichendorff, the super-
Romantic poet of forest magic; for they are identical with the
first six accompaniment notes of Schumann's own setting of that
poet's *Waldesgespräch*, Op. 39.

[Ex. 101]

[12] The bracketed notes of Ex. 100 (above) are no other than Beethoven's
chief source-motive, upside down. See my *Beethoven*, p. 578 ff.

There a lovely bride wanders the deep woods and falls into the clutches of the witch Lorelei.

No. 8 is a rousing *Hunt Song,* its straightaway quality conveying more than a hint of Mendelssohn. No. 9, *Parting,* is tremulous with romantic nostalgia.

Op. 99. *Bunte Blätter*

These are chips from the Master's work-bench. On account of their modest technical demands they are beloved by amateurs. No. 2, written in 1839, at the end of his great piano period, is strong, impressive, authentic Schumann. The wistful theme of No. 4 was later used by Brahms for the piano variations, Op. 9, which Johannes dedicated to Clara. Augusta Scheiber has shown me the similarity of this theme to that of Mendelssohn's *Andante con Variazioni,* Op. 82, composed 1841 and published posthumously in 1850.

This fourth number of the *Bunte Blätter,* entitled (somewhat confusingly) *Albumblätter,* was likewise composed in 1841, and published two years after his friend's variations. It would be interesting to know who was first in the field. Certainly Schumann's theme sounds more Mendelssohnian than the other's sounds Schumannian. And it is significant that Nos. 1, 5, 6, 7, 10, and 11 also have a Mendelssohnian tang ranging from faint to moderate.

No. 5 is the sort of rapid minor ballade-like piece that was dear to Schumann's heart. No. 6 is a waltz on the letters ASCH,[13] which was cut out of *Carnaval*.

[Ex. 104]

After so much Mendelssohn, No. 8 returns to the Schumann fold. No. 9 is entitled *Novelletto*. It is probably a cull from the *Novelletten*, Op. 21; for it was composed in their year, 1838.

[Ex. 105]

I like its offhand, perfectly relaxed playfulness, and think it worthy of its big brothers.

The richly shadowed *March*, No. 11, begins:

[Ex. 106]

[13] A reminder that *As* is A flat in German, and *H* is B natural.

It combines in succulent proportions the before-mentioned bit of Mendelssohn, and a generous slice of Schumann, with a little *Death and the Maiden*. There is more Schubert in the lovely Trio, which is also agreeably redolent of the scherzo of Schumann's own A Major Quartet, composed the previous year.

The *Abendmusik*, No. 12, is pure Schumann, except where, after the introduction, it makes one think of another piece in the same rhythm and key: the scherzo of Beethoven's *Hammerklavier* Sonata, Op. 106. The G Flat section is a delicious example of the sort of dark golden coloring which we found in the Trio of *Grillen*.

[Ex. 107]

My special favorite in this collection is the *Scherzo*, No. 13, written in the fertile symphonic year, 1841. For me there is a mysterious magic in the abrupt start:

[Ex. 108]

And in the Trio I enjoy meeting again that old friend, the *Carnaval* source-motive in its complete form (as already given in *Ende vom Lied*).[14] It is marked by a bracket:

14 See p. 322, Ex. 61.

[Ex. 109]

This *Scherzo* and the *Abendmusik* have been unaccountably neglected, and should come into their own.

Op. 111. *Three Fantasiestücke*

The *Fantasiestücke*, Op. 12, were by now well known. In this brief continuation of them, it is perhaps significant of the evolution of Schumann's esthetic philosophy that he dispensed with fancy literary titles.

The fiery excitement of No. 1, the poignant, wistful loveliness of No. 2, which might (among other things) be whispering

> Good-by, proud world, I'm going home,

and the virile, determined, ballade-like march of No. 3, fill music lovers with pride that, in his years of mental disintegration, Schumann could have pulled himself together and created these bits of fantasy. They need feel no shame in associating with the masterpieces of his youth.

Op. 118. *Three Piano Sonatas for Young People*

These little sonatas, each dedicated to one of his small daughters, were almost the last compositions finished by Schumann before the final catastrophe of 1853 that sent him into the Rhine and the asylum. It is remarkable to find two of them far superior in quality to the other works of that sinister period, and heavens above the lamentable accompaniments to the Bach 'cello suites that immediately preceded them. It is as if his love for children were so strong that it surmounted the barriers of illness to give us one more hour of his true self.

These childish sonatas are in simple Mozartian form, with

difficulties adapted to the technical resources of each small dedicatee—except when Father grew absent-minded, forgot the age
of the recipient, and ended the Second Sonata, for ten-year-old
Elise, with a "very spirited" movement called *Children's Party*,
to read which would embarrass many a famous adult pianist.
This reminds us of his occasionally failing to recognize his own
children when he encountered them in the street.

In all but the second alternating theme of the final *Rondeletto*,
the First Sonata, for eight-year-old Julie is a tiny masterpiece.
Its simplicity is almost as touching and winning as anything in
the *Album for the Young*. Schumann must have been especially
fond of the opening melody,

[Ex. 110]

as well he might, for he brought back an echo of it at the close
of the last sonata. Julie (the Schumann daughter whom Brahms
long afterward wished to marry) must have been entranced by
her third movement, *Doll's Cradle Song*, which is as charming
as its title:

[Ex. 111]

(Was it in greeting to Julie that Brahms started the *Andantino*
of his great Clarinet Quintet with an echo of this *Doll's Cradle
Song*?) The tripping second subject was a gay reminder of
Father's jolly children's Lied, *The Sandman*, Op. 79, No. 13.

Alas! Elise's Sonata No. 2 suddenly slumps down to the level
of "made" stuff, the characteristic product of those bad times
when Robert, like Saul in the Bible, knew that "the evil spirit
was upon him," and no young David of a Johannes was at hand
to exorcise it with his music. In the entire first movement the
composer's morbid obsession with a certain sixteenth-note figure [15] is painfully evident. It is nearly the same source-motive
that he had well-nigh done to death in the finales of the A Minor
Violin Sonata and of the A Minor String Quartet.

The Third Sonata, inscribed to twelve-year-old Marie, registers
a remarkable recovery, almost recapturing the quality of the
First. Near the beginning a gay greeting is waved to the often-
quoted "*Spring*" Violin Sonata of Beethoven. The *Gypsy Dance*
sparkles with authentic fire. In their simple comeliness, the
Andante and the *Child's Dream* show that, with the shades of
the prison-house nearly closing upon him, poor Schumann had
almost succeeded for the moment in becoming a glad, carefree
child again. But to us there is something wonderfully poignant
in catching such strains from a man who was very soon to hear
spirits dictating melodies to his pen. The *Child's Dream* was
his farewell to real composition. And it was a farewell that befitted the pioneer who had conceived the *Scenes from Childhood*
and the *Album for the Young*.

It is hard to understand why these sonatas, especially the
First, are not more used in teaching. For this they are ideal.

Op. 124. *Albumblätter*

Numbers 4, 15, and 17 of this late collection are culls from
Carnaval, the first and last of these being founded on the motto
ASCH. Among the Master's most tenderly comprehending and
appealing pages are the piteous *Premonition of Suffering*, No. 2,
Suffering without End, No. 8, the childishly simple and devout
Wiegenliedchen, No. 6, and the serene though not quite so child-
like *Schlummerlied*, No. 16:

[15] See pp. 337, 447, 453, and 482-4. As this figure, ascending two steps
and slipping back one, seems like a mountain climber struggling up a steep,
sandy slide, let us call it the Climb source-motive. Variants of it seem to
pick their way down rocky slopes.

[Ex. 112]

In the second part of the *Scherzino,* No. 3, Schumann is up to his old rhythmic prestidigitation, making ¼ time sound with ⅝:

[Ex. 113]

No. 10 is a tiny, semi-precious gem of a waltz; while No. 13 anticipates by a decade the charming theme of the F Major Quartet variations.[16]

[Ex. 114]

No. 17 is a little elfin puff of highly Schumannian thistledown— or feathery ASCH.

16 See p. 455, Ex. 216.

Op. 133. *Gesänge der Frühe*

These *Songs of Early Morning* were composed in 1853, and "dedicated to the lofty poetess Bettina." (I wonder if Robert had ever heard of this Bettina von Arnim's spiteful remarks about Clara at the time of the latter's first concert in Berlin!) There is a flash of the Schumann we love in the opening *Song*. Note the characteristic fifths:

Also in No. 2, which is a variation of No. 1. Then the work sadly degenerates into the "made," with the exception of the moving little hymn that starts No. 5.

POSTHUMOUS WORKS FOR PIANO

Scherzo

This is the movement which Schumann originally wrote for the *Concert sans Orchestra*, the Third Sonata, Op. 14. He wisely discarded it as not quite up to the mark; though the exciting Trio can hold up its head among his works.

Presto Passionato

Here is another scrapped movement. In 1835 Schumann put it on paper to end the Second Sonata, in G Minor, and then threw it out as inadequate. These pieces exhibit Schumann's love of rhythmical foolery. The former makes ⁶⁄₈ time sound as though the last beat of each bar were the first of the following. The latter suggests that ⁶⁄₁₆ time is ³⁄₈. There is a quality in both which might have induced another composer to let them stand.

CHAPTER 5

PIANO MUSIC FOR MORE THAN TEN FINGERS

FOR TWO PIANOS

Op. 46. *Andante and Variations*

ALTHOUGH Schumann composed this work in 1843, before he had quite recuperated from the exhaustion of the three fabulously creative years, 1840-42, it is one of his finest pieces, and a stand-by of all two-piano teams. Despite a theme that edges ever so slightly towards the sentimental, and a final variation for which the expressive word "dinky" might conceivably come to mind, it is a notable composition. With its subtle harmonic, rhythmic, and melodic wealth, and above all with the essence of true Schumann which it distills, the music more than makes up for those defects.

It breathes a lofty excitement. One feels that it was written for Clara with deep love. The high spots begin with the third variation, where that Schumannian emblem, the descending fifth, is used in the same pivotal way in which it had recently been employed in the Quintet.[1]

[*Ex. 116*]

[1] See p. 479, Ex. 240.

364

There is something stirringly impressive yet tender about the slow fifth variation; and the blood leaps to the fanfaresque summons of the seventh. In both one seems to hear a long-vanished brazen voice. For this work was originally written for the bizarre co-operation of a horn and two 'cellos with the pair of pianos, before being restricted to the latter. I suppose that Schumann chose these instruments because he was so fond of the deep, rich coloring which we have often remarked. But practical considerations supervened. It proved too hard to assemble such a combination. Besides, when the original work was tried at Dr. Härtel's in March 1843, it did not sound very well. Rescored for two pianos, it had its debut in August under the hands of Clara and Mendelssohn. And since then it has held its own with the best of everything written for this combination.

Works for Four Hands

In his final period Schumann, conscious of his enriched technic, was filled with ambition to continue the task which Schubert had begun, of building an original literature for four hands on the piano keys. The result was four works, of which

Op. 66. *Bilder aus Osten*

was the most important. The poet Rückert's *Makamen* provided the inspiration. And the most interesting thing about the series is the way in which Schumann's own individuality overpowered his attempts to give the music an exotic, oriental coloring.

No. 1 might be taken as a forerunner of Brahms' *Hungarian Dances*. No. 4, an unmistakable love-song, appropriately gives importance to the Clara source-motive,

[Ex. 117]

which, after the antiphonal folk-choirs of the vigorous No. 5, returns to play an important role in No. 6. This impressively closes and tops the series. It bears a heading such as none but the mystery-loving Schumann would have used. *"Reuig, andächtig" (contritely devout)* seems a bit mad, until we discover that it refers to Rückert's wise old rascal, Abu Seid.

Op. 85. *Twelve Four-Hand Piano Pieces*

Schumann's inveterate love of youth produced this continuation of the *Album for the Young,* "for little and big children." Except the closing *Abendlied,* which has come to be one of the Master's most beloved compositions, the series contains little of the real Schumann, except his humor and his tenderness for the little ones.

The droll, ungainly antics of the *Bear Dance,* No. 2, are sure to delight any child. The roguish paraphrase of the *Andante* from Mendelssohn's Violin Concerto that begins No. 3 might be over the heads of youngsters less musical than Schumann's own. But the gaiety of *Wreathmaking,* No. 4, of *Round Dance,* No. 8, and of *Hide and Seek,* No. 10, must have touched off millions of young laughs.

No. 6 is a vividly realized bit of juvenile *Sorrow.* And No. 11 is a spirited *Ghost Story* full of jolly shivers. One wonders at finding here that scrap of virtuosity, *At the Fountain,* No. 9. It is a trick piece, marked *"As fast as possible,"* and quite beyond the capacity of any but a wonder-child. The composer must have meant this to be played to, not by, his small friends.

It is interesting to hear the beautiful *Abendlied,* No. 12,

[Ex. 118]

which is usually played by stringed instruments, in its original setting for four hands. I like to remember that Joachim performed this in Bremen Cathedral in an entr'acte of the first complete [2] performance of Brahms' *German Requiem*. It was played in honor of Clara, who had put in a surprise appearance, and of her late husband, who had done so much to inspire the great oratorio.

Op. 109. *Ball Scenes*

Between the *Préambule* and the *Promenade* finale, these *Scenes* include the dances of many lands; but, as they lack the true Schumann quality, let us pass them.

Op. 130. *Children's Ball*

This was composed in 1853, just before the final catastrophe. The simple *Waltz* and the humorous *Ringelreihe*, with their childlike quality, would belong in an appendix to the *Album for the Young*, if only they contained more Schumann. It is amusing to find the opening piece, *Polonaise*, starting out with another merry greeting to Beethoven's "*Spring*" Violin Sonata.

As for the rest, they are gay and pleasant; but who would ever dream that Schumann had written them?

---

[2] Complete, that is, all but the present Part V, which was composed later.

CHAPTER 6

THE SONGS

B Y 1840 Schumann began to find the piano too restricted to deal with the ever growing luxuriance of his inspiration. So, as was natural for an amateur of poetry and a composer in love, he turned to song. And he entered this second field endowed with an even more astonishing ripeness and maturity than the *Papillons* had revealed at his public debut as a composer.

The best of the Schumann songs have the same inexhaustible vitality, freshness, and originality, the same vivid coloring, richness, and resource in melody, harmony and rhythm that delight us in the early piano works. And they surpass these in architectural excellence and directness, in the composer's own *innig* quality, and in freedom from what Dr. Daniel Gregory Mason well calls "eccentricities of manner and perversity of fancy."

Writing these songs stirred Schumann deeply; and, after the lapse of more than a century, they go straight to our own hearts with unerring power and intimacy. He began where his idol, Schubert, had left off; and at a bound placed himself side by side with that first great master of the Lied.

While he lacked the other's elemental might, world-embracing variety, and dithyrambic genius,[1] he equaled Schubert in naturalness of expression, lightness of touch, intimacy of appeal, and depth of poetic suggestion. And he surpassed him in harmonic richness and subtlety, in atmospheric opulence, psychological verisimilitude, knowledge of poetry, and in the *Innigkeit* and fervor of his love Lieder.

[1] And consequently made a complete success of only one ballad, *The Two Grenadiers*.

Schumann also performed an enormous service by mixing more absolute music in with lyric song than had ever before been heard in that field. He increased the significance of the piano part so that often it acquired the same importance as in a violin sonata. He heaped up the harmonic interest. Frequently, making voice and piano exchange traditional functions, he gave the keys the melody. Note how in *Das ist ein Flöten und Geigen* the piano is all-important, while the voice contributes a nearly negligible obligato. He allotted to the piano highly significant preludes, interludes, and postludes. Thus he took the Lied much further than Schubert up the path of evolution that leads from the basic folk-song to that point somewhere in the future where the singing voice will shed the burden of words.[1a]

Those wonderful, poignantly effective postludes in which the harmony summarizes the situation far better—if less concisely— than any voice could, were something new. In fact, they were such a startling novelty that decades elapsed before singers could be taught to wait them out instead of taking their bows as soon as the last word was uttered.

Composing as he did, without much regard for, or even knowledge of, any technic but that of the piano, made it simpler for Schumann to be original. The easier, more natural vocal patterns had long been used and overused. But this man pursued his musical dream almost regardless of the vehicle. Consequently, his vocal music bristles with formidable difficulties, and sometimes calls for a range that the singer does not possess.[2] However, nobody could justly say that Schumann's originality depends wholly on awkward writing; for some of his most novel compositions are also his most idiomatic.

[1a] The interweaving of voice and piano was taken over by Wolf, Brahms, Reger, Richard Strauss, and their successors.

[2] This is also one secret of Schumann's original way of writing for orchestral instruments. Very few composers have ever scored with less regard for practicability. The *Concertpiece for Four Horns and Orchestra*, Op. 86, is a case in point. It is full of lovely music which cannot be heard because the range is so high and the difficulties so horrendous that it needs almost the trump of an archangel to cope with them. I live in hopes that some enterprising conductor may yet produce this admirable *Concertpiece*, with a trumpet playing the part that is impossible for the first horn.

The best of the 260 solo Lieder have a considerably narrower range of subject matter than those of Schubert. Fourteen of them treat of happy love, eleven of unhappy love, five of nature, four are humorous, two treat of sadness, one of war, and one of the supernatural.[3] Thus, of these thirty-eight, two-thirds are love songs; which is natural considering the fevered condition of Schumann's affections during the great year which saw the birth of most of his best Lieder.

In the whole literature of song it would be hard to find a more triumphant delirium of ecstatic love than *Widmung*, which leads off the supreme songs of happy love:

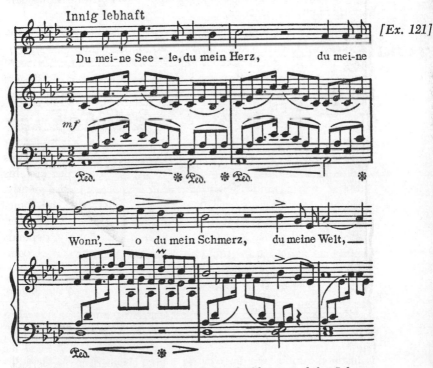

[Ex. 121]

[3] Compiling a list of this kind is a matter so highly personal that I do not expect any reader fully to endorse my choice. But then again, I do not expect any reader entirely to denounce it.

This torrent of pure inspiration appropriately opens the cycle *Myrthen,* Op. 25, which Robert brought Clara as a *Polterabend* [4] gift on the eve of their wedding.

Other great Lieder of happy love are: the delicate *Der Nussbaum,* which evenly holds the balance between voice and piano; *Du bist wie eine Blume,* in which the touching simplicity of the music perfectly agrees with that of Heine's words, and which has become the favorite among the myriad settings of this famous lyric. *Dein Bildniss wunderselig* appealed so strongly to Schumann himself that later he used it again in the F Major Trio.

In the same bright category are the first seven songs of the cycle, *Frauenliebe und Leben,* Op. 42, of which the second, *Er, der Herrlichste von Allen,*

[Ex. 122]

is justly the most popular; for its jubilant sweep is the perfect feminine counterpart to *Widmung.*

4 See p. 288.

This cycle offers a glaring contrast between the first-rate composer, Schumann, and the second-rate poet, Chamisso. However, if unequal composers and poets must collaborate, such a ratio is preferable to its opposite. For in song the music, always the main consideration, always injures the highly perishable word-melody of verse. So it is better not to have second-rate music usurp the center of the stage at the expense of immortal poetry.

Now in the *Frauenliebe,* Schumann's notes are so lordly in their prepotence over the mediocre words, that we scarcely wince when Chamisso, instead of remarking, "Let me weep," elegantly curls his little finger and declaims: "Let the unaccustomed adornment of moist pearls tremble, joyously bright, in this mine eye." Such a poetic effort would be fit to gain the suffrage of that Congressman who once characterized his home town of Duluth as "the zenith city of the unsalted seas."

The songs of happy love are rounded out by three from the great cycle, *Dichterliebe,* Op. 48. Though its melodic line is different, the first vocal phrase of the opening Lied, *Im wunderschönen Monat Mai*

[Ex. 123]

has a curious affinity with one of Beethoven's finest themes, the *Dona nobis pacem* of the *Missa Solennis*:

[Ex. 124]

This may be because each of these melodies avoids using any note which it has already used. As an expression of pure, pellucid love-ecstasy, this Schumann song has never been surpassed (even by Schubert himself)—unless by the fourth in the same series, *Wenn ich in deine Augen seh'*:

Langsam

Wenn ich in Dei - ne Au - gen seh', so

schwin-det all mein Leid und Weh;

[Ex. 125]

But this is said without prejudice to No. 5, *Ich will meine Seele tauchen.*

Few poets or composers have ever been able to express with equal power both the bright and the dark aspects of human passion; but Florestan and Eusebius were equal to the task. Among the eleven great depressive love songs there are jewels of as rare a luster as any among the manic Lieder. There is the superbly simple setting of *Die Lotosblume*, where, in defiance of those who smile at the pathetic fallacy, Heine identifies himself with a lotus flower unhappily in love. And the superb music makes us oblivious of the absurdity of the argument.

There is the final number of *Frauenliebe*, *Nun hast du mir den ersten Schmerz getan*, in which the sudden, dramatic change from the happiness of the preceding songs to stark tragedy is almost too poignant to bear. And the poignancy is heightened by the admirable postlude, with its echo of the love-dazzled opening Lied, *Seit ich ihn gesehen:*

[Ex. 126]

The simplicity of *Aus meinen Thränen spriessen* where, but for two measures, the melody keeps within the range of a fourth, recalls that other triumph of economy which we remarked in the *Novelletten.*[5] But it is not more elementally simple than the stark *Ich hab' im Traum geweinet. Ich grolle nicht,* one of the supreme moments in song literature, attains a depth of despair close to the limits of sanity:

Note the modern quality of its pioneering dissonances.

[5] See pp. 337-8, Ex. 82.

Die alten, bösen Lieder reminds one that Schumann was the
first composer to appreciate and reflect Heine's bitter irony,
which had gone quite over the head of the more naïve Schubert.
This powerful, astringent song completes the *Dichterliebe*, and
culminates in a most eloquent postlude. Here is the closing half
of it. Note how it anticipates the cadenza of the Piano Concerto:

[Ex. 128]

In *Der arme Peter I*, Eusebius again does justice to the gall and wormwood of Heine's bitterness. Other great Lieder of unhappy love are *Mit Myrthen und Rosen*, the sadly tender *Dein Angesicht*, and *Der schwere Abend*. That terrible song, *Der Spielmann*, seems to be another of those tactless references to the story of poor Ernestine which we noticed in connection with Opus 31.[6] Instead of loving the bridegroom, the bride loves the musician. And in the *Dichterliebe*, a song, *Ein Jüngling liebt ein Mädchen*, while not one of Schumann's best, treats of much the same theme: a girl loves a youth who is devoted to someone else; so that, in angry rebound, she weds the first man who crosses her path. The publication of such songs, so soon after jilting Ernestine, shows a strange disregard for the feelings of the girl who had recently stood up for him with loyal forgiveness in his struggle with Wieck.

The terribly convincing music of *Der Spielmann's* harrowing end, as it gets slower and more despairing, is a heart-breaking premonition of Robert's own end:

(*Wildly*)   *Wer heisst euch mit Fingern zeigen auf mich?*
(*Slower*)   *O Gott, bewahr uns gnädiglich*
              Dass keinen der Wahnsinn übermannt.
(*Adagio*)   *Bin selber ein armer Musikant.*

              (Who bids you point your fingers at me?
              O God, protect us mercifully
              When madness threatens with its ban.
              I'm only a poor music-man.)

And one of the two great songs of sadness, Goethe's *Wer sich der Einsamkeit ergibt*, to be sung "with profoundly melancholy expression," is another pitiful premonition of the composer's own last state. The other of these is *Die Nonne*, in which the nun envies the bride. Incidentally, I should like to refer those who, like Sir Henry Hadow, complain of the invariable monotony and repetitious symmetry of Schumann's rhythms,[7] to the admirably varied movement of this Lied.

[6] See p. 72.
[7] See p. 488 ff.

Mondnacht stands out among the songs of nature as a striking example of variety in unity. Except for eight measures near the end, the voice does nothing but repeat the selfsame motive:

[Ex. 129]

And yet there is not the slightest monotony.

Frühlingsnacht, filled to the delicate brim with the scents and sounds and veiled radiance that come to an exultant lover on a perfect *Spring Night,* gives us the very essence of Schumann's sensitive art. So does the simpler Spring song, *Frühlingsgruss.* Florestan must have been at the peak of exhilaration when he turned sun-worshiper in the folksy *An den Sonnenschein:*

[Ex. 130]

And as late as 1850, only four years before the catastrophe, he could still pay ardent tribute to nature in *Die Sennin*.

His sense of humor finds bubbling outlet in that delectable passage of *Abends am Strande*, where his tones hit off the dirty Laplanders, "with flat heads and enormous muzzles," who "squat about the fire and bake themselves fish, and squeak and yell, and squeak and yell." This music reminds us again how, as an urchin, Robert had achieved popularity among his fellow cave-pirates through his improvised caricatures at the piano.

There is the ebullient *Vom Schlaraffenland*, that pipe-dream of the fabulous Land of Cockayne. It is a tonal version of Pieter Brueghel's famous picture where the roast pigs run into men's arms, complete with knife and mustard, and their "digs" are roofed with pies of custard, where the eggs obligingly gambol away to boil themselves, and rare vintages flow straight into the lucky inhabitants' mouths as they loaf under the tree of heaven.

Then there is *Käuzlein*, a delicious vignette of a little tawny owl; and *Der Sandmann*, a choice appreciation of the way the Sandman comes stealing in upon a weary child. This is a perfect vocal companion-piece to the *Album for the Young*.

The Two Grenadiers, Schumann's one great dramatic ballad, ranks among the supreme compositions of its kind. The thrill of these strains can perhaps be traced back to Father August Schumann's hero-worship of Napoleon, and to Robert's own glimpse of that glamorous personage in Zwickau. I wonder if it is more than a coincidence that one of the composer's earliest poetic passions was Johann Wilhelm Gleim, whose best book was entitled *Prussian War Songs, by a Grenadier*. There is a specially moving place at the end of this ballad where, still more effectively than in the *Faschingsschwank*, the *Marseillaise* is ushered in:

[Ex. 131]

dann steig' ich gewaffnet her-vor aus dem Grab-den Kaiser, den Kaiser zu

schüt-zen!

It is remarkable that *Waldesgespräch* should be the only one of these best songs to employ the official machinery of Romanticism. I mean that supernatural midsummer-night's-dream apparatus of witches, elves, ghosts, nixies, kobolds, marble-like corpses with unusual talents, haunted grottoes, and such, so dearly beloved by the new movement. It is true that Schumann wrote a good deal in this vein; but nothing else wholly came off. Could it be that, deep down, he was not quite so double-dyed a Romantic as he has always been thought? It must be remembered that one of the chief earmarks of Romanticism was the attempt to marry literature and tone in program music; but this was a thing which Schumann abhorred as an inartistic hybrid. So far as this element of the movement is concerned, Berlioz, Liszt, and even Beethoven [8] were more Romantic than Schumann.

[8] Witness the *Pastoral* and *"Battle"* Symphonies.

In every age, many pioneers of Romanticism in the arts have attempted a facile originality and modernity by dragging in some alien art to co-operate with their own. There is nothing harder than to be original and still keep within the legitimate confines of one's own field. For this reason, Schumann and Chopin were the most admirable Romantics of the Nineteenth Century. They could be original and interesting without smearing the bread of music with the marmalade of fiction in order to make it palatable to those listeners, young and old, whose tastes were still infantile.

Schumann was more naturally a song-writer than Brahms. Only fourteen of the latter's 198 solo Lieder sound like full-weight Brahms; whereas all thirty-eight of Schumann's best, and a large proportion of his others, bear the Schumannian hallmark. But both sinned equally against their poets. And in the case of the elder composer, this was the more reprehensible, as he was by way of being a poet himself. He was one of those whom Tennyson was hitting when he growled: "Why do these damned musicians make me say a thing twice when I say it only once?"

We pass over the universal sin of misplacing accents. But like all too many other composers, Schumann would unblushingly alter a poem's meter, and even its form. He would go farther, and arbitrarily substitute words of his own minting; as at the close of *Das ist ein Flöten und Geigen*, where he changed

> *Dazwischen schluchzen und stöhnen*
> *Die guten Engelein*

to

> *Die lieblichen Engelein*

—a change not only censurable, but senseless. And there are scores of other instances as flagrant.

He would callously scramble together earlier and later versions of a poem-cycle, as he did with Heine's *Liederkreis*, Op. 24. He would light-heartedly leave whole stanzas out of a poem, and whole poems out of a series. Without so much as murmuring "By your leave," he would even appoint himself the collaborator of poets, living and dead, adding, subtracting, multiplying, and dividing at his own sweet will.

Such goings-on injure poetry all the more because—even at his best and most punctilious—the vocal composer cannot possibly avoid doing a good deal of injury to the poetry he sets. This, I know, is contrary to the general belief that the addition of great music to great verse heightens the beauty of the latter. None the less, it is sad but true that no song composer can help harming the very thing for which we most prize the poet—that "immediate jewel of his soul"—his word-music. This statement may make the reader indignant; but if he will read on, it can be proved.

In discussing songs, most writers have much to say about the different poets whom, as they phrase it, the composer has "interpreted." To my mind this question is as unimportant as the arbitrary alterations just mentioned. For, by the time that even as supreme a poet as Shakespeare has been musically "interpreted," he is quite undone. A Goethe becomes less than a Chamisso. And a Chamisso becomes less than that "Sweet Singer of Michigan" who once chanted:

> Alas for the South; her poets grow fewer;
> She was never much given to literature.

Few realize—and musicians least of all—that when you "set" a poem to music, you necessarily half-destroy that poem, though you substitute music-melody for word-melody. For what makes a poem a poem is not so much the argument as the word-music. Now the latter is even more delicate, subtle, and easily marred than any music-music; though I know of no composer who has ever realized its high perishability. The effect of word-music is dependent on meter, and still more so on tempo. The lines must be read or heard with the stresses and rhythm indicated by the poet; and at a pace which allows the ear to retain a certain vowel or consonant or rhyme until the correlative vowels or consonants or rhymes are reached. Slow down the natural pace even slightly, and this euphony goes glimmering.

But no musical setting can, in the nature of things, afford verse the natural tempo it requires.[9] The composer is compelled

[9] Except for humorous effect, in a patter-song.

to slow down this tempo to a point where verse is no longer verse. And if, by some miracle, any residuum of its music should survive, it is overlaid by the stronger sensuous appeal of the notes. It seems high time for some poet-musician who is jealous for the well-being of both the arts which he loves, to put in a word for that most helpless of all living things: poetry in the clutches of music.

A song is sung. The listener exclaims: "How lovely!" For he hears the words of some favorite poem, together with beautiful melody and harmony, and has the illusion of equally enjoying both poetry and music. Strictly speaking, however, what he should exclaim is, "What lovely music!" For, as the word-music of the poem has been killed, any enjoyment it affords him comes from the argument, plus his memory of the euphony of the lines when read at their natural tempo. If he is an infantile type of music-lover, he will like the notes all the better because the argument of the words turns the piece into a sort of program-music, thus saving him the imaginative effort of deciding what the music means to him.

"Hidden music" was what Schumann called his own poetry. And this presumptuous attitude towards verse is typical of composers. From them the music of verse is "hidden," and they themselves assume the proud task of discovering and supplying it. Perhaps if, like the true connoisseur, they were aware that, on the contrary, the music of verse is (at the right tempo) far from hidden, and is there for all to enjoy, they might learn a little more discretion in handling such fragile things of beauty as the wings of Keats' nightingale, and Shelley's dome of many-colored glass.

Composers are not the only people with a one-sided view of song. Such statements as the following are constantly cropping up in books:

Heine was composing his poems, which were so much melody poured into a literary form. Schumann set them free from the bondage of their words.[10]

[10] *The Arts*, by Hendrik Willem Van Loon, p. 521. (Simon and Schuster, New York, 1937.) Sir Henry Hadow declared that to know Heine one

"The bondage of their words," forsooth! No true poet would
agree that his poem is in bondage to its words. But what the
composer does to a great poem is very like what the firing-squad
does to its client: it sets him free from the bondage of life. And,
though the squad keeps right on living, the poem lies dead as
veal. Dr. John Erskine, who is both poet and musician, states
this more mildly when he declares that to set a beautiful poem
to music is "an impertinence."

Like modern warfare, then, the melodic and harmonic magic
of verse depends largely upon timing. The meter and natural
tempo must be faithfully reproduced, or else the thing for which
we most value poetry simply disappears. Now when, by some
miracle, a song composer succeeds in going almost fast enough
to let the ear grasp the correlative rhymes and vowel and consonant arpeggios of the poem, as Schumann did in *Widmung*,
and *Er, der Herrlichste von Allen*,[11] even then he often commits
sabotage by changing the poem's meter. In *Widmung*, Schumann
chopped up Rückert's four-stress, double-time lines into three-
stress, triple-time lines. In the other, he took three-quarters of
Chamisso's four-stress line, placed it upon the bed of Procrustes,
and elongated it to four stresses. In both he arbitrarily destroyed
the poet's unit of line-value. Such vandalism is almost as fatal
to the sensuous magic of poetry as is a too slow tempo.

In return for these injuries, poetry hits back by constricting
the infinitude of music within the narrow bounds of a finite program. No perfect product can be made out of two imperfect
ingredients.

The old poets who wrote lyrics to be sung could have been
no more aware of what music and poetry actually do to one another than the poets and composers of today seem to be.

Now, if you are still skeptical about all this, will you not try
a short and simple experiment? Take some great lyric which has
been set to music by no matter what composer. Note how long

must know Schumann's treatment of the *Buch der Lieder*. He would have
been more exact if he had written instead: "To know how Heine can be
manhandled, one must know, etc."

[11] Exclusive of preludes, interludes and postludes, *Widmung* slows up the
poem's natural pace 70 per cent, *Er, der Herrlichste*, 100 per cent.

it takes to sing. Then, discarding the music, and with one eye on your watch, read the words at precisely the composer's tempo. You will find that the musical setting has slowed down the poem's natural pace by from 70 to 1800 per cent [12]—so that there is little of its most precious part—its word-magic—left; for even a mere 50 per cent slowing would mar it. Only an argument remains. And that looks pretty dreary and forbidding amid the bombed-out ruins of the verbal melody.

Then please try one more experiment, which is even simpler. Hum, whistle, or play any great Schumann song—perhaps *Widmung*. Forget all about the words. Listen as if this were absolute music which might—in the infinite way of this particular art— mean a million different things to a million different imaginative people, and possibly a million more every time they reheard it. Then ask yourself whether, like the first man who ever saw a star, you cannot echo that line of Blanco White's famous sonnet:

> And lo! Creation widened in man's view.

After all, you surely prefer Handel's beautiful *Largo* as absolute music rather than in its original state of "bondage" to those lines about the plane tree in the opera *Serse*.

Trying to enjoy the word-melody of a song is a good deal like attempting to see an etching through a thick and highly colored stained glass window.

Some singers and composers who are unable to deny these obvious facts have told me that it is not fitting to be so logical about artistic matters. This, however, is not a question of the arts, but of the sciences underlying the arts of music and of verse. And since when has logic been out of place in science?

Naturally I am not proposing the absurd idea of entirely doing away with the combination of words and music. I am merely saying that this combination is artistically inferior to either poetry alone or music alone. Song, of course, will never die. It is instinctive; and is all the more deeply beloved because it is the

---

[12] The 1800 per cent *rit.* occurs in Handel's setting of "Sweet bird that shuns the voice of folly" from Milton's *Il Penseroso*. Ideas about the natural tempos of music and of verse, vary, of course, with the individual interpreter, though less than is generally realized.

first thing of striking beauty encountered in life, when Mother sang to the newcomer in his cradle. It is the first 'thing we enjoyed as children in church. It is associated in our minds with celebrations and love and happiness and the glory of the human voice.

Song should, however, be rated as on a lower artistic plane than instrumental music; because it is a sort of program music, and because it sabotages the word-melody and harmony of verse. When this fact is generally appreciated, composers will use more discretion in setting the very greatest poems "free from the bondage of their words," by altering their natural tempo and meter. And, in absolute music, composers will more and more use the textless voice as an orchestral instrument, lovely beyond words.

CHAPTER 7

THE SYMPHONIST

ON the thirtieth of June 1839, not many months before the miraculous year of song began, Schumann wrote to Hirschbach:

> Are you, perhaps, like me, who have always held vocal music to be on a lower plane than instrumental, and never thought it a high art? But don't tell anyone!

This opinion he never modified, except for a few months of the following year, during his frenzy of Lied composition. And for that modification who can blame a young man in love, to whom lyric poetry suggested such immortal melodies as *Widmung* and *Die Lotoshlume?*

Then came the reaction. His enthusiasm for the orchestra boiled over. The young genius felt as if his musical ideas were simply inexhaustible. He tossed the crutch of literature into the corner, to be resumed thereafter only now and then; and buried himself in the purest, deepest thing that a composer knows—absolute music.

And now it became more truly absolute than during the piano period. In *The Romantic Composers,* Dr. Daniel Gregory Mason neatly characterized this change:

> We see him in the compositions of this time paying less and less attention to those purely personal whims and fancies that had at first dominated his imagination, and beginning to work very earnestly toward objective beauty and impersonal expression. The fictitious characters, the mottoes, the stage directions, the whole elaborate machinery of allusion to extra-musical interests, are forgotten, and the

interest of the music itself becomes all in all. . . . Now what had been only occasional in the days when fancy and a self-involved emotional life absorbed him, grew to be normal and constant, and he became for the first time a liberal and devoted artist.

In a word, Schumann was growing up.

M. Basch deplores Schumann's keeping, in his symphonies, "to classic canons and sacrificing, in his admiration and imitation of the masters, the genial originality of his sensibility and of his imagination." As these things were just what Schumann did *not* do, I was puzzled until I read further. M. Basch goes on to declare that if Schumann's contemporaries had received his first efforts in this line with less coldness (though, as we have seen, the First Symphony was welcomed with signal warmth),

He would then perhaps have given us works which would have recalled, by their form, the Romanticism of the symphonic poems of Berlioz or of Liszt.

This explains M. Basch's surprising assertion! On the whole, the French of the Nineteenth Century preferred to have melody, harmony, and counterpoint tell them stories; which kept them from producing or hearing much absolute music. This French critic is about as wide of the mark as a critic could well be. For Schumann, far from slavishly stepping in the tracks of the older masters, created original and Schumannesquely Romantic versions of sonata, quartet, and symphony. And perhaps the most valuable service which he rendered Romanticism—that recurrent phase of the eternal art-cycle whose composers are usually all too prone to dally on the primrose path of fiction—was to set his face like a flint against the cheap program music so dear to the hearts of Berlioz, Liszt and their followers. The merit of these men lay neither in their forms nor in their musical ideas, but rather in their admirable pioneer contributions to the science of instrumentation. The same may be said today of Mahler.

On the other hand, a different school of critics is down on poor Schumann for a reason diametrically opposed to M. Basch's. It claims that he is not a real symphonist because he did not write sonatas for orchestra on the exact model of Beethoven's. But what ineluctable lawgiver has laid down the rule that, until the crack of doom, all symphonies worthy the name must be of one kind only? What final ukase has decreed: "Thou shalt have no other symphonic gods before me"?

I, for one, think that genius should have the last word in this matter. And I zestfully enjoy the Romantic variety that Schumann imported into sonata form. "In my Father's house are many mansions." Within the spacious city of art, side by side with all the tremendous epic monuments, there is abundant room for lyric symphonies like these. In them we find the same exultant joy in life, the same appealing melancholy, the same intimacy, dreamy tenderness, opulence of fancy and continuing excitement which we enjoy in the piano works, the songs, and the chamber music. In a word, we find the magnetic, endearing personality of a genius who now feels that the easy, improvisatorial style of his early period will not quite do for the larger forms; and who has been in some measure unconsciously influenced by the conservative spirit of his helpmate.

One of his aphorisms of about this time declares: "In any cause it is not good for a man to inherit too light a touch." Behind these words we may detect the voice of Clara. If Robert had but given more scope to the light touch of his first period, the symphonies might have been even more original and interesting than they turned out to be.

For example, the development section of sonata-form,[1] which was always his weakest point, would have benefited by his early freshness of improvisation. Just as Schubert had done in his trios, Schumann treated this section somewhat mechanically, by merely running large blocks of his subjects through various tonalities. And this sober economy of effort is the more striking because a person of Schumann's melodic resource, imaginative mobility and suppleness should have been ideally fitted to take a drop or so of thematic material, as the great masters could, pop it into his magic bottle, and then—presto-change!—pour out a stream so fertilizing that the desert blossoms like the rose, and the Arctic plateau becomes a luxuriant tropical jungle, starred with passion-flowers and aflutter with gorgeous Birds of Paradise.

[1] See Glossary, pp. 512-13, under Sonata Form.

If ever it was natural for any composer to go "all out" in this way, it would have seemed natural for Schumann. But I think that the strident outcry which the critics have raised because he did not do so is unjustified. If we refused to enjoy all composers who could not develop their material like Beethoven, we miserable perfectionists would have to subsist on a diet of pure L. v. B. and Brahms. And in these radio-saturated days, when the prudent listener is forced to ration his hearing of any one composer for fear of surfeit, how long would that last us?

Personally, I enjoy Schumann's innovations in the structure of sonata-form, such as his running all the movements together (Symphony No. 4), suppressing the second subject (A Minor Quartet), or delaying it until the development (Symphony No. 4, *Lebhaft*), or reserving an especially fine theme as a *bonne bouche* with which to spice a first movement coda (B Flat Symphony and Piano Quartet) or end a work (finales of Symphonies 2 and 4). I enjoy his peculiar way of winning breadth and unity through dovetailing two subjects together without a break (*passim*), and through the momentum of some incisive, elastic rhythm which, over long sweeps of music, impetuously carries all before it (Symphony No. 2: Scherzo with Trio I, first subjects of *Allegro ma non troppo* and of finale; Symphony No. 4, first movement). This last procedure, however, involves a risk of monotony which not even Florestan's impetuous enthusiasm and subtle resource are always equal to escaping.

The hypercritics would also have us believe that Schumann's symphonies are not worthy the name because, forsooth, they are all 'scrappy, short-winded, with the themes of a miniaturist.' The complete refutation of this inane criticism lies in the *Larghetto* of the First, the last three movements of the Second, and, above all, the opening subject of the Third—that great, sweeping, ultra-symphonic subject which inspired the corresponding theme of Brahms' corresponding symphony. As for the Fourth, such a criticism is hitting below the belt; for Schumann originally intended to call this work, not symphony but "symphonic fantasy"; which elastic name may fitly cover a multitude of unorthodox procedures.

In the field of orchestration Schumann undeniably had his

faults. As a rule he scored somewhat thickly, and was all too prone to double the parts. The strings are often lured to cruel and unusual reaches of the fingerboard, where the upper partials are killed, and the tone consequently dulled. The winds, too, are frequently made to perform awkward and ineffective feats. The extreme octaves are so rarely used that the musical outline tends to be "cabined, cribbed, confined." For instance, in *The Paradise and the Peri*, the first violins seldom escape the treble staff. There is not always enough interest in the lower voices. And the choice of instruments for a given task is not invariably above reproach.

Now, though this is all true, Schumann's instrumentation is still not nearly so black as it has long been the fashion to paint it. Hans von Bülow was a smart emitter of snap judgments. These were, like a railway time-table, subject to change without notice. I believe it was he who first remarked that Schumann's orchestral works were "piano-pieces badly arranged for orchestra." (Remember that Bülow was a grateful pupil of Schumann's chief enemy, old Wieck.) I agree with the anonymous writer [2] who declared:

Schumann was badly handicapped. But to say that his orchestral works are piano compositions arranged for orchestra is nonsense, and betrays the ignorance, not to say stupidity, of the man who utters such balderdash.

Folly of this sort is all too apt to be unthinkingly passed down, like a heritable disease, from generation to generation, in the manner of the now exploded notion that Brahms was an unhappy wretch who wrote nothing but sad, gray music.

Other critics go still further, and, parroting the wildly mistaken Clara, reproach Schumann's highly idiomatic piano music for being orchestral; while they simultaneously excoriate his orchestral and chamber works for being pianistic. Well, no composer can please all the people all the time, especially those who —come what may—must pull down great artists in order to build up a feeling of superiority. After all, this outcry against Schu-

[2] In *The Musical Courier* for Feb. 27, 1919.

mann's instrumentation is much ado about very little. Sir Donald Tovey has pointed out that:

The few outstanding defects in the published score are ridiculously easy to correct, and it is mistaken piety to leave them uncorrected. When a redistribution of the mass of wood-wind is advisable in order to bring the main theme out, we need not worry about the changes in tone-colour that may result. Unlike Beethoven, Schumann has not in such cases closely imagined a definite tone-colour that would be spoilt by any change. When obstacles to clearness have been removed, the resulting purity of tone is indeed rather new to listeners who have hitherto tried to hear Schumann's orchestra in its native fog; but the revelation is nevertheless that of Schumann's real intention.

A little effective retouching and a great conductor can do wonders. These symphonies had long been under a cloud in America. Then Toscanini came and revealed them to us in all their essential loveliness, since which time they have grown deservedly popular.

Schumann possessed the great essentials. Instrumentation is a thing that can be developed by study; but the more creative part of a composer's equipment is like the poet: born, not made. In this connection, Frederick Corder's contrast of Berlioz with Schumann is worth noting: [3]

Berlioz had hardly any melodic invention, nor feeling for harmony, yet he wrote with marvelous effectiveness. Schumann had an inexhaustible spring of both, yet a large proportion even of his vocal works has to be laid aside as uninteresting. But you cannot sit down to a pianoforte and play any work whatever of Berlioz for pleasure; whereas even Schumann's least successful pieces are pleasant to go through.

I have mentioned some serious drawbacks to the enjoyment of Schumann's orchestral scores as published. It is a startling commentary on the magnitude of his genius that, despite them all, and in the face of his strong introvert bias toward the subjective and the intimate, we can still find parts of his symphonies so spacious in scope, so lofty in spirit, so infectious and fresh,

[3] In *The Musical Times* for Aug. 1st, 1910.

so stirring and ennobling that they are worthy to stand with the best which has been thought and felt by the greatest of all sym phonists. Sir Henry Hadow spoke the truth:

After all, we have no right to require that an artist's whole gift should consist of masterpieces. We do not judge Wordsworth by his stories of the nursery, or Shelley by his two attempts at burlesque; we take the *Ode* and the *Sonnets*, *Prometheus* and *Adonais*, and let the failures go. In like manner we can discard some of Schumann's compositions . . . but when we have done so there will still be left a legacy that will enrich Music to the end of the world. It matters little whether his monument be large or small; in either case it is imperishable.

CHAPTER 8

THE SYMPHONIES

Op. 38. First (or *"Spring"*) Symphony, B Flat

IN her Life of Schumann, Miss Annie Patterson, the first Doctor of Music ever produced by Ireland, wrote of the B Flat Symphony:

It is very fresh and bright, and vividly brings, as the composer intended it should, the image of the fair but fleeting Spring before us.

Now, I feel sure that while Schumann was undoubtedly inspired to begin Opus 38 by a poem of Böttger's which ends:

Im Thale blüht der Frühling auf

(Down in the valley Spring is blooming),

he was not anxious to impose this program upon anyone else. He was far too sound a musician, far too reverent of the universality of his chosen art, to feel that the performer or the hearer of this work should invariably associate it with none but the precise images that floated through the composer's mind when he wrote it. I am convinced that he would have approved of those who identified his music with anything fresh, exuberant, and beautiful, like young love, or dawn in the mountains, or creative ecstasy, or the iridescent spray of surf on a sunny coastline. One fact makes me all the more certain that he would not have insisted on our exclusive preoccupation with "the fair but fleeting Spring." In the enthusiasm of the start he had thought of baptizing the four movements: *Spring's Coming, Evening, Merry Play*, and *Full Spring*.[1] But he soon saw the folly of thus

[1] How variously he thought of his own music at different times was

396

cramping the interpreter's and the listener's imagination, and blue-penciled the fancy titles as ill-conceived.

The slow Introduction starts with this forthright proclamation by the horns and trumpets,

[Ex. 132]

which anticipates the essence of the first movement's principal theme. In his valiant innocence of the science of orchestration, Robert originally wrote Ex. 132 a third lower. But those were the days of "natural" horns and trumpets, before valves had come into general use. And in rehearsal the effect of the "stopped" G and A was so comically feeble that the composer raised the tune to where it would sound respectable. Four years later he wrote Mendelssohn:

Do you still remember the first rehearsal in J. 1841—and the stopped trumpets and horns at the start? It sounded like a real cold-in-the-head. Even now, every time I think of it I am compelled to laugh.

A little Beethovenian gloom, a little tightening suspense, *poco a poco accelerando,* and the orchestra launches full tilt into the jubilant *Allegro molto vivace:*

[Ex. 133]

shown two years later in the letter to Taubert, part of which is quoted else-where: "Of the last movement I will tell you that I like to think of it as Spring's farewell."

This is the Schumann who has got his great piano music and songs out of his system, gone through dire tribulation to win the girl he so ardently adored, and then found marriage surpassing his loftiest expectations. He is at the height of his physical, mental, and emotional powers. Youth is delicious. Love is thrilling. Life is wonderful. He simply cannot contain himself, and pours out his exultation in this naïvely triumphant burst of music.

The second subject,

[Ex. 134]

seems less like an art product than something overheard in the forest beside a runlet where water falls, drop by drop, into a tiny pool. Its Eusebian peace offers a complete contrast to the Florestanic exaltations of Ex. 133.

It has been noted that Schumann's methods did not, as a rule, make for strong development sections. But in the one that now follows, it is remarkable what a degree of varied interest he is able to attain. For the wood-winds he invents a charming counterpoint to the first two bars of Ex. 133. He lets the flute turn itself into a song-bird (but one of those rare birds that possess the gift of absolute pitch), and fly away with the merry sixteenth notes of the second part of Ex. 133. And I agree with Kretzschmar [2] that

the place where the principal theme reappears in the broad rhythms of the Introduction, carried by trumpets and horns and with the utmost splendor of the orchestra, is one of the most glorious in the whole symphonic realm.

The recapitulation is very brief, in order to make room for a broadly modeled coda. This reminds one of that other coda which rounds out the finale of Beethoven's Eighth Symphony. It is like Beethoven's not alone in its imposing length and the

[2] *Führer durch den Konzertsaal,* Leipzig, 1888.

contour of notes 2-8, but also because it brings a new theme
more lovely than its predecessors.

[Ex. 135]

After the preceding pages of storm and stress, the peace of it is
welcome. And when fervently repeated by the full orchestra, its
climax gives a heartening reminder of the climax of *Widmung*.
What a close for a first movement of a First Symphony!

The high point of this work, however, is the *Larghetto*. Op. 38
has the same tonality and much the same emotional atmosphere·
as that other "*Spring*" Symphony composed thirty-five years before by Beethoven, as his Fourth. Schumann's preceding coda
has provided an ideal preparation for this sustained and impassioned love song:

[Ex. 136]

And the end of the slow movement does likewise more literally.
It lets the trombones anticipate what is to come by intoning a
solemn version of the main theme of the Scherzo.

In the midst of the *Larghetto*, just before the clarinet takes up

the theme, there is another look ahead—much farther ahead. The
first violins give out the rhythm

[Ex. 137]

that was, nine years later, to open Schumann's Third Symphony,
while playing the very tune that, forty-three years later, was to
open Brahms' (likewise) Third Symphony.

The peculiar syncopations that obstruct the even flow of Ex.
136, with their analogies in Exs. 135 and 137, may seem trite
to us of today; but in 1841 they were novelties of the very
first order. Schumann had already used this effect delightfully
in *Promenade, Grillen,* the *Faschingsschwank,* and many other
pieces. Towards the end of his career he unfortunately let this
sort of thing grow into a somewhat annoying mannerism.

After the sweetness of the *Larghetto,* the almost grim virility
of the Scherzo's opening is welcome before, relenting, it melts
into one of Schumann's airiest waltz tunes. It was highly original
to bring in two Trios; and the content of the first of these was
still more original. Beethoven had carried simplicity far in the
Trio of his *"Spring"* Symphony. Schumann, as we have seen, had
already gone him one simpler in the finale of the *Fantasie,* and
in the *Novelletten.*[3] But here in this Trio I, it is at first as if the
wood-winds, softly answering the strings,

[Ex. 138]

were literally winds in a wood, and the strings were those of an
aeolian harp. Only twice does the dialogue resolve itself into a
pert little scrap of man-made music, charmingly Schumannian.

The second Trio, with its scale-imitations, is a jolly juvenile
reminiscence of the *Solmisationsscherze,* or solmization games,
so beloved in olden times. The players had to sing very fast and

[3] See pp. 337-8.

give each note its proper designation of *do, re, mi,* etc., under pain of forfeit. The movement is brought to a close with the merest breath of Nature's wood-wind and aeolian harp theme.

The rondo finale crosses the t's and dots the i's of the first movement. But in order not to let the exuberance get entirely out of bounds, it starts with a threatening version of the *sol-fa* game in Trio II. This rising-scale motto reminds one of something similar in the corresponding movement of the Schubert C Major Symphony which Schumann, only two years before, had had the fabulous joy of unearthing.

[Ex. 139]

[Ex. 140]

When this finale was first performed, the filigree-like principal theme gave the dry-as-dusts a cruel shock. They cried havoc and damnation upon a man who dared imagine he could use such a frivolous tune in such a dignified and worthy work as a symphony.

[Ex. 141]

But Schumann would not listen to them. He liked this sort of material, and proceeded to use similar filigrees in the *Romanze* and Trio of the D Minor Symphony, in No. 16 of the *Peri*, and as the main theme of the F Major String Quartet's finale.

Next comes a delectable bit of horse-play. With malicious wit, the awkwardness of the ponderous "bull-fiddles" is caricatured.

They are overheard trying to carry on the violins' filigree tune;
but all they can make of it is a helpless

[Ex. 142]

while the agile fiddles mock the big fellows' flounderings with a
piercingly shrill figure—

[Ex. 143]

that reminds one of the sudden flash of a scarlet tanager among
lofty branches. According to Wasielewski [4] who played at the
first rehearsal of this symphony in the Gewandhaus, those elite
fiddlers of the world's best orchestra had so much trouble in
being good tanagers that Mendelssohn jovially advised them to
chalk upon their fingerboards the exact location of that elusive
high F. Which sheds light on the state of orchestral technic in
those days.

Presently the wood-winds, in rare fettle, start a snickering
little tune

[Ex. 144]

[4] *Robert Schumanns Biographie*, 1851.

which is harshly put down by the strings with the opening
motto (end of Ex. 144). The snickerers are quoting from the last
piece of the *Kreisleriana*.[5] But citation is far from ceasing there.
For the *Kreisleriana* theme was almost identical with the *Can-
zonetta* of Mendelssohn's E Flat String Quartet, Op. 12; which,
in turn, was quoted from J. S. Bach's jolly *Peasant Cantata*, and
from the *Quodlibet* which closes his *Thirty Variations*, where it
goes to the words:

> *Ich bin so lang nicht bei dir gewest.*

> (I've been so long away from you.)

And from what ancient folk-tune Bach took it, heaven may
know, but I do not.

This *Peasant Cantata* must have been a prime favorite with
Schumann; for we have now seen him using two tunes from it;
and each of these in two different compositions.[6]

We have heard the lively intruder put in its place by the
frowning motto, Ex. 144, in a very personal and amusing
fashion. But then the motto relents and turns genial. As we
listen, its rhythm transmutes itself into the real second subject.
This is one of those rich, intimate all-Schumann themes that we
tend to file away in memory:

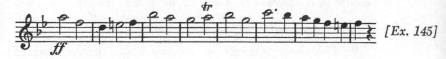

[Ex. 145]

And then the excitement grows, *accelerando,* until it suddenly
ends like a fragrant Spring storm.

Op. 52. *Overture, Scherzo and Finale*

According to the season of its birthday, this work should have
borne the nickname "*Spring*" rather than the one just described;
for it was sketched in April 1841. Schumann thought of calling

---

[5] There in ⁶⁄₈ time, but in the same key of G minor. See p. 332, Ex. 73.
[6] See pp. 282, 353, and 402.

it "*Symphonietta*," then decided not to. In offering it to Hofmeister for publication, he remarked: "The whole has a light, friendly character. I wrote it in a very joyful mood." And on finishing the *Overture*, he called it "siren-like."

Although in many places this composition gives evidence of Schumann's charm, it cannot compare in quality with any of the symphonies. Much of the thematic material is commonplace. Some of it recalls Mendelssohn; and the composer rides his hobby-horse of dotted rhythm to the point of wearisomeness. The best part is the infectious *Scherzo*, which begins:

[Ex. 146]

Op. 61. Second Symphony, C Major

Though this symphony came third in order of composition, it was published before its predecessor, the D Minor, and is known as the Second. A virile work, laid out on a tragic and epic scale broader in conception than the others, it was inspired by much the same sort of emotional stress that went to the making of Beethoven's Ninth.

The C Major epitomizes Schumann's whole development up to this point. We need not listen long before perceiving in it the fresh and fecund melodic and harmonic inspiration of the piano music, the charm and passion of the song period when he was beginning to master form and grasp the idea of thematic work for organic unity. Then we hear the note, at once lofty and intimate, of the chamber-music period, when he was penetrating so rapidly into the mysteries of counterpoint. Florestan, Eusebius, and Raro have now nearly finished their training, and merged into one great master at the summit of his ascent.

Unlike the Piano Concerto, this symphony has its obvious

weaknesses. They are: the rhythmic monotony of the first *Allegro's* dotted principal subject, the too exclusively modulatory development sections of this movement and of the finale, and Schumann's besetting sins against orchestration.

The older symphonists used introductions chiefly to put us into the proper frame of mind and spirit to enjoy what follows. But in the C Major, even more than in the B Flat and D Minor Symphonies, Schumann employs the introduction as a golden nutshell wherein to pack the kernel, the meat, of what is to come. Nearly every note of it is charged with tremendous thematic, as well as emotional, significance. It begins with horns and brasses giving out a fanfare-like motto which is to recur throughout the work. Below this we hear a writhing, snake-like down-and-up counterpoint in the strings: [7]

Compare the above motto for winds with the start of Haydn's "London" Symphony:

[7] A first cousin of the figure that starts the D Minor Symphony. See p. 417, Ex. 162.

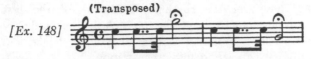

[Ex. 148]   (Transposed)

The counterpoint for strings in Ex. 147 is the source of the two
brief motives that do duty as second subject in the following
movement. And here is a microscopic bit from the Introduction,

[Ex. 149]

and the start of the full-sized first subject which it fathers:

[Ex. 150]

Allegro ma non troppo
Ob.
Bassoon   cresc.
Viola   p   H

Schumann even carried his thematic work so far as to insert,
at the fifteenth bar of the Introduction, a delicious wood-wind
passage which sounds like a full-fledged second subject if ever
a melody did, but which turns out, after all, merely to generate
the comparatively unimportant bridge-passage leading to the
second subject. In the cause of unity, he brought the same tune

in again, just for luck, at the *L'istesso tempo* which ends the finale.

This Introduction is one of the longest, most elaborate and significant in standard symphonic literature. It is the overture that gives us a miniature view, as if through the other end of the spy-glass, of the imminent drama.

Despite the drawbacks already mentioned, the first movement has a magnitude of spirit and a fervor that are heart-warming. This is especially true of the coda, *Con fuoco*. It works up to the brazen motto of Ex. 147, and is approached by a little theme in the wood-winds, somewhat reminiscent of the beginning and end of the famous "episode" in Beethoven's *Eroica*. Let those who like to exaggerate Schumann's undeniable failings as an orchestrator study here, for their edification, his exemplary and almost fabulous restraint in the employment of the much-abused trombones.

The Scherzo is Schumann's happiest essay in this form. Its main theme gives us some characteristic humor.

[*Ex. 151*]

It sounds like the irrepressible laughter of a bevy of girls. And the response of Trio I is like the slower and heavier laughter of the men. By the way, the happier phase of Mendelssohn's influence over his hero-worshiper was exerted at this point. Schumann had assigned to the strings the staccato triplets that begin Trio I; but Mendelssohn fortunately persuaded him to vary the tone-color by transferring them to the wood-winds.

These gusts of hilarity are interrupted by Trio II, with an almost prayerful folk-quality that is yet intensely Schumannian.

[*Ex. 152*]

The last eight notes of this example give a premonition, in severely stylized form, of the Schein source-motive that is to close the finale.[8] At the end of this infectious Scherzo we again hear the brazen motto of the Introduction.

The following movement has an even higher distinction; for this *Adagio espressivo* is the supreme point in all of Schumann's symphonies. The late Lawrence Gilman wrote:

> So far as profundity of feeling and felicity of instrumental speech are concerned, it has seemed to many that Schumann equalled nowhere else in his symphonic writing the page that makes this work so treasurous; the fervent *Adagio*—an utterance of such rich and moving poetry that, listening to it, you cannot help wondering if the bodily and spiritual malaise out of which this loveliness proceeded is not a condition that should occasionally be prayed for by certain composers enjoying perfect health.

This is reminiscent of Lincoln's famous plan for giving his other generals the same whisky used by that "drunkard," General Grant.

The principal theme begins:

[Ex. 153]

The bracketed notes are straight from the corresponding part of the Introduction (p. 405, Ex. 147). In this touching melody we have the more somber side of Eusebius at its most eloquent.

Several of Schumann's letters refer with special satisfaction to "my melancholy bassoon in the *Adagio*." This must mean that instrument's counterpoint to the oboe melody starting in the ninth measure; for all the other prominent bassoon passages are doubled by some other voice. The composer's satisfaction seems disproportionate until one remembers what a rare tour de force it is to write serious music so convincingly for an instrument that has nearly always been notoriously the clown of the orchestra.

[8] See pp. 313-14.

Twice near the end of this *Adagio* the trilling violins send up the signal for the gates of heaven to open. Brahms once wrote Clara that these passages made him see her "as if with the bodily eye."

The finale begins with four bars of a rising-scale motto very like that in the corresponding part of the First Symphony. Then we are lifted on a wave of vitality and youthful high spirits. The one flaw in our enjoyment of this infectious first subject is an unfortunate resemblance. Here is the start:

Allegro molto

[Ex. 154]

But this is the opening of Mendelssohn's *Italian* Symphony (transposed).

(Mendelssohn)
Allegro vivace

[Ex. 155]

The second theme of the finale, taken by a happy stroke of inspiration from the *Adagio* (Ex. 153), is later transformed and transfigured, with an imagination unusual in Schumann's development sections. And this helps to redeem an otherwise dull page. The world of this theme is stood upside down. And, curiously enough, as it stands on its head it sounds like something out of Italian opera. At last it is righted and laid to rest with pomp and circumstance—and three general pauses.

Thereupon, as in the finale of the D Minor Symphony, Schumann brings in an entirely new theme for the close. He must have loved it dearly; for he never gets back to the opening subject at all. At first it comes in beautiful but somewhat tentative form. But soon it is transfigured into the familiar Schein source-motive:

[Ex. 47]

This is one of those great, simple, universal themes that can never be forgotten. It is in the same class with the cantabile of the Quintet's funeral march, with *Widmung,* the start of the finale of the D Minor Trio, and the *Romanze* from the *"Spring"* Symphony. Note that the first half of Ex. 47 comes from bars 18-19 of the Introduction.

Schumann might be accused of borrowing one more feature of this finale—the ascending thirds after the lusty sixteenth-note passage for strings—from the Introduction to the Third Act of *Tristan,* if it were not for the circumstance that *Tristan* was composed more than a dozen years later. How annoyed Richard the Jackalhearted would have been if anyone had had the courage to point out that he had copied the man whom he had so condescendingly despised!

The finale works up to the brazen motto, then takes off from Earth into a western blaze of glory.

This symphony, so well interlocked, is further unified by the composer's singular pertinacity in keeping to the key of C Major. In writing of it, Mr. Gilman made one more remark which I cannot forbear quoting:

> It is good for us to be reminded occasionally that Schumann, after all, is a major composer. . . . Some of him . . . has faded. . . . But at his best he is indispensable. . . .

The music of our day, so cool and disabusing, repudiates by disdainful implication everything that was imaginative food and drink for the Romantics. But, regenerate and untrammeled though we may be—moving with crisp certainty, as no doubt we are, along the brightly lighted ways of life, which are no longer shadowed and mysterious, haunted with beauty and with terror, but as obvious and definite as a spotlight—we may gain something, perhaps, by remembering that . . . Schumann sought to transfigure human life and the world into their Platonic likenesses, perceiving them not only as they seem, but as what they essentially are.

Op. 97. Third (or *"Rhenish"*) Symphony, E Flat

In point of fact, this symphony was Schumann's Fourth and last. It begins abruptly with a great and truly symphonic subject which, for six measures, by means of deft syncopations achieves a fascinatingly elastic tension:

[Ex. 156]

Here, as in the second subject of the Piano Concerto's finale (p. 428, Ex. 182), ¾ time is made to sound like ³⁄₂ time. Only here, unlike there, the one is superposed upon the other in this tricky fashion

$$\left|\begin{array}{c|c|c|c|c|c}2 & 2 & 2 & 2 & 2 & 2 \\ \hline & 3 & 3 & & 3 & 3\end{array}\right|$$

In the second and third measures of Ex. 156, if we transpose the G's down an octave, we see that this splendid tune may have derived from a passage in the *Adagio* of Schumann's B Flat Symphony; and that both of these together were probably responsible for the way in which Brahms' Third Symphony begins:

Schumann B♭ Symphony

[Ex. 157]

Brahms F major Symphony *(transposed)*

[Ex. 158]

In this stirring movement, Schumann is nearly at his happiest. Note how convincingly the softly rounded feminine contours of the second subject

complement the strong masculinity of the first (Ex. 156). True, the development is of the lesser sort which the composer never surmounted. He juxtaposes and modulates instead of using the themes like seeds and making something quite new blossom from them. But this working-out portion is the very best of its limited kind. Nothing short of a miracle could have made such a lengthy example of an inferior sort of development into a thing so intensely moving and enthralling—every note of it.

Moreover, given the method, the return to the recapitulation in the home key of E Flat could not have been bettered by Beethoven himself. It is one of the treasures of orchestral literature. Up again to his old Puckish tricks, Schumann time after time makes us believe that the return is really coming, and then baffles and tantalizes us by sheering off. At last, after a long bout of kaleidoscopic modulation, our alertness is dulled by a *forte* variant for horns of the first subject, accompanied by a mysterious *pianissimo* trembling of the higher strings over an organ-point bass. An abrupt transition to the weird key of C Flat gives us to divine that the long-awaited event is still far off when the entire orchestra suddenly surges *fff* upon Ex. 156—and the wild waters of the Atlantic finally come bursting through the narrow Isthmus of Gibraltar! The movement ends in the glow of a triumphant coda.

Thus far the symphony, though it does not remind us of other composers, does not particularly remind us, either, of that earlier Schumann whose music seems most characteristic of him. The opening movement strikes a new note. That curious cross between a minuet and a Ländler, the Scherzo, brings forward a main theme which, without smacking much of its maker, manages to sound very like that favorite of youth, *The Happy Farmer,* all dressed up in gala attire, and sedately celebrating.

So not until the Trio do we find something upon which to pounce and label "the real Schumann."

Sehr mässig

[Ex. 159]

However, the modest little sixteenth note figure of the last example is made much of in the main part of this movement. We are already familiar with it

[Ex. 160]

as a form of the Climb source-motive.[9] One variant or another of this figure appears in the last four movements of the *"Rhenish."* By leaving it out of the remaining one, Schumann ran true to former idiosyncrasy.[10]

This Scherzo is charming, interesting, stirring music; but it is hardly of symphonic mold. And the same might truly be said of the *Nicht schnell,* a graceful little salon piece, tender and dainty, which, by the way, is orchestrated with more restraint and a happier lightness of touch than Schumann often showed. It might more appropriately have been written for piano, included

[9] See p. 361, Note.
[10] See pp. 460-61.

in the *Waldscenen* of the year before, and perhaps called
"*Tryst.*"

The obviously ecclesiastical character of the fourth movement,
marked *Feierlich* (Ceremonial), would stamp it as program
music, even if we did not know that it had been inspired by the
enthronement of an archbishop in Cologne Cathedral. That took
place one fine autumn day after Robert and Clara had come in
from the Belvedere with their hearts full of a marvelous view of
the Rhine and the Seven Hills.

Schumann at first entitled this fourth movement, "In the character of the accompaniment to a solemn ceremony." Then he
struck the inscription out "because one must not show people
one's heart." [11] Now, why is music not the place to show people
in words the devices and desires of one's own heart? Because
the very core of music is its infinite capacity to transcend any
one concrete meaning. So, if the composer rashly imposes a program by revealing the concrete image that is in his own heart
when he writes notes (but an image, for all that, none the more
true of the music than anyone else's idea about it), he may prevent the listener from independently asking himself what these
notes mean to him personally. And thus he will sin against the
holy ghost of music by seeking to make its infinitude finite.

This so-called "*Cathedral Scene,*" despite the odd, hectic ner-
vousness of the secular little Climb source-motive variant which
breaks into the prayerful voices of the pontifical trombones, is
in itself a superb, deeply moving piece—one of the composer's
best—and constitutes a splendid synthesis of the highest in ceremonial church music. But it is undeniably program music; and
as such does not belong in an unprogrammatic symphony.

The principal theme of the finale

[Ex. 161]

[11] A sentiment well in accord with his natural taciturnity.

opens with a variant of the Schein source-motive,

[Ex. 47]

A comparison of these two examples will show that all of the bracketed part of Ex. 161 except the first G, has the same melodic progression as Ex. 47.

Though this variant of the motive is not quite up to the standard of other forms of that rare melodic inspiration, it makes a bright, spirited finale subject. And the vivacity and humor of the companion themes bring us back to the old, fresh, witty, effervescent Schumann of the best period. Even the Climb source-motive turns infectiously vivacious. Twice the trumpets recall the first measure of the third movement; and towards the end sound moving echoes of the *"Cathedral Scene."*

The *"Rhenish"* is a composite work. Its two outer movements attain authentic symphonic stature. Its three inner ones, though they range from the delightful to the deeply stirring, belong almost anywhere but within the confines of a symphony.

Op. 120. Fourth Symphony, D Minor

When Schumann [12] tried his hand at a new form, he did not like to stop with one essay. After the *"Spring,"* and the *Overture, Scherzo and Finale,* he immediately started the D Minor Symphony. This was to have been his Second; but, after a single performance, he was dissatisfied and laid it upon the shelf. A decade after, he rewrote the wind parts, not always to the work's advantage, and finally published it as Number Four.

In originality of thematic material, it holds its own with Number One, though not with the other two. A few of the themes are, in themselves, so far from Schumann's usual distinctiveness that one wonders if he was not deliberately trying to see how much could be made of somewhat banal material.[13]

[12] Like Beethoven before him, and Brahms after him.
[13] The reader will recall his brilliantly humorous juggling with a hopelessly commonplace tune in the F Sharp Minor Sonata. See p. 304.

In originality of construction, however, this symphony so far surpasses the others that, to this day, it has remained a rock of offense to those academicians for whom "the rules" are sacrosanct. Not only do the movements run together without a break —an innovation eagerly copied by Liszt and his successors—but the exposition of the first movement has no second subject; that is to say, unless we lend this courtesy title to a little wisp of a phrase at measure fifteen, which is developed from the first bar of Ex. 163. What might have been a real second makes its unconventional entry in the development, from the start of which portion, the complete first subject eccentrically refuses to reappear. And ninety-nine listeners out of every hundred never realize the astounding fact that neither the first nor the second subject is given in the concluding section of the movement. This fact turns into a farce the time-honored term "recapitulation" by making that section simply a part of the development. The ear is perhaps kept from recognizing this odd procedure by the constant use of the first measure of Ex. 163 as accompanying figure in the closing section. Another unacademic quirk is the surprise appearance of a brand-new tune,[14] à la the C Major Symphony, in the coda of the finale.

And then there is the extraordinary development of thematic liaison work. The Introduction contains the germs of thematic material used in all the four following divisions. But this is only the start of the interlocking devices. The first and last movements have two themes in common. And there are thematic parallels between Scherzo and first movement, and between *Romanze* and Trio. So that the work is constantly being tied together by many a cross-band. Its parts are almost as closely related as the royal families of Europe.

The Introduction begins with a curious, writhing figure which reminds us of how the strings start the C Major Symphony. It culminates in a descending scale and ends [15] in a foreshadowing of the key motive of the whole symphony. Here are its most significant portions:

[14] See Ex. 176.
[15] *Accelerando*, like all of Schumann's symphonic introductions.

[Ex. 162]

At first sight, the main subject of the first movement looks none too interesting.

[Ex. 163]

And if we undress the important first measure by transposing the last six notes down an octave and stripping off the slurs, we have left a thing of the most abject banality:

[Ex. 164]

The rise of an octave, and the phrasing, were all that made its use possible as the most important motive in the symphony. This initial phrase functions, either as theme or as accompaniment, in almost every measure of the first movement. It helps mold the contour of the exquisite *Romanze*, reappears at the close of the Scherzo, and pops up again at the beginning of the finale.

Almost any other composer would have regarded Ex. 163 as little more than a mere figure, quite unfit for emotional expressiveness. But see how the resourceful Schumann fulfills the artist's supreme function, which is to reveal the beauty and significance of the apparently ugly and insignificant. Under his hands the difficult theme, taking on a strong character, expresses in turn, with equal ease and conviction, now the stormy power of an imperious will, now hesitation and doubt, and now a veritable frenzy of joyful excitement.

We have seen that this remarkable Ex. 163 almost entirely monopolizes the exposition. But, with a wealth of new ideas, the development strives to balance this initial singleness of thought. After the exposition has ended on the F major chord, there explodes a sudden *sforzando* E flat, to make everybody jump— very much as the practical joker L. v. B. did with his horseplay chords in the finale of that Eighth which I like to call the *Sinfonia Giocosa*. Then the poor little scrap of "pseudo" second subject receives some very flattering attention and is almost given "the resurrection and the life." After that, in subtle preparation for what ought by rights to be the real second subject, the trombones interject a mysterious phrase:

[Ex. 165]

which reminds one of Schubert's use of these instruments

Schubert *(transposed)*

[Ex. 166]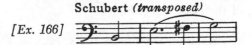

in the corresponding movement of his C Major Symphony.[16]

Now a splendid, solemn group, its significance underlined by fermatas, brings a theme destined to be the life and soul of that jolly celebration, the finale (see Ex. 172, p. 421).

[Ex. 167]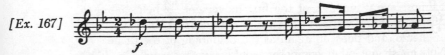

Best of all—and better late than never—comes the lovely piece of authentic Schumann which enjoys, if not the position, at least the significance of the real second subject:

[16] Notice that Schumann used for his simpler phrase only three of Schubert's four notes.

[Ex. 168]

a melody which, in the preceding century, had been roughly anticipated by old Florian Gassmann, the teacher of Beethoven's master, Salieri.

Allegro, Gassmann.

[Ex. 169]

Though the notes of this first movement are comparatively easy, its continual, protean changes of mood, and the rapid alternation between the caprices of Florestan and Eusebius, make it formidably difficult to play, conduct, or even analyze. Indeed, the listener who can find his way unerringly through the mazes of this elusive composition need fear no other problem in his study of musical form.

The *Romanze* begins with a folktune-like theme for solo 'cello and oboe. It is at once noble and poignantly intimate:

Ziemlich Langsam

[Ex. 170]

Notice that notes 3-9 are a slight elaboration of notes 3-8 in Ex. 163. Like the most natural thing in the world, this melody is followed by those parts of the Introduction already given at (a) and (b) of Ex. 162. And out of (b) there evolves a melody in sunny D major, adorned with a characteristic Schumannian filigree obligato for solo violin. We shall find the same combination again in the Trio of the Scherzo. The divided 'cellos, playing in thirds and sixths, lend this part a genial, mellow warmth.

In the Scherzo Florestan, almost above himself, begins with lusty exuberance by standing part (a) of Ex. 162 upon its head.

[Ex. 171]

Note the *Carnaval* source-motive, marked by a bracket.

The madly cavorting second part of the theme might easily suggest the consequences of a too practical joke. In fact, as a boy I was taught to remember this Scherzo by associating it with the start of the limerick:

> There was a young lady of Lynn
> Who sat on the point of a pin,

and then letting the ensuing notes suggest the resulting saltatory activities of the young lady.

The second part of the Scherzo is a jolly variation on the first half of Ex. 171. After the Trio with violin obligato already mentioned, and the repetition of the main movement, that Trio reappears to take a regretful, lingering farewell and to die away, as the composer would put it, 'as if in the distance.'

Now comes another of Schumann's characteristic introductions. The first violins brokenly whisper the start of Ex. 163, which they soon change into a blithe major. The brass battery registers grim exceptions. But with the help of the wood-winds, twittering like a flock of gay little birds, the brazen pessimists are over-ruled, *stringendo*, and the entire orchestra breaks tumultuously into a lively rendering of our old friend from the first movement, Ex. 167:

[Ex. 172]

The pessimists are allowed a word or two in working out a motive borrowed from the *Dona nobis* of Haydn's D Minor ("*Nelson*") Mass,

[Ex. 173]

and in the striking dissonances just before the development, where the composer is at his most original and modern. But, all in all, this is a movement of joyful exuberance; and we feel Schumann tingling with the consciousness that he is on the crest of the wave.

In music penned in such a state, especially in view of Schumann's extraordinary melodic fertility, it is astonishing to find one more borrowed tune. The second subject goes:

[Ex. 174]

With a little rhythmic disguise, this is essentially the same as a theme from the *Larghetto* of Beethoven's Second Symphony:

[Ex. 175]

The correspondence holds good even to the initial leap of an octave, and the phrasing. Faithful as his tune is to Beethoven, however, Schumann was miraculously able to make it the vehicle of his own peculiar capriciousness, charm, and youthful high spirits.

The development begins with an exciting fugato on the second half of Ex. 172. And so free is the form that it is hard to tell where this development merges into the recapitulation. But there is no doubt where the coda starts; for it immediately contributes a brand new and splendidly satisfying melody, twenty-four-karat Schumann, all the way through:

[Ex. 176]

The coda swings into a somewhat Italianate stretto, and this in turn into a *presto* fugato which has never yet failed to bring down the house.

Despite its borrowings, the D Minor will stand as the most Schumannian of the symphonies.

CHAPTER 9

THE CONCERTOS

Op. 54. Concerto for Piano and Orchestra, A Minor

WORDS so lamentably fail to do justice to this composition that one is tempted to imitate a certain Princeton undergraduate athlete. When called upon in class for a critical estimate of John Milton's masterpiece, he arose and muttered: "*Paradise Lost* is very good," and sat down.

One of the most original deeds of the original Schumann was to take the first long step towards the unexhibitionistic concerto. I mean the sort of work for solo instrument and orchestra in which we are not distracted from the music by the finger-twiddling of the soloist.

It is true that Mozart's D Minor and Beethoven's *"Emperor"* are very beautiful; but even these lay heavy stress upon virtuosity. Schumann's A Minor was the pioneer of that new, democratic form of concerto which might well be called a symphony with obligato for solo instrument. Brahms was to take up this new form and opulently enrich it. The new trend bore as its device: *The music's the thing!*

This innovation must have been hard for the conservatives of those days to swallow. Even so knowing a musician as August Reissmann, writing as late as 1865, felt obliged to blame as a defect this concerto's lack of pianistic show-off. When the beaver begins to build his house in the style of the *art nouveau,* the Reissmanns will admit the propriety of innovation in the time-honored musical laws of the Medes and Persians. But the truer the creative genius, the less he usually has in common with the

423

modistes of the moment. To be so woefully misjudged by contemporaries as Schumann was, is sometimes an indication of true greatness.

We of today have come to see that its democratic blending of piano and orchestra is chief among the A Minor's glories and virtues. And we are not sorry to miss that wallowing in the slough of mere technic which was the vice of most of the older concertos.

Opus 54 presents Schumann at his mellowest and most poetic. In structure, in coloring, in orchestration, in rhythmical resourcefulness, in inventive fertility he excels himself. Still retaining his youthful freshness, newness, verve, and spontaneity, he has "put away childish things," such as the capricious formlessness, moodiness, and too Puckish idiosyncrasy that sometimes did the piano works no good. By 1845 he had behind him most of his best music. And the evil years had not yet begun to touch and shrivel his spirit.

Preluded by three bold, energetic measures for piano alone, the wood-winds announce a principal theme at once sweet, soulful, and intimate—yet at the same time noble and spacious:

[Ex. 177]

Its breadth, pith, and rhythmic variety confute those who claim that Schumann was an incorrigible miniaturist and epigrammatist, who could not think symphonically and whose melodies all suffer from rhythmic monotony.

In the scherzo-variations of the A Major Quartet, we shall see him actually varying the theme before stating it.[1] And here in the opening movement of the Piano Concerto, we find him doing something equally original. Not only does he begin to develop both the first and second subjects before the development section is reached,[2] but also, to a slight extent, he even develops the first part of the second subject

[Ex. 178]

before he states it.

The second part of this second subject might almost be regarded as an offshoot of the first subject (Ex. 177). Roughly speaking, both have the same scalewise descent of five tones which we have seen as the Clara source-motive of the Piano Sonatas and the *Fantasie*.[3] This is only fitting; for the work was written for Clara and dedicated to her.[4]

The principal theme, as well such a glorious subject might, dominates the first movement, appearing in a protean profusion of keys, tempos, and rhythms: *Allegro affetuoso, Animato, Andante espressivo, Allegro, Più animato,* and *Allegro molto.* It moves in 4/4, 6/4, and 2/4 time. This vital movement consistently follows climactic order, building up from good to better. Some

[1] See p. 459.
[2] Brahms took over this procedure from him.
[3] See p. 297, Ex. 28.
[4] Mme. Olga Samaroff Stokowski feels that Ex. 178 is subsidiary thematic material which "never quite rises to the status of 'a second subject.'"

of its high lights are: the surprise appearance of the tender *Andante espressivo,*[5] the succulent clarinet part, and the wholly musical and unostentatious cadenza, with its exciting imitations. The mounting arpeggios of this delectable cadenza

[Ex. 179]

take us back to the Marschner tune with which, in the finale of the *Symphonic Etudes,*[6] Robert saluted his British friend Bennett.

An *adagio* would have failed of its effect after the *Andante espressivo.* Instead there comes a pert and dainty *Intermezzo.* It is a dialogue between piano and orchestra—

[Ex. 180]

INTERMEZZO
Andante grazioso

[5] Mme. Olga Samaroff Stokowski comments on this *Andante espressivo:* "It is an amazing proof of the fact that a minor theme, put into a different key in the major, can actually sound like a new theme!"

[6] See p. 325, Ex. 64.

Note the rapping "Victory" figure of the first four beats, a rhythm which has played such an important role in music, notably in Mozart's operas *passim* and Beethoven's Fifth Symphony. Here it is also found in the second and third measures of both Ex. 177 and of the main theme of the finale (Ex. 181), so that it attains the importance of a rhythmical germ-motive. Another trait which Ex. 180 has borrowed from both of these other themes is the upward leap of an octave as soon as the tune is well under way.

The *Intermezzo* goes on to make light keyboard filigrees fling graceful arms about a passionate 'cello melody. Towards the end of this unique movement there are passages for the solo instrument instinct with subtle mystery. One can almost see the composer fingering his puckered lips with a far-away smile. He is attending to supernal voices.

Not every listener realizes what a tour de force the main subject of the finale is. Here Schumann has actually remodeled his ideal first-movement theme into one ideally fitted to open a last movement:

[Ex. 181]

See how effectively its clear-cut rhythm contrasts with the teasing subtleties of motion in the theme next in importance of this unconventionally constructed rondo. There Schumann is most brilliantly up to the rhythmical sleight-of-hand that we

have so often encountered. The signature is ¾; but he has none
the less managed to make the music sound like 3/2 (indicated by
brackets). As there is nothing here for the theme to syncopate
against, all hints of the ¾ rhythm are lacking:

[Ex. 182]

At this point many an orchestral conductor has met his Waterloo; to the immense—if suppressed—glee of his armed forces,
each one of whom always feels that he could conduct that part
better.

Even if some other composer could perform a similar feat of
rhythmical magic, he would be at a loss how to get back to
normal with no awkward moments of transition. Not so Schumann. Witness the consummate ease and grace with which, after
four varied repetitions of the last example, he restores to us the
feeling for ¾ time:

[Ex. 183]

I like Dr. Daniel Gregory Mason's remark:

To do justice to the plastic beauty of this movement would require nothing less than a measure-by-measure analysis of its charmingly varied phraseology. To play it after the "Abegg Variations" is like passing from a schoolboy's singsong delivery of "The Boy Stood on the Burning Deck" to the reading of an ode of Shelley or a sonnet of Keats.

We who love Schumann's symphonies, but regret that they were so thickly scored, are tantalized when we discover that the Piano Concerto is orchestrated with admirable lightness. This may have come about because the composer, himself a pianist, took special pains to see that his own instrument—despite its unexhibitionistic employment—should not be drowned out.[6a]

Op. 92. *Introduction and Allegro Appassionato,* G Major. Concertpiece for Piano and Orchestra

This is one of Schumann's least-inspired compositions. The same may be said of—

Op. 134. *Concert Allegro with Introduction,* D Minor. For Piano and Orchestra

Throughout most of this work we hear little of the Schumann whom we know and appreciate. By the time he wrote it, disease had made such inroads on his creative powers that most of these pages sound as though they might have been set down, in moments of unusual inspiration, by some minor composer like

[6a] Grieg's Piano Concerto is a natural child of Schumann's Opus 54.

Grädener or Dietrich. It must have been a real pain to Brahms when he played this work, which had been dedicated to him by his beloved friend. Only toward the close does the composer seem to regain something of his old quality.

Op. 129. Concerto, A Minor, for 'Cello and Orchestra

In 1911, Marie Lipsius, the contemporary of Brahms who wrote under the pseudonym of La Mara, declared that this concerto had not 'permanently made its way.' Happily she was wrong. Though an effective composition for 'cello and orchestra is perhaps the most difficult problem that a maker of music is ever called upon to solve, Schumann's Opus 129 now stands, with the Dvořák and the one which bears the name of Haydn, at the head of the 'cellist's concerto repertory. In its own class this work enjoys a position as distinguished as the Quintet enjoys among piano quintets. Perhaps the fact that Schumann himself once took up the 'cello may help to explain why Opus 129 is of far higher quality than the Violin Concerto.

Having met in the earlier music with so much awkwardly unidiomatic writing for this difficult instrument, we are agreeably surprised when the first movement of the A Minor starts with a noble, all-'cello theme in the large fiddle's most effective register,

[Ex. 184]

and throughout holds with sympathetic understanding to the character of the instrument. In the pioneering spirit of the Piano Concerto, the composer lays more stress on the music itself than on the digital and carpal dexterity of the soloist.

The slow movement is equally noble, idiomatic and effective.

[Ex. 185]

The finale opens with a fiery subject somewhat akin to that which launches the corresponding movement of the A Minor Quartet.

[Ex. 186]

Schumann however, as he was prone to do in his last period, proceeeds to ride a certain not very interesting figure too hard, besides lapsing into some technically awkward writing. So that, like the closing movements of most concertos, and the final acts of most plays, this finale fails to sustain with perfect consistency the lofty level of the earlier sections. None the less the A Minor remains a noteworthy achievement, second to none among 'cello concertos.

Op. 131. *Fantasie*, C Major, for Violin and Orchestra. Without opus number, Concerto, D Minor, for Violin and Orchestra

Both of these compositions exasperate lovers of the Master, though for exactly opposite reasons: the *Fantasie*, because it offers so many bits of choice Schumann that the other parts strike one in the face like mailed fists; the Concerto, because its few scraps of the real Schumann are so sparsely strewn. This sparseness is, of course, highly venial; for the Concerto was written in the worst days of 1853, when the composer was struggling against his fatal illness.

The Violin Concerto has so little of the quality which Schumann-lovers wish it had that (if pronounced with a soft C after the manner of certain radio announcers) it might be called, in Dr. Carlisle Moore's expressive word-coinage, a "disconcerto." In his piety toward the Master's good name, Joseph Joachim was justified in endeavoring to keep the work from publication.

The most remarkable thing about this composition is the weird manner in which it was unearthed. One day in London, a few years ago, Miss Yelly d'Aranyi, the Hungarian violin virtuoso, perhaps inspired by Schumann's late enthusiasm for table-tipping, was toying with an improvised Ouija board made of an inverted tumbler. Suddenly she was directed by some source that claimed to be the spirit of Robert Schumann to go to Berlin in order to find and resurrect the manuscript of his Violin Concerto. She obeyed and, after a long search, actually discovered in the Prussian State Library not one but four manuscripts of the forgotten work.

CHAPTER 10

CHORAL WORKS AND OPERA

I N order to disprove their own limitations, geniuses are often seized by a longing to accomplish the impossible. Schumann ardently desired to succeed as a dramatic composer. He did not realize that he was too subjective, too intensely introverted.

His inability to realize this ambition cannot be attributed entirely to the failing powers of his last period; for during those years of brave struggle he produced such masterpieces as the Piano Concerto, the slow movement of the D Minor Trio, and the outer movements of the "*Rhenish*" Symphony. His powers failed more notably at just the times when he was engaged on the larger choral works and the opera *Genoveva* because the desperate endeavor to succeed in the kind of work for which he was least equipped always affected his shaky health more disastrously than did the sorts of composition for which he is best known and loved.

Perhaps another reason for his lack of success in this field was a preoccupation with the emotional life of woman, which grew out of his passion for Clara. This swung his choice toward subjects which allowed him gallantly to give special prominence to heroines like the Peri, the Rose, Margaret in *Faust,* and Genoveva. The *Frauenliebe* cycle was the up-beat to this procedure. While a subtle compliment to his wife, this matriarchal tendency was also something of a dramatic handicap.

His excursions into the alien field of dramatic composition threw the composer off his stride. In these long and elaborate works there are few pages that offer us bona-fide Schumann.

433

And for this reason they have virtually disappeared from the repertory.

In its day, *The Paradise and the Peri,* Op. 50, scored a considerable success. It pleased the Romantic public to have Schumann revive the secular oratorio of Handel and Haydn, giving it a new direction and a fashionable theme. Oriental subjects were just then all the mode; and his setting of Moore's best-selling poem, *Lalla Rookh,* chimed with the popular taste. In her raptures over the *Peri,* Dr. Annie Patterson tells about "the whole being embellished with the rich glow of the East, while underlying all are the universal emotions of patriotism, self-sacrificing love, and the dying sinner's repentance."

Despite its lack of dramatic quality and of the Schumann note, Part I of the *Peri* contains such charming music that, on a first hearing, the listener's hopes soar high. Alas! they are then progressively brought towards earth by the slackening of the inspiration, the lack of melodic, harmonic, rhythmical, and emotional contrast, and above all by the undramatic dead level. The oratorio is too consistently sweet. After an evening of it you feel as if you had taken a bath in liquid honey.

This was the one work of Schumann's that Mendelssohn liked. Perhaps he approved of its blameless smoothness, and the absence of that forward-looking originality which usually annoyed him in his admirer's music. There was nothing here to offend his conservative taste.

In the somewhat Lisztian Overture to *Faust,*[1] we are conscious of the same forcing of Schumann's real gift that troubles us here and there in the Violin Sonatas. The *Cathedral Scene* is the best portion of the incidental music; but while strong and impressive, it is neither dramatic nor Schumannian. There is, however, something pathetically autobiographical and convincing about the vaunts of the character "Anxiety" in the number marked *Midnight.*

[1] Without opus number.

The *Manfred Music*, Op. 115, is easily the best of the choral works. The Overture stands out among Schumann's other orchestral compositions for its fire, depth of ideas, instrumentation, and for its quite remarkable modernity of harmony and rhythm. The three opening chords exemplify his love of mystification; for they give no possible clue to the time-signature.[2]

Here are the more important themes:

In leidenschaftlichem tempo

[Ex. 187]

[Ex. 188]

[Ex. 189]

[2] As Mr. C. Dewar Simons has pointed out to me.

That this piece could be so splendid without sounding particularly like Schumann had always puzzled me. Then, one day,
the radio snapped on in the middle of something that reminded
me strongly of the prelude to *Manfred*. But it turned out to be
the *Ruy Blas Overture,* which Mendelssohn composed a decade
before his hero-worshiper had begun to wrestle with Byron's
poem. The resemblance was all the more odd because both
pieces sound unlike their respective composers. Perhaps the
more original and modern of the two musicians had been so
interested in Mendelssohn's attempt to emerge from his stylistic
rut that he unconsciously imitated the result.[2a]

A good deal of the music to the translation of Byron's griev-
ously maltreated *Manfred* has the real Schumannian quality.
Shorn of its words, No. 2 would fit comfortably among his lesser
piano pieces. No. 3 begins by echoing the theme of the *Symphonic Etudes*. No. 10, *The Conjuring-up of Astarte,* is the
spooky sort of music that young Robert might well have improvised for the entertainment of the young Wieck children, as an
accompaniment to his gooseflesh-raising ghost-stories. No. 11,
Manfred's Speech to Astarte, is lovely. At the words, *"wenn ich
dich einmal nur höre,"* it rises to the level of his best songs. This
high quality is maintained through the next two numbers and
the final *Cloister Song.*

The great pity about *Manfred* is the composer's choice of that
hybrid vehicle usually called "melodrama," which I prefer to
christen "melocution." Recitation accompanies ten of the fifteen
numbers. Now, the speaking voice necessarily clashes with
music, because it employs entirely different scales. So that "melocution" is as abhorrent to most musicians as conversation in the
audience during the performance of a string quartet. And things
go from bad to worse when the reciter, as in *Manfred,* competes,
not only against the instrumental music, but also against a four-
part chorus using another language, and each part singing different words to the same beat. Here is a bit of the resulting farrago from the closing scene:

[2a] Tchaikovsky's *Manfred* Symphony contains a pious allusion to the last
seven notes of Ex. 189.

MANFRED	Himmel!	Vorüber	ist's, mein	trüber Blick er-	kennt dich nicht, und	Alles schwimmt um mich,
SOPRANO	re-qui-	em,	re-qui-	em,	re- qui-	em ae-
ALTO	e--------	is		re--qui-	em	ae-----
TENOR			re- qui-	em,	re- qui-	em,
BASS		re- qui-	em	ae------	ter------	-------

[Ex. 190]

How pleased Byron would have been at this nonsense!

Some enterprising musician really ought to rescue *Manfred* from oblivion by making a wordless orchestral suite out of the most exquisite pages of the unfortunate work!

If we are inclined to begrudge the none too dramatic Beethoven's enormous expenditure of time and energy upon *Fidelio* —time and energy which might instead have yielded us further symphonies and quartets—we must begrudge even more the still less dramatic Schumann's suicidal expenditure upon his opera *Genoveva*, Op. 81, which, as much as anything else, drove him mad.

The *Genoveva* story, weak and undramatic in the first instance, was made still more so by Schumann's literary tinkering. Among other ill-advised changes, Golo, originally the leading character,[8] was shouldered from the spotlight in favor of the heroine, Genoveva. And when the composer had done his worst to the book, he innocently supposed that it had now become the ideal opera libretto.

The orchestral prelude is the best part of the opera, and, among all the overtures, ranks next to the *Manfred*. Its high point, one of the most charming moments in Schumann's orchestral work, is where one hears

The horns of elfland faintly blowing:

Now and again, through the four acts, the real Schumann gleams out like a will-o'-the-wisp, the next moment to be lost among the shadows that prophesy, all too plainly, the creative slackening of his final years.

[8] His leit-motive is a descending fifth.

Chapter 11

THE CHAMBER MUSIC

O N February 11th, 1838, Robert wrote to Clara in Vienna that he was preparing to compose three string quartets. The conservative girl, who wanted him to adopt the pellucid and forthright manner of the adored Mendelssohn, replied:

So you're going to write quartets? A question—but don't laugh me to scorn: are you, then, thoroughly acquainted with the instruments? I'm very much delighted over your plan. Only, please compose right clearly. It hurts me too much when people fail to understand you.

Here Clara was partly right, partly wrong. Robert reacted with vigorous anger against the second admonition. For what he understood by her "compose right clearly" was: "adapt your music to the current public taste." [1] On March 17th he answered:

You write that I am to make quartets, "only please compose right clearly." That sounds like some Dresdner Fräulein. Do you know what I said to myself when I read that? "Yes, so clearly that sight and hearing will fail you!" . . . And then: "Are you thoroughly acquainted with all the instruments?" Why, that's a matter of course, my Fräulein. How could I otherwise dare make so bold?

The Court-city of Dresden was, as we have seen, notoriously prim and reactionary in its musical taste. And when he compared Clara to a "Dresdner Fräulein," he was fighting to save that original, forward-looking individuality of his which had had such free play in the piano music and the songs. However, de-

---

[1] A year later we found Clara urging Robert to write a pot-boiler "suitable for the crowd." See p. 160.

spite his determined struggles, Clara, from her wedding-day on, was at times successful in Mendelssohnizing his music to some slight extent, making it more conventional and less utterly Schumannian.

On the other hand, her doubts as to his knowledge of the instruments were all too well justified. Despite his confident retort, Robert did not often succeed in handling the strings—or the winds either—so as to bring out all the resonance of the overtones and gain the maximum of effect with the minimum of technical agony. His worst failures in this regard are the finales of the first two String Quartets and the *L'istesso tempo* of the Quintet. There figures which would be easy and effective on the piano prove totally unidiomatic and highly awkward for the strings. Necessarily they lose a good deal of the effect which Schumann in his innocence must have anticipated when he conceived them.

In relation to the general excellence of his chamber music, however, this fault of ineffectiveness is even less impressive than we have seen it in the orchestral music. Great players can cover it up so completely that the ordinary hearer does not suspect its existence. And despite everything that can be brought against Schumann's chamber music, it often has delicious tonal effects, and remains among the freshest, most original, most fertile in invention, most charming, and most exciting in its class.

Let me emphasize the last adjective. One of the distinctive features of this man's best chamber music is its tensely exciting quality. I have heard many a quartetist refuse to play Schumann the last thing in the evening for fear that the glow and lift of it would keep him awake.

Except for the fault just discussed, Schumann started to write chamber music with as mature a mastery of the new vehicle as he had previously shown in starting piano and vocal composition. Indeed, benefiting by the former experiences, this mastery of chamber music began even more maturely. One can only think of Minerva and her precocious birthday exit from the head of Jove in the dignity of full-blown womanhood, with all the fixings.

The new phase started with string quartets; but before discussing them, let us look at the trios.

Op. 63. Trio in D Minor for Piano, Violin and 'Cello

The D Minor is a superb and justly renowned work. But M. Basch declares that it "goes higher and further" than even the Quintet. In this I can no more agree with him than when he states that the Scherzo proper of Opus 63 is "a dialogue led by the violoncello." In reality, it is nothing of the kind. For there the 'cello violates the canons of good ensemble style by slavishly doubling the violin all the way to the Trio. Among the French there seems to be a tendency to overestimate this D Minor Trio just as extremely as they have always underestimated Brahms.

In ensemble style the three Trios show a progressive improvement. While the First duplicates parts to an almost distressing degree, the Second doubles less and has much more polyphony. And the Third almost attains the ideal of perfect independence for each instrument. If Schumann had only been spared long enough to write as many Trios as Beethoven did, the too scanty literature for this combination might have been immensely enriched.

With all its faults, the exciting and varied D Minor is a fascinating work. It recaptures some of the wild fresh emotional overplus and vivacity of the early piano compositions, and sweeps us along for a glimpse through

> spirit casements opening for a flash
> On sunrise heavens of the long ago.

At the same time, it is emotionally well-balanced, with Eusebius and Florestan conducting alternate movements. The first, though marked *Mit Energie und Leidenschaft* (With energy and passion), belongs to the brooder rather than to the gay enthusiast. Its rich *Kreisleriana* gloom provides a foil for the vivacious Scherzo. While the noble but morbidly melancholy introspection of the slow movement is a perfect prelude to the jubilant young cavortings of the finale.

The principal theme of the opening movement is at once painful, magnificent, and astringent. The violin begins:

A splendid, energetic, and craggily dotted bridge-passage, anticipating the thousand and one dots of the Scherzo, leads to a second subject which is not in Schumann's happiest vein, consisting of material too dry and scanty to be so often repeated. Note that, at the end of the exposition, both subjects are cleverly, if freely, combined in counterpoint.

In the development, Schumann, after sipping like a bee from both subjects and from the craggy bridge-passage, does 'a thing he had frequently done before': he takes a leaf out of *Eroica* procedure by giving us, at *Tempo I, nur ruhiger,* a brand new "episode," *pianissimo* and *ponticello* for the strings, *una corda* for the piano. For some reason the exquisite page always brings to my own mind the more ethereal passages in Goethe's finest drama. This may be because, only a short time before writing it, Schumann had been working on the incidental music to *Faust.* At letter L, see how pointedly the violin emphasizes the composer's favorite descending fifth. Notice also the Bracketing source-motive, marked in Ex. 192 by a bracket.

The piano part—perhaps it would better be called the percussion part—of this first movement is written with a Gargantuan richness and a disregard of the weaker strings that are the joy of the *fort*ist, as distinguished from that rare and dodo-like creature, the *pian*ist. Most of the time the unfortunate fiddlers are toiling away on the least sonorous and effective reaches of the fingerboard while, with his powerful juggernaut, their percussive partner zestfully obliterates their efforts, and roars away to

leave not a rack behind.

Take, for example, the *molto crescendo* passage just before the recapitulation. The *fort*ist is in his glory. His right hand is crowned with juicy octaves and chords; his left, with a tremendous, lusty accompaniment in sixteenth notes. Ah, but two octaves below, on his feeble D string, behold the poor 'cellist vainly sweating to hold up his end of the canon! And if, by any chance, one of the fiddles is allotted an effective bit, there comes the greedy *fortist* rushing with loud cries of "me too!" and doubles it. I can count on the fingers of one hand remembered performances of this work in which the pianist had enough mastery, self-control, finger-control, musical piety, and greatheartedness to keep a reasonable balance with the strings.

The second movement suffers from a rush of dots to the head, and from the above-mentioned doubling of the strings. This Scherzo (proper) might just as well be in a violin sonata. It has this in common with many of the Haydn trios, that the 'cello, having nothing new to say, is really superfluous. And the monotony is increased when the Trio of this trio turns out to be merely a legato version in canon form of the Scherzo's main theme:

The slow movement, with the characteristic direction *Langsam, mit inniger Empfindung* (Slow, with heartfelt emotion), is worthy to stand with the corresponding portions of the C Major Symphony, the A Major String Quartet, and the Quintet, among Schumann's greatest *adagios*. Against a subtly woven tapestry of *una corda* piano harmony, the violin intones a complaint as somber and morbid as it is beautiful:

[Ex. 195]

Consider how peculiarly expressive the (marked) Bracketing source-motive is here. The 'cello refuses to yield wholly to this emotional atmosphere, and answers in a virile voice of confidence which seems to be infectious; for at *Bewegter* the violin begins a tender, heartening song, uniquely Schumannian. After four bars, the old morbid inhibitions threaten to creep in. But the 'cello will have none of that, and brightens the music until, at the climax of the movement, ten bars before *Tempo I*, even the principal subject is freed of its despair.

There is one more descent to the abyss; then a hold on the dominant of D major—and we plunge into the headlong excitements and exaltations of the finale. The direction *Mit Feuer* is supererogatory—for nobody could help playing it "with fire."

[Ex. 196]

The calmer second subject in quarter notes on the 'cello is almost a reminder of the early piano piece, *Arabeske*. It does little to damp the happiness, which takes on volume and momentum until it becomes an exultant outpouring of triumph. From the time when, in youth, I first attained the privilege of taking the 'cello part in a Schumann trio, I vowed to have this finale arranged for organ and played as a recessional at my wedding. And that dream came true.

Op. 80. Second Trio in F Major

This is Schumann's least important work for the combination. Its highlights are: the episode which begins the development of the opening movement with an improvement on Schumann's own song, *Dein Bildniss wunderselig;* [2] the deep and *innig* slow movement, and the canoned *allegretto* which does duty as scherzo.

In his reminiscences Carl Reinecke tells how in 1850, when Clara played him this still unpublished composition, Schumann asked him with a sly smile if he had noticed anything unusual about it. Seeing that the embarrassed disciple could not guess, he showed him that the first six bars of the slow movement maintain a strict canon between 'cello and piano. Such canons as these in the middle movements tickled Schumann immensely; and later he wrote Reinecke: "The beginning of the *Adagio* and the *Allegretto* always give me great pleasure when they come along." Did he implant in Brahms a liking for canonic imitation, and for *allegrettos* in place of scherzos?

The finales of both the First and Second Trios are *alla breve,* and both are jubilant. That in the former is the most spontaneous imaginable welling-up of triumphant joy. But that in the F Major sounds deliberately fabricated, a synthetic jubilance.

Op. 110. Third Trio in G Minor

This is a superbly unified work. Thematically it is even more closely interlocked than the F Major Quartet, which is welded together by the same general scheme of rising and falling arpeggios.[3] And in addition the subject matter is as closely interrelated as in the D Minor Symphony.

The dramatic opening movement at once brings forward the passionate young hothead that Schumann used to be, the strings competing in this fiery utterance:

[Ex. 197]

[2] Entitled *Intermezzo.* The theme returns as the second subject of the *Adagio.*
[3] See p. 457.

As he is prone to do, Schumann makes the second subject

[Ex. 198]

a good deal like the first, though the major mode and the appoggiaturas lend it more sentiment and grace. The two are at least first cousins. And, as in the corresponding part of the D Minor Trio, here he again combines both in counterpoint.

In its turn, the spacious and tender principal theme of the slow movement,

[Ex. 199]

bears a close resemblance to Ex. 198. The agitated up and down arpeggios of the middle section recall Ex. 197 while the *sforzando* ejaculations of the strings at *Schneller* again remind us of Ex. 198.

The rising and falling theme that begins the spirited Scherzo

[Ex. 200]

returns us to the wavelike tossing of Ex. 197; only this time the waves are choppy.

The second subject also heaves up and down, but more calmly. Oil has been poured upon the troubled waters.[4]

[Ex. 201]

[4] This theme also comes into the finale of the D Minor Violin Sonata, composed the same year, 1851.

The third subject is likewise an up-and-downer:

[Ex. 202]

This most jolly and uninhibited of strains was evidently dashed upon paper as if to cry: "To hell with discretion!" It is the very mood in which Richard Hovey wrote *Vagabondia*:

> Off with the fetters
> That chafe and restrain!
> Off with the chain! . . .
> Here we are free—
> Free as the wind is,
> Free as the sea,
> Free! . . .
>
> Midnights of revel,
> And noondays of song!
> Is it so wrong?
> Go to the Devil!

Notice that it brings in two of Schumann's perennially favorite devices: dotted rhythm and triplets gradually descending, like nimble toes feeling their way down a steep mountainside—a variation of the Climb source-motive.

The roughly burschikos and genuinely humorous finale bursts forth with this boisterous theme:

[Ex. 203]

Observe how craftily it combines the rising sixth of Ex. 198 with the stormy rise and fall of Ex. 197. The D major section borrows a tune (Ex. 201) from the Scherzo. And before the rowdy, bac- chanalian end, both the beloved dotted rhythm and the Climb source-motive triplets of Ex. 202 return to play their roles.

The fifth time that the 'cello has to tackle that awkward and uncellistic principal theme, Ex. 203, Schumann shows his dis- regard for string mechanism by putting the turn high up on the lowest and thickest wire string, where it is almost impossible to make the brute speak, and precisely where, on most 'cellos, the wolf-tone is least bearable. Perhaps, however, the practical joker R. S. did this deliberately to obtain the grotesque squeak almost sure to result, and to turn the laugh upon the tortured player. We must remember that the composer himself had once played at the 'cello.

This fine Trio has never been properly appreciated by the public at large, nor was it by Clara. In Paris I once heard it played as it should be, by that superb combination of artists, Thibaut, Casals, and Cortot. It followed the *"Archduke"* of Bee- thoven, and the Ravel. And, under the hands of those mighty colleagues, it gloriously held its own without the slightest sense of let-down. What more could one say for any trio? On that red- letter day, the part-writing sounded simply inevitable. Naturally all of Schumann's chamber works need great artists to do them justice. Nine hundred and ninety-nine pianists out of every thou- sand who undertake them are guilty of mayhem; though they can plead in extenuation that they are aided and abetted by Schumann himself.

Op. 88. *Fantasiestücke for Trio*, A Minor

This charming little work, so tender and intimate, is ideally suited, by the very qualities which make it less effective in pub- lic, for performance at home.

It opens with a *Romanze,* full of the simple, smiling appeal of the *Scenes from Childhood.* And this mood returns in later move-

ments, notably after the first part of the *Etwas lebhafter* in the
Humoreske.

This *Humoreske* is one more place where we search in vain
for the humor indicated in the title. It begins:

[Ex. 204]

Except for slight rhythmical differences, the first six notes of this
theme correspond with the beginning of Beethoven's *"Geister"*
Trio:

[Ex. 205]

which, as we happen to know, was often played in the Schumann establishment. The reader will recall that it was used to
fill in the time on that painful evening when Liszt was late, then
acted Puckishly and was bidden to hold his tongue.

The third movement, a glowing love duet, is the highlight of
the work:

[Ex. 206]

And the finale offers some of Schumann's most enlivening march music.

In the second and fourth movements, Opus 88 is marred by too much doubling of parts. This reminds us that it was composed in 1847, five years before the doublings of the D Minor Trio.

Chapter 12

THE STRING QUARTETS

Op. 41. Three Quartets for Two Violins, Viola, and 'Cello

IN these quartets did the composer use any of the themes that had gone into his earlier experiments with this vehicle? We wish that we knew.

First Quartet, A Minor

While Schumann's introductions are usually pregnant with material which he uses later, that of the A Minor Quartet has no thematic connection, but only one of mood, with what follows.

The richest, most productive, and most liberal of men have their curious little quirks of stinginess. In connection with the symphonies it has already been remarked how the opulent Schumann tended to economize on second subjects. And here too, in the *Allegro* of the A Minor, after the gracefully undulating principal theme

[Ex. 207]

has been stated and worked out a bit, the rest of the exposition is filled up with two fugatos on figures which are remotely de-

rived from the last example and which sound like a further
working out of it.

The *presto* Scherzo begins thus: [1]

[Ex. 208]

It is unified by the sort of all-embracing rhythmical momentum
described on page 392, and is one of the most exciting and successful movements of its kind in quartet literature.

The tranquil Trio, here called *Intermezzo,* with its warm,
caressing chromatic harmony, provides a blessedly satisfying
contrast. Characteristic syncopations tie one measure to another,
as in the *Larghetto* of the First Symphony (Ex. 136, p. 399).

The noble sublimities of the *Adagio*

[Ex. 209]

vaguely remind one of Beethoven's loftier moments, until one
realizes that, by leaving out the few more or less passing notes
that are enclosed in parentheses in Ex. 209, one has very much
the start of the *Adagio* in Beethoven's *Choral* Symphony.

(transposed)

[Ex. 210]

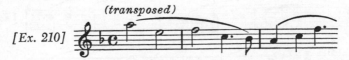

[1] Mme. Olga Samaroff Stokowski points out that Schumann uses this idea
"in the accompaniment of his song *Es leuchtet meine Liebe* (Op. 127, No.
3), and succeeds in altering its character by changing the time-signature
from ⅞ to 12⁄8, and the key from A minor to G minor."

But here again, as in his own D Minor Symphony,[2] Schumann, by a deft turn or two of his magic mental wrist, so thoroughly makes Beethoven his own that the resemblance, far from annoying, touches us. This lovely movement might well have been entitled *"Hommage à Beethoven."*

The manic but mystic exaltation of Ex. 200 alternates with loud, chromatic outcries of anguish, until exaltation finally wins the victory, and ends in a coda won from the movement's Introduction by the master hand which wrote the postludes of the *Frauenliebe* and the *Dichterliebe.*

Like the Scherzo, the *presto* finale is unified by a tremendous, tautly strung bow of rhythmic momentum. The excitement is maintained by the almost continuous employment of this Climb source-motive

[Ex. 211]

It starts with the energetic subject,

[Ex. 212]

From it many a stirring theme like this

[Ex. 213]

is whisked by an apparently effortless legerdemain. The most important of these tunes is the following:

[Ex. 214]

One feels that nothing less than a battery of trombones could do it full justice. It is particularly effective in the minor, with the first two notes an octave lower.

[2] See p. 421.

Towards the end of this finale, the sound and fury are dramatically held up by a few measures of simple bagpipe music, *Moderato*, and some soft, unearthly harmonies. Then comes the coda with its final frantic rush.

On this closing page—just as Beethoven had done in his E Minor Quartet, and as Brahms was to do afterwards in his A Minor—Schumann had his little fun with the lower strings. In the last run, which is made up of a series of Climb source-motives, the composer prescribed for those strings a D natural, instead of the D sharp which they would instinctively play. That run, by the bye, is the Waterloo of most 'cellists. For them it is in the same horrific class with the *L'istesso tempo* of the Quintet, the finale of the great Haydn Quartet in D, and the formidable Mozart *Divertimento* for string trio.

Because the first violin part is a little too prominent for good balance, and because it suffers more than the others from piano figures literally transcribed for the strings, this A Minor is somewhat less idiomatic quartet music than the other two numbers of Opus 41.

Second Quartet, F Major

From the first page of this work, one feels a more democratic equality of the four companions—out, as it were, on a bracing morning of brilliant sunshine, for a run over the moor. The long principal theme is a gloriously happy inspiration. It begins:

Watch the constantly changing and perfectly balanced movement. Who said that Schumann could not vary his rhythms if he wanted to? The play of motives, tossed from bow to bow, is as spontaneous as a swift game of Badminton doubles on the lawn.[3]

[3] Brahms lovers will find something pleasantly familiar about notes 2-4

The slim little new theme of less than four measures that sidles in at the end of the exposition is one more amusing instance of the opulent Schumann's parsimony with second subjects. It is like a millionaire's grudging a full-sized net for the Badminton court.

A decade before this, a tiny *Larghetto*, later published as No. 13 of the *Albumblätter* (see p. 362, Ex. 114), anticipated the lovely, caressing theme of the *Andante, quasi Variazioni*, which hesitantly begins as follows:

[Ex. 216]

This long, delicious melody has been unjustly accused of copying the *Adagio* of Beethoven's E Flat Quartet, Opus 127. Except that both are sets of variations in 1⅔ time, all they have in common is that certain phrases in both start on the ninth beat of the measure—surely a distant and venial resemblance! These small likenesses are less than skin-deep. The emotional tone of the two movements differs enormously.

The syncopated harmonies of the first variation have the rich, dusky quality that we have often noticed in Schumann's works, from *Grillen* on. In its simplicity, the second variation with the delicious rolling basses, is as touching as a child's folk tune.

The last two variations before the theme returns sound as if they belonged in the *Scenes from Childhood*. The *Molto più lento* might well have fitted in there under some such name as *The Swan Boat*, while the *Un poco più vivace* could perhaps have functioned as *Elves at Hopscotch*.

of Ex. 215, for they form the F A F of Johannes' personal motto, *Frei aber froh* (Free but glad). Brahms was nine years old when the F Major was written. The story goes that, in his early twenties, he adopted this motto as a match for Joachim's F A E, *Frei aber einsam* (Free but lonely). But that was at the very time when Johannes had just learned to know and love Schumann and his music. It is interesting to speculate whether the older master's F Major Quartet may not have had a finger in the motto pie.

The Scherzo, with its rapidly flitting ups and downs,

has an eerie quality. But in the Trio it finds the good common earth with a bump. There the 'cello is made to appear as a ridiculous and perhaps love-sick lout, at whose clumsy naïveté the shriller strings cannot keep from giggling helplessly. Then the first violin travesties the bull-fiddler's emotion in a burlesque tune for which the German language has the perfect word, *schmachtend*, but which we can only call languishing. The whole rare page once again brings to mind a vision of little Robert, perched before the piano and wittily improvising while his cronies double up in malicious mirth.

The finale, a curious blend of sonata-form and rondo, starts, like the last movement of the *"Spring"* Symphony, with one of those delicate, sunny, filigree-like and decorative themes of which Schumann was so fond:

The second subject, too, is highly Schumannian:

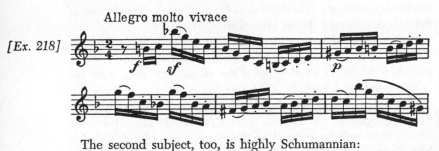

At the end of it (below the bracket) appears the favorite Schein source-motive.

Some commentators assure us that the hideously awkward solo for the largest instrument at *animato* is "roughly humorous." What I personally find funny there is the spectacle of the agonized 'cellist struggling with pianistic strains quite inappropriate for his unwieldy fiddle, while the rest sit smugly back in comfort to enjoy his flounderings. It is certainly no joke for the luckless soloist, who has already, in the Trio of the Scherzo, been laughed at quite sufficiently.

This milestone of a quartet marks Schumann's first essay at thematic work in chamber music. The exciting up-and-down arpeggios in the development section of the first movement, which are evolved by stylization out of the principal theme (Ex. 215), constitute a germ-motive. This comes again in the third variation of the *Andante*. It reappears, and with the most literal emphasis, as the main theme of the Scherzo (Ex. 217) and—slightly dressed up—both as the principal theme of the finale (Ex. 218) and just before the end of the first section.

Following the first three superb movements, this finale usually brings a sense of anticlimax. One day while the composer was engaged upon it, Mendelssohn dropped in and proposed a walk. Schumann refused because he had to finish a piece of work. The next time the other appeared, he was shown the completed manuscript of the finale. He looked it through, shook his head, and remarked to Clara: "He had better have come out walking with me!"

Taken together with his famous suggestions for improving the Second Symphony and the Quintet,[4] the incident would show that Mendelssohn was no mean critic of Schumann's work. All the same, this least satisfactory among the latter's dozen string quartet movements grows mightily on one, the more it is played and heard. The pianistic passages annoy one less and less; and the essential beauty of the music radiates increasingly from underneath the somewhat crabbèd style.

Granted that the finales of the first two quartets have unstringlike moments which make the fiddlers groan and curse. Theoretically they are not written very well for the vehicle. But, as in the

[4] See pp. 407 and 473.

case of the symphonies, the plus-es far outweigh the minus-es. Parts of these closing movements are superb. I mean especially the strong, trombone-like subject in the First; and in the Second, that gay filigree of a principal theme and the Schein source-motive of Ex. 48. They are highly original departures from conventional and hackneyed lines of quartet-writing, and all the more welcome for that.

Despite the shortcomings of its finale, the Second is a better quartet than the First. And the Third is a signal advance over the Second. Even Beethoven's first sheaf of half a dozen string quartets could not begin to show such a rapid advance in quality. If it had, his B Flat Quartet, Op. 18, No. 6, would have been as good as his Eleventh Quartet in F Minor, Op. 95, actually is. Too bad that Schumann could not have kept on and written sixteen!

Third Quartet, A Major

The Introduction starts with a falling fifth, and the first movement promptly follows suit. As we have long noticed Schumann's partiality for falling fifths, we feel that this may be a significant hint about what is to come. And we are not mistaken.

Somebody once attached the syllables *"Cla-ra"* to the opening measure of the *Allegro molto moderato,*

and they have clung to it ever since. Indeed, the sunny, *schwärmerisch* character of the A Major Quartet suggests that Robert was very much enamored when he wrote it.

The second subject is even lovelier than the first.

The importance of its falling fifths (marked by brackets) makes us wonder if this distant allusion to the Haydn source-motive [5] may not be a loose sort of germ-motive, meant to bind the whole composition thematically together. The idea is strengthened when, after much insistence on the two notes, accompanied by celestial harmonies, and after a brief recapitulation [6] and coda, the movement comes full circle by melting away with a delicious low falling fifth on the 'cello.

So far as I am aware, no commentator has ever called attention to one curious feature of the exciting variations that do duty for a scherzo. The theme, *Un poco Adagio,* passionately sung in turn by first violin, viola, and 'cello,

is not stated until after the appearance of the first three variations upon it—a novel application of the appoggiatura idea. Therefore this *Assai agitato* movement resembles that parlor game (also *assai agitato*) in which one player is sent from the room, the rest decide on a subject, and the banished player returns and tries to guess that subject from the guarded answers he receives about its main characteristics.[7]

The first two variations provide fair enough clues to the enigma:

<hr />

[5] See pp. 285 and 344.

[6] As Schumann has used only the first subject in the development, he gives us no more than a dainty whiff of it at the beginning and end of the recapitulation.

[7] Beethoven faintly suggested this innovation by starting the variations of the *Eroica* with the bass of the theme. D'Indy uses a method similar to Schumann's in his *Istar Variations,* and Sibelius, in his symphonies.

But the third variation, a tempestuous fugato, that starts with an ascending fifth and descends in a variant of the Climb source-motive,

Listesso tempo

[Ex. 223]

strays so far from the subject as to be scarcely "playing the game."

Then, after the beauties of Ex. 221 have been discovered (or disclosed) and exploited, there ensues a veritable orgy of high jinks:

Tempo risoluto

[Ex. 224]

The coda brings back the spirit of passionate beauty, as a legacy of the theme. Roll back and forth on your tongue, reader, and exquisitely savor the wonderful and characteristically Schumannian modulation from E Flat Major to F Sharp Major:

[Ex. 225]

And now one of the most original movements in the whole of quartet literature closes with soft after-echoes of the orgy (Ex. 224) pulsing deep in the 'cello. Note that the falling fifth ends the bass of most of the sections, up to the orgy, which features fifths, both rising and falling.

In the slow movement there is much insistence upon the rising fourth, which is the inversion of the falling fifth. But then, in the finale, Schumann surprisingly abandons this quasi germ-motive.

It is as though it had suddenly struck him that, in the previous quartet, he might have worked the device too hard and, for fear of monotony, decided to carry it no further here.

The nobly soaring *Adagio molto* is Romanticism at its most moving and impressive.

[Ex. 226]

It is especially so when, after the pathetic remonstrance of the viola, and the broken utterance of the second subject, the principal theme comes back towards the end, supported by 'cello pizzicati as mellow as cathedral chimes.

The finale is a tremendous, scintillating rondo, designed for that Utopian combination, four really musical virtuosi. Its main theme, which begins

[Ex. 227]

appears seven times, a stupendous total. Fascinating though this theme is, when taken together with the similar movement of the elaborate coda it all adds up to a saturnalia of dotted rhythm that must have immensely pleased the dot-minded Schumann. But as for us, we sometimes feel that there may be a few dots too many. However, this is looking the gift-gallop of Pegasus in the hoof.

The second theme,

[Ex. 228]

is a characteristic Schumannism that had already been used in his third *Novellette*. The third theme has a family relationship to the second.

[Ex. 229]

And in the fourth theme

[Ex. 230]

Schumann showed that he could Schumannize Bach just as easily as he could do it to Marschner, Haydn, Beethoven, or— von Fricken; [8] for this theme is won from the E Major Gavotte of Johann Sebastian's Sixth *French Suite*.

All these melodies are strong, incisive, colorful affairs. And when the second coming of Ex. 230 sweeps with masterful triumph into the exciting coda, and the good companions lash their foaming steeds half a league onward to infinity—one may well understand why a prudent fiddler might refuse to put such a Florestanic page last on the program, for fear of a white night.[8a]

How indulgently time has treated these quartets! How superbly they have worn! Though the famous Quintet, if heard at discreetly spaced intervals, is highly impressive, the significant fact remains that one can hear and play all the numbers of Opus 41 more often without satiety. And that is a convincing test.

A third of a century ago, Dr. Daniel Gregory Mason criticized these string quartets with great severity,[9] going so far as to call them "patchy or dry." It is good to find that, since then, he has had not only a change of mind, but also the candor to admit it.

[8] Ernestine's adoptive father, from whom he took the theme of the *Symphonic Etudes*.

[8a] This coda exerted an obvious influence upon the corresponding portion of the finale of Tchaikovsky's Fifth Symphony.

[9] In *The Romantic Composers*, p. 141.

Recently he wrote [10] that, in comparison with the Quintet and the Piano Quartet,

the string quartets are the profounder works, containing some of their composer's greatest music . . . This is as we should expect; for Beethoven had shown that the quartet is the fit medium for deep spiritual expression, and Schumann's exuberant nature had been deeply spiritualized by the sufferings and difficulties of his middle years; Florestan had become a little chastened, but Eusebius was finer and sweeter than ever.

[10] In the *International Cyclopedia of Music and Musicians,* 1943, p. 1686.

CHAPTER 13

THE PIANO QUARTET AND QUINTET

Op. 47. Quartet for Piano, Violin, Viola and 'Cello. E Flat

HERE we have an excellent chamber music style. On the whole, it is idiomatic, with doubling at a minimum, and with the piano part written more discreetly than in the Trios. In common with the more popular Quintet, the Piano Quartet has the key of E Flat, and the same jubilant, triumphant spirit. Florestan is caracoling through gala days upon his high horse.

Both compositions give the impression of welling up out of an inexhaustible reservoir of spontaneous inspiration. Masterly thematic work welds each into unity; and the contrapuntal imitations appear to spring up as naturally as anemones in April; while the contrasts of atmosphere are as varied and dramatic as Nature's own.

Like Beethoven's great String Quartet in E Flat, Opus 127, Schumann's Piano Quartet opens with a slow and solemn Introduction that hints at what is immediately to follow.[1] And both lead to glad *allegros* of much the same emotional tone, except that Schumann's, which starts:

[1] The four notes which start Schumann's first movement (Ex. 231) are, incidentally, the same as those out of which Beethoven constructed the Scherzo of the Quartet in B Flat, Op. 130.

From the autograph score of the Trio in D Minor, Opus 63,
for Piano, Violin, and 'Cello

[Ex. 231]

is, on the whole, the more exciting.

There is a change of mood when the closing portion of the first subject,

[Ex. 232]

which is derived from its opening portion (Ex. 231), launches into a passionate 'cello solo. In this lovely theme there is for me something staunch, faithful, true, and intimately Schumannian.[2]

But, in the second subject, the excitement grows:

[Ex. 233]

Note the Haydn source-motive under the bracket.

It was characteristic of Schumann's form to restrict the modulatory development to one subject, here, the first; and to produce, in the coda, a brand-new theme as fine as any that preceded it:

[Ex. 234]

[2] A study of its rhythmic variety is suggested for those who follow Sir Henry Hadow in deploring the alleged symmetrical monotony of Schumann's metrical designs. See p. 488 ff.

And he gives it to the 'cello's best register, as if to atone in advance for the ineffective start of the imminent Scherzo. The delightful movement ends with all the neat, epigrammatic force of the corresponding portion of the *Choral* Symphony.

The Scherzo begins with a rapid staccato figure, the 'cello's weakest register doubling the piano,

[Ex. 235]

and ineffectually striving to make headway.[3] However, as in the symphonies, Schumann's ignorance of the finer points of instrumentation cannot take overmuch from the interest and inspiration of what he has to say.

The contrapuntal imitations of Trio I are capital. In its simplicity, Trio II reminds one of the aeolian harps of the *Spring* Symphony's Trio I. And its alternation of high and low chords takes us back to that part of the *Faschingsschwank* which was inspired by Beethoven's E Flat Sonata, Op. 31, No. 3.[4] As a striking novelty of form, the second part of this Trio II elaborately develops the *Carnaval* source-motive part of the main Scherzo.

The *Andante cantabile* is like the first movement in featuring the 'cello. And this reminds us that the Piano Quartet was dedicated to one of the most eminent amateur 'cellists of the day, Count Matvei Wielhorsky. Alas! the long solo which opens the movement, too saccharine in feeling and too mechanical in construction, is the weakest part of the work.

But the following portion in A flat more than atones for the temporary lapse. It fulfills the brief promise of solemn joy that gleamed for a moment from the Introduction. This is one of my favorite passages, not alone in Schumann, but in all chamber music. Its glowing intimacy, its deep, happy peace, at once

---

[3] The *Carnaval* source-motive is marked by a bracket.
[4] See p. 345, Ex. 92.

soothes and uplifts. It is a useful strain to memorize, for it can console one in misery and reach a helping hand over many a difficult stile. This should be on everybody's mental shelf of first-aid remedies. A few bars of the piano part will give the gist of the inestimable page:

[Ex. 236]

Both following Ex. 236, and after the *A tempo*, many of the composer's beloved descending fifths (including the Haydn source-motive) ratify the proceedings. At *Tempo I*, the violin whispers an anticipation of the finale.

The end of the slow movement adds one more to the many examples of Schumann's instrumental innocence. He wanted to close with a 13-bar organ-point on B flat. So his eager, original mind had the 'cellist tune his C string down a tone, and support his colleagues with a B flat in octaves. On paper, this looks like a brilliant solution. But in reality, when the 'cellist relaxes his lowest string to the required depth, gets down to brass B flats, and begins to repeat his solo, he finds that the retuning has upset the quality of the whole 'cello. And when he comes to the organ-point, his lowest string refuses to stay at B flat, and he has to twist it down again, while the performance suffers—a fine example of the unfortunately frequent discrepancy between theory and practice.

The mettlesome finale opens with a jolly fugato on a real fugue theme—a variant of the Climb source-motive,

[Ex. 237]

and a handsome cantilena for the strings.

Then memory takes a hand. At letter B comes an allusion to letter B of the slow movement. With the change of key to four flats, the strings put in a reminder of Trio I (inverted on the following page), while the piano harks back to the first contrasting theme of the Fifth *Novellette*. All the motives of this finale are engaging and are worked out with unusual subtlety. After the exciting close, one is tempted to throw things aloft and shout "hurrah!"

In its own generation, despite the somewhat lush principal theme of the *Andante cantabile*, Opus 47 was the best piano quartet which had appeared since Mozart's two. And ever since that day, except for Brahms' three, it has remained the best.

Op. 44. Quintet for Piano, Two Violins, Viola, and 'Cello. E Flat.

Opus 44 occupies an even more distinguished position in chamber music than Opus 47, for it was the first great piano quintet to be written. And it has been equaled by only two others: the Brahms and the Franck.

Dr. Annie Patterson, who has already been quoted on the First Symphony, writes of this work for strings and "that wonderful domestic instrument," the piano, that Wasielewski

considers it a true picture of a wanderer or mountaineer climbing ever higher till the glorious prospect of a fair landscape bursts upon one's view from the highest summit.

Hence these critics might well have applied to Opus 44 the term which Longfellow, in an off moment, pinned upon his well known poem, *Excelsior*. The *"Excelsior"* Quintet! Could the bathos of programmatists-at-any-price sink to more absurd depths? [5]

There is an even more sparkling abundance of vitality and spontaneous inspiration in the Quintet than in the Piano Quartet; and not a single weak spot.

The *Allegro brillante* sets forth like the Olympians launching a carnival. In this famous opening, Schumann's indebtedness to Mozart seems to have escaped notice. The Quintet begins:

[5] The suggestion recalls another ingenious proposal in connection with the same poem. It was made by A. E. Housman, author of *A Shropshire Lad*. He felt that the cause of Anglo-Saxon, hands-across-the-sea solidarity might be furthered if British and American poets would only join in collaboration. He, for one, was ready to do so; but the only American poet he knew of was Henry Wadsworth Longfellow, who was no longer on hand. And the only creation of this bard with which he was acquainted was *Excelsior*. All this, however, would not deter him. By knocking out alternate lines of Longfellow and substituting his own make, a very fine international collaboration would result. So Housman furthered Anglo-Saxon unity as follows:

> The shades of night were falling fast;
> The rain was falling faster;
> When through an Alpine village passed
> An Alpine village pastor.

And the composite poem went on to chronicle the lamentable adventures of the wretched pastor in the deluge, as he toiled ever onward and upward to the heights. If Dr. Patterson had but known of this gem of song, she might perhaps have associated the somber slow movement of the Quintet with the feelings of the pastor when, footsore, weary, and fully saturated, he arrived at the summit, only to be confronted by the slippery descent. She might have identified this descent with the notorious *L'istesso tempo* of the Scherzo, down which so many hapless 'cellists have slithered to their doom.

Immediately after bringing up her striking poetic analogy, Dr. Patterson recommends "as being well worth a careful analysis . . . the best known of the string quartets, Op. 47." She should have added that this work is to be found only in the land of Shangri-La; for Op. 47 is the Quartet for Piano and Strings.

And Mozart's Piano Quartet, in the same key of E Flat, starts

with the same pedal point on E flat, and virtually the same harmony. Yet Schumann deftly makes this quotation his own.

As the movement goes on, see how even the little parenthetical ejaculations of the strings assume significance. The resolute fire of Ex. 238 brings out the delectable wistfulness of the second part of the first subject. And both parts provide a perfect approach to the second subject, one of the tunes most characteristic of Schumann, sung antiphonally by 'cello and viola: [6]

[Ex. 240]

[6] The two examples quoted here from the first movement are so Schumannian that they will be further studied in Chap. XIV.

The development belongs exclusively to Ex. 238. Through almost the whole length of it runs a figure taken from its own third and fourth bars, but with the tempo doubled. This favorite maneuver is again carried out at the first change of key in the finale, with that movement's first subject. Schumann sometimes used such a speeded-up figure for its own sake, and at other times as accompaniment for its own slower version. And he handed the idea down to Brahms.

The recapitulation maintains the balance of excitement and of luscious cantabile; and the coda intensifies the initial atmosphere of jubilation.

The slow movement, *In modo d'una Marcia,* mingles so much exalted beauty with its sorrow that it manages to be at the same time somber, comforting, and reassuring. We feel that if those glorious, dusky strains of the first theme are really true—and Schumann convinces us that they are—then there can be no adequate ground for despair.

In modo d'una Marcia
un poco largamente
molto piano ma marcato

[Ex. 241]

And the C major song that follows foretastes the bliss of a better world.

This beatitude, however, is roughly broken into by the agonized staccato triplets of the *Agitato,* which to our amazement turns out to be none other than Ex. 241 in a whirlwind of despair. But this temporary irruption of human frailty only makes the return of the first part the more impressive and satisfying.[6a]

The Scherzo, with its constant runs up and down, begins by reminding us melodically of the first number of the *Papillons.*[7] The effect achieved by little more than ascending and descend-

---

[6a] This slow movement, which is sometimes called the "Funeral March," influenced the *Dumka* of Dvořák's Piano Quintet.

[7] See p. 280, Ex. 2.

ing scales on all the instruments is astonishing. I wonder if Schumann was inspired by the humorous Trio of the Minuet of Haydn's String Quartet in the same key, Op. 76, No. 6, where the elder genius does equally expert conjuring with the same unpromising material.

Trio I is almost wholly made up of our old friend, the Haydn source-motive,[8]

TRIO

[Ex. 242]

which we have surmised to have some special significance for Robert in connection with Clara. This surmise is strengthened by the facts that the Quintet is dedicated to her; that her half-brother, Woldemar Bargiel, began his First Trio with the same motive; and that, in Brahms' F Sharp Minor Sonata, Opus 2, which he dedicated to Clara, the Haydn serves as the principal theme of the finale.

On December 6th, 1842, Clara was ill and unable to assist in the first private performance of the Quintet. Mendelssohn, who read the piano part famously, very properly objected that Trio II was not lively enough, and persuaded Robert to write the present one, thus incurring the maledictions of many generations of 'cellists. For that notorious *L'istesso tempo,* which is pure piano music for strings, and consists mainly of an awkward variant of the Climb source-motive, offers the 'cellist one of the most difficult passages in all chamber music.

The rousing finale opens with a theme perfectly adapted to its function:

Allegro, ma non troppo

[Ex. 243]

sempre marcato

[8] See pp. 285 and 344.

It is as convincing a start for a last movement as Ex. 238 is for a first.[9]

The first part of the second subject

[Ex. 244]

reminds us again of Schumann's much-quoted song, *Dein Bildniss wunderselig*.[10] And then we find it cleverly turned into an accompaniment for the main part of the second subject:

[Ex. 245]

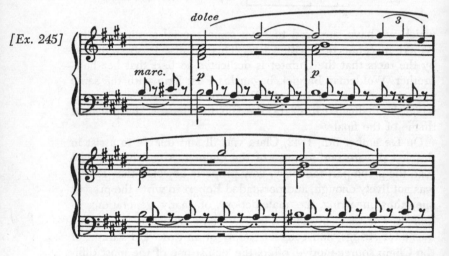

This is excellent counterpoint; but the supreme contrapuntal tour de force in Schumann's music comes near the triumphant culmination of the movement. There the principal theme (Ex. 243) is most convincingly and gloriously combined with the crashing melody that opens the Quintet (Ex. 238). Thus the serpent of music bites its own tail, a fitting symbol of the immortality which is assured for this mighty work.

[9] Note the Haydn source-motive under the bracket. Here it is diluted by a passing note (in parentheses).
[10] See p. 445.

CHAPTER 14

WHAT MAKES SCHUMANN'S MUSIC SCHUMANNIAN?

BEFORE considering the qualities which made Schumann's music distinctively his own, let us look at some general characteristics of the man himself.

From the outset he was highly original. Hans Pfitzner was right:

> Not Beethoven and not Mozart and not Wagner nor any other composer started his creative work with such originality, such self-contained perfection, as Robert Schumann.

Even when he appropriated tunes from Haydn, Beethoven, Marschner, and others, he put them so thoroughly through his own mill that they emerged good Schumann. But he borrowed and imitated less than almost any other music maker. Mendelssohn was the only contemporary composer who left any considerable trace on Schumann's work. Despite this, in his melody, harmony, counterpoint, form, and above all in his rhythm, he was very much himself, and exerted a powerful influence upon the development of the art.

Jean Paul counted for less in his music than Schumann himself imagined. Where in it can we find the sentimentality and the long-winded discursiveness that now make that undeniably gifted author so hard to read? Even the musician's letters and critical writings are like nobody else's; and his literary side, with its gift of the humorous, the epigrammatic, and the allusive, and its leaning toward symbolism and mystery left its mark upon his compositions. Taking little, he gave much.

That this was not for lack of light-fingered ability is shown in *Carnaval* by his masterly imitations of Chopin and Paganini. And other composers were not the only ones whom he could hit off. Remember the gay crowd, each individual neatly characterized, in *Carnaval, Papillons,* and the *Davidsbündler Dances;* to say nothing of the stuffed shirt in the Scherzo of the F Sharp Minor Sonata.

This musico-literary gift, however, was one of Schumann's least important. Not the aptness of the music to the title which he thought up later delights us most, but the music in and for itself.

He was the most admirable of all the Romantics. Romanticism forms one side of the infinite spiral of the arts. Its fresh, personal originality revivifies the old, architecturally-minded Classicism, after the latter has at length degenerated into mere arid formalism. Then, when the final, fantastic orgy of extravagance in which every Romantic impulse ends has provoked the inevitable revulsion, the dying movement enriches the new Classicism with the treasure-trove of its novel discoveries.

This contrast between the opposite sides of the spiral looks somewhat as follows:

CLASSICISM		ROMANTICISM
Form	vs.	Content
Necessity		Free-will
Authority		Individualism

But the notion of either pure Classicism or pure Romanticism is abhorrent. The former is Fascism; the latter, raving Anarchy. The ideal—though almost unattainable—is a balance of both in perfect equipoise.[1]

---

[1] Egon Kenton's thoughts on reading this part of my ms. are to appear in his forthcoming book on chamber music:

"This is one of mankind's dream goals which, I think, can be merely approached but never realized. To me the Romantics are the pioneers, who open up new territories by pushing the frontiers further. The Classicists are the homesteaders, who create order and form, and incorporate the newly acquired territory into civilized life.

"It is only natural that man, and immeasurably more so the artist, strives to achieve something beautiful, something great. The next man wants to go

One reason why we love Schumann so truly is that his Romanticism was leavened by much well-restrained Classicist wisdom. For example, he knew enough to steer clear of the chief vice of Romanticism: too much dependence upon the art of poetry. Unlike most of his contemporaries, he despised the infantilism of program-music.

It is amazing to find works at once so virile and rich in passion as Schumann's, and so singularly chaste. As has been suggested, this may be because the maternal Clara satisfied the demands of his mother-fixation.[1a] But it is also astonishing to find in this ultra-masculine man an actual streak of primness, as evidenced by the story of Dr. Schad.

It was probably in the early months of 1850 that Schumann set for soprano, alto, and piano a lyric by Dr. Christian Schad, *Sommerruh, wie schön bist du!* [2] and wrote the poet:

First of all, an apology for changing the text of the enclosed song. The beginning quite gave me the atmosphere of a moonlit summer night. Then the poem takes a somewhat sensual turn; and that may

one better, and expands the Classical form of his predecessor. Sometimes the genius, believing that he has exhausted the possibilities of his Classical form, himself does the expanding, as Michelangelo or Beethoven did, and paves the way for Romanticism. The Romantics do the same. The Romantic style's essence being that it gives free rein to individual expression, they carry this liberation of form and expression to a *non plus ultra*, to a point beyond which it is impossible to proceed. Add to this the devastating effect of the epigonoi, the horde of minor composers who imitate the turn of melody, the harmony, and the form of any genius, and who, as André Gide says in his *Prétextes*, make a *tabula rasa* for the next style, which will be Classical again."

[1a] See p. 157. In his comments on the ms. of this book, Egon Kenton writes:

"I am not partial to reducing everything in life to Freudian terms; but Schumann's mother-fixation explains the adolescent quality of his ardor, which is constantly fired by love, without ever becoming sensual. (This explains as well the story of Dr. Schad, and his changing of the text.) The phenomenon is unique in musical genius. It makes Schumann's music so lovable. Lovable for youngsters and adolescents, who find themselves mirrored in it. Lovable for us oldsters, for it brings back to us those years when we were full of enthusiasm, rapture, passion and guileless love. And this is why I had to think of Schumann when I first saw the Raphael frescoes in the Villa Farnesina."

[2] Not in the *Thematic Catalogue,* but published, 1850, in Schad's *Deutsche Musenalmanach.*

be permitted in a poem. In music it is otherwise—here it is repugnant, especially sung by a woman. So I have, *as a mere proposal*, put in a couple of other lines, in place of which you may put still others, if only the initial atmosphere of the poem is preserved.

And what was this "somewhat sensual turn"?—

> *Leise Wellen kräuselnd blinken,*
> *Wie wenn weisse Schultern winken,*
> *Mondverklärte Liebesruh.*

> (Wavelets gently rippling shimmer,
> As white shoulders, beckoning, glimmer
> On moon-transfigured lovers' peace.)

Instead, Schumann substituted the following:

> *Welch ein Leben, himmlisch Weben!*
> *Engel durch die Lüfte schweben*
> *Ihrer blauen Heimath zu.*

The translation must be free:

> Life recurring, heavenly stirring,
> Angels through the ether whirring
> To their azure fatherland.

In thus proposing angels in place of white shoulders, Schumann gave a remarkable exhibition of Comstockery, besides treating the poetry with his customary lack of consideration.

When we consider the chastity of what William J. Henderson called his "intense, concentrated emotional force," we sometimes find its tremendously arousing quality mysterious. For example, there are no Tristanic ardors in the string quartets. And yet they are wildly exciting.

What is there about a characteristic page of the Master's work that makes us exclaim: "Schumann!"?

There is the cut of his melody, by which we can distinguish him very much as we can look at an Englishman's jacket and diagnose: "Savile Row." Take, for example, the second subject of the opening movement of the Quintet:

Here, in measures 1, 5, 9, and 16-17, we have a delayed variant of the Haydn source-motive of falling fifths.[3] Measures 3-4 show his way of inverting motives; for they are nothing but measures 1 2 stood upon their adorable heads. This example well illustrates the composer's habit of using the same interval often in a melody, alternating positive and contrary motion.[4]

The seven dotted phrases hint at Schumann's fondness for dotted tunes which, as we have seen, all too often run riot. Here we find bars 1-2 recurring twice, each time a step higher, illustrating his partiality for sequences.

In the first five pairs of measures, note how the same rhythmical pattern,

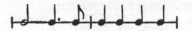

occurs five times, though—strangely enough—without monotony. Instead, Schumann gets a rare refrain-value out of this risky procedure. In like manner a poet can escape monotony and win refrain-value out of lines which he repeats in a triolet or rondeau.

Characteristic of Schumann's rare depressive melodies is the broken utterance of *Ich grolle nicht*:

[3] See pp. 285, 344, and 473. The multitude of Haydn source-motives in Schumann's pages is too great to enumerate here.

[4] The slow movement of the Piano Quartet offers another example of this device. Elgar uses it better in the theme of the *Enigma Variations*.

[Ex. 127]

And akin to it in spirit is the great tune which opens the slow movement of the D Minor Trio:

[Ex. 195]

Note the highly Schumannian Bracketing source-motive (marked by a bracket).[5] Along with the gasping pauses, and the peculiarly individual syncopations that retard and trouble the flow of melody, like boulders half blocking a narrow stream, this painfully labored Bracketing way of attaining the goal of the

[5] See p. 307, N.

desired note sets upon this movement the sign of the despairing Eusebius. *Thema,* which is No. 34 in the *Album for the Young,*

[Ex. 246]

is so full of both varieties of this source-motive that brackets are not needed. I know of no other composer who used it so freely as Schumann.

At the start of the Fifth *Novellette,* however, the motive that was despairing in the last example actually sounds merry (at letter a):

[Ex. 81]

As already pointed out,[6] the example is especially interesting because it gives, in compact compass, three of Schumann's most individual idioms of melodic speech.

All of this composer's source-motives except the Haydn seem to have escaped the notice of the commentators. A backward glance at them will give us a bird's-eye view of his most characteristic turns of melody. The reader should bear firmly in mind that all source-motives are necessarily simple enough to belong among those commonplaces of music which are more or less employed by all composers; but that only frequent use as thematic material, and a highly individual treatment, can justify calling any phrase the source-motive of a particular composer.

In Ex. 81 (b) marks the Haydn source-motive,[7] the most striking use of which we found in the *Impromptus* and the Quintet. And (c) shows one of the many variants of the downhill Climb source-motive.[8] Other variants of this will be met

[6] See p. 337.
[7] See p. 479, N. 3.
[8] See p. 361, N.

in the bumpy, spine-jarring descent that opens the Piano Concerto, where the soloist stumbles at every step over appoggiaturas; in the main theme of the Piano Quartet finale, and the gradual descent of triplets in the last movement of the G Minor Trio. There are also the highly personal climbing methods of *Fabel*:

 [Ex. 247]

which seem like the eccentric hoppings-down of some pert little winged creature. In *Vision*, the fourteenth *Albumblatt*, an amusingly awkward, and apparently involuntary, descent is made in triplets. These must be attempting to scramble up a very deliberate avalanche or a descending escalator; for, with one exception, each ascending triplet begins lower than the preceding.

Sehr rasch

 [Ex. 248]

The uphill Climb figures, as well, often seem to be in similar difficulties; perhaps struggling up a steep sand slide where one slips back so and so much for every foot of elevation won. This sort of thing goes on in the second of the *Waldscenen*, and in the Scherzo of the *Four Piano Pieces*, Op. 32, which limps upwards in the favorite dotted rhythm. A good deal of the *Toccata* consists of up-and-down Climb, complicated and slowed up by a heavy burden of difficult technic.

The form of this source-motive suitable for very steep terrain, where one foot takes a good step and drags the other halfway up after it, persists like a veritable obsession through the finale of the A Minor Quartet:

 [Ex. 211]

It has much to say in the *"Rhenish"* Symphony and in the finale of the A Minor Violin Sonata.

We have seen how Schumann made especially characteristic use of the five descending steps of the Clara source-motive [9] in the three Piano Sonatas, the *Fantasie,* and his other works *passim.*

And we are aware of how peculiarly he made his own that legacy of the musical ages, the Schein source-motive.[9a]

[Ex. 47]

The *Carnaval* source-motive [10] is somewhat less simple than most of the others. It keeps popping up in the most unexpected places, and usually with a strong tang of its maker,[11] as in *Ende vom Lied:*

Etwas lebhafter

[Ex. 61]

---

[9] See p. 297.

[9a] See especially, pp. 313-14.

[10] See p. 295.

[11] Usually in abbreviated form, it is to be found in the 4th *Intermezzo,* Op. 4 (bass of the *Alternativo*); twice (diminished and inverted, bars 19-20) in the bass of *Warum?;* in notes 4-8 of the second *Kreisleriana;* inverted and reversed, in the *Etwas langsamer* of the 7th *Novellette,* bars 4-6; and inverted at the wind-up of the Quintet's *Allegro brillante.* In the minor, it starts the Scherzo of the Piano Quartet, and is the most important phrase in the movement. It steals into the accompaniment of *The Two Grenadiers,* after the words about "the trample of whinnying horses." We find it in the finale of the Piano Concerto; at the start of *Nachklänge aus dem Theater,* Op. 68, No. 25; in the second of the *Four Fugues,* Op. 72; in the second of the *Waldscenen* (bar 2); reversed at the start of the Scherzo of the *"Rhenish"* Symphony; at *Lebhafter* (bars 4-5) of *Bunte Blätter* No. 13; at bar 3 of *Lebhaft* in *Manfred,* No. 4; and finally, in the minor, at bars 5-6 of the Scherzo of the D Minor Symphony.

Another rather peculiarly Schumannian effect is the Swirling source-motive in Variation Seven (Etude Eight) of the *Symphonic Etudes*.

[Ex. 63]

A fine example of it comes on the last page of the *Humoreske*, Op. 20.[12]

Schumann has stamped his trade-mark upon the sort of filigree tune that starts the finales of the First Symphony

Allegro animato

[Ex. 141]

and of the F Major Quartet (see p. 456, Ex. 218), and which appears in the middle section of *Abschied,* the ninth of the

[12] See p. 324. There is a little of this in Op. 6, No. 12; more in *Vogel als Prophet;* at *In tempo* in the sixth *Kreisleriana;* and at bar 10 of the Introduction to the *Concert Allegro,* Op. 134.

Waldscenen, and in the dainty violin postlude to the wedding
chorus which is No. 22 in *The Pilgrimage of the Rose.* These are
so truly decorative that they remind us of the filigree fiddle
obligatos in the inside movements of the D Minor Symphony.
This sort of tune, as used by Schumann, shocked the pedants of
his time. But we moderns credit him with striking a new and
highly original note. Perhaps his expertness as a writer of song
accompaniments led him to its discovery.

He also coined the sort of march that has Schumann written
all over it, like the rousing one that begins the *Novelletten:*

[Ex. 76]

Other characteristic marches are: the stirring middle movement
of the *Fantasie,* the finale of the *Fantasiestücke,* Op. 88, the
charming little *Soldiers' March* which comes second in the
Album; and not least, that highly original one in ¾ time which
winds up *Carnaval:*

[Ex. 249]

The characteristic pucker of Schumann's lips in the later portraits may well have come because his themes are so eminently
whistle-able that he was always whistling the new melodies as
they came crowding in upon him. It would be hard to imagine

such later composers as Hindemith or Varese, Berg or Webern developing a similar pucker.[13]

In the early days, Schumann was led by the pressure of his teeming invention, and by his ignorance of the science underlying his art, to pour out a spate of melodies with the artlessness of a bird, and not trouble his head about what to do with them. Then, as little by little he acquired knowledge and learned the importance of organic unity, his themes grew away from the miniature toward the monumental, developed longer breath, and became more and more adapted for thematic development. Compare the theme of Op. 1 (p. 278, Ex. 1) with the principal themes of the outer movements of the Quintet, Op. 44 (pp. 470, Ex. 238, and 473, Ex. 243), which are so splendidly worked out and then combined.

Sometimes, however, toward the end of his life, under the pressure of illness, instead of mastering his material he let it master him. Like the luckless sorcerer's apprentice, he evoked a powerful spirit, only to have it get out of hand. Such painful moments occur in the first movement of the C Major Symphony, in the finale of the 'Cello Concerto, and in the *Lebhaft* of the young folks' Sonata, Op. 118, No. 2.

Schumann's melody often has a uniquely tender and intimate quality for which the Germans have the expressive word, *innig*. Think of the slow movements of the F Sharp Minor and the G Minor Sonatas, the opening one of the *Fantasie*, the variations of the F Major Quartet, *Träumerei* and *Der Dichter spricht*, the second *Romance*, Op. 28, that other *Romance* which begins the *Fantasiestücke* for Trio, the *Little Romance* in the *Album*, *Ende vom Lied*, and such songs as *Dein Bildniss wunderselig*, *Im wunderschönen Monat Mai*, and *Wenn ich in deine Augen seh*.

A good deal of nonsense has been written about the so-called "miniature" quality of Schumann's melodies. M. Basch stresses the notion that the chief difference between his music and that of the Classicist period before him was this: the Classicists had large, general ideas which they expressed in music; but Schumann had only small and very particularized ones.

---

[13] Though I am told that Schönberg has one. Perhaps this was developed back in the *Verklärte Nacht* period.

This is not true. There were large, universal ideas back of the sonatas, the *Fantasie,* the chamber music, and most of the symphonies. But even if it *were* true, the art of music is much too powerful and spacious a thing to allow itself to be thus strait-jacketed. Fortunately the concrete image that a composer has in his mind possesses no power to brand upon his music an indelible caption which others must accept. The melody that he perhaps formed on a radiant morning while he was whipping a trout-stream may convey to the first listener who hears it "the shadow of a mighty rock within a weary land"; to the second, roast duck with champagne; and to the third, the major love of his life.

In the field of rhythm, Schumann was at his most individual, masterly, and original. First let us look at a very serious charge which, half a century ago, Sir Henry Hadow brought against him, and which, uncritically passed down the years, has done him a great deal of undeserved harm.

Sir Henry contrasted the start of Beethoven's A Major 'Cello Sonata

[Ex. 250]

with the start of Schumann's Quintet:

[Ex. 251]
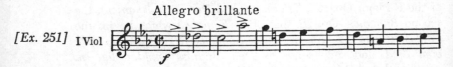

He pointed out that in the former

no two bars present the same figure, yet the whole is a unity; [but that] in the latter a set of parallel clauses are balanced antithetically: the same rhythmic figure is preserved in all. . . . The former [which Sir Henry calls "the Continuous"] is the typical method of Beethoven; the latter [which he calls "the Discrete"], that of Schumann. . . . Of course Beethoven employed both methods . . . but it is incontestable that in the power of varying and developing his figures is to be found one of his greatest claims to supremacy as an artist. This power Schumann seldom or never brought into active operation. . . . There are very few of Beethoven's instrumental melodies to which it would be possible to adapt metrical words; there is scarcely one of Schumann's which could not be so treated.

When I read this charge, I became like Doubting Thomas, or the man from Missouri: I wanted to be shown. In default of an an exhibitor, I devoted some weeks to going through a great part of Schumann's compositions, to see whether or not he could get away from symmetry, and could rhythmically vary his tunes as Beethoven had in the Third 'Cello Sonata.

And here is what I found. The rhythm in Schumann's first fourteen opuses is nearly all of the "Discrete" type. But with the *Scenes from Childhood,* Op. 15, comes a sudden change. And from there on to the end, almost half of his thematic material is of the "Continuous" rhythmic type. It is worthy of note that the best songs of the three great cycles, *Myrthen, Frauenliebe,* and *Dichterliebe,* are all "Continuous." Through most of *Peri,* the composer evidently made a valiant and successful effort to overcome the besetting rhythmical symmetry of his youth; but after the twentieth number, he grew weary and relaxed his vigilance. Of the forty-four pieces in the *Album,* more than two-thirds are "Discrete." But that is easily explained on the ground that symmetry is a natural and effective means of simplifying music for a child's understanding.

With growing maturity, Schumann became more and more clever at achieving a satisfying asymmetry; and the subtleties of this in the *Stücke im Volkston,* for 'Cello and Piano, Op. 102, are masterly. In Nos. 1 and 3, with delightful originality he enhances the asymmetry by starting the same phrase successively on different parts of the measure.[14] Here is the start of No. 1—

Mit Humor

[Ex. 252]

[14] This maneuver was inherited by Brahms, as witness, for example, the first movement of the D Major Symphony.

In No. 2 he complicates matters further by alternating periods three and four bars long, usually arranging them: 3, 4, 4, 3. No. 5 even goes so far as to scramble together periods 5, 6, and 4 measures long. The irregular periods of *Grillen* were noticed on page 320.

On occasion Schumann could invent tunes as rhythmically diverse as any of Beethoven's. For instance, the second part of the first subject of the Piano Quartet's opening movement starts by admirably varying its unsymmetrical rhythm from bar to bar:

[Ex. 232]

So does *Er, der Herrlichste:*

[Ex. 253]

If, before hurling his monstrous accusation, Sir Henry had only taken the trouble to look up the facts, succeeding generations of equally careless critics would not have mechanically inherited the false notion, and done their bit in prolonging a gross injustice.

Even, however, when Schumann is what Sir Henry calls "Discrete," he often gives us a mysterious and special sort of pleasure. The start of the Quintet, with a rhythm symmetrical as the build of a four-winged dragonfly, but with intervals richly varied, develops magical refrain-values. And sometimes, as in the slow movement of the Piano Quartet, he seems deliberately to rub in the symmetry for the pleasure of the relief when, after the third time of asking, the tune suddenly tails off into an agreeably contrasting motion.

Schumann's rhythm is always original, vigorous, and vital. The abundant variety and verve of his galloping dotted figures

(when not overdone) lend the music zest, excitement, and youth.
He revels in such elastic drum figures as

and

But he can be just as young and electric without the dots, as in
his favorite

[music notation], [music notation]

or

[music notation]

And he loves to repeat these in the rising sequences which are
one of the chief characteristics of the Romantic movement. With
his mastery of rhythm, Schumann leads all the Romantics in
freshness, youthful initiative, and tempestuous dash.

His love of mischief was transmuted into all manner of delightful rhythmical tricks, to try the interpreter, mystify the
hearer, and lend the music additional wearing quality. We have
seen how, in the finale of the F Sharp Minor Sonata, he makes
¾ time sound with ²⁄₄, subtly and excitingly playing off the
metrical stress against the natural motive stress: [15]

[Ex. 36]

---

[15] See p. 305.

And we have seen him in *Des Abends* pitting ⅔ against ⅜; [16] and in the finale of the Piano Concerto, making ¾ sound like 3⁄2, to the confusion of the lesser conductors.[17] These are only a few of his tricks. He bequeathed them to Brahms who, in the slow movement of the B Flat Concerto, made 6⁄4 suggest 3⁄2. These examples show Schumann the polyrhythmist as the equal of Schuman the polyphonist.

His mastery of syncopation, his varied resourcefulness in achieving elasticity by holding over from the weak to the strong parts of the measure, mark him as a specialist in the many ways of skinning the cat of accentuation.

A word of caution about Schumann's tempos. After his death, his metronome was found to be badly out of kilter. It ran too fast, so that his numerical tempo indications are nearly always too slow. One of his editors, Dr. Hans Bischoff, has corrected the original tempo designation of 73 for a quarter note in the opening number of *Gesänge der Frühe*, to 96. And where the composer gave 72 for an eighth note in No. 4, Bischoff amended it to 132, or almost twice as fast. Could the defective metronome have led him to make that famous howler in the G Minor Sonata: "As fast as possible," then, "Still faster"?

As a harmonist, Schumann is just as guileful a tease as in his rhythmical alarums and excursions—just as shifty a springer of pleasant disappointments, just as crafty a misleader of the trusting conventional ear. To his taste, there was not enough rich mystery in the chord progressions of the blameless Dittersdorf

[16] See p. 318.
[17] See p. 428.

or of the predictable Haydn. He loved unforeseen about-faces and delectable surprises.

What a jolt the innocent ear of his day must have received from the unprepared chord of the minor ninth that ushers in the *Genoveva Overture!*

Langsam

[Ex. 254]

Dr. Daniel Gregory Mason [18] has neatly described Schumann's Puckish harmonic side:

Strong unprepared dissonances, entrances of chords before we expect them, delays of the expected ones, entire evasions of the seemingly inevitable, and felicitous transitions into the seemingly impossible are a constant feature of his program. He loves to hit upon a note as if by accident, and then to justify and even emphasize it . . . ; to wound our ears with the harshest intervals, and then compel our acquiescence by a resulting felicity, as in the introduction to the F Sharp Minor Sonata; to toss us restlessly upon a chromatic sea and bring us out at last into diatonic tranquillity, as in the first two pages of the "Toccata." At the beginning of the "Kreisleriana" he keeps the right hand half a pace ahead of the left, thus producing great richness of tone as well as emphasizing the vigorous progression of the bass.

Schumann's talent for improvising must have enriched his harmonic sense. Sir Hubert Parry wrote that

he loved to use the pedal all that was possible, and had but little objection to hearing all the notes of the scale sounding at once. He is said to have liked dreaming to himself, by rambling through all sorts

[18] In *The Romantic Composers*, pp. 121-22.

of harmonies with the pedal down; and the glamour of crossing rhythms and the sound of clashing and antagonistic notes was most thoroughly adapted to his nature.

Thus he became the pioneer of modern dissonance. And it is interesting to find him, at twenty, putting this aphorism into the mouth of Eusebius:

> The enemies of chromaticism should realize that there was once a time when the seventh was as conspicuous as, say, a diminished octave is now; and that through the development of the harmonic sense it has become possible to depict passion with finer shadings. And this has placed music in the ranks of the highest vehicles of art which has a script and a sign for all soul-states.

He loved, as well, solid, massive, resonant chords. And the deep, rich, dusky coloring that we have remarked in connection with the First *Novellette, Grillen,* and other pieces, was an original contribution to tone-color.

Musicians have often wondered why, amid much that is superbly idiomatic in Schumann's writing for piano, there should be such a curious admixture of the awkwardly unpianistic. The pianist Ann Slade Frey has suggested to me that this admixture may have been caused by the technical handicap resulting from the accident to his finger.

This theory has now been unexpectedly confirmed. Some years ago, Mr. Morton Krouse, a Philadelphia lawyer and pianist, while playing basket-ball, broke the ring-finger of his right hand (the same that Schumann injured), and has never fully recovered its use. He writes me:

> Long before I met you, I noticed that Schumann's piano works were much easier to play with my crippled finger than those of any other composer. For example, in most parts the Schumann Piano Concerto is easier for me than many passages in Bach's *Two-Voiced Inventions,* just because the fingering seems to suit my right hand much better. Whereas *Papillons,* written before his accident, is just as difficult for me as any other composer's works of approximately the same technical caliber. Any pianist who broke his ring-finger would notice how much more easily he could play Schumann than anybody else.

It may also well be that some of the Master's melodic and harmonic—as well as technical—originality was born of his accident.

Schumann made each form that he touched his own. In sonata-form, for example, witness his treatment of the second subject. Sometimes he would entirely omit it; sometimes reduce it to a mere rudiment; sometimes build it upon the rhythm of the first subject, or use a modification of that subject as its accompaniment.

We have seen him carrying on Beethoven's innovation of producing wholly new thematic material in his developments and codas. Like that Master, he sometimes bewilders the pedants by approaching the traditional dominant key of the second subject by a detour through tonalities that are not according to the musical Hoyle. And notice his eager, impetuous, youthful way of cogging his subjects into one another without pausing for breath, as in the *Manfred Overture*.

He wrote the D Minor Symphony to be played continuously, thus establishing a precedent for the *Faust* Symphony of Liszt, the D Minor of Franck, and the Seventh of Sibelius. He welded his movements thematically together by new procedures. One of these was a continual reference back to the material of the long, eloquent introductions of the Second and Fourth Symphonies.

At a time when the Variation form of classical days had been degraded, by such luminaries as Herz and Hünten, down to the level of a mere vehicle of fireworks, Schumann, in the *Symphonic Etudes* and the *Andante and Variations,* filled it again with pure poetry.

And even more happened to the concerto at his hands. He helped to root mere exhibitionism out of it; because he realized that when the main interest of a performance is such a petty thing as mere digital dexterity, the musical center of gravity becomes the center of levity. Schumann's Piano Concerto prepared the way for Brahms to transmute the form into that nobler thing, a symphony with obligato.

Schumann is, *par excellence,* the exemplar of eternal youth, with its prevailing high spirits and its occasional quickly passing glooms. As a rule, the French fail to understand this. M. Basch cannot find in his music "de la gaieté, de la sérénité." He is very strongly of the opinion that Schumann was miserable because he was so aware that the exaltations of his manic phase would be inexorably followed by the miseries of the depressive. But the available evidence goes to show that he believed each manic state would last indefinitely. M. Camille Bellaigue actually declares: [19]

> His irritated complaint never appeased itself. He was of those who did not wish to be consoled. Almost never did he smile.

If these gentlemen were right, there would be a morbid quality in most of Schumann. But in fact, morbidity, such as in *Manfred* (where it fits the text), is very rarely found there. We hear none in the symphonies except in the slow movement of the C Major, which was written in illness. There is none in the concertos, none in the chamber music (except in the first and slow movements of the D Minor Trio, and a little in the Violin Sonatas). Even the Funeral March of the Quintet, though appropriately sad, is far from morbid. There is none of this quality in the great songs, except in *Ich grolle nicht*, where Heine had already started the ball of morbidity rolling. And there is very little in the piano music.

That cock will not fight; for Schumann, on the contrary, is the tone-poet of eternal youth, with its fresh vitality, sparkle, clear-eyed health and laughter. And even most of the "lines written in dejection" during his grievous phases, belying their sad origin, bubble over with those bright qualities. Delacroix believed that the very great men are "those who have kept, until the age when the intelligence has developed its full power, a part of that impetuosity of impression . . . which is the hall-mark of youth." If ever a composer did that, it was Schumann.

It is beyond me how anyone could think Schumann chronically morbid if he had ever heard, say, the *Polonaise* in the *Papillons, Glückes genug*, the Third *Novellette*, the *Allegro* and *Scherzino* of the *Faschingsschwank*, the Third String Quartet, *Er, der Herrlichste*, the finale of the D Minor Trio, the *Soldatenmarsch* from the *Album*, or *Der Sandmann*.

[19] In *Un Siècle de musique française*, Paris, Delagrave, p. 191.

However, another Frenchman, Robert de Launay,[20] has formed so just an estimate of Schumann's rare humanity as to help atone for the gross misconceptions of his fellow-countrymen:

More than to the intelligence, it is to the heart that this soul unveils itself. Those of others, it is true, are grander, and more loftily dominate the centuries. None, not even that of Beethoven, is more winged with love, more human, more rare, and more like Tancred's enchanted forest where, from every tree, there escape sighs, laughs, or groans.

[20] In *L'âme chantante de Robert Schumann*, Paris, Frischbacher, p. 46.

APPENDICES

ACKNOWLEDGMENTS

FOR criticizing the manuscript and proofs of this book, hearty thanks are due the following friends: Miss Marion Bauer, Mr. Emil Bloch, Mrs. Clifford Braider, Mr. Felix O. Derrick, Mrs. Samuel Harrell Ferebee, Mr. Samuel Harrell Ferebee, Mr. Norman Hoyte, Mr. Egon Kenton, Mrs. Annie Nathan Meyer, Mrs. Elizabeth C. Moore, Miss Helen Morgan, Mr. Harvey Officer, Mr. Harrison Potter, Mrs. Augusta Scheiber, Mrs. Helene Scheu-Riesz, Mr. William Sloane, Mme. Olga Samaroff Stokowski, and Miss Helen K. Taylor.

For other help I wish to thank: Miss Adelaide Ahrling, Mr. Theobald Bayer, Mr. Elmer Gordon, Miss Ilona Hagen, Mr. Gwynn Hoffman, Mrs. Alice H. McCullen, Mr. Edwin McKinley, Mr. Morris Nathan, Miss Sarah Ann Scheiber, Miss Ida R. Weirich, Miss Blanche Winogran, the music libraries of Albany, Boston and New York, and especially Miss Dorothy Lawton, Director of the New York Music Library.

Any biography which requires as many years of research as this book has called for, needs subsidization for the same reason that a symphony orchestra needs it. I wish to acknowledge the generosity of Mrs. Ira Nelson Morris, who encouraged me to begin Schumann research, and subsidized it for the first twelve months. After the second year, the work would have had to be abandoned but for the vigorous and great-hearted intervention of Mrs. Annie Nathan Meyer, who found able assistants in Mrs. Clifford Braider and Mrs. Edgar Stillman Kelley. This committee raised a Schumann Fund, substantial contributions to which have been made by: Mrs. Clifford Braider, Mr. and Mrs. Morris Llewellyn Cooke, Mrs. Colgate W. Darden, Mr. and Mrs. Horatio Ford, Mr. Henry Harkness Flagler, Mrs. John Henry Hammond, Mrs. Annie Nathan Meyer, Mrs. Ira Nelson Morris,

Mrs. Dushayne Penniman, Mrs. Frederick G. Platt, Miss Caroline Schauffler, Dr. Goodrich Schauffler, Mr. Henry Schauffler, and two anonymous donors, one of them a well-known national institution.

A large number of music-lovers, including many of the leading musicians of America, have also assisted the Fund by subscribing early for the book at a considerable advance over the publication price.

Special thanks are due to Miss Marion Bauer for reading proof of the music cuts, arranging several musical examples and helping to prepare the Glossary; to Mr. George H. Engelhard for advice on Saxon marriage laws; to Mrs. Else Kurzbauer for her painstaking care in copying the musical examples; to Dr. Daniel Gregory Mason and the Macmillan Co. for their kind permission to quote from *The Romantic Composers;* to Mrs. Elizabeth C. Moore for brilliant editorial work, proof-reading, and preparing the Indexes and much of the other back-matter; to Dr. Artur Rodzinski for information about the retouching of Schumann's orchestration; to Mrs. Augusta Scheiber for reading proof of the music cuts, refreshing my memory of Schumann's piano- and piano-chamber music, and arranging private performances of his choral works; to *The Musical Courier* for its generous permission to reproduce a number of illustrations; and to Mrs. C. Dewar Simons for many months of splendid research. Last but not least comes a vote of thanks to Mr. William Sloane, Miss Helen K. Taylor, Mr. Maurice Kaplan, and the rest of the staff of that extraordinary and almost unheard-of phenomenon, the creatively minded publishing house of Holt.

R. H. S.

Ogunquit, Maine,
June 15th, 1945

SOME BOOKS BY AND ABOUT SCHUMANN

Robert Schumanns gesammelte Schriften über Musik und Musiker. 2 vols., 5th ed., edited by Martin Kreisig. Leipzig, 1914, Breitkopf and Härtel.
Thematisches Verzeichniss sämmtlicher im Druck erschienenen Werke Robert Schumanns. Leipzig, n.d., Schuberth.

LETTERS

Jugendbriefe, Robert Schumanns. Ed. by Clara Schumann. Leipzig, 1885, Breitkopf.
Der junge Schumann. Edited by Alfred Schumann. 1910.
Neue Folge. 2nd ed., edited by F. Gustav Jansen. Leipzig, 1904, Breitkopf.
Schumanns Leben in Briefen, edited by Hermann Erler. 2 vols., Berlin, 1887, Ries and Erler.

BIOGRAPHIES

Abert, H. *Robert Schumann.* 3rd ed. Berlin, 1918, Harmonie.
Basch, Victor. *Schumann,* Paris, 1926, Alcan.
Batka, R. *Robert Schumann.* Leipzig, n.d., Reclam.
Bedford, Herbert. *Schumann: His Life and Work.* New York, 1925, Harper.
Burk, John N. *Clara Schumann, a Romantic Biography,* New York, 1940, Random House.
Calvocoressi, D. *Schumann,* Paris, 1912.
Dahms, Walter. *Schumann.* Berlin, 1922, Schuster and Löffler.
Fuller-Maitland, J. A. *Schumann.* London, 1888, Sampson Low, Marston.
La Mara. *Robert Schumann,* Leipzig, 1911.

Litzmann, Berthold. *Clara Schumann*. 3 vols., 3rd ed., Leipzig, 1906, Breitkopf.

Mauclaire, Camille. *Schumann*. Paris, 1906 (in *Musiciens célèbres*).

Niecks, Frederick. *Robert Schumann*. London, 1925, Dent.

Reimann, Heinrich. *Robert Schumanns Leben und Werke*. Leipzig, 1887.

Reissmann, August. *Robert Schumann*. Berlin, 1865, Guttentag.

Schneider, Louis, and Mareschal, Marcel. *Schumann, sa vie et ses œuvres*. Paris, 1905, Bibliothèque Charpentier.

Schumann, Eugenie. *Robert Schumann*. Leipzig, 1931, Kœhler and Amelang.

——. *The Schumanns and Johannes Brahms*. New York, 1927, Dial Press.

Spitta, Philipp. *Robert Schumann, ein Lebensbild*. Leipzig, 1882, Breitkopf.

Wasielewski, Wilhelm Joseph v. *Robert Schumann*. 4th ed., Leipzig, 1906, Breitkopf.

MISCELLANEOUS

Chantavoine, Jean. *La jeunesse de Schumann*. Paris, 1912 (in *Musiciens et Poètes*).

Cobbett's Cyclopedic Survey of Chamber Music.

Grove's Dictionary of Music and Musicians.

Hadow, Sir Henry. *Studies in Modern Music*. New York, 1893-94, Macmillan.

International Cyclopedia of Music and Musicians, Dodd, Mead.

Jansen, F. Gustav. *Die Davidsbündler*. Leipzig, 1883, Breitkopf.

Kohut, Adolf. *Friedrich Wieck*.

Korte, Werner. *Robert Schumann*. Potsdam, 1937, Athenaion.

Mason, Daniel Gregory. *The Romantic Composers*. New York, 1906, Macmillan.

Möbius, P. *Über Robert Schumanns Krankheit*. Halle, 1906, Marhold.

Ninck, Martin. *Schumann und die Romantik in der Musik*. Heidelberg, 1929, Kampmann.

Pascal, Dr. *Les Maladies mentales de Robert Schumann* (in *Journal de Psychologie Normal et Pathologique*, Mch.-Apr. 1908).

Pitrou, R. *La Vie intérieure de Robert Schumann*, Paris, 1925, Laurens.

Pohl, R. *Erinnerungen an Robert Schumann*. Berlin, Janke (in *Deutsche Revue*, Vol. II, Aug.-Sept. 1878).

Reinecke, Carl. *Und manche Schatten steigen auf.*

Tessmer, Hans. *Der Klingende Weg*. Regensburg, 1923, Bosse.

Wasielewski, Wilhelm Joseph v. *Schumanniana*. Bonn, 1883, Strauss.

Wieck, Marie. *Aus dem Kreise Wieck-Schumann*. 2nd ed., Dresden, 1914.

GLOSSARY

Some Technical Terms Every Music Lover Should Know

APPOGGIATURA: A short note of embellishment suspending or delaying a note of melody.

ABSOLUTE MUSIC: That type of music to which no program or literary interpretation is attached by the composer. Sometimes called pure music.

ACOUSTICS: That branch of the science of physics dealing with the phenomena of sound.

ANSWER: The response to the fugue (q. v.) [1] subject. It resembles that subject but is in another key.

ARIA: One of the more ambitious instrumental forms originally used vocally in the older operas.

AUGMENTATION: Repeating a subject in notes of greater value: halves for quarters, etc. The opposite of diminution.

AUTHENTIC CADENCE: A closing formula consisting of the dominant triad (on the fifth degree) followed by the tonic triad (on the first degree).

BAGATELLE: A short simple composition, usually in song form.

BASSO OSTINATO: A bass part in which the same melodic figure obstinately recurs.

BINARY FORM: Two-part form. A movement with two themes.

CADENCE: (From Latin: *cadere*, to fall.) The close (fall) or ending of a phrase, period, part, movement, or work. The harmonic formula by which a phrase or period is ended, giving a sense of temporary or complete finality. Cadences are authentic, plagal, perfect, deceptive, etc.

[1] Literally "which see."

506

CADENZA (Italian for *cadence*): An improvised florid passage usually brought in at or near the end of an instrumental movement or vocal aria. In the eighteenth century the cadenza was the part of the concerto best designed to exhibit the soloist's technical ability, introducing his own development of the subject matter of the movement. Later, not trusting to the powers of the artist, the composer himself wrote the cadenza. It is still the custom for composers or performers to compose new cadenzas to standard works, such as Kreisler wrote for the Beethoven violin concerto.

CANON: A composition in which a subject sung or played in one voice is imitated note for note in the others, either at the same or at a different pitch. The old-fashioned round is in canon form (e.g., *Three Blind Mice*).

CAVATINA: A short aria (q. v.). The term is occasionally used for a songlike instrumental piece or movement.

CHAMBER MUSIC: Music meant to be played in a small hall or room by a limited number of soloists, or a group of instrumentalists, such as wood-wind combinations, string quartet, trio, etc., with or without piano.

CHORAL: Psalm or hymn tune. A broad simple song for many voices (chorale).

CHORD: The simultaneous sounding of tones built up in thirds from a given root or fundamental. A three-voiced chord is a triad; four-voiced, a chord of the seventh, etc. Today chords are sometimes arbitrarily built up in intervals other than the time-honored thirds.

CHROMATIC SCALE: One that proceeds in half steps.

CODA: A concluding phrase or section added to a vocal or instrumental work, not strictly necessary for completeness, but making a more positive and effective close. It may also occur at the end of a principal section or even of a period.

CONCERTO: In Beethoven's time, an elaborate work for solo instrument and orchestra. In form it is virtually a sonata (q. v.), usually of three movements.

CONTRAPUNTAL: Pertaining to counterpoint. Contrapuntal forms are canons (q. v.) and fugues (q. v.).

COUNTERPOINT: (Point against point. Point is an old term for note.) Two or more melodies written to sound simultaneously. Polyphonic or many-voiced style. Horizontal music as opposed to vertical or harmonic music.

CYCLICAL FORM: A composition laid out in a series of movements (as a suite or a sonata). Today we apply the term to inter-movement thematic relation.

DEVELOPMENT: The working out of a theme, subject, or group of subjects by every device for variation, expansion, etc., at the composer's command. The second section in fugue (q. v.) and in sonata-form (q. v.). Also called free fantasia, development section, or working-out portion.

DIATONIC: A scale proceeding by consecutive tone degrees, or a melody containing no tones foreign to the key.

DIMINUTION: Repeating a subject in notes of shorter duration: e.g., quarters for halves, eighths for quarters, etc. The opposite of augmentation.

DIVERTIMENTO (DIVERTISSEMENT): An early instrumental composition usually consisting of more than four movements, and of a cheerful, entertaining character.

DOMINANT: The fifth step of the scale; dominant harmony, the triad on the fifth degree (e.g., the dominant chord of the key of G major is D–F sharp–A).

DYNAMICS: Contrasts between loud and soft, and progressions from one to the other: one of the means of producing expression in music.

ECOSSAISE: A dance of Scottish origin.

ENSEMBLE: A particular combination of instruments or voices, as chorus, string quartet, orchestra, etc. Team-work of instruments or voices. Chamber music is sometimes called ensemble music.

EXPOSITION: The thematic or subject matter set forth in the first part of a fugue or sonata.

FIGURE: A small melodic tone-group or motive.

FIGURED-BASS: A system of numeral-notation of a bass part to indicate the intended harmony. A stenographic method of writing keyboard music. Also called thoroughbass.

FINALE: The final movement of a composition in several movements.

FORM: The plan of a piece of music. The arrangement of material into symmetrical and effective order, as in the rondo, minuet, scherzo, sonata-form movement, etc. (q. v.).

FUGATO: A part of a composition built in the manner of a fugue (q. v.) but not carried out with its complication or completeness. The theme begins in one part and is successively imitated by the other parts.

FUGUE (From Latin: *fuga*, flight): An enlarged and elaborately developed canon (q. v.). The highest form of contrapuntal art. A fugue has a subject (q. v.), an answer (the subject repeated more or less exactly a fifth above), a counter-subject (a theme planned to dovetail contrapuntally into the answer), and episodes developed from the subject matter. Sometimes the first part, or exposition, is brought back with the subject inverted (*see* Inversion), augmented (*see* Augmentation), or diminished (*see* Diminution). The stretto (q. v.), in which the subject is shortened by telescoping in order to build up the climax of the composition, is followed by a coda (q. v.) in which there is often a long organ-point (q. v.) before the final cadence (q. v.). As it may be divided into exposition, developing portion, and recapitulation, it may be regarded as the precursor of sonata-form. Fugues are both instrumental and vocal. It has been jestingly said that in a fugue the voices come in one by one and the listeners go out one by one.

GERM-MOTIVE: A musical phrase which recurs, more or less disguised, in different movements of the same composition; used as an interlocking device to lend the whole work thematic unity. (E.g., the motive A S C H which runs through *Carnaval*, see p. 291, and the rising and falling arpeggio which binds together the four movements of the F Major Quartet, see p. 457.)

HARMONY: The science which treats of chords—their construction, interrelation, and logical progression.

IMITATION: An echoing of the theme in other voice-parts but usually higher or lower than the original statement.

INTERVAL: The distance from one tone to another; the difference in pitch between two tones.

INTRODUCTION: A passage or movement at the beginning of a work, leading up to the principal subject (q. v.) or exposition (q. v.).

INVERSION:

(a) Turning the two tones of an interval upside down.

(b) Changing the position of the tones of a chord so that some other than its root serves as bass.

(c) Reversing the intervals of a melodic line so that they go in contrary motion to their original order.

(d) In counterpoint, exchanging the position of two lines of melody so that, e.g., soprano becomes alto, and vice versa.

KEY: Any particular scale or tone series binding the triads of that scale into a unity through relation to a tonal center that gives the key its name. "Key" and "scale" are used interchangeably. (Key of D.) (*See* Tonality.)

LEITMOTIF: A term first used by Von Wolzogen in connection with the Wagnerian music-drama. A motive intimately identified with some character, situation, or idea in opera. The lineal descendant of the germ- and source-motive (q. v.).

MASS: A choral setting, with or without accompaniment, of certain portions of the Eucharistic service in the Roman Church. Sung in Latin.

MINUET: A dance of French origin originally consisting of two eight-bar phrases in ¾ time and of moderate pace. A second minuet was added, contrasted in feeling and usually written in three-part harmony, from which it derived the name Trio. Beethoven speeded this form up and altered it emotionally into the scherzo (q. v.).

MODE: A type or species of scale. Today we have the major and minor modes in all keys, corresponding to the major and minor scales. The term was used in Hindu, Greek, and church music (Gregorian and Ambrosian modes).

MODULATION: The process of changing, in the course of a movement, from one key or tonality (q. v.) to another.

MOTIVE, MOTIF: A short melodic figure or note-group used as a structural basis for developing a composition.

MOVEMENT:

(a) Rhythmic motion.

(b) A principal division of a compound or cyclical work, such as a suite or sonata.

ORATORIO: An extended composition for solo voices, chorus, and orchestra, without stage setting or acting, usually illustrating some sacred subject.

ORGAN-POINT, sometimes called PEDAL-POINT: A stationary bass held for a considerable time, over which other voices move freely. (See the close of *Carnaval, Più stretto,* first 16 measures, and the *"Rhenish"* Symphony, Trio of Scherzo, p. 413, Ex. 159.)

OVERTONES, also called UPPER PARTIALS: Tones of higher pitch which are present in a regular, mathematical series in every perfect musical sound. The higher overtones are more dissonant and—fortunately—fainter.

PLAGAL CADENCE: A closing formula which consists of the triad upon the fourth degree of the scale followed by the tonic triad (q. v.).

PROGRAM MUSIC: A purely instrumental composition to which a detailed poetic program is affixed by the composer. Such a program, however, no more represents the exclusive meaning of the music than any other which may be attached to the piece by its millions of hearers. Music is too infinite to allow even its composer to pin it down to any one program. Calverley's line applies here:

And as to the meaning, it's what you please.

RECAPITULATION: The restatement of a sonata or fugue exposition (q. v.). Succeeds the development (q. v.) with certain traditional changes in key relations.

RONDO: A piece derived from the old round dance in which the main theme or subject is frequently repeated, separated by secondary themes, e.g., on the model ABACA or ABACADA.

SCALE: A definite succession of tones within an octave, written on successive staff degrees. There are many varieties, ranging from the pentatonic, or five-tone scale of the Chinese, Scots, and many primitive races, and the modal scales of the Greeks and of the Medieval Church, to the diatonic major and minor, and chromatic scales in use today, as well as the whole-tone scale of Debussy, etc.

SCHERZO: Literally the joke movement. Usually the third movement in a larger instrumental work. Consists of two short sections built on three-part song-form (q. v.). The second section is known as the Trio. The typical scherzo usually begins fast, light, staccato, and in three-quarter time. Its Trio often brings in contrasting slower, smoother, and mellower music. This is followed by the more or less literal repetition of the first part. Schumann often has two Trios.

SEQUENCE: The frequent repetition of the same melodic figure, starting on a different degree of the scale.

SONATA: (From Latin and Italian *sonare:* to sound; hence a "sound-piece.") An instrumental composition of three or four contrasting and more or less related movements. Most sonatas are for piano, or for piano and another instrument. Trios, quartets, quintets, etc., are really sonatas for groups of instruments. A symphony is a sonata for orchestra. The first movement is customarily in so-called sonata-form. The second, often a slow movement, is generally in extended three-part song-form. The third is usually in minuet or scherzo form. The fourth is frequently in rondo form, occasionally in sonata-form. Variation form may be used in any movement of a sonata.

SONATA-FORM: The form in which the first movement of the standard sonata is constructed. It is a development of the three-part song-form. The basic material of the typical sonata-form is found in two contrasting subjects, the first and the second, sometimes called "the masculine" and "the feminine," or vice versa, each of which may consist of one or more themes closely related by mood and key. The three main divisions of the form consist of:

(1) Exposition:
    (a) First subject in key of tonic, and modulation to
    (b) Second subject in complementary key which is usually dominant, or relative major if (a) is in the minor.

(2) Development: in which these subjects are worked out with much modulation (q. v.), according to the imaginative fertility and technical resource of the composer.

(3) Recapitulation: a virtual repetition of the Exposition with prescribed changes of key (second subject in tonic, etc.).

The following diagram graphically represents the typical structure of sonata-form:

SONG-FORM:

(a) The small, or simple, in two or three parts;

(b) the large, or extended, in two or three parts.

(a) is the smallest independent form in use and is so named because it is in the form of a song. Much folk music and many songs are in the small two- and three-part song-forms. The *Figurirter Choral, Album for the Young*, No. 42, is simple, or small, two-part song-form (A+B), while *Nordisches Lied*, No. 41, is in simple three-part song-form (A+B+A). The third part is often a repetition, more or less exact, of the first part, and often a coda (q. v.) is added.

The large two-part song-forms embrace the old dance-forms such as Allemandes, Sarabandes, also Themes for Variations, and occasionally an entire movement. Many minuets, scherzos, and slow movements are in large three-part song-form, e.g., *Adagio molto* of A Major String Quartet, Op. 41, No. 3: A+B+A+Coda.

SOURCE-MOTIVE: A musical phrase that recurs, more or less identically, in a number of distinct compositions and produces in the group an effect of thematic unity. (See p. 479 ff.)

STRETTO: In a fugue (q. v.) a passage in which the subject and answer are introduced in close succession, so as to overlap and crowd upon each other, producing an effect of climax.

SUBDOMINANT: The fourth degree of the scale. Subdominant harmony, the triad on the fourth degree (e.g., in the key of G major, the subdominant chord is C—E—G).

SUBJECT: A melodic figure or phrase taken as a theme for treatment throughout a movement. Used specifically in a fugue and as a general term in all forms of composition. Opposed to Answer (q. v.).

SUITE: A collection of idealized dance tunes put together in contrasting tempos, rhythms, and moods. Also called partita. A precursor of the form of composition in several movements which finds its highest perfection in the Beethoven sonata. Bach, Handel, Couperin, etc., wrote suites.

SYMPHONY: A sonata for large orchestra.

SYNCOPATION: Shifting the accent to the normally weak or unaccented part of the beat or measure and holding it over the strong or accented part, thus robbing the naturally strong rhythmic position of its normal accent. This rhythmic disturbance is often carried over from one measure to another by means of tied notes. See B Flat Symphony, *Larghetto*, p. 399, Ex. 136, bars 3-4 and 5-6.

THEMATIC WORK: The development of themes (*see* Development). The use in longer compositions of more or less disguised germ-motives (q. v.).

THEME: A subject of a composition, or part of a subject.

THOROUGHBASS: Loosely, harmonic composition. Also Figured-bass (q. v.).

TONALITY: All relations between degrees of a scale connected with a tonal center. A key or mode.

TONIC: The first tone of the scale (for instance, G in the scale of G).

TONIC CHORD: The chord based on the first tone of the scale, e.g., G—B—D in the scale of G.

TRIAD: A three-voiced chord, consisting of a root, third, and fifth. Triads are major, minor, augmented, and diminished.

TUTTI: Denotes the entrance of the full orchestra after passages for individual instruments.

VARIATION: The amplification or modification of a given theme. A form of composition called Theme and Variations.

THE COMPOSITIONS OF ROBERT SCHUMANN

NOTE.—*The first date given is that of composition; the second, that of publication. A single date is that of both. If you wish to find a work and do not know its opus number, consult the Music Indexes, pp. 558-74.*

OPUS NO.

1. THEME ON THE NAME ABEGG with Variations, for piano. 1830; 1832.
2. PAPILLONS, for piano. 1829-31; 1832.
3. SIX PIANO STUDIES on Paganini Caprices, for piano. First set. (See also Op. 10.) 1832.
4. INTERMEZZI for piano. Two books. 1832; 1833.
5. IMPROMPTUS on a Theme by Clara Wieck, for piano. 1833. Rev. ed. 1850.
6. DAVIDSBÜNDLERTÄNZE. 18 Characteristic pieces for piano. 1837; 1838. Rev. ed. 1850.
7. TOCCATA for piano in C major. 1830. Rev. 1833. Pub. 1834.
8. ALLEGRO for piano in B minor. 1831; 1835.
9. CARNAVAL—Scènes mignonnes composées pour le pianoforte sur quatre notes. 1834-35; 1837.

1—Préambule	13—Chopin
2—Pierrot	14—Estrella
3—Arlequin	15—Reconnaissance
4—Valse noble	16—Pantalon et Colombine
5—Eusebius	17—Valse allemande
6—Florestan	18—Paganini
7—Coquette	19—Aveu
8—Réplique	20—Promenade
9—Sphinxes	21—Pause
10—Papillons	22—Marche des "Davidsbündler"
11—Lettres dansantes	contre les Philistins
12—Chiarina	

OPUS NO.

10. SIX CONCERT ETUDES on Paganini Caprices, for piano. Second set. (See also Opus 3.) 1833; 1835.

11. SONATA No. 1 for piano in F sharp minor. 1833-35; 1836.

12. FANTASIESTÜCKE for piano. 1837; 1838.

1—*Des Abends*	5—*In der Nacht*
2—*Aufschwung*	6—*Fabel*
3—*Warum?*	7—*Traumeswirren*
4—*Grillen*	8—*Ende vom Lied*

13. SYMPHONIC ETUDES, for piano, in C sharp minor. 1834; 1837. Rev. ed. 1852.

14. SONATA No. 3 for piano in F minor (*Concert sans orchestre*). 1835; 1836. Rev. ed. 1853.

15. KINDERSCENEN, easy piano pieces. 1838; 1839.

1—*Von fremden Ländern und Menschen*	7—*Träumerei*
	8—*Am Camin*
2—*Curiose Geschichte*	9—*Ritter vom Steckenpferd*
3—*Hasche-Mann*	10—*Fast zu ernst*
4—*Bittendes Kind*	11—*Fürchtenmachen*
5—*Glückes genug*	12—*Kind im Einschlummern*
6—*Wichtige Begebenheit*	13—*Der Dichter spricht*

16. KREISLERIANA—eight fantasies for the piano. 1838. Rev. ed. 1850.

17. FANTASIE for the piano in C major. 1836; 1839.

18. ARABESKE for piano in C major. 1839.

19. BLUMENSTÜCK for piano in D flat major. 1839.

20. HUMORESKE for piano in B flat major. 1839.

21. NOVELLETTEN for piano. 1838; 1839.

22. SONATA No. 2 for piano in G minor. 1833-35; last movement 1838; 1839.

23. NACHTSTÜCKE. Four piano pieces. 1839; 1840.

24. LIEDERKREIS I, cycle of nine songs (Heine). 1840.

1—*Morgens steh' ich auf*
2—*Es treibt mich hin*
3—*Ich wandelte unter den Bäumen*
4—*Lieb' Liebchen*
5—*Schöne Wiege meiner Leiden*
6—*Warte, warte, wilder Schiffsmann*

OPUS NO.

> 7—*Berg' und Burgen schau'n herunter*
> 8—*Anfangs wollt' ich fast verzagen*
> 9—*Mit Myrthen und Rosen*

25. MYRTHEN, cycle of twenty-six songs (Goethe, Rückert, Byron, Moore, Heine, Burns, J. Mosen). 1840.

> 1—*Widmung*
> 2—*Freisinn*
> 3—*Der Nussbaum*
> 4—*Jemand (Mein Herz ist betrübt)*
> 5—*Sitz' ich allein*
> 6—*Setze mir nicht*
> 7—*Die Lotosblume*
> 8—*Talismane*
> 0 *Lied der Suleika*
> 10—*Die Hochländer Wittwe*
> 11—*Mutter! Mutter!*
> 12—*Lass mich ihm am Busen hangen*
> 13—*Hochländers Abschied*
> 14—*Hochländisches Wiegenlied*
> 15—*Aus den hebräischen Gesängen*
> 16—*Rätsel*
> 17—*Leis' rudern hier*
> 18—*Wenn durch die Piazzetta*
> 19—*Hauptmanns Weib*
> 20—*Weit, weit*
> 21—*Was will die einsame Träne*
> 22—*Niemand*
> 23—*Im Westen*
> 24—*Du bist wie eine Blume*
> 25—*Aus den östlichen Rosen*
> 26—*Zum Schluss*

26. FASCHINGSSCHWANK aus Wien, for piano in B flat major. 1839; 1841.

27. LIEDER UND GESÄNGE, Book I. (See also Opp. 51, 77, 96.) Five songs (Hebbel, Burns, Chamisso, Rückert, Zimmermann). 1840; 1849.

> 1—*Sag' an, o lieber Vogel mein*
> 2—*Dem rothen Röslein gleicht mein Lieb*

OPUS NO.

> 3—*Was soll ich sagen?*
> 4—*Jasminstrauch*
> 5—*Nur ein lächelnder Blick*

28. DREI ROMANZEN, for piano, in B flat minor, F sharp major, and B major. 1839; 1840.
29. DREI GEDICHTE von Emanuel Geibel. With piano accompaniment. No. 1 for two sopranos. No. 2 for three sopranos. No. 3 (*Zigeunerleben*) for small chorus, triangle and tambourine *ad libitum*. 1840; 1841.
30. DREI GEDICHTE von Emanuel Geibel. 1840; 1841.

> 1—*Der Knabe mit den Wunder-*   2—*Der Page*
>   *horn*   3—*Der Hidalgo*

31. DREI GESÄNGE (Chamisso). 1840; 1841.

> 1—*Die Löwenbraut*   3—*Die rothe Hanne*
> 2—*Die Kartenlegerin*

32. VIER CLAVIERSTÜCKE. 1838-39; 1841.

> 1—*Scherzo in B flat major*   3—*Romanze in D minor*
> 2—*Gigue in G minor*   4—*Fughette in G minor*

33. SECHS LIEDER, for four-part male voices unaccompanied. (Mosen, Heine, Goethe, Reinick.) 1840; 1842.

> 1—*Der träumende See*   4—*Der Zecher als Doctrinair*
> 2—*Die Minnesänger*   5—*Rastlose Liebe*
> 3—*Die Lotosblume*   6—*Frühlingsglöckchen*

34. VIER DUETTE. Soprano and tenor. (Reinick, Burns, Grün.) 1840; 1841.

> 1—*Liebesgarten*   3—*Unter'm Fenster*
> 2—*Liebhabers Ständchen*   4—*Familien-Gemälde*

35. ZWÖLF GEDICHTE von Justinus Kerner. Two books. 1840; 1841.

> 1—*Lust der Sturmnacht*
> 2—*Stirb, Lieb' und Freud'*
> 3—*Wanderlied*
> 4—*Erstes Grün*
> 5—*Sehnsucht nach der Waldgegend*
> 6—*Auf das Trinkglas eines verstorbenen Freundes*

OPUS NO.

7—*Wanderung*
8—*Stille Liebe*
9—*Frage*
10—*Stille Tränen*
11—*Wer machte dich so krank?*
12—*Alte Laute*

36. SECHS LIEDER. For soprano or tenor, from Reinick. 1840; 1842.

1—*Sonntags am Rhein*   4—*An den Sonnenschein*
2—*Ständchen*   5—*Dichters Genesung*
3—*Nichts Schöneres*   6—*Liebesbotschaft*

37. ZWÖLF LIEDER from Rückert's *Liebesfrühling*. Two books. Nos. 2, 4, and 11 by Clara Schumann, Op. 12. 1840; 1841.

1—*Der Himmel hat eine Thräne geweint*
2—*Er ist gekommen*
3—*O ihr Herren*
4—*Liebst du um Schönheit*
5—*Ich hab' in mich gesogen*
6—*Liebste, was kann denn uns scheiden*
7—*Schön ist das Fest des Lenzes*
8—*Flügel! Flügel!*
9—*Rose, Meer und Sonne*
10—*O Sonn', o Meer, o Rose!*
11—*Warum willst du And're fragen*
12—*So wahr die Sonne scheinet*

38. SYMPHONY No. 1 in B flat major ("*Spring*"). Composed 1841. Published, parts 1841. Ed. for piano duet 1842. Score 1853.

39. LIEDERKREIS II, cycle of twelve songs of Eichendorff. 1840; 1842.

1—*In der Fremde*   7—*Auf einer Burg*
2—*Intermezzo*   8—*In der Fremde*
3—*Waldesgespräch*   9—*Wehmut*
4—*Die Stille*   10—*Zwielicht*
5—*Mondnacht*   11—*Im Walde*
6—*Schöne Fremde*   12—*Frühlingsnacht*

40. FÜNF LIEDER. (Four poems from the Danish of H. C. Andersen; one from modern Greek, translated by Chamisso.) 1840; 1842.

OPUS NO.

1—*Märzveilchen*   4—*Der Spielmann*
2—*Muttertraum*   5—*Verrathene Liebe*
3—*Der Soldat*

41. THREE STRING QUARTETS: in A minor, in F major, in A major. 1842; 1843 (parts) and 1849 (score).

42. FRAUENLIEBE UND LEBEN, cycle of eight songs of Chamisso. 1840; 1843.

1—*Seit ich ihn gesehen*
2—*Er, der Herrlichste von Allen*
3—*Ich kann's nicht fassen*
4—*Du Ring an meinem Finger*
5—*Helft mir, ihr Schwestern*
6—*Süsser Freund, du blickest*
7—*An meinem Herzen*
8—*Nun hast du mir den ersten Schmerz getan*

43. DREI ZWEISTIMMIGE LIEDER. Three two-part songs with pf. accompaniment. (Reinick and others.) 1840; 1844.

1—*Wenn ich ein Vöglein wär'*
2—*Herbstlied*
3—*Schön Blümelein*

44. PIANO QUINTET in E flat major for piano, two violins, viola, and 'cello. 1842; 1843.

45. ROMANZEN UND BALLADEN, Book I (Eichendorff and Heine). (See also Opp. 49, 53, 64.) 1840; 1844.

1—*Der Schatzgräber*
2—*Frühlingsfahrt*
3—*Abends am Strande*

46. ANDANTE AND VARIATIONS for two pianos in B flat major. 1843; 1844.

47. PIANO QUARTET in E flat major for piano, violin, viola, and 'cello. 1842; 1845.

48. DICHTERLIEBE, cycle of sixteen songs of Heine. Two books. 1840; 1844.

1—*Im wunderschönen Monat Mai*
2—*Aus meinen Tränen spriessen*
3—*Die Rose, die Lilie*

OPUS NO.

4 *Wenn ich in deine Augen seh'*
5—*Ich will meine Seele tauchen*
6—*Im Rhein, im heiligen Strome*
7—*Ich grolle nicht*
8—*Und wüssten's die Blumen*
9—*Das ist ein Flöten und Geigen*
10—*Hör' ich das Liedchen klingen*
11—*Ein Jüngling liebt ein Mädchen*
12—*Am leuchtenden Sommermorgen*
13—*Ich hab' im Traum geweinet*
14—*Allnächtlich im Traume*
15—*Aus alten Märchen winkt es*
16—*Die alten, bösen Lieder*

49. ROMANZEN UND BALLADEN, Book II (Heine and Fröhlich).
(See also Opp. 45, 53, 64.) 1840; 1844.

1—*Die beiden Grenadiere*
2—*Die feindlichen Brüder*
3—*Die Nonne*

50. DAS PARADIES UND DIE PERI. For solo voices, chorus, and orchestra. (From Moore's *Lalla Rookh*.) 1843; 1844-45.
51. LIEDER UND GESÄNGE, Book II. Five songs (Geibel, Rückert, etc.). (See also Opp. 27, 77, 96.) 1842; 1850.

1—*Sehnsucht*
2—*Volksliedchen*
3—*Ich wand're nicht*
4—*Auf dem Rhein*
5—*Liebeslied*

52. OVERTURE, SCHERZO, AND FINALE in E major for orchestra. 1841; 1846 and 1854.
53. ROMANZEN UND BALLADEN, Book III. (See also Opp. 45, 49, 64.) 1840; 1845.

1—*Blondel's Lied*
2—*Loreley*
3—*Der arme Peter*, three songs by Heine:
  (*a*) *Der Hans und die Grete*
  (*b*) *In meiner Brust*
  (*c*) *Der arme Peter wankt vorbei*

OPUS NO.

54. PIANO CONCERTO in A minor. Composed, first movement, 1841; Intermezzo and Finale, 1845. Published, parts 1846, score 1862.

55. FÜNF LIEDER (BURNS). For mixed chorus unaccompanied. 1846; 1847.

    1—Das Hochlandmädchen
    2—Zahnweh
    3—Mich zieht es nach dem Dörfchen hin
    4—Die alte gute Zeit
    5—Hochlandbursch

56. STUDIES FOR PEDAL PIANO. Six pieces in canon form. 1845.

57. BELSATZÀR. Ballad by Heine for voice. 1840; 1846.

58. SKETCHES FOR PEDAL PIANO. 1845; 1846.

59. VIER GESÄNGE, for mixed chorus unaccompanied (Mörike, Rückert, etc.). 1846; 1848.

    1—Nord oder Süd   3—Jägerlied
    2—Am Bodensee (a and b)   4—Gute Nacht

60. SIX FUGUES ON THE NAME BACH, for organ or Pedal Piano. 1845; 1847.

61. SYMPHONY No. 2 in C major. 1845-46; 1848.

62. DREI GESÄNGE. For male chorus unaccompanied. (Eichendorff, Rückert, Klopstock.) 1847; 1848.

    1—Der Eidgenossen Nachtwache
    2—Freiheitslied
    3—Schlachtgesang

63. TRIO No. 1 in D minor for piano, violin, and 'cello. 1847; 1848.

64. ROMANZEN UND BALLADEN, Book IV. (Mörike and Heine.) (See also Opp. 45, 49, 53.) 1841 and 1847; 1847.

    1—Die Soldatenbraut
    2—Das verlassene Mägdlein
    3—Tragödie, three songs by Heine:
        (a) Entflieh' mit mir
        (b) Es fiel ein Reif
        (c) Auf ihrem Grab (duet for soprano and tenor)

65. RITORNELLE (F. Rückert). Seven canons for male voices unaccompanied. 1847; 1849.

66. BILDER AUS OSTEN. Six impromptus for piano duet. 1848; 1849.

OPUS NO.

67. ROMANZEN UND BALLADEN. For chorus. Book I (Goethe, Mörike, Chamisso, Burns). (See also Opp. 75, 145, 146.) 1849.

1—Der König in Thule	4—Ungewitter
2—Schön Rohtraut	5—John Anderson
3—Haideröslein	

68. ALBUM FOR THE YOUNG. Forty (later forty-three) piano pieces. Part I for small folk; Part II for more grown-up folk. 1848; 1849 and 1851.

Part I:

1—Melodie	10—Fröhlicher Landmann
2—Soldatenmarsch	11—Sicilianisch
3—Trällerliedchen	12—Knecht Rupprecht
4—Ein Choral	13—Mai, lieber Mai
5—Stückchen	14—Kleine Studie
6—Armes Waisenkind	15—Frühlingsgesang
7—Jägerliedchen	16—Erster Verlust
8—Wilder Reiter	17—Kleiner Morgenwanderer
9—Volksliedchen	18—Schnitterliedchen

Part II:

19—Kleine Romanze	32—Sheherazade
20—Ländliches Lied	33—"Weinlesezeit—Fröh-
21—* * *	liche Zeit!"
22—Rundgesang	34—Thema
23—Reiterstück	35—Mignon
24—Ernteliedchen	36—Lied italienischer
25—Nachklänge aus dem	Marinari
Theater	37—Matrosenlied
26—* * *	38—Winterzeit I
27—Canonisches Liedchen	39—Winterzeit II
28—Erinnerung	40—Kleine Fuge
29—Fremder Mann	41—Nordisches Lied
30—* * *	42—Figurierter Choral
31—Kriegslied	43—Sylvesterlied

69. ROMANZEN, part-songs for female voices. Book I (Eichendorff, Kerner, Mörike, Uhland). (See also Op. 91.) 1849.

1—Tamburinschlägerin	4—Soldatenbraut
2—Waldmädchen	5—Meerfey
3—Klosterfräulein	6—Die Capelle

OPUS NO.

70. ADAGIO UND ALLEGRO in A flat major for piano and horn (or 'cello, or violin). 1849.

71. ADVENTLIED (Rückert), for soprano solo and chorus with orchestral accompaniment. Composed 1848. Published, piano edition 1849; score 1866.

72. VIER FUGEN for piano. 1845; 1850.

73. FANTASIESTÜCKE for piano and clarinet (or violin, or 'cello). Three pieces. 1849.

74. SPANISCHES LIEDERSPIEL, for one, two, and four voices with piano accompaniment. Nine songs translated from Spanish by Geibel. 1849.

1—*Erste Begegnung*	6—*Melancholie*
2—*Intermezzo*	7—*Geständnis*
3—*Liebesgram*	8—*Botschaft*
4—*In der Nacht*	9—*Ich bin geliebt*
5—*Es ist verraten*	10—*Der Contrabandiste* (appendix)

75. ROMANZEN UND BALLADEN for chorus unaccompanied. Book II (Eichendorff, Burns, etc.). (See also Opp. 67, 145, 146.) 1849; 1850.

1—*Schnitter Tod*	4—*Der Rekrut*
2—*Im Walde*	5—*Vom verwundeten Knaben*
3—*Der traurige Jäger*	

76. VIER MÄRSCHE for piano. 1849.

77. LIEDER UND GESÄNGE. Book III (Eichendorff, v. Fallersleben, etc.). (See also Opp. 27, 51, 96.) 1840-50; 1851.

1—*Der frohe Wandersmann*	4—*Stiller Vorwurf*
2—*Mein Garten*	5—*Aufträge*
3—*Geisternähe*	

78. VIER DUETTE for soprano and tenor with piano accompaniment (Rückert, Kerner, Goethe, Hebbel). 1849; 1850.

1—*Tanzlied*	3—*Ich denke dein*
2—*Er und Sie*	4—*Wiegenlied*

79. SONGS FOR YOUNG PEOPLE. Twenty-nine songs (v. Fallersleben, Uhland, Goethe, Schiller, etc.). 1849.

1—*Der Abendstern*	3—*Frühlingsbotschaft*
2—*Schmetterling*	4—*Frühlingsgruss*

OPUS NO.

5—*Vom Schlaraffenland*	18—*Die wandelnde Glocke*
6—*Sonntag*	19—*Frühlingslied* (duet)
7, 8—*Zigeunerliedchen*	20—*Frühlingsankunft*
(a, b)	21—*Die Schwalben*
9—*Des Knaben Berglied*	22—*Kinderwacht*
10—*Mailied*	23—*Des Sennen Abschied*
11—*Käuzlein*	24—*Er ist's*
12—*Hinaus in's Freie!*	25—*Spinnlied*
13—*Der Sandmann*	26—*Des Buben Schützenlied*
14—*Marienwürmchen*	27—*Schneeglöckchen*
15—*Die Waise*	28—*Lied Lynceus des*
16—*Das Glück*	*Thürmers*
17—*Weihnachtslied*	29—*Mignon*

80. TRIO No. 2 in F major for piano, violin and 'cello. 1847; 1850.

81. GENOVEVA, opera in four acts, after Tieck and Hebbel. Composed 1847-48. Published, score 1850; piano edition 1851.

82. WALDSCENEN. Nine piano pieces. 1848-49; 1851.

1—*Eintritt*	6—*Herberge*
2—*Jäger auf der Lauer*	7—*Vogel als Prophet*
3—*Einsame Blumen*	8—*Jagdlied*
4—*Verrufene Stelle*	9—*Abschied*
5—*Freundliche Landschaft*	

83. DREI GESÄNGE (Rückert, Eichendorff, etc.). 1850.

1—*Resignation*
2—*Die Blume der Ergebung*
3—*Der Einsiedler*

84. BEIM ABSCHIED ZU SINGEN. Song (Feuchtersleben) for chorus with accompaniment of wind instruments or piano. 1847; 1850.

85. ZWÖLF VIERHÄNDIGE CLAVIERSTÜCKE. For children little and big. 1849; 1850.

1—*Geburtstagsmarsch*	7—*Turniermarsch*
2—*Bärentanz*	8—*Reigen*
3—*Gartenmelodie*	9—*Am Springbrunnen*
4—*Beim Kränzewinden*	10—*Versteckens*
5—*Kroatenmarsch*	11—*Gespenstermärchen*
6—*Trauer*	12—*Abendlied*

OPUS NO.

86. CONCERTSTÜCK in F major for four horns and orchestra. 1849; 1851.

87. DER HANDSCHUH. Ballad (Schiller) for voice with piano accompaniment. 1850; 1851.

88. FANTASIESTÜCKE for piano, violin, and 'cello. 1842; 1850.

1—Romanze   3—Duett

2—Humoreske   4—Finale

89. SECHS GESÄNGE (Wilfried von der Neun). 1850.

1—Es stürmet am Himmel   4—Abschied vom Walde

2—Heimliches Verschwinden   5—In's Freie

3—Herbstlied   6—Röselein

90. SECHS GEDICHTE (N. Lenau), and REQUIEM. 1850; 1851.

1—Lied eines Schmiedes   5—Einsamkeit

2—Meine Rose   6—Der schwere Abend

3—Kommen und Scheiden   7—Requiem (old Catholic

4—Die Sennin   poem)

91. ROMANZEN for female voices, with *ad libitum* piano accompaniment. Book II. (Kerner, Mörike, Rückert, etc.) (See also Op. 69.) 1849; 1851.

1—Rosmarien   4—Das verlassene Mägdlein

2—Jäger Wohlgemut   5—Der Bleicherin Nachtlied

3—Der Wassermann   6—In Meeres Mitten

92. INTRODUCTION AND ALLEGRO APPASSIONATO in G major for piano and orchestra. 1849; 1852.

93. MOTET, *Verzweifle nicht im Schmerzensthal* (Rückert) for double male chorus with *ad libitum* organ accompaniment. 1849; 1851.

94. DREI ROMANZEN for oboe (or violin, or clarinet) with piano accompaniment. 1849; 1851.

95. DREI GESÄNGE (from Byron's *Hebrew Melodies*) for voice with harp or piano accompaniment. 1849; 1851.

1—Die Tochter Jephthas

2—An den Mond

3—Dem Helden

OPUS NO.

96. LIEDER UND GESÄNGE. Book IV (Goethe, v. Platen, v. der Neun). (See also Opp. 27, 51, 77.) 1850; 1851.

1—*Nachtlied*	4—*Gesungen*
2—*Schneeglöckchen*	5—*Himmel und Erde*
3—*Ihre Stimme*	

97. SYMPHONY No. 3 in E flat major ("*Rhenish*"). Composed 1850. Published, score 1851; piano duet edition 1852.

98. LIEDER, GESÄNGE, UND REQUIEM FÜR MIGNON (from Goethe's *Wilhelm Meister*). 1849; 1851.

Part I (98a), Songs for voice and piano
1—*Kennst du das Land?*
2—*Ballade des Harfners*
3—*Nur wer die Sehnsucht kennt*
4—*Wer nie sein Brod mit Thränen ass*
5—*Heiss' mich nicht reden*
6—*Wer sich der Einsamkeit ergiebt*
7—*Singet nicht in Trauertönen*
8—*An die Thüren will ich schleichen*
9—*So lasst mich scheinen*

Part II (98b), Requiem for chorus, solo voices, and orchestra.

99. BUNTE BLÄTTER, fourteen piano pieces. Composed at different times; 1852.

1-3—*Drei Stücklein*	11—*Marsch*
4-8—*Fünf Albumblätter*	12—*Abendmusik*
9—*Novelletto*	13—*Scherzo*
10—*Präludium*	14—*Geschwindmarsch*

100. OVERTURE TO SCHILLER'S *Bride of Messina*, in C minor. 1850-51; 1851.

101. MINNESPIEL from Rückert's *Liebesfrühling*, for one, two, and four voices. 1849; 1852.

1—*Meine Töne still und heiter*
2—*Liebster, deine Worte stehlen*
3—*Ich bin dein Baum, o Gärtner*
4—*Mein schöner Stern, ich bitte dich*
5—*Schön ist das Fest des Lenzes*

OPUS NO.

6—*O Freund, mein Schirm, mein Schutz*
7—*Die tausend Grüsse, die wir dir senden*
8—*So wahr die Sonne scheinet*

102. FÜNF STUCKE IM VOLKSTON, for 'cello (or violin) and piano. 1849; 1851.

103. MÄDCHENLIEDER (Elisabeth Kulmann) for two sopranos or soprano and alto, with piano accompaniment. 1851.

1—*Mailied*   3—*An die Nachtigall*
2—*Frühlingslied*   4—*An den Abendstern*

104. SIEBEN LIEDER (Elisabeth Kulmann). 1851.

1—*Mond, meiner Seele Liebling*
2—*Viel Glück zur Reise*
3—*Du nennst mich armes Mädchen*
4—*Der Zeisig*
5—*Reich' mir die Hand*
6—*Die letzten Blumen starben*
7—*Gekämpft hat meine Barke*

105. SONATA No. 1 for violin and piano, in A minor. 1851; 1852.

106. SCHÖN HEDWIG, ballad (Hebbel) for declamation with piano accompaniment. 1849; 1853.

107. SECHS GESÄNGE (Ullrich, Mörike, Heyse, etc.). 1851-52; 1852.

1—*Herzeleid*   4—*Die Spinnerin*
2—*Die Fensterscheibe*   5—*Im Walde*
3—*Der Gärtner*   6—*Abendlied*

108. NACHTLIED von F. Hebbel, for chorus and orchestra. 1849; 1852 and 1853.

109. BALLSCENEN. Nine characteristic pieces for piano four hands. 1851; 1853.

1—*Préambule*   6—*Mazurka*
2—*Polonaise*   7—*Ecossaise*
3—*Walzer*   8—*Walzer*
4—*Ungarisch*   9—*Promenade*
5—*Française*

110. TRIO No. 3 in G minor for piano, violin, and 'cello. 1851; 1852.

111. DREI FANTASIESTÜCKE for piano. 1851; 1852.

OPUS NO.

112. DER ROSE PILGERFAHRT. Fairy tale after a poem by Moritz Horn, for solo voices, chorus, and orchestra. 1851; 1852.

113. MÄRCHENBILDER, four pieces for piano and viola (or violin). 1851; 1852.

114. DREI LIEDER. Three trios (Rückert, etc.) for female voices with piano accompaniment. 1853.

> 1—Nänie
> 2—Triolett
> 3—Spruch

115. MANFRED. Overture and incidental music to the dramatic poem by Byron. Composed 1848 (Overture) and 1849 (the rest). Published, Overture 1852; piano edition of the whole 1853; whole score 1862.

116. DER KONIGSSOHN. Ballad (Uhland) for solo voices, chorus, and orchestra. 1851; 1853.

117. VIER HUSARENLIEDER (N. Lenau) for baritone with piano accompaniment. 1851; 1852.

> 1—Der Husar, trara!
> 2—Der leidige Frieden
> 3—Den grünen Zeigern
> 4—Da liegt der Feinde gestreckte Schaar

118. DREI CLAVIER-SONATEN FÜR DIE JUGEND. 1853; 1854.

119. DREI LIEDER. (Pfarrius). 1851; 1853.

> 1—Die Hütte
> 2—Warnung
> 3—Der Bräutigam und die Birke

120. SYMPHONY No. 4 in D minor. Composed 1841, and performed 1841 as "second symphony." Newly instrumentated 1851, and known as "fourth symphony." Published, parts, and edition for piano duet 1853; score 1854. 1841 version published 1896.

121. SONATA No. 2 for violin and piano, in D minor. 1851; 1853.

122. No. 1 BALLADE VOM HAIDEKNABEN (Hebbel) for declamation with piano. 1852; 1853.

No. 2 DIE FLÜCHTLINGE. Ballad (Shelley) for declamation with piano. 1852; 1853.

530 THE COMPOSITIONS OF ROBERT SCHUMANN

123. FESTIVAL OVERTURE on the *Rheinweinlied*, for orchestra and chorus. 1853; 1857.

124. ALBUMBLÄTTER. Twenty piano pieces. 1832-45; 1854.

1—*Impromptu*	11—*Romanze*
2—*Leides Ahnung*	12—*Burla*
3—*Scherzino*	13—*Larghetto*
4—*Walzer*	14—*Vision*
5—*Phantasietanz*	15—*Walzer*
6—*Wiegenliedchen*	16—*Schlummerlied*
7—*Ländler*	17—*Elfe*
8—*Leid ohne Ende*	18—*Botschaft*
9—*Impromptu*	19—*Phantasiestück*
10—*Walzer*	20—*Canon*

125. FÜNF HEITERE GESÄNGE (Mörike, etc.). 1851; 1853.

1—*Die Meerfee*	4—*Frühlingslied*
2—*Husarenabzug*	5—*Frühlingslust*
3—*Jung Volkers Lied*	

126. SIEBEN CLAVIERSTÜCKE IN FUGHETTENFORM. 1853; 1854.

127. LIEDER UND GESÄNGE. Five songs (Kerner, Heine, Shakespeare, Strachwitz). 1850-51; 1854.

1—*Sängers Trost*	4—*Mein altes Ross*
2—*Dein Angesicht*	5—*Schlusslied des Narren*
3—*Es leuchtet meine Liebe*	

128. OVERTURE TO SHAKESPEARE'S *Julius Caesar*. 1851; 1855.

129. VIOLONCELLO CONCERTO in A minor. 1850; 1854.

130. KINDERBALL. Six easy dances for piano four hands. 1853; 1854.

1—*Polonaise*	4—*Ecossaise*
2—*Walzer*	5—*Française*
3—*Menuett*	6—*Ringelreihe*

131. FANTASIE for violin in C major, with orchestral or piano accompaniment. 1853; 1854.

132. MÄRCHENERZÄHLUNGEN. Four pieces for clarinet (or violin), viola, and piano. 1853; 1854.

133. GESÄNGE DER FRÜHE. Five piano pieces. 1853; 1855.

134. CONCERT-ALLEGRO WITH INTRODUCTION in D minor, for piano and orchestra. 1853; 1855.

OPUS NO.

135. CEDICHTE DER KÖNICIN MARIA STUART. Five songs (old English poems). 1852; 1855.

    1—*Abschied von Frankreich*
    2—*Nach der Geburt ihres Sohnes*
    3—*An die Königin Elisabeth*
    4—*Abschied von der Welt*
    5—*Gebet*

136. OVERTURE TO GOETHE's *Hermann und Dorothea*, in B minor. No. 1 of the posthumous works. 1851; 1857.

137. FÜNF GESÄNGE. Five hunting songs (Laube) for four-part male chorus, with *ad libitum* accompaniment of four horns. No. 2 of the posthumous works. 1849; 1857.

138. SPANISCHE LIEBES-LIEDER. Ten songs from Spanish folk-songs and romances (translated by Geibel) for one, two, and four voices with piano duet accompaniment. No. 3 of the posthumous works. 1849; 1857.

139. DES SÄNGERS FLUCH. Ballad (after Uhland) for solo voices, chorus, and orchestra. No. 4 of the posthumous works. 1852; 1858.

140. VOM PAGEN UND DER KÖNIGSTOCHTER. Four ballads (Geibel) for solo voices, chorus, and orchestra. No. 5 of the posthumous works. 1852; 1858.

141. VIER DOPPELCHÖRIGE GESÄNGE (Rückert, Goethe, etc.). Unaccompanied. No. 6 of the posthumous works.

    1—*An die Sterne*   3—*Zuversicht*
    2—*Ungewisses Licht*   4—*Talismane*

142. VIER GESÄNGE (Kerner, Heine, etc.). No. 7 of the posthumous works. 1852; 1858.

    1—*Trost im Gesange*   3—*Mädchenschwermut*
    2—*Lehn' deine Wang'*   4—*Mein Wagen rollet langsam*

143. DAS GLÜCK VON EDENHALL. Ballad (after Uhland) for male voices, solo, and chorus, with orchestral accompaniment. No. 8 of the posthumous works. 1853; 1860.

144. NEUJAHRSLIED (Rückert) for chorus with orchestral accompaniment. No. 9 of the posthumous works. 1849-50; 1861.

OPUS NO.

145. ROMANZEN UND BALLADEN. For chorus unaccompanied. Book III (Uhland, Burns, etc.). (See also Opp. 67, 75, 146.) 1849; 1860.

1—*Der Schmidt*	4—*John Anderson*
2—*Die Nonne*	5—*Vom Gänsebuben*
3—*Der Sänger*	

146. ROMANZEN UND BALLADEN. For chorus unaccompanied. Book IV (Uhland, Burns, etc.). (See also Opp. 67, 75, 145.) 1849; 1860.

1—*Brautgesang*	4—*Sommerlied*
2—*Bänkelsänger Willie*	5—*Das Schifflein*
3—*Der Traum*	

147. MASS for four-part chorus with orchestral accompaniment. No. 10 of the posthumous works. Composed 1852. Published, piano edition 1862, score 1863.

148. REQUIEM for chorus and orchestra. No. 11 of the posthumous works. 1852; 1864.

Without Opus Numbers

SCENES FROM GOETHE'S *Faust*. For solo voices, chorus, and orchestra. Composed 1844-47-48-49-50-53. Published, piano edition 1858, score 1859.

DER DEUTSCHE RHEIN. Patriotic song (Becker) for solo voice and chorus with piano accompaniment. 1840.

SOLDATENLIED (v. Fallersleben).

SCHERZO UND PRESTO PASSIONATO for piano. Nos. 12 and 13 of the posthumous works. Published 1866. The Scherzo intended for the Sonata Op. 14; and the Presto as finale of the Sonata Op. 22.

CANON on "To Alexis" in A flat major.

SIX VIOLIN SONATAS by Johann Sebastian Bach, with piano accompaniment by Robert Schumann. 1854.

SIX 'CELLO SONATAS by Johann Sebastian Bach, with piano accompaniment by Robert Schumann. 1854.

VIOLIN CONCERTO in D minor. 1853; 1937.

RECORDED WORKS OF SCHUMANN

NOTE.—*The following list includes only such recordings as may be bought now in this country. In recent years, the importation of European recordings has declined steadily, so that most of them are virtually inaccessible now. But it has been thought advisable to list all such foreign Schumann records, at the end of our principal list (see p. 538), since there is a possibility that with the return of peace they will again be available.*

OPUS NO.	RECORD NO.
2. PAPILLONS—Alfred Cortot	V-1819/20
7. TOCCATA in C major	
—Josef Lhevinne	V-8766
—Simon Barere	V-14263
—Anatole Kitain	C-DX901
9. CARNAVAL (complete)	
—Sergei Rachmaninoff	VM-70
—Myra Hess	VM-476
—Arr. for orchestra by Glazunov (and perhaps others)—London Philharmonic, Goossens	VM-513
12. FANTASIESTÜCKE	
—Complete—Harold Bauer	VM-379
—Separately:	
No. 2, *Aufschwung*—W. Bachaus	V-1445
No. 7, *Traumeswirren*—V. Horowitz	V-1654
13. SYMPHONIC ETUDES—Edward Kilenyi	CM-X162
15. KINDERSCENEN	
—Complete—B. Moiseivitch	V-7705/6

15. KINDERSCENEN (Cont.)
   —Separately:
   No. 7, *Träumerei*
      —Arr. for violin and piano, Spalding — V-1727
      Zimbalist — C-17105D
      Elman — V-1482
      —Arr. for 'cello and piano, Casals — V-1178
      Feuermann — C-DX855
      —Arr. for orchestra, Minneapolis Sym- — V-8285
      phony, Ormandy
16. KREISLERIANA, Alfred Cortot — VM-493
17. FANTASIE in C major, W. Bachaus — VM-463
18. ARABESKE in C major, V. Horowitz — V-1713
21. NOVELLETTES, Harold Bauer — V-7122
22. PIANO SONATA No. 2 in G minor
   —M. Levitzki — V-8363/4
   —S. Gorodnitzki — CM-X186
23, No. 4. NACHTSTÜCK in F major, W. Bachaus — V-14978
25. MYRTHEN—separately:
   No. 1. *Widmung*
      —Lotte Lehmann (S) — D-20376
      —Risë Stevens (Ms) — C-17297D
      —Richard Tauber (T) — D-20349
      —Herbert Janssen (B) — V-1931
   No. 3. *Der Nussbaum*
      —Lotte Lehmann (S) — D-20375
      —Marian Anderson (C) — V-14610
      —Richard Tauber (T) — D-20348
   No. 7. *Die Lotosblume*
      —Lotte Lehmann (S) — D-20377
      —Richard Tauber (T) — D-20350
      —Herbert Janssen (B) — V-1931
   No. 24. *Du bist wie eine Blume*—Lotte Leh-
      mann (S) — V-1859
   No. 25. *Aus den östlichen Rosen*—Richard
      Tauber (T) — D-20349
27, No. 3. *Was soll ich sagen?*—Karl Erb (T) — V-4402
28, No. 2. ROMANZE in F sharp major, Artur
   Rubinstein — V-14949
29, No. 3. *Zigeunerleben*, chorus—Wiener Sänger-
   knaben and organ — D-25825

OPUS NO.	RECORD NO.

79. LIEDER-ALBUM FÜR DIE JUGEND (Cont.)

No. 9. *Mailied*, duet—M. Wilson and R.
Rodgers (in English) ... V-24542

No. 13. *Marienwürmchen*—Lotte Lehmann
(S) ... D-20377

No. 21. *Kinderwacht*—Helen Jepson (S)
(in English) ... in V-4288

82. WALDSCENEN

—Separately:

No. 3. *Einsame Blumen*—arr. for orchestra ... in V-22162

No. 7. *Vogel als Prophet*—Paderewski ... V-1426

85, No. 12. *Abendlied* (no recording of original
4-hand version)

—Arr. for violin and piano—A. Spalding ... V-1727

—Arr. for 'cello and piano—P. Casals ... V-6630

—Arr. for 'cello and organ—G. Piatigorsky ... D-25139

—Arr. for organ—C. Courboin ... V-14279

90, No. 1. *Lied eines Schmiedes*—George Henschel
(B) ... C-4129

94, No. 2. ROMANZE in A major—L. Coossens
(oboe) and G. Moore (pf) ... C-69816/7D

97. SYMPHONY No. 3 in E flat major (*"Rhenish"*)

—N. Y. Philharmonic-Symphony, Bruno
Walter ... CM-464

—Paris Conservatory Orchestra, P. Coppola ... VM-237

101, No. 4. *Mein schöner Stern*—Povla Frijsh (S) ... V-16149

103, No. 4. *An den Abendstern*, duet—V. Anderson
and V. Morris ... C-DB1233

104, No. 2. *Viel Glück zur Reise*—Povla Frijsh (S) ... V-16169

105. SONATA No. 1 for violin and piano—A. Busch
and R. Serkin ... VM-551

115. MANFRED (overture and incidental music)

—Overture—B.B.C. Symphony, A. Boult ... V-11713/4

—*Alpenkuhreigen*—Symphony Orchestra, M.
von Schillings ... D-25475

120. SYMPHONY No. 4 in D minor

—Chicago Symphony Orchestra, F. Stock ... CM-475

—London Symphony Orchestra, B. Walter ... VM-837

—Minneapolis Symphony Orchestra, E. Or-
mandy ... VM-201

OPUS NO.   RECORD NO.

129. VIOLONCELLO CONCERTO in A minor—Piati-
gorsky with London Philharmonic, Barbirolli   VM-247
VIOLIN CONCERTO in D minor—Menuhin with
N. Y. Philharmonic-Symphony, Barbirolli   VM-451

Schumann Recordings
Rarely Available Now, But Perhaps Available Later

OPUS NO.

9. CARNAVAL (complete)
—Alfred Cortot   G-DB1252/4
—Arr. for orchestra, London Symphony,
Ronald   G-DB1840/2
12, No. 1. FANTASIESTÜCKE: *Des Abends*—Cortot   G-DB3338
13. SYMPHONIC ETUDES—Cortot   G-DB1325/7
15. KINDERSCENEN (complete)
—Cortot   G-DB2581/2
—Elly Ney   G-DB4471/2
28, No. 2. *Romanze*—Moiseivitch   G-C3260
48. DICHTERLIEBE (complete)—Gerhard Hüsch   G-DB2940/2
50. DAS PARADIES UND DIE PERI—one number: *Nun
ruhe sanft*—Hildegarde Erdmann, chorus, and
orchestra   G-EH1250
54. PIANO CONCERTO in A minor—Cortot, with London Philharmonic, Ronald   GM-209
65. RITORNELLE—Vienna Male Chorus   G-ER287
73, No. 1. FANTASIESTÜCKE—Reginald Kell, clarinet   G-C3170
94, No. 2. *Romanze*—Menuhin   G-DB3438
113. MÄRCHENBILDER—Ginot and Benvenuti   G-K8096/7
124, No. 16. *Schlummerlied*—Mark Hambourg   G-B4385

Friedrich August
Gottlob SCHUMANN .. m .. Johanna Christiane Schnabel   Adolf Bargiel .. m .. (2) . Marianne Tromlitz .. m .. (1) .. Friedrich WIECK .. m .. (2) .. Clementine Fechner
1778-1826   (1795)   1771-1836   d. 1841   1785-1873

Eduard	Karl	Julius	Emilie	ROBERT ALEXANDER .. m .. CLARA JOSEPHINE		Alwin	Gustav	Klemens	Marie	Cäcilie
1797-1839	1801-1849	1805-1833	1807-1826	June 8, 1810- Sept. 13, 1819		1821-1885	d. 1823	1830-1833	1832-1916	1834
(wife Theresa)	(wife Rosalie d. 1833)			July 29, 1856 May 20, 1896						

Woldemar
1828-1897

Marie	Elise	Julie	Emil	Ludwig	Ferdinand	Eugenie	Felix
b. 1841	b. 1843	b. 1845	b. 1846	b. 1848	b. 1849	b. 1851	b. 1854

KEY TO THE SCHUMANN FAMILY CHART

The upper left-hand half of the chart shows Schumann's parents, his sister, and his brothers and their wives. The upper right-hand half makes clear the complex relationships due to Friedrich Wieck's two marriages. Wieck married (1) Marianne Tromlitz, and by her had Clara, Alwin, and Gustav. He married (2) Clementine Fech-ner, by whom his children were Klemens, Marie, and Cäcilie. His first wife Marianne, after her divorce from Wieck, married (2) Adolf Bargiel, and their child was the composer Bargiel. Thus Clara had Alwin and Gustav Wieck as whole brothers; Klemens, Marie, and Cäcilie Wieck as halfbrother and halfsisters; and Woldemar Bargiel as halfbrother.

INDEXES

INDEX I—GENERAL

541

INDEX II—SCHUMANN'S INSTRUMENTAL WORKS

NOTE.—*When the final page number in an entry is preceded by (R), the reader is being directed to the page on which the recording of the work is listed.*

558

INDEX III—SCHUMANN'S VOCAL WORKS

Note.—*When the final page number in an entry is preceded by (R), the reader is being directed to the page on which the recording of the work is listed.*

566

CATALOG OF DOVER BOOKS

Books Explaining Science

THE STRANGE STORY OF THE QUANTUM, AN ACCOUNT FOR THE GENERAL READER OF THE GROWTH OF IDEAS UNDERLYING OUR PRESENT ATOMIC KNOWLEDGE, B. Hoffmann. Presents lucidly and expertly, with least amount of mathematics, the problems and theories which led to modern quantum physics. Dr. Hoffmann begins with the closing years of the 19th century, when certain trifling discrepancies were noticed, and with illuminating analogies and examples takes you through the brilliant concepts of Planck, Einstein, Pauli, Broglie, Bohr, Schroedinger, Heisenberg, Dirac, Sommerfeld, Feynman, etc. This edition includes a new, long postscript carrying the story through 1958. "Of the books attempting an account of the history and contents of our modern atomic physics which have come to my attention, this is the best," H. Margenau, Yale University, in "American Journal of Physics." 32 tables and line illustrations. Index. 275pp. 5⅜ x 8.   T518 Paperbound **$1.45**

*THE EVOLUTION OF SCIENTIFIC THOUGHT FROM NEWTON TO EINSTEIN, A. d'Abro. A detailed account of the evolution of classical physics into modern relativistic theory and the concomitant changes in scientific methodology. The breakdown of classical physics in the face of non-Euclidean geometry and. the electromagnetic equations is carefully discussed and then an exhaustive analysis of Einstein's special and general theories of relativity and their implications is given. Newton, Riemann, Weyl, Lorentz, Planck, Maxwell, and many others are considered. A non-technical explanation of space, time, electromagnetic waves, etc. as understood today. "Model of semi-popular exposition," NEW REPUBLIC. 21 diagrams. 482pp. 5⅜ x 8.
T2 Paperbound **$2.00**

*THE RISE OF THE NEW PHYSICS (formerly THE DECLINE OF MECHANISM), A. d'Abro. This authoritative and comprehensive 2 volume exposition is unique in scientific publishing. Written for intelligent readers not familiar with higher mathematics, it is the only thorough explanation in non-technical language of modern mathematical-physical theory. Combining both history and exposition, it ranges from classical Newtonian concepts up through the electronic theories of Dirac and Heisenberg, the statistical mechanics of Fermi, and Einstein's relativity theories. "A must for anyone doing serious study in the physical sciences," THE FRANKLIN INSTITUTE. 97 illustrations. 991pp. 2 volumes.   T3 Vol. 1, Paperbound **$2.00**
T4 Vol. 2, Paperbound **$2.00**

THE STORY OF X-RAYS FROM RÖNTGEN TO ISOTOPES, A. R. Bleich, M.D. This book, by a member of the American College of Radiology, gives the scientific explanation of x-rays, their applications in medicine, industry and art, and their danger (and that of atmospheric radiation) to the individual and the species. You learn how radiation therapy is applied against cancer, how x-rays diagnose heart disease and other ailments, how they are used to examine mummies for information on diseases of early societies, and industrial materials for hidden weaknesses. 54 illustrations show x-rays of flowers, bones, stomach, gears with flaws, etc. 1st publication. Index. xix + 186pp. 5⅜ x 8.   T622 Paperbound **$1.35**

SPINNING TOPS AND GYROSCOPIC MOTION, John Perry. A classic elementary text of the dynamics of rotation — the behavior and use of rotating bodies such as gyroscopes and tops. In simple, everyday English you are shown how quasi-rigidity is induced in discs of paper, smoke rings, chains, etc., by rapid motions; why a gyrostat falls and why a top rises: precession; how the earth's motion affects climate; and many other phenomena. Appendix on practical use of gyroscopes. 62 figures. 128pp. 5⅜ x 8.   T416 Paperbound **$1.00**

PIONEERS OF SCIENCE, O. Lodge. An authoritative, yet elementary history of science by a leading scientist and expositor. Concentrating on individuals—Copernicus, Brahe, Kepler, Galileo, Descartes, Newton, Laplace, Herschel, Lord Kelvin, and other scientists—the author presents their discoveries in historical order, adding biographical material on each man and full, specific explanations of their achievements. The full, clear discussion of the accomplishments of post-Newtonian astronomers are features seldom found in other books on the subject. Index. 120 illustrations. xv + 404pp. 5⅜ x 8.   T716 Paperbound **$1.50**

BRIDGES AND THEIR BUILDERS, D. B. Steinman & S. R. Watson. Engineers, historians, and every person who has ever been fascinated by great spans will find this book an endless source of information and interest. Greek and Roman structures, Medieval bridges, modern classics such as the Brooklyn Bridge, and the latest developments in the science are retold by one of the world's leading authorities on bridge design and construction. BRIDGES AND THEIR BUILDERS is the only comprehensive and accurate semi-popular history of these important measures of progress in print. New, greatly revised, enlarged edition. 23 photos; 26 line-drawings. Index. xvii + 401pp. 5⅜ x 8.   T431 Paperbound **$2.00**

FAMOUS BRIDGES OF THE WORLD, D. B. Steinman. An up-to-the-minute new edition of a book that explains the fascinating drama of how the world's great bridges came to be built. The author, designer of the famed Mackinac bridge, discusses bridges from all periods and all parts of the world, explaining their various types of construction, and describing the problems their builders faced. Although primarily for youngsters, this cannot fail to interest readers of all ages. 48 illustrations in the text. 23 photographs. 99pp. 6⅛ x 9¼.   T161 Paperbound **$1.00**

CATALOG OF DOVER BOOKS

HOW DO YOU USE A SLIDE RULE? by A. A. Merrill. A step-by-step explanation of the slide rule that presents the fundamental rules clearly enough for the non-mathematician to understand. Unlike most instruction manuals, this work concentrates on the two most important operations: multiplication and division. 10 easy lessons, each with a clear drawing, for the reader who has difficulty following other expositions. 1st publication. Index. 2 Appendices. 10 illustrations. 78 problems, all with answers. vi + 36 pp. 6⅛ x 9¼. **T62 Paperbound 60¢**

CALCULUS REFRESHER FOR TECHNICAL MEN. A. A. Klaf. Not an ordinary textbook but a unique refresher for engineers, technicians, and students. An examination of the most important aspects of differential and integral calculus by means of 756 key questions. Part I covers simple differential calculus: constants, variables, functions, increments, derivatives, logarithms, curvature, etc. Part II treats fundamental concepts of integration: inspection, substitution, transformation, reduction, areas and volumes, mean value, successive and partial integration, double and triple integration. STRESSES PRACTICAL ASPECTS! A 50 page section gives applications to civil and nautical engineering, electricity, stress and strain, elasticity, industrial engineering, and similar fields. 756 questions answered. 556 problems; solutions to odd numbers. 36 pages of constants, formulae. Index. v + 431pp. 5⅜ x 8. **T370 Paperbound $2.00**

TRIGONOMETRY REFRESHER FOR TECHNICAL MEN, A. A. Klaf. A modern question and answer text on plane and spherical trigonometry. Part I covers plane trigonometry: angles, quadrants, trigonometrical functions, graphical representation, interpolation, equations, logarithms, solution of triangles, slide rules, etc. Part II discusses applications to navigation, surveying, elasticity, architecture, and engineering. Small angles, periodic functions, vectors, polar coordinates, De Moivre's theorem, fully covered. Part III is devoted to spherical trigonometry and the solution of spherical triangles, with applications to terrestrial and astronomical problems. Special time-savers for numerical calculation. 913 questions answered for you! 1738 problems; answers to odd numbers. 494 figures. 14 pages of functions, formulae. Index. x + 629pp. 5⅜ x 8. **1371 Paperbound $2.00**

*HIGHER MATHEMATICS FOR STUDENTS OF CHEMISTRY AND PHYSICS, J. W. Mellor. Not abstract, but practical, drawing its problems from familiar laboratory material, this book covers theory and application of differential calculus, analytic geometry, functions with singularities, integral calulus, infinite series, solution of numerical equations, differential equations, Fourier's theorem and extensions, probability and the theory of errors, calulus of variations, determinants, etc. "If the reader is not familiar with this book, it will repay him to examine it," CHEM. & ENGINEERING NEWS. 800 problems. 189 figures. 2 appendices; 30 tables of integrals, probability functions, etc. Bibliography. xxi + 641pp. 5⅜ x 8. **S193 Paperbound $2.00**

*GEOMETRY OF FOUR DIMENSIONS, H. P. Manning. Unique in English as a clear concise introduction to this fascinating subject. Treatment is primarily synthetic and Euclidean, although hyperplanes and hyperspheres at infinity are considered by non-Euclidean forms. Historical introduction and foundations of 4-dimensional geometry; perpendicularity; simple angles; angles of planes; higher order; symmetry; order, motion; hyperpyramids, hypercones, hyperspheres; figures with parallel elements; volume, hypervolume in space; regular polyhedroids. Glossary of terms. 74 illustrations. ix + 348pp. 5⅜ x 8. **S182 Paperbound $1.95**

*INTRODUCTION TO SYMBOLIC LOGIC AND ITS APPLICATIONS, Rudolph Carnap. One of the clearest, most comprehensive, and rigorous introductions to modern symbolic logic, by perhaps its greatest living master. Not merely elementary theory, but demonstrated applications in mathematics, physics, and biology. Symbolic languages of various degrees of complexity are analyzed, and one constructed. "A creation of the rank of a masterpiece," Zentralblatt Für Mathematik und Ihre Grenzgebiete. Over 300 exercises. 5 figures. Bibliography. Index. xvi + 241pp. 5⅜ x 8. **S453 Paperbound $1.85**

HOW TO CALCULATE QUICKLY, H. Sticker. A tried and true method for increasing your "number sense" — the ability to see relationships between numbers and groups of numbers. Addition, subtraction, multiplication, division, fractions, and other topics are treated through techniques not generally taught in schools: left to right multiplication, division by inspection, etc. This is not a collection of tricks which work only on special numbers, but a detailed well-planned course, consisting of over 9,000 problems that you can work in spare moments. It is excellent for anyone who is inconvenienced by slow computational skills. 5 or 10 minutes of this book daily will double or triple your calculation speed. 9,000 problems, answers. 256pp. 5⅜ x 8. **T295 Paperbound $1.00**

FADS AND FALLACIES IN THE NAME OF SCIENCE, Martin Gardner. Formerly entitled IN THE NAME OF SCIENCE, this is the standard account of various cults, quack systems, and delusions which have masqueraded as science: hollow earth fanatics, Reich and orgone sex energy, dianetics, Atlantis, multiple moons, Forteanism, flying saucers, medical fallacies like iridiagnosis, zone therapy, etc. A new chapter has been added on Bridey Murphy, psionics, and other recent manifestations in this field. This is a fair reasoned appraisal of eccentric theory which provides excellent innoculation against cleverly masked nonsense. "Should be read by everyone, scientist and non-scientist alike," R. T. Birge, Prof. Emeritus of Physics, Univ. of California; Former President, American Physical Society. Index. x + 365pp. 5⅜ x 8. **T394 Paperbound $1.50**

CATALOG OF DOVER BOOKS

PHILOSOPHY AND THE PHYSICISTS, L. Susan Stebbing. A philosopher examines the philosophical aspects of modern science, in terms of a lively critical attack on the ideas of Jeans and Eddington. Such basic questions are treated as the task of science, causality, determinism, probability, consciousness, the relation of the world of physics to the world of everyday experience. The author probes the concepts of man's smallness before an inscrutable universe, the tendency to idealize mathematical construction, unpredictability theorems and human freedom, the supposed opposition between 19th century determinism and modern science, and many others. Introduces many thought-stimulating ideas about the implications of modern physical concepts. xvi + 295pp.   T480 Paperbound **$1.65**

WHAT IS SCIENCE?, N. Campbell. The role of experiment and measurement, the function of mathematics, the nature of scientific laws, the difference between laws and theories, the limitations of science, and many similarly provocative topics are treated clearly and without technicalities by an eminent scientist. "Still an excellent introduction to scientific philosophy," H. Margenau in PHYSICS TODAY. "A first-rate primer . . . deserves a wide audience," SCIENTIFIC AMERICAN. 192pp. 5⅜ x 8.   S43 Paperbound **$1.25**

THE NATURE OF PHYSICAL THEORY, P. W. Bridgman. A Nobel Laureate's clear, non-technical lectures on difficulties and paradoxes connected with frontier research on the physical sciences. Concerned with such central concepts as thought, logic, mathematics, relativity, probability, wave mechanics, etc. he analyzes the contributions of such men as Newton, Einstein, Bohr, Heisenberg, and many others. "Lucid and entertaining . . . recommended to anyone who wants to get some insight into current philosophies of science," THE NEW PHILOSOPHY. Index. xi + 138pp. 5⅜ x 8.   S33 Paperbound **$1.25**

EXPERIMENT AND THEORY IN PHYSICS, Max Born. A Nobel Laureate examines the nature of experiment and theory in theoretical physics and analyzes the advances made by the great physicists of our day: Heisenberg, Einstein, Bohr, Planck, Dirac, and others. The actual process of creation is detailed step-by-step by one who participated. A fine examination of the scientific method at work. 44pp. 5⅜ x 8.   S308 Paperbound **75¢**

THE PSYCHOLOGY OF INVENTION IN THE MATHEMATICAL FIELD, J. Hadamard. The reports of such men as Descartes, Pascal, Einstein, Poincaré, and others are considered in this investigation of the method of idea-creation in mathematics and other sciences and the thinking process in general. How do ideas originate? What is the role of the unconscious? What is Poincaré's forgetting hypothesis? are some of the fascinating questions treated. A penetrating analysis of Einstein's thought processes concludes the book. xiii + 145pp. 5⅜ x 8.
T107 Paperbound **$1.25**

THE BIRTH AND DEVELOPMENT OF THE GEOLOGICAL SCIENCES, F. D. Adams. The most complete and thorough history of the earth sciences in print. Geological thought from earliest recorded times to the end of the 19th century—covers over 300 early thinkers and systems: fossils and hypothetical explanations of them, vulcanists vs. neptunists, figured stones and paleontology, generation of stones, and similar topics. 91 illustrations, including medieval, renaissance woodcuts, etc. 632 footnotes and bibliographic notes. Index. 511pp. 5⅜ x 8.
T5 Paperbound **$2.00**

A HISTORY OF ASTRONOMY FROM THALES TO KEPLER, J. L. E. Dreyer. Formerly titled A HISTORY OF PLANETARY SYSTEMS FROM THALES TO KEPLER. This is the only work in English which provides a detailed history of man's cosmological views from prehistoric times up through the Renaissance. It covers Egypt, Babylonia, early Greece, Alexandria, the Middle Ages, Copernicus, Tycho Brahe, Kepler, and many others. Epicycles and other complex theories of positional astronomy are explained in terms nearly everyone will find clear and easy to understand. "Standard reference on Greek astronomy and the Copernican revolution," SKY AND TELESCOPE. Bibliography. 21 diagrams. Index. xvii + 430pp. 5⅜ x 8.   S79 Paperbound **$1.98**

A SHORT HISTORY OF ASTRONOMY, A. Berry. A popular standard work for over 50 years, this thorough and accurate volume covers the science from primitive times to the end of the 19th century. After the Greeks and Middle Ages, individual chapters analyze Copernicus, Brahe, Galileo, Kepler, and Newton, and the mixed reception of their startling discoveries. Post-Newtonian achievements are then discussed in unusual detail: Halley, Bradley, Lagrange, Laplace, Herschel, Bessel, etc. 2 indexes. 104 illustrations, 9 portraits. xxxi + 440pp. 5⅜ x 8.
T210 Paperbound **$2.00**

THE STORY OF ALCHEMY AND EARLY CHEMISTRY, J. M. Stillman. "Add the blood of a red-haired man"—a recipe typical of the many quoted in this authoritative and readable history of the strange beliefs and practices of the alchemists. Concise studies of every leading figure in alchemy and early chemistry through Lavoisier, in this curious epic of superstition and true science, constructed from scores of rare and difficult Greek, Latin, German, and French texts. Foreword by S. W. Young. 246-item bibliography. Index. xiii + 566pp. 5⅜ x 8.
S628 Paperbound **$2.45**

A CONCISE HISTORY OF MATHEMATICS, D. Struik. A lucid, easily followed history of mathematical ideas and techniques from the Ancient Near East up to modern times. Requires no mathematics but will serve as an excellent introduction to mathematical concepts and great mathematicians through the method of historical development. 60 illustrations including Egyptian papyri, Greek mss., portraits of 31 eminent mathematicians. Bibliography. xix + 299pp. 5⅜ x 8.   T255 Paperbound **$1.75**

CATALOG OF DOVER BOOKS

HISTORY OF MATHEMATICS, D. E. Smith. Most comprehensive non-technical history of math in English. Discusses the lives and works of over a thousand major and minor figures, from Euclid to Descartes, Gauss, and Riemann. Vol. I: A chronological examination, from primitive concepts through Egypt, Babylonia, Greece, the Orient, Rome, the Middle Ages, the Renaissance, and up to 1900. Vol. 2: The development of ideas in specific fields and problems, up through elementary calculus. Two volumes, total of 510 illustrations, 1355pp. 5⅜ x 8.   T429,430 Paperbound the set **$5.00**

GUIDE TO THE LITERATURE OF MATHEMATICS AND PHYSICS, N. G. Parke III. Over 5000 entries included under approximately 120 major subject headings, of selected most important books, monographs, periodicals, articles in English, plus important works in German, French, Italian, Spanish, Russian (many recently available works). Covers every branch of physics, math, related engineering. Includes author, title, edition, publisher, place, date, number of volumes, number of pages. A 40-page introduction on the basic problems of research and study provides useful information on the organization and use of libraries, the psychology of learning, etc. This reference work will save you hours of time. 2nd revised edition. Indices of authors, subjects. 464pp. 5⅜ x 8.   S447 Paperbound **$2.49**

THE STUDY OF THE HISTORY OF MATHEMATICS, THE STUDY OF THE HISTORY OF SCIENCE, G. Sarton. Two books bound as one. Each volume contains a long introduction to the methods and philosophy of each of these historical fields, covering the skills and sympathies of the historian, concepts of history of science, psychology of idea-creation, and the purpose of history of science. Prof. Sarton also provides more than 80 pages of classified bibliography. Complete and unabridged. Indexed. 10 illustrations. 188pp. 5⅜ x 8.   T240 Paperbound **$1.25**

THE DIDEROT PICTORIAL ENCYCLOPEDIA OF TRADES AND INDUSTRY, MANUFACTURING AND THE TECHNICAL ARTS IN PLATES SELECTED FROM "L'ENCYCLOPÉDIE OU DICTIONNAIRE RAISONNÉ DES SCIENCES, DES ARTS, ET DES MÉTIERS" OF DENIS DIDEROT, edited with text by C. Gillispie. The first modern selection of plates from the high point of 18th century French engraving, Diderot's famous Encyclopedia. Over 2000 illustrations on 485 full page plates, most of them original size, illustrating the trades and industries of one of the most fascinating periods of modern history, 18th century France. These magnificent engravings provide an invaluable source of fresh, copyright-free material to artists and illustrators, a lively and accurate social document to students of cultures, an outstanding find to the lover of fine engravings. The plates teem with life, with men, women, and children performing all of the thousands of operations necessary to the trades before and during the early stages of the industrial revolution. Plates are in sequence, and show general operations, closeups of difficult operations, and details of complex machinery. Such important and interesting trades and industries are illustrated as sowing, harvesting, beekeeping, cheesemaking, operating windmills, milling flour, charcoal burning, tobacco processing, indigo, fishing, arts of war, salt extraction, mining, smelting iron, casting iron, steel, extracting mercury, zinc, sulphur, copper, etc., slating, tinning, silverplating, gilding, making gunpowder, cannons, bells, shoeing horses, tanning, papermaking, printing, dying, and more than 40 other categories. Besides being a work of remarkable beauty and skill, this is also one of the largest collections of working figures in print. 920pp. 9 x 12. Heavy library cloth.   T421 Two volume set **$18.50**

THE VALUE OF SCIENCE, Henri Poincaré. Many of the most mature ideas of the "last scientific universalist" conveyed with charm and vigor for both the beginning student and the advanced worker. Discusses the nature of scientific truth, whether order is innate in the universe or imposed upon it by man, logical thought versus intuition (relating to mathematics through the works of Weierstrass, Lie, Klein, Riemann), time and space (relativity, psychological time, simultaneity), Hertz's concept of force, interrelationship of mathematical physics to pure math, values within disciplines of Maxwell, Carnot, Mayer, Newton, Lorentz, etc. Index. iii + 147pp. 5⅜ x 8.   S469 Paperbound **$1.35**

SCIENCE AND METHOD, Henri Poincaré. Procedure of scientific discovery, methodology, experiment, idea-germination—the intellectual processes by which discoveries come into being. Most significant and most interesting aspects of development, application of ideas. Chapters cover selection of facts, chance, mathematical reasoning, mathematics, and logic; Whitehead, Russell, Cantor; the new mechanics, etc. 288pp. 5⅜ x 8.   S222 Paperbound **$1.35**

SCIENCE AND HYPOTHESIS, Henri Poincaré. Creative psychology in science. How such concepts as number, magnitude, space, force, classical mechanics were developed and how the modern scientist uses them in his thought. Hypothesis in physics, theories of modern physics. Introduction by Sir James Larmor. "Few mathematicians have had the breadth of vision of Poincaré, and none is his superior in the gift of clear exposition," E. T. Bell. Index. 272pp. 5⅜ x 8.   S221 Paperbound **$1.35**

ON MATHEMATICS AND MATHEMATICIANS, R. E. Moritz. A ten year labor of love by the discerning and discriminating Prof. Moritz, this collection has rarely been equalled in its ability to convey the full sense of mathematics and the personalities of great mathematicians. A collection of anecdotes, aphorisms, reminiscences, philosophies, definitions, speculations, biographical insights, etc., by great mathematicians and writers: Descartes, Mill, De Morgan, Locke, Berkeley, Kant, Coleridge, Whitehead, Sylvester, Klein, and many others. Also, glimpses into the lives of mathematical giants from Archimedes to Euler, Gauss, and Weierstrass. To mathematicians, a superb book for browsing; to writers and teachers, an unequalled source of quotation; to the layman, an exciting revelation of the fullness of mathematics. Extensive cross index. 410pp. 5⅜ x 8.   T489 Paperbound **$1.95**

Classics of Science

*OPTICKS, Sir Isaac Newton. An enormous storehouse of insights and discoveries on light, reflection, color, refraction, theories of wave and corpuscular propagation of light, optical apparatus, and mathematical devices which have recently been reevaluated in terms of modern physics and placed in the top-most ranks of Newton's work. Foreword by Albert Einstein. Preface by I. B. Cohen of Harvard U. 7 pages of portraits, facsimile pages, letters, etc. cxvi + 412pp. 5⅜ x 8.   S205 Paperbound **$2.00**

A SURVEY OF PHYSICAL THEORY, M. Planck. Lucid essays on modern physics for the general reader by the Nobel laureate and creator of the quantum revolution. Planck explains how the new concepts came into being; explores the clash between theories of mechanics, electrodynamics, and thermodynamics; and traces the evolution of the concept of light through Newton, Huygens, Maxwell, and his own quantum theory, providing unparalleled insights into his development of this momentous modern concept. Bibliography. Index. vii + 121pp. 5⅜ x 8.
T650 Paperbound **$1.15**

DE RE METALLICA, Georgius Agricola. Written over 400 years ago, for 200 years the most authoritative first-hand account of the production of metals, translated in 1912 by former President Herbert Hoover and his wife, and today still one of the most beautiful and fascinating volumes ever produced in the history of science! 12 books, exhaustively annotated, give a wonderfully lucid and vivid picture of the history of mining, selection of sites, types of deposits, excavating pits, sinking shafts, ventilating, pumps, crushing machinery, assaying, smelting, refining metals, making salt, alum, nitre, glass, and many other topics. This definitive edition contains all 289 of the 16th century woodcuts which made the original an artistic masterpiece. It makes a superb gift for geologists, engineers, libraries, artists, historians, and everyone interested in science and early illustrative art. Biographical, historical introductions. Bibliography, survey of ancient authors. Indices. 289 illustrations. 672pp. 6¾ x 10¾.
Deluxe library edition.   S6 Clothbound **$10.00**

CHARLES BABBAGE AND HIS CALCULATING ENGINES, edited by P. Morrison and E. Morrison. Friend of Darwin, Humboldt, and Laplace, Babbage was a leading pioneer in large-scale mathematical machines and a prophetic herald of modern operational research—true father of Harvard's relay computer Mark I. His Difference Engine and Analytical Engine were the first successful machines in the field. This volume contains a valuable introduction on his life and work; major excerpts from his fascinating autobiography, revealing his eccentric and unusual personality; and extensive selections from "Babbage's Calculating Engines," a compilation of hard-to-find journal articles, both by Babbage and by such eminent contributors as the Countess of Lovelace, L. F. Menabrea, and Dionysius Lardner. 11 illustrations. Appendix of miscellaneous papers. Index. Bibliography. xxxviii + ·3 pp. 5⅜ x 8.   T12 Paperbound **$2.00**

A SOURCE BOOK IN MATHEMATICS, D. E. Smith. English translations of the original papers that announced the great discoveries in mathematics from the Renaissance to the end of the 19th century: succinct selections from 125 different treatises and articles, most of them unavailable elsewhere in English—Newton, Leibniz, Pascal, Riemann, Bernoulli, etc. 24 articles trace developments in the field of number, 18 cover algebra, 36 are on geometry, and 13 on calculus. Biographical-historical introductions to each article. Two volume set. Index in each. Total of 115 illustrations. Total of xxviii + 742pp. 5⅜ x 8.   T552 Vol I Paperbound **$1.85**
T553 Vol II Paperbound **$1.85**
The set, boxed **$3.50**

*THE WORKS OF ARCHIMEDES WITH THE METHOD OF ARCHIMEDES, edited by T. L. Heath. All the known works of the greatest mathematician of antiquity including the recently discovered METHOD OF ARCHIMEDES. This last is the only work we have which shows exactly how early mathematicians discovered their proofs before setting them down in their final perfection. A 186 page study by the eminent scholar Heath discusses Archimedes and the history of Greek mathematics. Bibliography. 563pp. 5⅜ x 8.   S9 Paperbound **$2.00**

*THE THIRTEEN BOOKS OF EUCLID'S ELEMENTS, edited by T. L. Heath. This is the complete EUCLID — the definitive edition of one of the greatest classics of the western world. Complete English translation of the Heiberg text with spurious Book XIV. Detailed 150 page introduction discusses aspects of Greek and medieval mathematics: Euclid, texts, commentators, etc. Paralleling the text is an elaborate critical exposition analyzing each definition, proposition, postulate, etc., and covering textual matters, mathematical analyses, refutations, extensions, etc. Unabridged reproduction of the Cambridge 2nd edition. 3 volumes. Total of 995 figures, 1426pp. 5⅜ x 8.   S88, 89, 90 — 3 vol. set, Paperbound **$6.00**

CLASSICS OF CARDIOLOGY, F. A. Willius, T. E. Keys. Monumental collection of 52 papers by great researchers, physicians on the anatomy, physiology and pathology of the heart and the circulation, and the diagnosis and therapy of their diseases. These are the original writings of Harvey, Sénac, Auenbrugger, Withering, Stokes, Einthoven, Osler, and 44 others from 1628 to 1912. 27 of the papers are complete, the rest in major excerpts; all are in English. The biographical notes and introductory essays make this a full history of cardiology—with exclusively first-hand material. 103 portraits, diagrams, and facsimiles of title pages. Chronological table. Total of xx + 858pp. 5⅝ x 8⅜. Two volume set.   S912 Vol I Paperbound **$2.00**
S913 Vol II Paperbound **$2.00**
The set **$4.00**

CATALOG OF DOVER BOOKS

*A PHILOSOPHICAL ESSAY ON PROBABILITIES, P. Laplace. Without recource to any mathematics above grammar school, Laplace develops a philosophically, mathematically and historically classical exposition of the nature of probability: its functions and limitations, operations in practical affairs, calculations in games of chance, insurance, government, astronomy, and countless other fields. New introduction by E. T. Bell. viii + 196pp. S166 Paperbound **$1.35**

*DIALOGUES CONCERNING TWO NEW SCIENCES, Galileo Galilei. A classic of experimental science which has had a profound and enduring influence on the entire history of mechanics and engineering. Galileo based this, his finest work, on 30 years of experimentation. It offers a fascinating and vivid exposition of dynamics, elasticity, sound, ballistics, strength of materials, and the scientific method. Translated b H. Crew and A. de Salvio. 126 diagrams. Index. xxi + 288pp. 5⅜ x 8. S99 Paperbound **$1.65**

DE MAGNETE, William Gilbert. This classic work on magnetism founded a new science. Gilbert was the first to use the word "electricity," to recognize mass as distinct from weight, to discover the effect of heat on magnetic bodies; invented an electroscope, differentiated between static electricity and magnetism, conceived of the earth as a magnet. Written by the first great experimental scientist, this lively work is valuable not only as an historical landmark, but as the delightfully easy to follow record of a perpetually searching, ingenious mind. Translated by P. F. Mottelay. 25 page biographical memoir. 90 fix. lix + 368pp. 5⅜ x 8. S470 Paperbound **$2.00**

*THE GEOMETRY OF RENÉ DESCARTES. The great work which founded analytic geometry. The renowned Smith-Latham translation faced with the original French text containing all of Descartes' own diagrams! Contains: Problems the Construction of Which Requires Only Straight Lines and Circles; On the Nature of Curved Lines; On the Construction of Solid or Supersolid Problems. Notes. Diagrams. 258pp. S68 Paperbound **$1.50**

Nature and Biology

THE AUTOBIOGRAPHY OF CHARLES DARWIN AND SELECTED LETTERS, edited by Francis Darwin. The personal record of the professional and private life of the author of "Origin of the Species," whose ideas have shaped our thinking as have few others. His early life; the historic voyage aboard the "Beagle," the furor surrounding evolution and his replies; revealing anecdotes; reminiscences by his son; letters to Henslow, Lyell, Hooker, Huxley, Wallace, Kingsley, and others; his thought on religion and vivisection. Appendix. Index. 365pp. 5⅜ x 8. T479 Paperbound **$1.65**

THE LIFE OF PASTEUR, R. Vallery-Radot. 13th edition of this definitive biography, cited in Encyclopaedia Britannica. Authoritative, scholarly, well-documented with contemporary quotes, observations; gives complete picture of Pasteur's personal life; especially thorough presentation of scientific activities with silkworms, fermentation, hydrophobia, inoculation, etc. Introduction by Sir William Osler. Index. 505pp. 5⅜ x 8. T632 Paperbound **$2.00**

LOUIS PASTEUR, S. J. Holmes. A brief, very clear, and warmly understanding biography of the great French scientist by a former Professor of Zoology in the University of California. Traces his home life, the fortunate effects of his education, his early researches and first theses, and his constant struggle with superstition and institutionalism in his work on microorganisms, fermentation, anthrax, rabies, etc. New preface by the author. T197 Paperbound **$1.00**

THE ORIGIN OF LIFE, A. I. Oparin. This is the first modern statement of the theory that life evolved from complex nitro-carbon compounds. A historical introduction covers theories of the origin of life from the Greeks to modern times and then the techniques of biochemistry as applied to the problem by Dr. Oparin. The exposition presupposes a knowledge of chemistry but can be read with profit by everyone interested in this absorbing question. "Easily the most scholarly authority on the question," NEW YORK TIMES. Bibliography. Index. xxv + 270pp. 5⅛ x 8. S213 Paperbound **$1.75**

FREE! All you do is ask for it!

A WAY OF LIFE, by Sir William Osler. An inspirational classic that has helped countless business and professional men since the beloved physician and philosopher first delivered it at Yale in 1913. In warm human terms Osler tells how he managed to make the most of every day by an edifying mental and physical regimen. Illustrated. **FREE**

STUDIES ON THE STRUCTURE AND DEVELOPMENT OF VERTEBRATES, Edwin S. Goodrich. This definitive study by the greatest modern comparative anatomist covers the skeleton, fins and limbs, head region morphology, skull, skeletal viseral arches and labial cartilages, middle ear and ear ossicles, visceral clefts and gills, subdivisions of body cavity, vascular, respiratory, excretory, and peripheral nervous systems of vertebrates from fish to the higher mammals. 754 pictures. 69 page biographical study by C. C. Hardy. Bibliography of 1186 references. "For many a day this will certainly be the standard textbook," Journal of Anatomy. Index. Two volumes total 906pp. 5⅜ x 8. 2 volume set S449-50 Paperbound **$5.00**

CATALOG OF DOVER BOOKS

HEREDITY AND YOUR LIFE, A. M. Winchester. Authoritative, concise explanation of human genetics, in non-technical terms. What factors determine characteristics of future generations, how they may be altered; history of genetics, application of knowledge to control health, intelligence, number of entire populations. Physiology of reproduction, chromosomes, genes, blood types, Rh factor, dominant, recessive traits, birth by proxy, sexual abnormalities, radiation, much more. Index. 75 illus. 345pp. 5⅜ x 8. **T598 Paperbound $1.45**

FROM MAGIC TO SCIENCE, Charles Singer. Great historian of science examines aspects of medical science from the Roman Empire through the Renaissance. Especially valuable are the sections on early herbals, probably the best coverage of this subject available, and on "The Visions of Hildegarde of Bingen" which are explained by physiological means. Also covered are Arabian and Galenic influences, astrology, the Sphere of Pythagoras, Leonardo da Vinci, Vesalius, Paracelsus, et al. Frequent quotations and translations. New introduction by the author. New unabridged, corrected edition. 158 unusual illustrations from classical and medieval sources. Index. xxvii + 365pp. 5⅜ x 8. **T390 Paperbound $2.00**

A SHORT HISTORY OF ANATOMY AND PHYSIOLOGY FROM THE GREEKS TO HARVEY, C. Singer. An intermediate history formerly entitled THE EVOLUTION OF ANATOMY, this work conveys the thrill of discovery as the nature of the human body is gradually clarified by hundreds of scientists from the Greeks to the Renaissance. Diogenes, Hippocrates, and other early workers, up to Leonardo da Vinci, Vesalius, Harvey, and others, with 139 illustrations from medieval manuscripts, classical sculpture, etc. Index. 221pp. 5⅜ x 8. **T389 Paperbound $1.75**

INTRODUCTION TO THE STUDY OF EXPERIMENTAL MEDICINE, Claude Bernard. The only major work of Claude Bernard now available in English, this classic records Bernard's efforts to transform physiology into an exact science. He examines the roles of chance and error and incorrect hypothesis in leading to scientific truth and describes many classic experiments on the action of curare, carbon monoxide, and other poisons, the functions of the pancreas, the glycogenic function of the liver, and many others. Introduction. Foreword by I. B. Cohen. xxv + 266pp. 5⅜ x 8. **T400 Paperbound $1.50**

A WAY OF LIFE AND OTHER SELECTED WRITINGS, Sir William Osler. Physician and humanist, Osler writes brilliantly on philosophy, religion, and literature in "The Student Life," "Books and Men," "Creators, Transmuters, and Transmitters," "The Old Humanities and the New Science," and the title essay. His medical history is equally acute in discussions of Thomas Browne, Gui Patin, Robert Burton, Michael Servetus, William Beaumont, Laënnec. 5 more of his best essays. 5 photographs. Introduction by G. L. Keynes, M.D., F.R.C.S. Index. xx + 278pp. 5⅜ x 8. **T488 Paperbound $1.50**

FRUIT KEY AND TWIG KEY TO TREES AND SHRUBS, W. M. Harlow. Bound together in one volume for the first time, these handy and accurate keys to fruit and twig identification are the only guides of their sort with photographs (up to 3 times natural size). "Fruit Key": Key to over 120 different deciduous and evergreen fruits. 139 photographs and 11 line drawings. Synoptic summary of fruit types. Bibliography. 2 Indexes (common and scientific names). "Twig Key": Key to over 160 different twigs and buds. 173 photographs. Glossary of technical terms. Bibliography. 2 Indexes (common and scientific names). Two volumes bound as one. Total of xvii + 126pp. 5⅝ x 8⅜. **T511 Paperbound $1.25**

TREES OF THE EASTERN AND CENTRAL UNITED STATES AND CANADA, W. M. Harlow. A revised edition of a standard middle-level guide to native trees and important escapes. More than 140 trees are described in detail, and illustrated with more than 600 drawings and photographs. Supplementary keys will enable the careful reader to identify almost any tree he might encounter. xiii + 288pp. 5⅜ x 8. **T395 Paperbound $1.35**

INSECT LIFE AND INSECT NATURAL HISTORY, S. W. Frost. A work emphasizing habits, social life, and ecological relations of insects, rather than more academic aspects of classification and morphology. Prof. Frost's enthusiasm and knowledge are everywhere evident as he discusses insect associations, and specialized habits like leaf-rolling, leaf-mining, and case-making, the gall insects, the boring insects, aquatic insects, etc. He examines all sorts of matters not usually covered in general works, such as: insects as human food, insect music and musicians, insect response to electric and radio waves, use of insects in art and literature. The admirably executed purpose of this book, which covers the middle ground between elementary treatment and scholarly monographs, is to excite the reader to observe for himself. Over 700 illustrations. Extensive bibliography. x + 524pp. 5⅜ x 8.

T517 Paperbound $2.25

COMMON SPIDERS OF THE UNITED STATES, J. H. Emerton. Here is a nature hobby you can pursue right in your own cellar! Only non-technical, but thorough, reliable guide to spiders for the layman. Over 200 spiders from all parts of the country, arranged by scientific classification, are identified by shape and color, number of eyes, habitat and range, habits, etc. Full text, 501 line drawings and photographs, and valuable introduction explain webs, poisons, threads, capturing and preserving spiders, etc. Index. New synoptic key by S. W. Frost. xxiv + 225pp. 5⅜ x 8. T223 Paperbound **$1.35**

HOW TO KNOW THE FERNS, F. T. Parsons. Ferns, among our most lovely native plants, are all too little known. This modern classic of nature lore will enable the layman to identify any American fern he may come across. After an introduction on the structure and life of ferns, the 57 most important ferns are fully pictured and described (arranged upon a simple identification key). Index of Latin and English names. 61 illustrations and 42 full-page plates. xiv + 215pp. 5⅜ x 8. T740 Paperbound **$1.25**

RACING PIGEONS, C. Osman. A complete, practical, up-to-date, and authoritative book on racing pigeons by a British expert. Covers the anatomy of the pigeon, the homing instinct, the pigeon's life cycle, food and feeding, lofts and aviaries, breeding winners, preparing for races, winning systems, common diseases, and much more. Indispensable for beginner and expert alike. 24 photographs by the author. 10 line drawings. Index. 192pp. 5⅛ x 7⅛. T513 Clothbound **$3.00**

Psychology

YOGA: A SCIENTIFIC EVALUATION, Kovoor T. Behanan. A complete reprinting of the book that for the first time gave Western readers a sane, scientific explanation and analysis of yoga. The author draws on controlled laboratory experiments and personal records of a year as a disciple of a yoga, to investigate yoga psychology, concepts of knowledge, physiology, "supernatural" phenomena, and the ability to tap the deepest human powers. In this study under the auspices of Yale University Institute of Human Relations, the strictest principles of physiological and psychological inquiry are followed throughout. Foreword by W. A. Miles, Yale University. 17 photographs. Glossary. Index. xx + 270pp. 5⅜ x 8. T505 Paperbound **$1.65**

CONDITIONED REFLEXES: AN INVESTIGATION OF THE PHYSIOLOGICAL ACTIVITIES OF THE CEREBRAL CORTEX, I. P. Pavlov. Full, authorized translation of Pavlov's own survey of his work in experimental psychology reviews entire course of experiments, summarizes conclusions, outlines psychological system based on famous "conditioned reflex" concept. Details of technical means used in experiments, observations on formation of conditioned reflexes, function of cerebral hemispheres, results of damage, nature of sleep, typology of nervous system, significance of experiments for human psychology. Trans. by Dr. G. V. Anrep, Cambridge Univ. 235-item bibliography. 18 figures. 445pp. 5⅜ x 8. S614 Paperbound **$2.25**

EXPLANATION OF HUMAN BEHAVIOUR, F. V. Smith. A major intermediate-level introduction to and criticism of 8 complete systems of the psychology of human behavior, with unusual emphasis on theory of investigation and methodology. Part I is an illuminating analysis of the problems involved in the explanation of observed phenomena, and the differing viewpoints on the nature of causality. Parts II and III are a closely detailed survey of the systems of McDougall, Gordon Allport, Lewin, the Gestalt group, Freud, Watson, Hull, and Tolman. Biographical notes. Bibliography of over 800 items. 2 Indexes. 38 figures. xii + 460pp. 5½ x 8¾. T253 Clothbound **$6.00**

SEX IN PSYCHO-ANALYSIS (formerly CONTRIBUTIONS TO PSYCHO-ANALYSIS), S. Ferenczi. Written by an associate of Freud, this volume presents countless insights on such topics as impotence, transference, analysis and children, dreams, symbols, obscene words, masturbation and male homosexuality, paranoia and psycho-analysis, the sense of reality, hypnotism and therapy, and many others. Also includes full text of THE DEVELOPMENT OF PSYCHO-ANALYSIS by Ferenczi and Otto Rank. Two books bound as one. Total of 406pp. 5⅜ x 8. T324· Paperbound **$1.85**

BEYOND PSYCHOLOGY, Otto Rank. One of Rank's most mature contributions, focussing on the irrational basis of human behavior as a basic fact of our lives. The psychoanalytic techniques of myth analysis trace to their source the ultimates of human existence: fear of death, personality, the social organization, the need for love and creativity, etc. Dr. Rank finds them stemming from a common irrational source, man's fear of final destruction. A seminal work in modern psychology, this work sheds light on areas ranging from the concept of immortal soul to the sources of state power. 291pp. 5⅜ x 8. T485 Paperbound **$1.75**

ILLUSIONS AND DELUSIONS OF THE SUPERNATURAL AND THE OCCULT, D. H. Rawcliffe. Holds up to rational examination hundreds of persistent delusions including crystal gazing, automatic writing, table turning, mediumistic trances, mental healing, stigmata, lycanthropy, live burial, the Indian Rope Trick, spiritualism, dowsing, telepathy, clairvoyance, ghosts, ESP, etc. The author explains and exposes the mental and physical deceptions involved, making this not only an exposé of supernatural phenomena, but a valuable exposition of characteristic types of abnormal psychology. Originally titled "The Psychology of the Occult." 14 illustrations. Index. 551pp. 5⅜ x 8. T503 Paperbound **$2.00**

THE PRINCIPLES OF PSYCHOLOGY, William James. The full long course, unabridged, of one of the great classics of Western literature and science. Wonderfully lucid descriptions of human mental activity, the stream of thought, consciousness, time perception, memory, imagination, emotions, reason, abnormal phenomena, and similar topics. Original contributions are integrated with the work of such men as Berkeley, Binet, Mills, Darwin, Hume, Kant, Royce, Schopenhauer, Spinoza, Locke, Descartes, Galton, Wundt, Lotze, Herbart, Fechner, and scores of others. All contrasting interpretations of mental phenomena are examined in detail — introspective analysis, philosophical interpretation, and experimental research. "A classic," JOURNAL OF CONSULTING PSYCHOLOGY. "The main lines are as valid as ever," PSYCHO-ANALYTICAL QUARTERLY. "Standard reading . . . a classic of interpretation," PSYCHIATRIC QUARTERLY. 94 illustrations. 1408pp. 2 volumes. 5⅜ x 8.   Vol. 1, T381 Paperbound **$2.50**
Vol. 2, T382 Paperbound **$2.50**

Puzzles, Mathematical Recreations

SYMBOLIC LOGIC and THE GAME OF LOGIC, Lewis Carroll. "Symbolic Logic" is not concerned with modern symbolic logic, but is instead a collection of over 380 problems posed with charm and imagination, using the syllogism, and a fascinating diagrammatic method of drawing conclusions. In "The Game of Logic" Carroll's whimsical imagination devises a logical game played with 2 diagrams and counters (included) to manipulate hundreds of tricky syllogisms. The final section, "Hit or Miss" is a lagniappe of 101 additional puzzles in the delightful Carroll manner. Until this reprint edition, both of these books were rarities costing up to $15 each. Symbolic Logic: Index. xxxi + 199pp. The Game of Logic: 96pp. 2 vols. bound as one. 5⅜ x 8.   T492 Paperbound **$1.50**

PILLOW PROBLEMS and A TANGLED TALE, Lewis Carroll. One of the rarest of all Carroll's works, "Pillow Problems" contains 72 original math puzzles, all typically ingenious. Particularly fascinating are Carroll's answers which remain exactly as he thought them out, reflecting his actual mental process. The problems in "A Tangled Tale" are in story form, originally appearing as a monthly magazine serial. Carroll not only gives the solutions, but uses answers sent in by readers to discuss wrong approaches and misleading paths, and grades them for insight. Both of these books were rarities until this edition, "Pillow Problems" costing up to $25, and "A Tangled Tale" $15. Pillow Problems: Preface and Introduction by Lewis Carroll. xx + 109pp. A Tangled Tale: 6 illustrations. 152pp. Two vols. bound as one. 5⅜ x 8.   T493 Paperbound **$1.50**

AMUSEMENTS IN MATHEMATICS, Henry Ernest Dudeney. The foremost British originator of mathematical puzzles is always intriguing, witty, and paradoxical in this classic, one of the largest collections of mathematical amusements. More than 430 puzzles, problems, and paradoxes. Mazes and games, problems on number manipulation, unicursal and other route problems, puzzles on measuring, weighing, packing, age, kinship, chessboards, joiners', crossing river, plane figure dissection, and many others. Solutions. More than 450 illustrations. vii + 258pp. 5⅜ x 8.   T473 Paperbound **$1.25**

THE CANTERBURY PUZZLES, Henry Dudeney. Chaucer's pilgrims set one another problems in story form. Also Adventures of the Puzzle Club, the Strange Escape of the King's Jester, the Monks of Riddlewell, the Squire's Christmas Puzzle Party, and others. All puzzles are original, based on dissecting plane figures, arithmetic, algebra, elementary calculus and other branches of mathematics, and purely logical ingenuity. "The limit of ingenuity and intricacy," The Observer. Over 110 puzzles. Full Solutions. 150 illustrations. vii + 225pp. 5⅜ x 8.   T474 Paperbound **$1.25**

MATHEMATICAL RECREATIONS, M. Kraitchik. One of the most thorough compilations of unusual mathematical problems for beginners and advanced mathematicians. Historical problems from Greek, Medieval, Arabic, Hindu sources. 50 pages devoted to pastimes derived from figurate numbers, Mersenne numbers, Fermat numbers, primes and probability. 40 pages of magic, Euler, Latin, panmagic squares. 25 new positional and permutational games of permanent value: fairy chess, latruncles, reversi, jinx, ruma, lasca, tricolor, tetrachrome, etc. Complete rigorous solutions. Revised second edition. 181 illustrations. 333pp. 5⅜ x 8.
T163 Paperbound **$1.75**

MATHEMATICAL EXCURSIONS, H. A. Merrill. Even if you hardly remember your high school math, you'll enjoy the 90 stimulating problems contained in this book and you will come to understand a great many mathematical principles with surprisingly little effort. Many useful shortcuts and diversions not generally known are included: division by inspection, Russian peasant multiplication, memory systems for pi, building odd and even magic squares, square roots by geometry, dyadic systems, and many more. Solutions to difficult problems. 50 illustrations. 145pp. 5⅜ x 8.   T350 Paperbound **$1.00**

MAGIC SQUARES AND CUBES, W. S. Andrews. Only book-length treatment in English, a thorough non-technical description and analysis. Here are nasik, overlapping, pandiagonal, serrated squares; magic circles, cubes, spheres, rhombuses. Try your hand at 4-dimensional magical figures! Much unusual folklore and tradition included. High school algebra is sufficient. 754 diagrams and illustrations. viii + 419pp. 5⅜ x 8.   T658 Paperbound **$1.85**

CATALOG OF DOVER BOOKS

MATHEMATICAL PUZZLES OF SAM LOYD, Vol. I selected, edited by M. Gardner. Choice puzzles by the greatest American puzzle creator and innovator. Selected from his famous collection, "Cyclopedia of Puzzles," they retain the unique style and historical flavor of the originals. There are posers based on arithmetic, algebra, probability, game theory, route tracing, topology, counter, sliding block, operations research, geometrical dissection. Includes the famous "14-15" puzzle which was a national craze, and his "Horse of a Different Color" which sold millions of copies. 117 of his most ingenious puzzles in all, 120 line drawings and diagrams. Solutions. Selected references. xx + 167pp. 5⅜ x 8.   T498 Paperbound **$1.00**

MATHEMATICAL PUZZLES OF SAM LOYD, Vol. II, selected and edited by Martin Gardner. The outstanding 2nd selection from the great American innovator's "Cyclopedia of Puzzles": speed and distance problems, clock problems, plane and solid geometry, calculus problems, etc. Analytical table of contents that groups the puzzles according to the type of mathematics necessary to solve them. 166 puzzles, 150 original line drawings and diagrams. Selected references. xiv + 177pp. 5⅜ x 8.   T709 Paperbound **$1.00**

CALIBAN'S PROBLEM BOOK: MATHEMATICAL, INFERENTIAL AND CRYPTOGRAPHIC PUZZLES, H. Phillips (Caliban), S. T. Shovelton, G. S. Marshall. 105 ingenious problems by the greatest living creator of puzzles based on logic and inference. Rigorous, modern, piquant; reflecting their author's unusual personality, these intermediate and advanced puzzles all involve the ability to reason clearly through complex situations; some call for mathematical knowledge, ranging from algebra to number theory. Solutions. xi + 180pp. 5⅜ x 8.
                   T736 Paperbound **$1.25**

MATHEMATICAL PUZZLES FOR BEGINNERS AND ENTHUSIASTS, G. Mott-Smith. 188 mathematical puzzles based on algebra, dissection of plane figures, permutations, and probability, that will test and improve your powers of inference and interpretation. The Odic Force, The Spider's Cousin, Ellipse Drawing, theory and strategy of card and board games like tit-tat-toe, go moku, salvo, and many others. 100 pages of detailed mathematical explanations. Appendix of primes, square roots, etc. 135 illustrations. 2nd revised edition. 248pp. 5⅜ x 8.
                   T198 Paperbound **$1.00**

MATHEMAGIC, MAGIC PUZZLES, AND GAMES WITH NUMBERS, R. V. Heath. More than 60 new puzzles and stunts based on the properties of numbers. Easy techniques for multiplying large numbers mentally, revealing hidden numbers magically, finding the date of any day in any year, and dozens more. Over 30 pages devoted to magic squares, triangles, cubes, circles, etc. Edited by J. S. Meyer. 76 illustrations. 128pp. 5⅜ x 8.   T110 Paperbound **$1.00**

ARITHMETICAL EXCURSIONS: AN ENRICHMENT OF ELEMENTARY MATHEMATICS, H. Bowers and J. Bowers. A lively and lighthearted collection of facts and entertainments for anyone who enjoys manipulating numbers or solving arithmetical puzzles: methods of arithmetic never taught in school, little-known facts about the most simple numbers, and clear explanations of more sophisticated topics; mysteries and folklore of numbers, the "Hin-dog-abic" number system, etc. First publication. Index. 529 numbered problems and diversions, all with answers. Bibliography. 60 figures. xiv + 320pp. 5⅜ x 8.   T770 Paperbound **$1.65**

CRYPTANALYSIS, H. F. Gaines. Formerly entitled ELEMENTARY CRYPTANALYSIS, this introductory-intermediate level text is the best book in print on cryptograms and their solution. It covers all major techniques of the past, and contains much that is not generally known except to experts. Full details about concealment, substitution, and transposition ciphers; periodic mixed alphabets, multafid, Kasiski and Vigenere methods, Ohaver patterns, Playfair, and scores of other topics. 6 language letter and word frequency appendix. 167 problems, now furnished with solutions. Index. 173 figures. vi + 230pp. 5⅜ x 8.
                   T97 Paperbound **$1.95**

CRYPTOGRAPHY, L. D. Smith. An excellent introductory work on ciphers and their solution, the history of secret writing, and actual methods and problems in such techniques as transposition and substitution. Appendices describe the enciphering of Japanese, the Baconian biliteral cipher, and contain frequency tables and a bibliography for further study. Over 150 problems with solutions. 160pp. 5⅜ x 8.   T247 Paperbound **$1.00**

PUZZLE QUIZ AND STUNT FUN, J. Meyer. The solution to party doldrums. 238 challenging puzzles, stunts and tricks. Mathematical puzzles like The Clever Carpenter, Atom Bomb; mysteries and deductions like The Bridge of Sighs, The Nine Pearls, Dog Logic; observation puzzles like Cigarette Smokers, Telephone Dial; over 200 others including magic squares, tongue twisters, puns, anagrams, and many others. All problems solved fully. 250pp. 5⅜ x 8.
                   T337 Paperbound **$1.00**

101 PUZZLES IN THOUGHT AND LOGIC, C. R. Wylie, Jr. Brand new problems you need no special knowledge to solve! Take the kinks out of your mental "muscles" and enjoy solving murder problems, the detection of lying fishermen, the logical identification of color by a blindman, and dozens more. Introduction with simplified explanation of general scientific method and puzzle solving. 128pp. 5⅜ x 8.   T367 Paperbound **$1.00**

THE BOOK OF MODERN PUZZLES, G. L. Kaufman. A completely new series of puzzles as fascinating as crossword and deduction puzzles but based upon different principles and techniques. Simple 2-minute teasers, word labyrinths, design and pattern puzzles, logic and observation puzzles — over 150 braincrackers. Answers to all problems. 116 illustrations. 192pp. 5⅜ x 8.
T143 Paperbound **$1.00**

NEW WORD PUZZLES, G. L. Kaufman. 100 ENTIRELY NEW puzzles based on words and their combinations that will delight crossword puzzle, Scrabble and Jotto fans. Chess words, based on the moves of the chess king; design-onyms, symmetrical designs made of synonyms; rhymed double-crostics; syllable sentences; addle letter anagrams; alphagrams; linkograms; and many others all brand new. Full solutions. Space to work problems. 196 figures. vi + 122pp. 5⅜ x 8.
T344 Paperbound **$1.00**

MAZES AND LABYRINTHS: A BOOK OF PUZZLES, W. Shepherd. Mazes, formerly associated with mystery and ritual, are still among the most intriguing of intellectual puzzles. This is a novel and different collection of 50 amusements that embody the principle of the maze: mazes in the classical tradition; 3-dimensional, ribbon, and Möbius-strip mazes; hidden messages; spatial arrangements; etc.—almost all built on amusing story situations. 84 illustrations. Essay on maze psychology. Solutions. xv + 122pp. 5⅜ x 8.
T731 Paperbound **$1.00**

HOUDINI ON MAGIC, Harry Houdini. One of the greatest magicians of modern times explains his most prized secrets. How locks are picked, with illustrated picks and skeleton keys; how a girl is sawed into twins; how to walk through a brick wall — Houdini's explanations of 44 stage tricks with many diagrams. Also included is a fascinating discussion of great magicians of the past and the story of his fight against fraudulent mediums and spiritualists. Edited by W.B. Gibson and M.N. Young. Bibliography. 155 figures, photos. xv + 280pp. 5⅜ x 8.
T384 Paperbound **$1.25**

MATHEMATICS, MAGIC AND MYSTERY, Martin Gardner. Why do card tricks work? How do magicians perform astonishing mathematical feats? How is stage mind-reading possible? This is the first book length study explaining the application of probability, set theory, theory of numbers, topology, etc., to achieve many startling tricks. Non-technical, accurate, detailed! 115 sections discuss tricks with cards, dice, coins, knots, geometrical vanishing illusions, how a Curry square "demonstrates" that the sum fo the parts may be greater than the whole, and dozens of others. No sleight of hand necessary! 135 illustrations. xii + 174pp. 5⅜ x 8.
T335 Paperbound **$1.00**

MAGIC TRICKS & CARD TRICKS, W. Jonson. Two books bound as one. 52 tricks with cards, 37 tricks with coins, bills, eggs, smoke, ribbons, slates, etc. Details on presentation, misdirection, and routining will help you master such famous tricks as the Changing Card, Card in the Pocket, Four Aces, Coin Through the Hand, Bill in the Egg, Afghan Bands, and over 75 others. If you follow the lucid exposition and key diagrams carefully, you will finish these two books with an astonishing mastery of magic. 106 figures. 224pp. 5⅜ x 8. T909 Paperbound **$1.00**

Entertainments, Humor

PAPER FOLDING FOR BEGINNERS, W. D. Murray and F. J. Rigney. A delightful introduction to the varied and entertaining Japanese art of origami (paper folding), with a full, crystal clear text that anticipates every difficulty; over 275 clearly labeled diagrams of all important stages in creation. You get results at each stage, since complex figures are logically developed from simpler ones. 43 different pieces are explained: sailboats, frogs, roosters, etc. 6 photographic plates. 279 diagrams. 95pp. 5⅝ x 8⅜.
T713 Paperbound **$1.00**

ODDITIES AND CURIOSITIES OF WORDS AND LITERATURE, C. Bombaugh, edited by M. Gardner. The largest collection of idiosyncratic prose and poetry techniques in English, a legendary work in the curious and amusing bypaths of literary recreations and the play technique in literature—so important in modern works. Contains alphabetic poetry, acrostics, palindromes, scissors verse, centos, emblematic poetry, famous literary puns, hoaxes, notorious slips of the press, hilarious mistranslations, and much more. Revised and enlarged with modern material by Martin Gardner. 368pp. 5⅜ x 8.
T759 Paperbound **$1.50**

A NONSENSE ANTHOLOGY, collected by Carolyn Wells. 245 of the best nonsense verses ever written, including nonsense puns, absurd arguments, mock epics and sagas, nonsense ballads, odes, "sick" versus, dog-Latin verses, French nonsense verses, songs. By Edward Lear, Lewis Carroll, Gelett Burgess, W. S. Gilbert, Hilaire Belloc, Peter Newell, Oliver Herford, etc., 83 writers in all plus over four score anonymous nonsense verses. A special section of limericks, plus famous nonsense such as Carroll's "Jabberwocky" and Lear's "The Jumblies" and much excellent verse virtually impossible to locate elsewhere. For 50 years considered the best anthology available. Index of first lines specially prepared for this edition. Introduction by Carolyn Wells. 3 indexes: Title, Author, First lines. xxxiii + 279pp.
T499 Paperbound **$1.25**

CATALOG OF DOVER BOOKS

THE BAD CHILD'S BOOK OF BEASTS, MORE BEASTS FOR WORSE CHILDREN, and A MORAL ALPHA-BET, H. Belloc. Hardly an anthology of humorous verse has appeared in the last 50 years without at least a couple of these famous nonsense verses. But one must see the entire volumes—with all the delightful original illustrations by Sir Basil Blackwood—to appreciate fully Belloc's charming and witty verses that play so subacidly on the platitudes of life and morals that beset his day—and ours. A great humor classic. Three books in one. Total of 157pp. 5⅜ x 8.
T749 Paperbound **$1.00**

THE DEVIL'S DICTIONARY, Ambrose Bierce. Sardonic and irreverent barbs puncturing the pomposities and absurdities of American politics, business, religion, literature, and arts, by the country's greatest satirist in the classic tradition. Epigrammatic as Shaw, piercing as Swift, American as Mark Twain, Will Rogers, and Fred Allen, Bierce will always remain the favorite of a small coterie of enthusiasts, and of writers and speakers whom he supplies with "some of the most gorgeous witticisms of the English language." (H. L. Mencken) Over 1000 entries in alphabetical order. 144pp. 5⅜ x 8.
T487 Paperbound **$1.00**

THE PURPLE COW AND OTHER NONSENSE, Gelett Burgess. The best of Burgess's early nonsense, selected from the first edition of the "Burgess Nonsense Book." Contains many of his most unusual and truly awe-inspiring pieces: 36 nonsense quatrains, the Poems of Patagonia, Alphabet of Famous Goops, and the other hilarious (and rare) adult nonsense that place him in the forefront of American humorists. All pieces are accompanied by the original Burgess illustrations. 123 illustrations. xiii + 113pp. 5⅜ x 8.
T772 Paperbound **$1.00**

THE HUMOROUS VERSE OF LEWIS CARROLL. Almost every poem Carroll ever wrote, the largest collection ever published, including much never published elsewhere: 150 parodies, burlesques, riddles, ballads, acrostics, etc., with 130 original illustrations by Tenniel, Carroll, and others. "Addicts will be grateful . . . there is nothing for the faithful to do but sit down and fall to the banquet," N. Y. Times. Index to first lines. xiv + 446pp. 5⅜ x 8.
T654 Paperbound **$1.85**

DIVERSIONS AND DIGRESSIONS OF LEWIS CARROLL. A major new treasure for Carroll fans! Rare privately published humor, fantasy, puzzles, and games by Carroll at his whimsical best, with a new vein of frank satire. Includes many new mathematical amusements and recreations, among them the fragmentary Part III of "Curiosa Mathematica." Contains "The Rectory Umbrella," "The New Belfry," "The Vision of the Three T's," and much more. New 32-page supplement of rare photographs taken by Carroll. x + 375pp. 5⅜ x 8.
T732 Paperbound **$1.50**

THE COMPLETE NONSENSE OF EDWARD LEAR. This is the only complete edition of this master of gentle madness available at a popular price. A BOOK OF NONSENSE, NONSENSE SONGS, MORE NONSENSE SONGS AND STORIES in their entirety with all the old favorites that have delighted children and adults for years. The Dong With A Luminous Nose, The Jumblies, The Owl and the Pussycat, and hundreds of other bits of wonderful nonsense. 214 limericks, 3 sets of Nonsense Botany, 5 Nonsense Alphabets, 546 drawings by Lear himself, and much more. 320pp. 5⅜ x 8.
T167 Paperbound **$1.00**

PECK'S BAD BOY AND HIS PA, George W. Peck. The complete edition, containing both volumes, of one of the most widely read American humor books. The endless ingenious pranks played by bad boy "Hennery" on his pa and the grocery man, the outraged pomposity of Pa, the perpetual ridiculing of middle class institutions, are as entertaining today as they were in 1883. No pale sophistications or subtleties, but rather humor vigorous, raw, earthy, imaginative, and, as folk humor often is, sadistic. This peculiarly fascinating book is also valuable to historians and students of American culture as a portrait of an age. 100 original illustrations by True Williams. Introduction by E. F. Bleiler. 347pp. 5⅜ x 8.
T497 Paperbound **$1.35**

FABLES IN SLANG & MORE FABLES IN SLANG, George Ade. 2 complete books of major American humorist in pungent colloquial tradition of Twain, Billings. 1st reprinting in over 30 years includes "The Two Mandolin Players and the Willing Performer," "The Base Ball Fan Who Took the Only Known Cure," "The Slim Girl Who Tried to Keep a Date that was Never Made," 42 other tales of eccentric, perverse, but always funny characters. "Touch of Genius," H. L. Mencken. New introduction by E. F. Bleiler. 86 illus. 208pp. 5⅜ x 8.
T533 Paperbound **$1.00**

SINGULAR TRAVELS, CAMPAIGNS, AND ADVENTURES OF BARON MUNCHAUSEN, R. E. Raspe, with 90 illustrations by Gustave Doré. The first edition in over 150 years to reestablish the deeds of the Prince of Liars exactly as Raspe first recorded them in 1785—the genuine Baron Munchausen, one of the most popular personalities in English literature. Included also are the best of the many sequels, written by other hands. Introduction on Raspe by J. Carswell. Bibliography of early edition. xliv + 192pp. 5⅜ x 8.
T698 Paperbound **$1.00**

HOW TO TELL THE BIRDS FROM THE FLOWERS, R. W. Wood. How not to confuse a carrot with a parrot, a grape with an ape, a puffin with nuffin. Delightful drawings, clever puns, absurd little poems point out farfetched resemblances in nature. The author was a leading physicist. Introduction by Margaret Wood White. 106 illus. 60pp. 5⅜ x 8.
T523 Paperbound **75¢**

THE WIT AND HUMOR OF OSCAR WILDE, ed. by Alvin Redman. Wilde at his most brilliant, in 1000 epigrams exposing weaknesses and hypocrisies of "civilized" society. Divided into 49 categories—sin, wealth, women, America, etc.—to aid writers, speakers. Includes excerpts from his trials. books. plays, criticism. Formerly "The Epigrams of Oscar Wilde." Introduction by Vyvyan Holland, Wilde's only living son. Introductory essay by editor. 260pp. 5⅜ x 8.   T602 Paperbound **$1.00**

Chess, Checkers, Games, Go

THE ADVENTURE OF CHESS, Edward Lasker. A lively history of chess, from its ancient beginnings in the Indian 4-handed game of Chaturanga, through to the great players of our day, as told by one of America's finest masters. He introduces such unusual sidelights and amusing oddities as Maelzel's chess-playing automaton that beat Napoleon 3 times. Major discussion of chess-playing machines and personal memories of. Nimzovich, Capablanca, etc. 5-page chess primer. 11 illustrations, 53 diagrams. 296pp. 5⅜ x 8.   S510 Paperbound **$1.45**

A TREASURY OF CHESS LORE, edited by Fred Reinfeld. A delightful collection of anecdotes, short stories, aphorisms by and about the masters, poems, accounts of games and tournaments, photography. Hundreds of humorous, pithy, satirical, wise, and historical episodes, comments, and word portraits. A fascinating "must" for chess players; revealing and perhaps seductive to those who wonder what their friends see in the game. 48 photographs (14 full page plates) 12 diagrams. xi + 306pp. 5⅜ x 8.   T458 Paperbound **$1.75**

FREE! All you do is ask for it!

HOW DO YOU PLAY CHESS? by Fred Reinfeld. A prominent expert covers every basic rule of chess for the beginner in 86 questions and answers: moves, powers of pieces, rationale behind moves, how to play forcefully, history of chess, and much more. Bibliography of chess publications. 11 board diagrams. 48 pages.   **FREE**

THE PLEASURES OF CHESS, Assiac. Internationally known British writer, influential chess columnist, writes wittily about wide variety of chess subjects: Anderssen's "Immortal Game;" only game in which both opponents resigned at once; psychological tactics of Reshevsky, Lasker; varieties played by masters for relaxation, such as "losing chess;" sacrificial orgies; etc. These anecdotes, witty observations will give you fresh appreciation of game. 43 problems. 150 diagrams. 139pp. 5⅜ x 8.   T597 Paperbound **$1.25**

WIN AT CHESS, F. Reinfeld. 300 practical chess situations from actual tournament play to sharpen your chess eye and test your skill. Traps, sacrifices, mates, winning combinations, subtle exchanges, show you how to WIN AT CHESS. Short notes and tables of solutions and alternative moves help you evaluate your progress. Learn to think ahead playing the "crucial moments" of historic games. 300 diagrams. Notes and solutions. Formerly titled CHESS QUIZ. vi + 120pp. 5⅜ x 8.   T438 Paperbound **$1.00**

THE ART OF CHESS, James Mason. An unabridged reprinting of the latest revised edition of the most famous general study of chess ever written. Also included, a complete supplement by Fred Reinfeld, "How Do You Play Chess?", invaluable to beginners for its lively question and answer method. Mason, an early 20th century master, teaches the beginning and intermediate player more than 90 openings, middle game, end game, how to see more moves ahead, to plan purposefully, attack, sacrifice, defend, exchange, and govern general strategy. Supplement. 448 diagrams. 1947 Reinfeld-Bernstein text. Bibliography. xvi + 340pp. 5⅜ x 8. T463 Paperbound **$1.85**

THE PRINCIPLES OF CHESS, James Mason. This "great chess classic" (N. Y. Times) is a general study covering all aspects of the game; basic forces, resistance, obstruction, opposition, relative values, mating, typical end game situations, combinations, much more. The last section discusses openings, with 50 games illustrating modern master play of Rubinstein, Spielmann, Lasker, Capablanca, etc., selected and annotated by Fred Reinfeld. Will improve the game of any intermediate-skilled player, but is so forceful and lucid that an absolute beginner might use it to become an accomplished player. 1946 Reinfeld edition. 166 diagrams. 378pp. 5⅜ x 8.   T646 Paperbound **$1.85**

LASKER'S MANUAL OF CHESS, Dr. Emanuel Lasker. Probably the greatest chess player of modern times, Dr. Emanuel Lasker held the world championship 28 years, independent of passing schools or fashions. This unmatched study of the game, chiefly for intermediate to skilled players, analyzes basic methods, combinations, position play, the aesthetics of chess, dozens of different openings, etc., with constant reference to great modern games. Contains a brilliant exposition of Steinitz's important theories. Introduction by Fred Reinfeld. Tables of Lasker's tournament record. 3 indices. 308 diagrams. 1 photograph. xxx + 349pp. 5⅜ x 8. T640 Paperbound **$2.00**

WIN AT CHECKERS, M. Hopper. (Formerly CHECKERS). The former World's Unrestricted Checker Champion discusses the principles of the game, expert's shots and traps, problems for the beginner, standard openings, locating your best move, the end game, opening "blitzkrieg" moves, ways to draw when you are behind your opponent, etc. More than 100 detailed questions and answers anticipate your problems. Appendix. 75 problems with solutions and diagrams. Index. 79 figures. xi + 107pp. 5⅜ x 8.   T363 Paperbound **$1.00**

GAMES ANCIENT AND ORIENTAL, AND HOW TO PLAY THEM, E. Falkener. A connoisseur's selection of exciting and different games: Oriental varieties of chess, with unusual pieces and moves (including Japanese shogi); the original pachisi; go; reconstructions of lost Roman and Egyptian games; and many more. Full rules and sample games. Now play at home the games that have entertained millions, not on a fad basis, but for millennia. 345 illustrations and figures. iv + 366pp. 5⅜ x 8.   T739 Paperbound **$1.85**

GO AND GO-MOKU, Edward Lasker. A fascinating Oriental game, Go, is winning new devotees in America daily. Rules that you can learn in a few minutes—a wealth of combinations that makes it more profound than chess! This is an easily followed step-by-step explanation of this 2000-year-old game, beginning with fundamentals. New chapter on advanced strategy in this edition! Also contains rules for Go-Moku, a very easy sister game. 72 diagrams. xix + 215pp. 5⅜ x 8.   T613 Paperbound **$1.45**

Fiction

FLATLAND, E. A. Abbott. A science-fiction classic of life in a 2-dimensional world that is also a first-rate introduction to such aspects of modern science as relativity and hyperspace. Political, moral, satirical, and humorous overtones have made FLATLAND fascinating reading for thousands. 7th edition. New introduction by Banesh Hoffmann. 16 illustrations. 128pp. 5⅜ x 8.   T1 Paperbound **$1.00**

THE WONDERFUL WIZARD OF OZ, L. F. Baum. Only edition in print with all the original W. W. Denslow illustrations in full color—as much a part of "The Wizard" as Tenniel's drawings are of "Alice in Wonderland." "The Wizard" is still America's best-loved fairy tale, in which, as the author expresses it, "The wonderment and joy are retained and the heartaches and nightmares left out." Now today's young readers can enjoy every word and wonderful picture of the original book. New introduction by Martin Gardner. A Baum bibliography. 23 full-page color plates. viii + 268pp. 5⅜ x 8.   T691 Paperbound **$1.45**

THE MARVELOUS LAND OF OZ, L. F. Baum. This is the equally enchanting sequel to the "Wizard," continuing the adventures of the Scarecrow and the Tin Woodman. The hero this time is a little boy named Tip, and all the delightful Oz magic is still present. This is the Oz book with the Animated Saw-Horse, the Woggle-Bug, and Jack Pumpkinhead. All the original John R. Neill illustrations, 10 in full color. 287 pp. 5⅜ x 8.   T692 Paperbound **$1.45**

FIVE GREAT DOG NOVELS, edited by Blanche Cirker. The complete original texts of five classic dog novels that have delighted and thrilled millions of children and adults throughout the world with their stories of loyalty, adventure, and courage. Full texts of Jack London's "The Call of the Wild"; John Brown's "Rab and His Friends"; Alfred Ollivant's "Bob, Son of Battle"; Marshall Saunders's "Beautiful Joe"; and Ouida's "A Dog of Flanders." 21 Illustrations from the original editions. 495pp. 5⅜ x 8.   T777 Paperbound **$1.50**

The Space Novels of Jules Verne

TO THE SUN? and OFF ON A COMET!, Jules Verne. Complete texts of two of the most imaginative flights into fancy in world literature display the high adventure that have kept Verne's novels read for nearly a century. Only unabridged edition of the best translation, by Edward Roth. Large, easily readable type. 50 illustrations selected from first editions. 462pp. 5⅜ x 8.   T634 Paperbound **$1.75**

FROM THE EARTH TO THE MOON and ALL AROUND THE MOON, Jules Verne. Complete editions of 2 of Verne's most successful novels, in finest Edward Roth translations, now available after many years out of print. Verne's visions of submarines, airplanes, television, rockets, interplanetary travel; of scientific and not-so-scientific beliefs; of peculiarities of Americans; all delight and engross us today as much as when they first appeared. Large, easily readable type. 42 illus. from first French edition. 476pp. 5⅜ x 8.   T633 Paperbound **$1.75**

3 ADVENTURE NOVELS by H. Rider Haggard. Complete texts of "She," "King Solomon's Mines," "Allan Quatermain." Qualities of discovery, desire for immortality, search for the primitive, for what is unadorned by civilization, have kept these novels of African adventure excitingly alive to readers from R. L. Stevenson to George Orwell. 636pp. 5⅜ x 8.   T584 Paperbound **$2.00**

THE CASTING AWAY OF MRS. LECKS AND MRS. ALESHINE, F. R. Stockton. A charming light novel by Frank Stockton, one of America's finest humorists (and author of "The Lady, or the Tiger?"). This book has made millions of Americans laugh at the reflection of themselves in two middle-aged American women involved in some of the strangest adventures on record. You will laugh, too, as they endure shipwreck, desert island, and blizzard with maddening tranquillity. Also contains complete text of "The Dusantes," sequel to "The Casting Away." 49 original illustrations by F. D. Steele. vii + 142pp. 5⅜ x 8.

T743 Paperbound **$1.00**

THREE PROPHETIC NOVELS OF H. G. WELLS. Complete texts of 3 timeless science fiction novels by the greatest master of the art, with remarkable prophecies of technological and social changes that are really taking place!—"When the Sleeper Wakes" (first printing in 50 years), "A Story of the Days to Come," and "The Time Machine" (only truly complete text available). Introduction by E. F. Bleiler. "The absolute best of imaginative fiction," N. Y. Times. 335pp. 5⅜ x 8.

T605 Paperbound **$1.45**

SEVEN SCIENCE FICTION NOVELS, H. G. Wells. Full unabridged texts of 7 science-fiction novels of the master. Ranging from biology, physics, chemistry, astronomy, to sociology and other studies, Mr. Wells extrapolates whole worlds of strange and intriguing character. "One will have to go far to match this for entertainment, excitement, and sheer pleasure . . ." NEW YORK TIMES. Contents: The Time Machine, The Island of Dr. Moreau, The First Men in the Moon, The Invisible Man, The War of the Worlds, The Food of the Gods, In The Days of the Comet. 1015pp. 5⅜ x 8.

T264 Clothbound **$3.95**

28 SCIENCE FICTION STORIES OF H. G. WELLS. Two full unabridged novels, MEN LIKE GODS and STAR BEGOTTEN, plus 26 short stories by the master science-fiction writer of all time! Stories of space, time, invention, exploration, future adventure—an indispensible part of the library of everyone interested in science and adventure. PARTIAL CONTENTS: Men Like Gods, The Country of the Blind, In the Abyss, The Crystal Egg, The Man Who Could Work Miracles, A Story of the Days to Come, The Valley of Spiders, and 21 more! 928pp. 5⅜ x 8.

T265 Clothbound **$3.95**

DAVID HARUM, E. N. Westcott. This novel of one of the most loveable, humorous characters in American literature is a prime example of regional humor. It continues to delight people who like their humor dry, their characters quaint, and their plots ingenuous. First book edition to contain complete novel plus chapter found after author's death. Illustrations from first illustrated edition. 192pp. 5⅜ x 8.

T580 Paperbound **$1.15**

GESTA ROMANORUM, trans. by Charles Swan, ed. by Wynnard Hooper. 181 tales of Greeks, Romans, Britons, Biblical characters, comprise one of greatest medieval story collections, source of plots for writers including Shakespeare, Chaucer, Gower, etc. Imaginative tales of wars, incest, thwarted love, magic, fantasy, allegory, humor, tell about kings, prostitutes, philosophers, fair damsels, knights, Noah, pirates, all walks, stations of life. Introduction. Notes. 500pp. 5⅜ x 8.

T535 Paperbound **$1.85**

Social Sciences

SOCIAL THOUGHT FROM LORE TO SCIENCE, H. E. Barnes and H. Becker. An immense survey of sociological thought and ways of viewing, studying, planning, and reforming society from earliest times to the present. Includes thought on society of preliterate peoples, ancient non-Western cultures, and every great movement in Europe, America, and modern Japan. Analyzes hundreds of great thinkers: Plato, Augustine, Bodin, Vico, Montesquieu, Herder, Comte, Marx, etc. Weighs the contributions of utopians, sophists, fascists and communists; economists, jurists, philosophers, ecclesiastics, and every 19th and 20th century school of scientific sociology, anthropology, and social psychology throughout the world. Combines topical, chronological, and regional approaches, treating the evolution of social thought as a process rather than as a series of mere topics. "Impressive accuracy, competence, and discrimination . . . easily the best single survey," Nation. Thoroughly revised, with new material up to 1960. 2 indexes. Over 2200 bibliographical notes. Three volume set. Total of 1586pp. 5⅜ x 8.

T901 Vol I Paperbound **$2.35**
T902 Vol II Paperbound **$2.35**
T903 Vol III Paperbound **$2.35**
The set **$7.05**

FOLKWAYS, William Graham Sumner. A classic of sociology, a searching and thorough examination of patterns of behaviour from primitive, ancient Greek and Judaic, Medieval Christian, African, Oriental, Melanesian, Australian, Islamic, to modern Western societies. Thousands of illustrations of social, sexual, and religious customs, mores, laws, and institutions. Hundreds of categories: Labor, Wealth, Abortion, Primitive Justice, Life Policy, Slavery, Cannibalism, Uncleanness and the Evil Eye, etc. Will extend the horizon of every reader by showing the relativism of his own culture. Prefatory note by A. G. Keller. Introduction by William Lyon Phelps. Bibliography. Index. xiii + 692pp. 5⅜ x 8.

T508 Paperbound **$2.49**

PRIMITIVE RELIGION, P. Radin. A thorough treatment by a noted anthropologist of the nature and origin of man's belief in the supernatural and the influences that have shaped religious expression in primitive societies. Ranging from the Arunta, Ashanti, Aztec, Bushman, Crow, Fijian, etc., of Africa, Australia, Pacific Islands, the Arctic, North and South America, Prof. Radin integrates modern psychology, comparative religion, and economic thought with first-hand accounts gathered by himself and other scholars of primitive initiations, training of the shaman, and other fascinating topics. "Excellent," NATURE (London). Unabridged reissue of 1st edition. New author's preface. Bibliographic notes. Index. x + 322pp. 5⅜ x 8.
T393 Paperbound **$1.85**

PRIMITIVE MAN AS PHILOSOPHER, P. Radin. A standard anthropological work covering primitive thought on such topics as the purpose of life, marital relations, freedom of thought, symbolism, death, resignation, the nature of reality, personality, gods, and many others. Drawn from factual material gathered from the Winnebago, Oglala Sioux, Maori, Baganda, Batak, Zuni, among others, it does not distort ideas by removing them from context but interprets strictly within the original framework. Extensive selections of original primitive documents. Bibliography. Index. xviii + 402pp. 5⅜ x 8.
T392 Paperbound **$2.00**

THE POLISH PEASANT IN EUROPE AND AMERICA, William I. Thomas, Florian Znaniecki. A seminal sociological study of peasant primary groups (family and community) and the disruptions produced by a new industrial system and immigration to America. The peasant's family, class system, religious and aesthetic attitudes, and economic life are minutely examined and analyzed in hundreds of pages of primary documentation, particularly letters between family members. The disorientation caused by new environments is scrutinized in detail (a 312 page autobiography of an immigrant is especially valuable and revealing) in an attempt to find common experiences and reactions. The famous "Methodological Note" sets forth the principles which guided the authors. When out of print this set has sold for as much as $50. 2nd revised edition. 2 vols. Vol. 1: xv + 1115pp. Vol. 2: 1135pp. Index. 6 x 9.
T478 Clothbound 2 vol. set **$12.50**

Music

A GENERAL HISTORY OF MUSIC, Charles Burney. A detailed coverage of music from the Greeks up to 1789, with full information on all types of music: sacred and secular, vocal and instrumental, operatic and symphonic. Theory, notation, forms, instruments, innovators, composers, performers, typical and important works, and much more in an easy, entertaining style. Burney covered much of Europe and spoke with hundreds of authorities and composers so that this work is more than a compilation of records . . . it is a living work of careful and first-hand scholarship. Its account of thoroughbass (18th century) Italian music is probably still the best introduction on the subject. A recent NEW YORK TIMES review said, "Surprisingly few of Burney's statements have been invalidated by modern research . . . still of great value." Edited and corrected by Frank Mercer. 35 figures. Indices. 1915pp. 5⅜ x 8. 2 volumes.
T36 The Set, Clothbound **$12.50**

A DICTIONARY OF HYMNOLOGY, John Julian. This exhaustive and scholarly work has become known as an invaluable source of hundreds of thousands of important and often difficult to obtain facts on the history and use of hymns in the western world. Everyone interested in hymns will be fascinated by the accounts of famous hymns and hymn writers and amazed by the amount of practical information he will find. More than 30,000 entries on individual hymns, giving authorship, date and circumstances of composition, publication, textual variations, translations, denominational and ritual usage, etc. Biographies of more than 9,000 hymn writers, and essays on important topics such as Christmas carols and children's hymns, and many other unusual and valuable information. A 200 page double-columned index of first lines — the largest in print. Total of 1786 pages in two reinforced clothbound volumes. 6¼ x 9¼.
The set, T333 Clothbound **$15.00**

MUSIC IN MEDIEVAL BRITAIN, F. Ll. Harrison. The most thorough, up-to-date, and accurate treatment of the subject ever published, beautifully illustrated. Complete account of institutions and choirs; carols, masses, and motets; liturgy and plainsong; and polyphonic music from the Norman Conquest to the Reformation. Discusses the various schools of music and their reciprocal influences; the origin and development of new ritual forms; development and use of instruments; and new evidence on many problems of the period. Reproductions of scores, over 200 excerpts from medieval melodies. Rules of harmony and dissonance; influence of Continental styles; great composers (Dunstable, Cornysh, Fairfax, etc.); and much more. Register and index of more than 400 musicians. Index of titles. General Index. 225-item bibliography. 6 Appendices. xix + 491pp. 5⅝ x 8¾.
T705 Clothbound **$10.00**

THE MUSIC OF SPAIN, Gilbert Chase. Only book in English to give concise, comprehensive account of Iberian music; new Chapter covers music since 1941. Victoria, Albéniz, Cabezón, Pedrell, Turina, hundreds of other composers; popular and folk music; the Gypsies; the guitar; dance, theatre, opera, with only extensive discussion in English of the Zarzuela; virtuosi such as Casals; much more. "Distinguished . . . readable," Saturday Review. 400-item bibliography. Index. 27 photos. 383pp. 5⅜ x 8.
T549 Paperbound **$2.00**

CATALOG OF DOVER BOOKS

WILLIAM LAWES, M. Lefkowitz. This is the definitive work on Lawes, the versatile, prolific, and highly original "King's musician" of 17th century England. His life is reconstructed from original documents, and nearly every piece he ever wrote is examined and evaluated: his fantasias, pavans, violin "sonatas," lyra viol and bass viol suites, and music for harp and theorbo; and his songs, masques, and theater music to words by Herrick ("Gather Ye Rosebuds"), Jonson, Suckling, Shirley, and others. The author shows the innovations of dissonance, augmented triad, and other Italian influences Lawes helped introduce to England. List of Lawes' complete works and several complete scores by this major precursor of Purcell and the 18th century developments. Index. 5 Appendices. 52 musical excerpts, many never before in print. Bibliography. x + 320pp. 5⅜ x 8. **T706 Clothbound $10.00**

JOHANN SEBASTIAN BACH, Philipp Spitta. The complete and unabridged text of the definitive study of Bach. Written some 70 years ago, it is still unsurpassed for its coverage of nearly all aspects of Bach's life and work. There could hardly be a finer non-technical introduction to Bach's music than the detailed, lucid analyses which Spitta provides for hundreds of individual pieces. 26 solid pages are devoted to the B minor mass, for example, and 30 pages to the glorious St. Matthew Passion. This monumental set also includes a major analysis of the music of the 18th century: Buxtehude, Pachelbel, etc. "Unchallenged as the last word on one of the supreme geniuses of music," John Barkham, SATURDAY REVIEW SYNDICATE. Total of 1819pp. 2 volumes. Heavy cloth binding. 5⅜ x 8. **T252 Clothbound $12.50**

THE LIFE OF MOZART, O. Jahn. Probably the largest amount of material on Mozart's life and works ever gathered together in one book! Its 1350 authoritative and readable pages cover every event in his life, and contain a full critique of almost every piece he ever wrote, including sketches and intimate works. There is a full historical-cultural background, and vast research into musical and literary history, sources of librettos, prior treatments of Don Juan legend, etc. This is the complete and unaltered text of the definitive Townsend translation, with foreword by Grove. 5 engraved portraits from Salzburg archives. 4 facsimiles in Mozart's hand. 226 musical examples. 4 Appendixes, including complete list of Mozart's compositions, with Köchel numbers (fragmentary works included). Total of xxviii + 1352pp. Three volume set, Bound in 2 volumes.

T85 Clothbound $5.00
T86 Clothbound $5.00
The set $10.00

THE FUGUE IN BEETHOVEN'S PIANO MUSIC, J. V. Cockshoot. The first study of a neglected aspect of Beethoven's genius: his ability as a writer of fugues. Analyses of early studies and published works demonstrate his original and powerful contributions to composition. 34 works are examined, with 143 musical excerpts. For all pianists, teachers, students, and music-minded readers with a serious interest in Beethoven. Index. 93-item bibliography. Illustration of original score for "Fugue in C." xv + 212pp. 5⅜ x 8⅜. **T704 Clothbound $6.00**

BEETHOVEN'S QUARTETS, J. de Marliave. The most complete and authoritative study ever written, enjoyable for scholar and layman alike. The 16 quartets and Grand Fugue are all analyzed bar by bar and theme by theme, not over-technically, but concentrating on mood and effects. Complete background material for each composition: influences, first reviews, etc. Preface by Gabriel Fauré. Introduction and notes by J. Escarra. Translated by Hilda Andrews. 321 musical examples. xxiii + 379pp. 5⅜ x 8. **T694 Paperbound $1.85**

STRUCTURAL HEARING: TONAL COHERENCE IN MUSIC, Felix Salzer. Written by a pupil of the late Heinrich Schenker, this is not only the most thorough exposition in English of the Schenker method but also extends the Schenker approach to include modern music, the middle ages, and renaissance music. It explores the phenomenon of tonal organization by means of a detailed analysis and discussion of more than 500 musical pieces. It casts new light for the reader acquainted with harmony upon the understanding of musical compositions, problems of musical coherence, and connection between theory and composition. "Has been the foundation on which all teaching in music theory has been based at this college," Leopold Mannes, President of The Mannes College of Music. 2 volumes. Total of 658pp. 6½ x 9¼. **The set, T418 Clothbound $8.00**

ON STUDYING SINGING, Sergius Kagen. An intelligent method of voice-training, which leads you around pitfalls that waste your time, money, and effort. Exposes rigid, mechanical systems, baseless theories, deleterious exercises. "Logical, clear, convincing . . . dead right," Virgil Thomson, N.Y. Herald Tribune. "I recommend this volume highly," Maggie Teyte, Saturday Review. 119pp. 5⅜ x 8. **T622 Paperbound $1.25**

ROMAIN ROLLAND'S ESSAYS ON MUSIC, ed. by David Ewen. 16 best essays by great critic of our time, Nobel Laureate, discuss Mozart, Beethoven, Gluck, Handel, Berlioz, Wagner, Wolf, Saint-Saëns, Metastasio, Lully, Telemann, Grétry, "Origins of 18th Century 'Classic' Style," and musical life of 18th century Germany and Italy. "Shows the key to the high place that Rolland still holds in the world of music," Library Journal. 371pp. 5⅜ x 8. **T550 Paperbound $1.50**

Language Books and Records

Say It language phrase books

These handy phrase books (128 to 196 pages each) make grammatical drills unnecessary for an elementary knowledge of a spoken foreign language. Covering most matters of travel and everyday life each volume contains:

Over 1000 phrases and sentences in immediately useful forms — foreign language plus English.

Modern usage designed for Americans. Specific phrases like, "Give me small change," and "Please call a taxi."

Simplified phonetic transcription you will be able to read at sight.

The only completely indexed phrase books on the market.

Covers scores of important situations: — Greetings, restaurants, sightseeing, useful expressions, etc.

These books are prepared by native linguists who are professors at Columbia, N.Y.U., Fordham and other great universities. Use them independently or with any other book or record course. They provide a supplementary living element that most other courses lack. Individual volumes in:

Russian 75¢	Danish 75¢	Italian 75¢
Hebrew 75¢	German 75¢	Spanish 80¢
Japanese 75¢	Portuguese 75¢	Swedish 75¢
Dutch 75¢	French 60¢	Modern Greek 75¢
Esperanto 75¢	Norwegian 75¢	Yiddish 75¢
	Polish 75¢	Turkish 75¢

English for Spanish-speaking people 60¢
English for Italian-speaking people 60¢
English for German-speaking people 60¢

Large clear type. 128-196 pages each. 3½ x 5¼. Sturdy paper binding.

Say It Correctly language records

These are the best inexpensive pronunciation aids on the market. Spoken by native linguists associated with major American universities, each record contains:

15 minutes of speech — 12 minutes of normal but relatively slow speech, 2 minutes at normal conversational speed

120 basic phrases and sentences covering nearly every aspect of everyday life and travel — introducing yourself, travel in autos, buses, taxis, etc., walking, sightseeing, hotels, restaurants, money, shopping, etc.

32 page booklet containing everything on the record plus English translations and an easy-to-follow phonetic guide

Clear, high fidelity quality recordings

Unique bracketing system and selection of basic sentences enabling you to expand the use of your SAY IT CORRECTLY records with a dictionary so as to fit thousands of additional situations and needs

Use this record to supplement any course or text. All sounds in each language are illustrated perfectly for you. Imitate the speaker in the pause which follows each foreign phrase in the slow section and you will be amazed at the increased ease and accuracy of your pronunciation. Available, one language per record, for

French	Spanish	German
Italian	Dutch	Modern Greek
Japanese	Portuguese	Swedish
Russian	Polish	Hebrew
English (for German-speaking people)		Arabic
English (for Spanish-speaking people)		Serbo-Croatian
		Turkish

7" (33⅓ rpm) record, album, booklet. **$1.00** each.

CATALOG OF DOVER BOOKS

Listen and Learn language records

LISTEN & LEARN is the only language record course designed especially to meet your travel and everyday needs. It is available in separate sets for FRENCH, SPANISH, GERMAN, JAPANESE, RUSSIAN, or ITALIAN, and each set contains three 33⅓ rpm long-playing records—1½ hours of recorded speech by eminent native speakers who are professors at Columbia, New York University, Queens College.

Check the following special features found only in LISTEN & LEARN:

- **Dual-language recording.** 812 selected phrases and sentences, over 3200 words, spoken first in English, then in their foreign language euivalents. A suitable pause follows each foreign phrase, allowing you time to repeat the expression. You learn by unconscious assimilation.
- **128 to 206-page manual** contains everything on the records, plus a simple phonetic pronunciation guide.
- **Indexed for convenience. The only set on the market** that is completely indexed. No more puzzling over where to find the phrase you need. Just look in the rear of the manual.
- **Practical.** No time wasted on material you can find in any grammar. LISTEN & LEARN covers central core material with phrase approach. Ideal for the person with limited learning time.
- **Living, modern expressions,** not found in other courses. Hygienic products, modern equipment, shopping—expressions used every day, like "nylon" and "air-conditioned."
- **Limited objective.** Everything you learn, no matter where you stop, is immediately useful. You have to finish other courses, wade through grammar and vocabulary drill, before they help you.
- **High-fidelity recording.** LISTEN & LEARN records equal in clarity and surface-silence any record on the market costing up to $6.

"Excellent . . . the spoken records . . . impress me as being among the very best on the market," **Prof. Mario Pei,** Dept. of Romance Languages, Columbia University. "Inexpensive and well-done . . . it would make an ideal present," CHICAGO SUNDAY TRIBUNE. "More genuinely helpful than anything of its kind which I have previously encountered," **Sidney Clark,** well-known author of "ALL THE BEST" travel books.

UNCONDITIONAL GUARANTEE. Try LISTEN & LEARN, then return it within 10 days for full refund if you are not satisfied. The only course on the market guaranteed after you **actually use it.**

Each set contains three 33⅓ records, manual, and album.

SPANISH	the set **$5.95**	GERMAN	the set **$5.95**
FRENCH	the set **$5.95**	ITALIAN	the set **$5.95**
RUSSIAN	the set **$5.95**	JAPANESE	the set **$5.95**
PORTUGUESE	the set **$5.95**	MODERN GREEK	the set **$5.95**

Trubner Colloquial Manuals

These unusual books are members of the famous Trubner series of collouial manuals. They have been written to provide adults with a sound colloquial knowledge of a foreign language, and are suited for either class use or self-study. Each book is a complete course in itself, with progressive, easy to follow lessons. Phonetics, grammar, and syntax are covered, while hundreds of phrases and idioms, reading texts, exercises, and vocabulary are included. These books are unusual in being neither skimpy nor overdetailed in grammatical matters, and in presenting up-to-date, colloquial, and practical phrase material. Bilingual presentation is stressed, to make thorough self-study easier for the reader.

COLLOQUIAL HINDUSTANI, A. H. Harley, formerly Nizam's Reader in Urdu, U. of London. 30 pages on phonetics and scripts (devanagari & Arabic-Persian) are followed by 29 lessons, including material on English and Arabic-Persian influences. Key to all exercises. Vocabulary. 5 x 7½. 147pp. Clothbound **$1.75**

COLLOQUIAL PERSIAN, L. P. Elwell-Sutton. Best introduction to modern Persian, with 90 page grammatical section followed by conversations, 35 page vocabulary. 139pp.
Clothbound **$1.75**

COLLOQUIAL ARABIC, DeLacy O'Leary. Foremost Islamic scholar covers language of Egypt, Syria, Palestine, & Northern Arabia. Extremely clear coverage of complex Arabic verbs & noun plurals; also cultural aspects of language. Vocabulary. xviii + 192pp. 5 x 7½.
Clothbound **$1.75**

COLLOQUIAL GERMAN, P. F. Doring. Intensive thorough coverage of grammar in easily-followed form. Excellent for brush-up, with hundreds of colloquial phrases. 34 pages of bilingual texts. 224pp. 5 x 7½. Clothbound **$1.75**

COLLOQUIAL SPANISH, W. R. Patterson. Castilian grammar and colloquial language, loaded with bilingual phrases and colloquialisms. Excellent for review or self-study. 164pp. 5 x 7½.
Clothbound **$1.75**

COLLOQUIAL FRENCH, W. R. Patterson. 16th revision on this extremely popular manual. Grammar explained with model clarity, and hundreds of useful expressions and phrases; exercises, reading texts, etc. Appendixes of new and useful words and phrases. 223pp. 5 x 7½.
Clothbound **$1.75**

COLLOQUIAL CZECH, J. Schwarz, former headmaster of Lingua Institute, Prague. Full easily followed coverage of grammar, hundreds of immediately useable phrases, texts. Perhaps the best Czech grammar in print. "An absolutely successful textbook," JOURNAL OF CZECHO-SLOVAK FORCES IN GREAT BRITAIN. 252pp. 5 x 7½. Clothbound **$3.00**

COLLOQUIAL RUMANIAN, G. Nandris, Professor of University of London. Extremely thorough coverage of phonetics, grammar, syntax; also included 70 page reader, and 70 page vocabulary. Probably the best grammar for this increasingly important language. 340pp. 5 x 7½.
Clothbound **$2.50**

COLLOQUIAL ITALIAN, A. L. Hayward. Excellent self-study course in grammar, vocabulary, idioms, and reading. Easy progressive lessons will give a good working knowledge of Italian in the shortest possible time. 5 x 7½. Clothbound **$1.75**

Other Language Aids

AN ENGLISH-FRENCH-GERMAN-SPANISH WORD FREQUENCY DICTIONARY, H. S. Eaton. An indispensable language study aid, this is a semantic frequency list of the 6000 most frequently used words in 4 languages—24,000 words in all. The lists, based on concepts rather than words alone, and containing all modern, exact, and idiomatic vocabulary, are arranged side by side to form a unique 4-language dictionary. A simple key indicates the importance of the individual words within each language. Over 200 pages of separate indexes for each language enable you to locate individual words at a glance. Will help language teachers and students, authors of textbooks, grammars, and language tests to compare concepts in the various languages and to concentrate on basic vocabulary, avoiding uncommon and obsolete words. 2 Appendixes. xxi + 441pp. 6½ x 9¼. T738 Paperbound **$2.45**

NEW RUSSIAN-ENGLISH AND ENGLISH-RUSSIAN DICTIONARY, M. A. O'Brien. Over 70,000 entries in the new orthography! Many idiomatic uses and colloquialisms which form the basis of actual speech. Irregular verbs, perfective and imperfective aspects, regular and irregular sound changes, and other features. One of the few dictionaries where accent changes within the conjugation of verbs and the declension of nouns are fully indicated. "One of the best," Prof. E. J. Simmons, Cornell. First names, geographical terms, bibliography, etc. 738pp. 4½ x 6¼. T208 Paperbound **$2.00**

DICTIONARY OF SPOKEN RUSSIAN, English-Russian, Russian-English. Based on phrases and complete sentences, rather than isolated words; recognized as one of the best methods of learning the idiomatic speech of a country. Over 11,500 entries, indexed by single words, with more than 32,000 English and Russian sentences and phrases, in immediately useable form. Probably the largest list ever published. Shows accent changes in conjugation and declension; irregular forms listed in both alphabetical place and under main form of word. 15,000 word introduction covering Russian sounds, writing, grammar, syntax. 15 page appendix of geographical names, money, important signs, given names, foods, special Soviet terms, etc. Travellers, businessmen, students, government employees have found this their best source for Russian expressions. Originally published as U.S. War Department Technical Manual TM 30-944. iv + 573pp. 5⅝ x 8⅜.   T496 Paperbound **$2.75**

DICTIONARY OF SPOKEN SPANISH, Spanish-English, English-Spanish. Compiled from spoken Spanish, emphasizing idiom and colloquial usage in both Castillian and Latin-American. More than 16,00 entries containing over 25,000 idioms—the largest list of idiomatic constructions ever published. Complete sentences given, indexed under single words—language in immediately useable form, for travellers, businessmen, students, etc. 25 page introduction provides rapid survey of sounds, grammar, syntax, with full consideration of irregular verbs. Especially apt in modern treatment of phrases and structure. 17 page glossary gives translations of geographical names, money values, numbers, national holidays, important street signs, useful expressions of high frequency, plus unique 7 page glossary of Spanish and Spanish-American foods and dishes.   Originally published as U.S. War Department Technical Manual TM 30-900. fv + 513pp. 5⅜ x 8.   T495 Paperbound **$1.75**

FREE! All you do is ask for it!

96 MOST USEFUL PHRASES FOR TOURISTS AND STUDENTS in English, French, Spanish, German, Italian. A handy folder you'll want to carry with you. How to say "Excuse me," "How much is it?", "Write it down, please," etc., in four foreign languages.

DUTCH-ENGLISH AND ENGLISH-DUTCH DICTIONARY, F. G. Renier. For travel, literary, scientific or business Dutch, you will find this the most convenient, practical and comprehensive dictionary on the market. More than 60,000 entries, shades of meaning, colloquialisms, idioms, compounds and technical terms. Dutch and English strong and irregular verbs. This is the only dictionary in its size and price range that indicates the gender of nouns. New orthography. xvii + 571pp. 5½ x 6¼.   T224 Clothbound **$2.75**

LEARN DUTCH, F. G. Renier. This book is the most satisfactory and most easily used grammar of modern Dutch. The student is gradually led from simple lessons in pronunciation, through translation from and into Dutch, and finally to a mastery of spoken and written Dutch. Grammatical principles are clearly explained while a usefuly, practical vocabulary is introduced in easy exercises and readings. It is used and recommended by the Fulbright Committee in the Netherlands. Phonetic appendices. Over 1200 exercises; Dutch-English, English-Dutch vocabularies. 181pp. 4¼ x 7¼.   T441 Clothbound **$2.25**

INVITATION TO GERMAN POETRY record. Spoken by Lotte Lenya. Edited by Gustave Mathieu, Guy Stern. 42 poems of Walther von der Vogelweide, Goethe, Hölderlin, Heine, Hofmannsthal, George, Werfel, Brecht, other great poets from 13th to middle of 20th century, spoken with superb artistry. Use this set to improve your diction, build vocabulary, improve aural comprehension, learn German literary history, as well as for sheer delight in listening. 165-page book contains full German text of each poem; English translations; biographical, critical information on each poet; textual information; portraits of each poet, many never before available in this country. 1 12" 33⅓ record; 165-page book; album.   The set **$4.95**

ESSENTIALS OF RUSSIAN record, A von Gronicka, H. Bates-Yakobson. 50 minutes spoken Russian based on leading grammar will improve comprehension, pronunciation, increase vocabulary painlessly. Complete aural review of phonetics, phonemics—words contrasted to highlight sound differences. Wide range of material: talk between family members, friends; sightseeing; adaptation of Tolstoy's "The Shark;" history of Academy of Sciences; proverbs, epigrams; Pushkin, Lermontov, Fet, Blok, Maikov poems. Conversation passages spoken twice, fast and slow, let you anticipate answers, hear all sounds but understand normal talk speed. 12" 33 record, album sleeve. 44-page manual with entire record text. Translation on facing pages, phonetic instructions.   The set **$4.95**

Note: For students wishing to use a grammar as well, set is available with grammar-text on which record is based, Gronicka and Bates-Yakobson's "Essentials of Russian" (400pp., 6 x 9, clothbound; Prentice Hall), an excellent, standard text used in scores of colleges, institutions.
                                   Augmented set: book, record, manual, sleeve **$10.70**

SPEAK MY LANGUAGE: SPANISH FOR YOUNG BEGINNERS, M. Ahlman, Z Gilbert. Records provide one of the best, and most entertaining, methods of introducing a foreign language to children. Within the framework of a train trip from Portugal to Spain, an English speaking child is introduced to Spanish by a native companion. (Adapted from a successful radio program of the N. Y. State Educational Department.) Though a continuous story, there are a dozen specific categories of expressions, including greetings, numbers, time, weather, food, clothes, family members, etc. Drill is combined with poetry and contextual use. Authentic background music is heard. An accompanying book enables a reader to follow the records, and includes a vocabulary of over 350 recorded expressions. Two 10″ 33⅓ records, total of 40 minutes. Book. 40 illustrations. 69pp. 5¼ x 10½. **T890 The set $4.95**

MONEY CONVERTER AND TIPPING GUIDE FOR EUROPEAN TRAVEL, C. Vomacka. A small, convenient handbook crammed with information on currency regulations and tipping for every European country including the Iron Curtain countries, plus Israel, Egypt, and Turkey. Currency conversion tables for every country from U.S. to foreign and vice versa. The only source of such information as phone rates, postal rates, clothing sizes, what and when to tip, duty-free imports, and dozens of other valuable topics. 128pp. 3½ x 5¼. **T260 Paperbound 60¢**

Literature, History of Literature

ARISTOTLE'S THEORY OF POETRY AND THE FINE ARTS, edited by S. H. Butcher. The celebrated Butcher translation of this great classic faced, page by page, with the complete Greek text. A 300 page introduction discussing Aristotle's ideas and their influence in the history of thought and literature, and covering art and nature, imitation as an aesthetic form, poetic truth, art and morality, tragedy, comedy, and similar topics. Modern Aristotelian criticism discussed by John Gassner. lxxvi + 421pp. 5⅜ x 8. **T42 Paperbound $2.00**

FOUNDERS OF THE MIDDLE AGES, E. K. Rand. This is the best non-technical discussion of the transformation of Latin pagan culture into medieval civilization. Covering such figures as Tertullian, Gregory, Jerome, Boethius, Augustine, the Neoplatonists, and many other literary men, educators, classicists, and humanists, this book is a storehouse of information presented clearly and simply for the intelligent non-specialist. "Thoughtful, beautifully written," AMERICAN HISTORICAL REVIEW. "Extraordinarily accurate," Richard McKeon, THE NATION. ix + 365pp. 5⅜ x 8. **T369 Paperbound $1.85**

INTRODUCTIONS TO ENGLISH LITERATURE, edited by B. Dobrée. Goes far beyond ordinary histories, ranging from the 7th century up to 1914 (to the 1940's in some cases.) The first half of each volume is a specific detailed study of historical and economic background of the period and a general survey of poetry and prose, including trends of thought, influences, etc. The second and larger half is devoted to a detailed study of more than 5000 poets, novelists, dramatists; also economists, historians, biographers, religious writers, philosophers, travellers, and scientists of literary stature, with dates, lists of major works and their dates, keypoint critical bibliography, and evaluating comments. The most compendious bibliographic and literary aid within its price range.

Vol. I. THE BEGINNINGS OF ENGLISH LITERATURE TO SKELTON, (1509), W. L. Renwick, H. Orton. 450pp. 5⅛ x 7⅞. **T75 Clothbound $3.50**

Vol. II. THE ENGLISH RENAISSANCE, 1510-1688, V. de Sola Pinto. 381pp. 5⅛ x 7⅞. **T76 Clothbound $3.50**

Vol. III. AUGUSTANS AND ROMANTICS, 1689-1830, H. Dyson, J. Butt. 320pp. 5⅛ x 7⅞. **T77 Clothbound $3.50**

Vol. IV. THE VICTORIANS AND AFTER, 1830-1914, E. Batho, B. Dobree. 360pp. 5⅛ x 7⅞. **T78 Clothbound $3.50**

EPIC AND ROMANCE, W. P. Ker. Written by one of the foremost authorities on medieval literature, this is the standard survey of medieval epic and romance. It covers Teutonic epics, Icelandic sagas, Beowulf, French chansons de geste, the Roman de Troie and many other important works of literature. It is an excellent account for a body of literature whose beauty and value has only recently come to be recognized. Index. xxiv + 398pp. 5⅜ x 8. **T355 Paperbound $1.95**

THE POPULAR BALLAD, F. B. Gummere. Most useful factual introduction; fund of descriptive material; quotes, cites over 260 ballads. Examines, from folkloristic view, structure; choral, ritual elements; meter, diction, fusion; effects of tradition. editors; almost every other aspect of border, riddle, kinship, sea, ribald, supernatural, etc., ballads. Bibliography. 2 indexes. 374pp. 5⅜ x 8. **T548 Paperbound $1.65**

Philosophy, Religion

GUIDE TO PHILOSOPHY, C. E. M. Joad. A modern classic which examines many crucial problems which man has pondered through the ages: Does free will exist? Is there plan in the universe? How do we know and validate our knowledge? Such opposed solutions as subjective idealism and realism, chance and teleology, vitalism and logical positivism, are evaluated and the contributions of the great philosophers from the Greeks to moderns like Russell, Whitehead, and others, are considered in the context of each problem. "The finest introduction," BOSTON TRANSCRIPT. Index. Classified bibliography. 592pp. 5⅜ x 8.
T297 Paperbound **$2.00**

HISTORY OF ANCIENT PHILOSOPHY, W. Windelband. One of the clearest, most accurate comprehensive surveys of Greek and Roman philosophy. Discusses ancient philosophy in general, intellectual life in Greece in the 7th and 6th centuries B.C., Thales, Anaximander, Anaximenes, Heraclitus, the Eleatics, Empedocles, Anaxagoras, Leucippus, the Pythagoreans, the Sophists, Socrates, Democritus (20 pages), Plato (50 pages), Aristotle (70 pages), the Peripatetics, Stoics, Epicureans, Sceptics, Neo-platonists, Christian Apologists, etc. 2nd German edition translated by H. E. Cushman. xv + 393pp. 5⅜ x 8. T357 Paperbound **$1.75**

ILLUSTRATIONS OF THE HISTORY OF MEDIEVAL THOUGHT AND LEARNING, R. L. Poole. Basic analysis of the thought and lives of the leading philosophers and ecclesiastics from the 8th to the 14th century—Abailard, Ockham, Wycliffe, Marsiglio of Padua, and many other great thinkers who carried the torch of Western culture and learning through the "Dark Ages": political, religious, and metaphysical views. Long a standard work for scholars and one of the best introductions to medieval thought for beginners. Index. 10 Appendices. xiii + 327pp. 5⅜ x 8. T674 Paperbound **$1.85**

PHILOSOPHY AND CIVILIZATION IN THE MIDDLE AGES, M. de Wulf. This semi-popular survey covers aspects of medieval intellectual life such as religion, philosophy, science, the arts, etc. It also covers feudalism vs. Catholicism, rise of the universities, mendicant orders, monastic centers, and similar topics. Unabridged. Bibliography. Index. viii + 320pp. 5⅜ x 8.
T284 Paperbound **$1.75**

AN INTRODUCTION TO SCHOLASTIC PHILOSOPHY, Prof. M. de Wulf. Formerly entitled SCHOLASTICISM OLD AND NEW, this volume examines the central scholastic tradition from St. Anselm, Albertus Magnus, Thomas Aquinas, up to Suarez in the 17th century. The relation of scholasticism to ancient and medieval philosophy and science in general is clear and easily followed. The second part of the book considers the modern revival of scholasticism, the Louvain position, relations with Kantianism and Positivism. Unabridged. xvi + 271pp. 5⅜ x 8.
T296 Clothbound **$3.50**
T283 Paperbound **$1.75**

A HISTORY OF MODERN PHILOSOPHY, H. Höffding. An exceptionally clear and detailed coverage of western philosophy from the Renaissance to the end of the 19th century. Major and minor men such as Pomponazzi, Bodin, Boehme, Telesius, Bruno, Copernicus, da Vinci, Kepler, Galileo, Bacon, Descartes, Hobbes, Spinoza, Leibniz, Wolff, Locke, Newton, Berkeley, Hume, Erasmus, Montesquieu, Voltaire, Diderot, Rousseau, Lessing, Kant, Herder, Fichte, Schelling, Hegel, Schopenhauer, Comte, Mill, Darwin, Spencer, Hartmann, Lange, and many others, are discussed in terms of theory of knowledge, logic, cosmology, and psychology. Index. 2 volumes, total of 1159pp. 5⅜ x 8.
T117 Vol. 1, Paperbound **$2.00**
T118 Vol. 2, Paperbound **$2.00**

ARISTOTLE, A. E. Taylor. A brilliant, searching non-technical account of Aristotle and his thought written by a foremost Platonist. It covers the life and works of Aristotle; classification of the sciences; logic; first philosophy; matter and form; causes; motion and eternity; God; physics; metaphysics; and similar topics. Bibliography. New Index compiled for this edition. 128pp. 5⅜ x 8. T280 Paperbound **$1.00**

THE SYSTEM OF THOMAS AQUINAS, M. de Wulf. Leading Neo-Thomist, one of founders of University of Louvain, gives concise exposition to central doctrines of Aquinas, as a means toward determining his value to modern philosophy. religion. Formerly "Medieval Philosophy Illustrated from the System of Thomas Aquinas." Trans. by E. Messenger. Introduction. 151pp. 5⅜ x 8. T568 Paperbound **$1.25**

THE PHILOSOPHICAL WORKS OF DESCARTES. The definitive English edition of all the major philosophical works and letters of René Descartes. All of his revolutionary insights, from his famous "Cogito ergo sum" to his detailed account of contemporary science and his astonishingly fruitful concept that all phenomena of the universe (except mind) could be reduced to clear laws by the use of mathematics. An excellent source for the thought of men like Hobbes, Arnauld, Gassendi, etc., who were Descarte's contemporaries. Translated by E. S. Haldane and G. Ross. Introductory notes. Index. Total of 842pp. 5⅜ x 8.
T71 Vol. 1, Paperbound **$2.00**
T72 Vol. 2, Paperbound **$2.00**

THE CHIEF WORKS OF SPINOZA. An unabridged reprint of the famous Bohn edition containing all of Spinoza's most important works: Vol. I: The Theologico-Political Treatise and the Political Treatise. Vol. II: On The Improvement Of Understanding, The Ethics, Selected Letters. Profound and enduring ideas on God, the universe, pantheism, society, religion, the state, democracy, the mind, emotions, freedom and the nature of man, which influenced Goethe, Hegel, Schelling, Coleridge, Whitehead, and many others. Introduction. 2 volumes. 826pp. 5⅜ x 8.
T249 Vol. I, Paperbound **$1.50**
T250 Vol. II, Paperbound **$1.50**

LEIBNIZ, H. W. Carr. Most stimulating middle-level coverage of basic philosophical thought of Leibniz. Easily understood discussion, analysis of major works: "Theodicy," "Principles of Nature and Grace," Monadology"; Leibniz's influence; intellectual growth; correspondence; disputes with Bayle, Malebranche, Newton; importance of his thought today, with reinterpretation in modern terminology. "Power and mastery," London Times. Bibliography. Index. 226pp. 5⅜ x 8.
T624 Paperbound **$1.35**

AN ESSAY CONCERNING HUMAN UNDERSTANDING, John Locke. Edited by A. C. Fraser. Unabridged reprinting of definitive edition; only complete edition of "Essay" in print. Marginal analyses of almost every paragraph; hundreds of footnotes; authoritative 140-page biographical, critical, historical prolegomena. Indexes. 1170pp. 5⅜ x 8.
T530 Vol. 1 (Books 1, 2) Paperbound **$2.25**
T531 Vol. 2 (Books 3, 4) Paperbound **$2.25**
2 volume set **$4.50**

THE PHILOSOPHY OF HISTORY, G. W. F. Hegel. One of the great classics of western thought which reveals Hegel's basic principle: that history is not chance but a rational process, the realization of the Spirit of Freedom. Ranges from the oriental cultures of subjective thought to the classical subjective cultures, to the modern absolute synthesis where spiritual and secular may be reconciled. Translation and introduction by J. Sibree. Introduction by C. Hegel. Special introduction for this edition by Prof. Carl Friedrich. xxxix + 447pp. 5⅜ x 8.
T112 Paperbound **$1.85**

THE PHILOSOPHY OF HEGEL, W. T. Stace. The first detailed analysis of Hegel's thought in English, this is especially valuable since so many of Hegel's works are out of print. Dr. Stace examines Hegel's debt to Greek idealists and the 18th century and then proceeds to a careful description and analysis of Hegel's first principles, categories, reason, dialectic method, his logic, philosophy of nature and spirit, etc. Index. Special 14 x 20 chart of Hegelian system. x + 526pp. 5⅜ x 8.
T254 Paperbound **$2.00**

THE WILL TO BELIEVE and HUMAN IMMORTALITY, W. James. Two complete books bound as one. THE WILL TO BELIEVE discusses the interrelations of belief, will, and intellect in man; chance vs. determinism, free will vs. determinism, free will vs. fate, pluralism vs. monism; the philosophies of Hegel and Spencer, and more. HUMAN IMMORTALITY examines the question of survival after death and develops an unusual and powerful argument for immortality. Two prefaces. Index. Total of 429pp. 5⅜ x 8.
T291 Paperbound **$1.65**

THE WORLD AND THE INDIVIDUAL, Josiah Royce. Only major effort by an American philosopher to interpret nature of things in systematic, comprehensive manner. Royce's formulation of an absolute voluntarism remains one of the original and profound solutions to the problems involved. Part one, 4 Historical Conceptions of Being, inquires into first principles, true meaning and place of individuality. Part two, Nature, Man, and the Moral Order, is application of first principles to problems concerning religion, evil, moral order. Introduction by J. E. Smith, Yale Univ. Index. 1070pp. 5⅜ x 8.
T561 Vol. 1 Paperbound **$2.25**
T562 Vol. 2 Paperbound **$2.25**
the set **$4.50**

THE PHILOSOPHICAL WRITINGS OF PEIRCE, edited by J. Buchler. This book (formerly THE PHILOSOPHY OF PEIRCE) is a carefully integrated exposition of Peirce's complete system composed of selections from his own work. Symbolic logic, scientific method, theory of signs, pragmatism, epistemology, chance, cosmology, ethics, and many other topics are treated by one of the greatest philosophers of modern times. This is the only inexpensive compilation of his key ideas. xvi + 386pp. 5⅜ x 8.
T217 Paperbound **$1.95**

EXPERIENCE AND NATURE, John Dewey. An enlarged, revised edition of the Paul Carus lectures which Dewey delivered in 1925. It covers Dewey's basic formulation of the problem of knowledge, with a full discussion of other systems, and a detailing of his own concepts of the relationship of external world, mind, and knowledge. Starts with a thorough examination of the philosophical method; examines the interrelationship of experience and nature; analyzes experience on basis of empirical naturalism, the formulation of law, role of language and social factors in knowledge; etc. Dewey's treatment of central problems in philosophy is profound but extremely easy to follow. ix + 448pp. 5⅜ x 8.
T471 Paperbound **$1.85**

CATALOG OF DOVER BOOKS

MIND AND THE WORLD-ORDER, C. I. Lewis. Building upon the work of Peirce, James, and Dewey, Professor Lewis outlines a theory of knowledge in terms of "conceptual pragmatism." Dividing truth into abstract mathematical certainty and empirical truth, the author demonstrates that the traditional understanding of the a priori must be abandoned. Detailed analyses of philosophy, metaphysics, method, the "given" in experience, knowledge of objects, nature of the a priori, experience and order, and many others. Appendices. xiv + 446pp. 5⅜ x 8. T359 Paperbound **$1.95**

SCEPTICISM AND ANIMAL FAITH, G. Santayana. To eliminate difficulties in the traditional theory of knowledge, Santayana distinguishes between the independent existence of objects and the essence our mind attributes to them. Scepticism is thereby established as a form of belief, and animal faith is shown to be a necessary condition of knowledge. Belief, classical idealism, intuition, memory, symbols, literary psychology, and much more, discussed with unusual clarity and depth. Index. xii + 314pp. 5⅜ x 8.

T236 Paperbound **$1.50**

LANGUAGE AND MYTH, E. Cassirer. Analyzing the non-rational thought processes which go to make up culture, Cassirer demonstrates that beneath both language and myth there lies a dominant unconscious "grammar" of experience whose categories and canons are not those of logical thought. His analyses of seemingly diverse phenomena such as Indian metaphysics, the Melanesian "mana," the Naturphilosophie of Schelling, modern poetry, etc., are profound without being pedantic. Introduction and translation by Susanne Langer. Index. x + 103pp. 5⅜ x 8. T51 Paperbound **$1.25**

SUBSTANCE AND FUNCTION, EINSTEIN'S THEORY OF RELATIVITY, E. Cassirer. In this double-volume, Cassirer develops a philosophy of the exact sciences that is historically sound, philosophically mature, and scientifically impeccable. Such topics as the concept of number, space and geometry, non-Euclidean geometry, traditional logic and scientific method, mechanism and motion, energy, relational concepts, degrees of objectivity, the ego, Einstein's relativity, and many others are treated in detail. Authorized translation by W. C. and M. C. Swabey. xii + 465pp. 5⅜ x 8. T50 Paperbound **$2.00**

*THE ANALYSIS OF MATTER, Bertrand Russell. A classic which has retained its importance in understanding the relation between modern physical theory and human perception. Logical analysis of physics, prerelativity physics, causality, scientific inference, Weyl's theory, tensors, invariants and physical interpretations, periodicity, and much more is treated with Russell's usual brilliance. "Masterly piece of clear thinking and clear writing," NATION AND ATHENAEUM. "Most thorough treatment of the subject," THE NATION. Introduction. Index. 8 figures. viii + 408pp. 5⅜ x 8. 231 Paperbound **$1.95**

CONCEPTUAL THINKING (A LOGICAL INQUIRY), S. Körner. Discusses origin, use of general concepts on which language is based, and the light they shed on basic philosophical questions. Rigorously examines how different concepts are related; how they are linked to experience; problems of the field of contact between exact logical, mathematical, and scientific concepts, and the inexactness of everyday experience (studied at length). This work elaborates many new approaches to the traditional problems of philosophy—epistemology, value theories, metaphysics, aesthetics, morality. "Rare originality . . . brings a new rigour into philosophical argument," Philosophical Quarterly. New corrected second edition. Index. vii + 301pp. 5⅜ x 8 T516 Paperbound **$1.75**

INTRODUCTION TO SYMBOLIC LOGIC, S. Langer. No special knowledge of math required — probably the clearest book ever written on symbolic logic, suitable for the layman, general scientist, and philosopher. You start with simple symbols and advance to a knowledge of the Boole-Schroeder and Russell-Whitehead systems. Forms, logical structure, classes, the calculus of propositions, logic of the syllogism, etc., are all covered. "One of the clearest and simplest introductions," MATHEMATICS GAZETTE. Second enlarged, revised edition. 368pp. 5⅜ x 8. S164 Paperbound **$1.75**

LANGUAGE, TRUTH AND LOGIC, A. J. Ayer. A clear, careful analysis of the basic ideas of Logical Positivism. Building on the work of Schlick, Russell, Carnap, and the Viennese School, Mr. Ayer develops a detailed exposition of the nature of philosophy, science, and metaphysics; the Self and the World; logic and common sense, and other philosophic concepts. An aid to clarity of thought as well as the first full-length development of Logical Positivism in English. Introduction by Bertrand Russell. Index. 160pp. 5⅜ x 8. T10 Paperbound **$1.25**

ESSAYS IN EXPERIMENTAL LOGIC, J. Dewey. Based upon the theory that knowledge implies a judgment which in turn implies an inquiry, these papers consider the inquiry stage in terms of: the relationship of thought and subject matter, antecedents of thought, data and meanings. 3 papers examine Bertrand Russell's thought, while 2 others discuss pragmatism and a final essay presents a new theory of the logic of values. Index. viii + 444pp. 5⅜ x 8. T73 Paperbound **$1.95**

TRAGIC SENSE OF LIFE, M. de Unamuno. The acknowledged masterpiece of one of Spain's most influential thinkers. Between the despair at the inevitable death of man and all his works and the desire for something better, Unamuno finds that "saving incertitude" that alone can console us. This dynamic appraisal of man's faith in God and in himself has been called "a masterpiece" by the ENCYCLOPAEDIA BRITANNICA. xxx + 332pp. 5⅜ x 8. T257 Paperbound **$1.95**

CATALOG OF DOVER BOOKS

THE SENSE OF BEAUTY, G. Santayana. A revelation of the beauty of language as well as an important philosophic treatise, this work studies the "why, when, and how beauty appears, what conditions an object must fulfill to be beautiful, what elements of our nature make us sensible of beauty, and what the relation is between the constitution of the object and the excitement of our susceptibility." "It is doubtful if a better treatment of the subject has since been published," PEABODY JOURNAL. Index. ix + 275pp. 5⅜ x 8.
T238 Paperbound **$1.00**

THE IDEA OF PROGRESS, J. B. Bury. Practically unknown before the Reformation, the idea of progress has since become one of the central concepts of western civilization. Prof. Bury analyzes its evolution in the thought of Greece, Rome, the Middle Ages, the Renaissance, to its flowering in all branches of science, religion, philosophy, industry, art, and literature, during and following the 16th century. Introduction by Charles Beard. Index. xl + 357pp. 5⅜ x 8.
T40 Paperbound **$1.95**

HISTORY OF DOGMA, A. Harnack. Adolph Harnack, who died in 1930, was perhaps the greatest Church historian of all time. In this epoch-making history, which has never been surpassed in comprehensiveness and wealth of learning, he traces the development of the authoritative Christian doctrinal system from its first crystallization in the 4th century down through the Reformation, including also a brief survey of the later developments through the Infallibility decree of 1870. He reveals the enormous influence of Greek thought on the early Fathers, and discusses such topics as the Apologists, the great councils, Manichaeism, the historical position of Augustine, the medieval opposition to indulgences, the rise of Protestantism, the relations of Luther's doctrines with modern tendencies of thought, and much more. "Monumental work; still the most valuable history of dogma . . . luminous analysis of the problems . . . abounds in suggestion and stimulus and can be neglected by no one who desires to understand the history of thought in this most important field," Dutcher's Guide to Historical Literature. Translated by Neil Buchanan. Index. Unabridged reprint in 4 volumes. Vol I: Beginnings to the Gnostics and Marcion. Vol II & III: 2nd century to the 4th century Fathers. Vol IV & V: 4th century Councils to the Carlovingian Renaissance. Vol VI & VII: Period of Clugny (c. 1000) to the Reformation, and after. Total of cii + 2407pp. 5⅜ x 8.

T904 Vol I	Paperbound	**$2.50**
T905 Vol II & III	Paperbound	**$2.50**
T906 Vol IV & V	Paperbound	**$2.50**
T907 Vol VI & VII	Paperbound	**$2.50**
	The set	**$10.00**

THE GUIDE FOR THE PERPLEXED, Maimonides. One of the great philosophical works of all time and a necessity for everyone interested in the philosophy of the Middle Ages in the Jewish, Christian, and Moslem traditions. Maimonides develops a common meeting-point for the Old Testament and the Aristotelian thought which pervaded the medieval world. His ideas and methods predate such scholastics as Aquinas and Scotus and throw light on the entire problem of philosophy or science vs. religion. 2nd revised edition. Complete unabridged Friedländer translation. 55 page introduction to Maimonides's life, period, etc., with an important summary of the GUIDE. Index. lix + 414pp. 5⅜ x 8.   T351 Paperbound **$1.85**

ASTROLOGY AND RELIGION AMONG THE GREEKS AND ROMANS, Franz Cumont. How astrololgy developed, spread, and took hold of superior intellects, from ancient Babylonia through Rome of the fourth century A.D. You see astrology as the base of a learned theology, the influence of the Neo-Pythagoreans, forms of oriental mysteries, the devotion of the emperors to the sun cult (such as the Sol Invictus of Aurelian), and much more. The second part deals with conceptions of the world as formed by astrology, the theology bound up with them, and moral and eschatological ideas. Introduction. Index. 128pp. 5⅜ x 8.
T581 Paperbound **$1.35**

AFTER LIFE IN ROMAN PAGANISM, Franz Cumont. Deepest thoughts, beliefs of epoch between republican period and fall of Roman paganism. Contemporary settings, hidden lore, sources in Greek, Hebrew, Egyptian, prehistoric thought. Secret teachings of mystery religions, Hermetic writings, the gnosis, Pythagoreans, Orphism; sacrifices, nether world, immortality; Hades, problem of violent death, death of children; reincarnation, ecstasy, purification; etc. Introduction. Index. 239pp. 5⅜ x 8.   T573 Paperbound **$1.35**

Dover publishes books on art, music, philosophy, literature, languages, history, social sciences, psychology, handicrafts, orientalia, puzzles and entertainments, chess, pets and gardens, books explaining science, intermediate and higher mathematics mathematical physics, engineering, biological sciences, earth sciences, classics of science, etc. Write to:

> *Dept. catrr.*
> *Dover Publications, Inc.*
> *180 Varick Street, N. Y. 14, N. Y.*